STRUCTURAL POLYMERS

P. M. Ogibalov, N. I. Malinin, V. P. Netrebko,
B. P. Kishkin

STRUCTURAL POLYMERS

Testing Methods

VOLUME II

Translated from Russian by J. Eliassaf

A HALSTED PRESS BOOK

JOHN WILEY & SONS
New York · Toronto

ISRAEL PROGRAM FOR SCIENTIFIC TRANSLATIONS
Jerusalem · London

Sole distributors for the Western Hemisphere and Japan

HALSTED PRESS, a division of
JOHN WILEY & SONS, INC., NEW YORK

Library of Congress Cataloging in Publication Data
Main entry under title:

Structural polymers.

Translation of *Konstruktsionnye polimery.*
"A Halsted Press book."
Includes bibliographies.
1. Polymers and polymerization–Testing.
I. Ogibalov, Petr Matveevich.
TA455.P58K6513 620.1'923 73-16434
ISBN 0-470-65285-3 Vol. II

Distributors for the U.K., Europe, Africa and
the Middle East

JOHN WILEY & SONS, LTD., CHICHESTER

Distributed in the rest of the world by

KETER PUBLISHING HOUSE JERUSALEM LTD.
ISBN 0 7065 1338 X
IPST cat. no. 22065

This book is a translation from Russian of
KONSTRUKTSIONNYE POLYMERY · KNIGA VTORAYA
Izdatel'stvo Moskovskogo Universiteta
1972

Printed in Israel

CONTENTS

Chapter I

STABILITY AND WAVE PROPAGATION

This chapter presents theoretical and experimental formulations and solutions of the problem of the stability of polymeric rods, plates and shells under conditions of creep. The propagation of waves in an elastoviscoplastic medium is studied and specific examples are considered. The formulation and solution of the stability of cylindrical shells under thermal shock is also treated.

§1. FORMULATION AND SOLUTION OF PROBLEMS OF STABILITY UNDER CREEP CONDITIONS FOR THIN-WALLED ELEMENTS MADE FROM HOMOGENEOUS MATERIALS

There are many formulations of the problem of the stability of thin-walled elements under creep conditions. However, the most accurate formulation from the mechanical-mathematical point of view is that of Rabotnov and Shesterikov /1/. It will be discussed now.

Hardening theory is chosen as the starting physical hypothesis. According to this theory the creep process is described by an equation relating the stress to the magnitude and rate of plastic strain:

$$\Phi(\sigma,\ p,\ \dot{p}) = 0 \quad \left(p = \varepsilon - \frac{\sigma}{E}\right). \tag{1.1}$$

Here p denotes creep, $\dot{p}$ strain rate and σ stress.

In the initial formulation /1/ the problem of the stability of, for example, a rod consists in finding the possibility of bending the rod at an infinitesimal rate, while the creep rate under compression remains finite. It follows that this formulation excludes the possibility of studying load removal. The latter can be studied only when we look for finite bending. However, Shanley's formulation /2, 3/ results in the limit of vanishingly small creep rates.

We shall consider in some detail in the initial (starting) formulation methods which have been advanced in order to determine the stability regions of a straight rod subject to creep, based on investigating the rod performance after applying some very small perturbation. Application of the creep law in form (1.1) for a rod compressed by a longitudinal force P yields the equation of motion in the form

$$\rho F \frac{\partial^2 y}{\partial t^2} + P \frac{\partial^2 y}{\partial x^2} + EI \frac{\partial^4 y}{\partial x^4} - \\ - \left\{\exp\left[-\int \frac{\mu}{\nu} dt\right]\right\} \int_0^t \frac{E\lambda}{\nu} \left\{\exp\left[\int \frac{\mu}{\nu} dt\right]\right\} \times \\ \times \left(P \frac{\partial^2 y}{\partial x^2} + \rho F \frac{\partial^2 y}{\partial t^2}\right) dt = 0 \qquad (1.2)$$

$$\left(\nu = \frac{\partial \Phi}{\partial \dot{p}},\ \lambda = \frac{\partial \Phi}{\partial \sigma},\ \mu = \frac{\partial \Phi}{\partial p}\right),$$

where ρ is density, F cross-sectional area, y the deflection, I the moment of inertia, E the modulus of elasticity, t time; x is a running coordinate along the rod of length a.

For a hinged rod,

$$y = \tau(t) \sin \frac{\pi x}{a}. \qquad (1.3)$$

If

$$P_* = \frac{\pi^2}{a^2} EI,\ k = \frac{1}{P_*} \frac{a^2}{\pi^2} \rho F,\ \beta = \frac{P}{P_*}.$$

then substitution of (1.3) in (1.2) leads to the following equation for τ:

$$\tau(1-\beta) + k\ddot{\tau} - \exp\left[-\int_0^t \frac{\mu}{\nu} dt\right] \int_0^t \frac{E\lambda}{\nu} (k\ddot{\tau} - \beta\tau) \times \\ \times \left\{\exp\left[\int \frac{\mu}{\nu} dt\right] dt = 0. \qquad (1.4)$$

At the instant of perturbation ($t = 0$),

$$\tau(0)(1-\beta) + k\ddot{\tau}(0) = 0. \qquad (1.5)$$

One can derive the following differential equation from (1.4):

$$\dddot{\tau}+\frac{\mu-E\lambda}{\nu}\ddot{\tau}+\frac{1}{k}(1-\beta)\dot{\tau}+\frac{1}{k\nu}[\mu+\beta E\lambda-\beta\mu]\tau=0. \quad (1.6)$$

On the assumption of constant coefficients, the solution of the latter equation can be expressed in the form /1/

$$\tau=Ae^{st}, \quad (1.7)$$

and the stability region is determined from the limiting condition for τ, corresponding to nonpositive real parts of s. This condition is satisfied when the coefficient of τ in (1.6) is larger than zero, since the remaining coefficients are always positive ($\beta<1$ implies that the load is less than the Euler critical load). Therefore the inequality

$$\mu+\beta E\lambda-\mu\beta\geqslant 0 \quad (1.8)$$

determines the region of stability.

Shesterikov /4/ has shown that inequality (1.8) may give very underestimated critical times. Actually, the corresponding relation (1.1) for steady-state creep is

$$\dot{p}-\varphi(\sigma)=0 \text{ or } \mu=0,\ \lambda=-\varphi', \quad (1.9)$$

and from inequality (1.8) it follows that the critical time is zero. A similar result was also obtained by a more comprehensive stability criterion for creep /5/.

Shesterikov /4/ has given other evaluations of the critical time which are based on his dynamical stability criterion for creep. Consider the evaluation of the critical time of stability for creep in the case of a rod. Steady- and nonsteady-state creep will be discussed.

For steady-state creep at given σ, all the coefficients in equation (1.6) are constant.

We seek a particular solution in the form (1.7). The characteristic equation satisfying (1.6) is

$$u^3+u^2+k_1(1-\beta)u-\beta k_1=0, \quad (1.10)$$

where

$$s=-E\lambda u,\ k_1^{-1}=k(E\lambda)^2,\ \theta=-E\lambda t.$$

Since $\beta k_1 > 0$, there exists one real positive root u_1. The two other roots are given by the expression

$$u_{2,3} = -\frac{1+u_1}{2} \pm \sqrt{\mathcal{D}} \left(\mathcal{D} = \frac{(1+u_1)^2}{4} - k_2,\ k_2 = \frac{k_1}{1+u_1}\right). \quad (1.11)$$

It is evident that u_2 and u_3 have negative real parts.

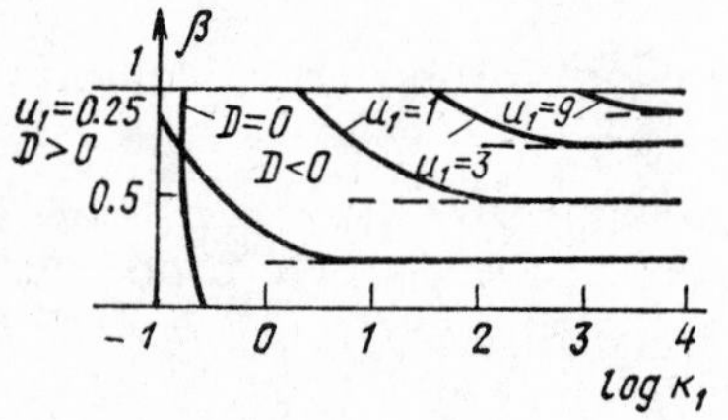

FIGURE 1.1.

The characteristic regions of change in parameters β and k_1 are shown in Figure 1.1, where the lines $u_1 =$ const are plotted. Dashed lines indicate asymptotic values of $\beta = \frac{u_1}{1+u_1}$. There are three cases determined by the value of $\mathcal{D}$.

1. When $\mathcal{D} > 0$, roots u_2 and u_3 are real, different and negative, and the solution of equation (1.6) is

$$\tau = A_1 e^{u_1 \theta} + A_2 e^{u_2 \theta} + A_3 e^{u_3 \theta}. \quad (1.12)$$

2. When $\mathcal{D} = 0$, $u_2 = u_3 = -\frac{(1+u_1)}{2}$ and the solution of (1.6) is

$$\tau = A_1 e^{u_1 \theta} + (A_2 + A_3 \theta) \exp\left(-\frac{1+u_1}{2}\theta\right). \quad (1.13)$$

3. When $\mathcal{D} < 0$, roots u_2 and u_3 are conjugate and the solution of (1.6) is

$$\tau = A_1 e^{u_1 \theta} [A_2 \sin \sqrt{-\mathcal{D}}\,\theta + A_3 \cos \sqrt{-\mathcal{D}}\,\theta] \exp\left(-\frac{1+u_1}{2}\theta\right). \quad (1.14)$$

At $t = 0$, the initial conditions $\tau = \tau_0$, $\dot{\tau} = \dot{\tau}_0$ and (1.5) enable A_1, A_2 and A_3 to be determined.

Consider first, separately, the two limiting conditions of the problem subject to initial data

$$\tau(0)=\tau_0\neq 0,\quad \dot{\tau}(0)=0.$$

1. If $\mathcal{D}>0$, then in (1.12)

$$\begin{aligned} A_1 &= \frac{u_1(1+u_1)}{2u_1(1+u_1)+k_2}\tau_0, \\ A_2 &= -\frac{u_1(u_1-1)-2k_2-2u_1\sqrt{\mathcal{D}}}{2(3u_1+1-2\sqrt{\mathcal{D}})\sqrt{\mathcal{D}}}\tau_0, \\ A_3 &= \frac{u_1(u_1-1)-2k_2+2u_1\sqrt{\mathcal{D}}}{2(3u_1+1+2\sqrt{\mathcal{D}})\sqrt{\mathcal{D}}}\tau_0. \end{aligned} \quad (1.15)$$

Typical graphs of the dependence of τ on t are shown in Figure 1.2, which presents plots of $\frac{\tau}{\tau_0}$ vs. θ for $k_1=0.1$ ($\mathcal{D}>0$). The critical state is determined by the condition

$$\begin{aligned} &(u_1^2+u_1^3)\sqrt{\mathcal{D}}\left\{2\exp(\theta u_1)-\exp\left[\left(-\frac{1+u_1}{2}+\sqrt{\mathcal{D}}\right)\theta\right]-\right. \\ &\left.-\exp\left[\left(-\frac{1+u_1}{2}-\sqrt{\mathcal{D}}\right)\theta\right]\right\}=\left\{\frac{u_1^2-u_1^4}{2}+(2u_1+u_1^2)k_2+\right. \\ &\left.+k_2^2\right\}\left\{\exp\left[\left(-\frac{1+u_1}{2}+\sqrt{\mathcal{D}}\right)\theta\right]-\right. \\ &\left.-\exp\left[\left(-\frac{1+u_1}{2}-\sqrt{\mathcal{D}}\right)\theta\right]\right\}. \end{aligned} \quad (1.16)$$

This equation can be solved numerically for any k_2 and u_1. When evaluating the solution, the approximate condition

$$\theta=-2\frac{\Psi'(0)}{\Psi''(0)}, \quad (1.17)$$

can be used, where $\tau=\Psi(0)$. From (1.17) we derive

$$\theta=\frac{k_2^2+(2u_1+u_1^2)k_2-2u_1^3(1+u_1)}{[2u_1(1+u_1)+k_2](1+u_1)k_2}. \quad (1.18)$$

In the numerical example

$$\beta=\frac{1}{2},\ k=\frac{25}{256},\ \left(u_1=\frac{1}{4}\right)$$

the value $\theta=0.341$ was found from (1.16) and $\theta=0.343$ from (1.18). From the physical standpoint the case under consideration corresponds to rods made from a very tough material.

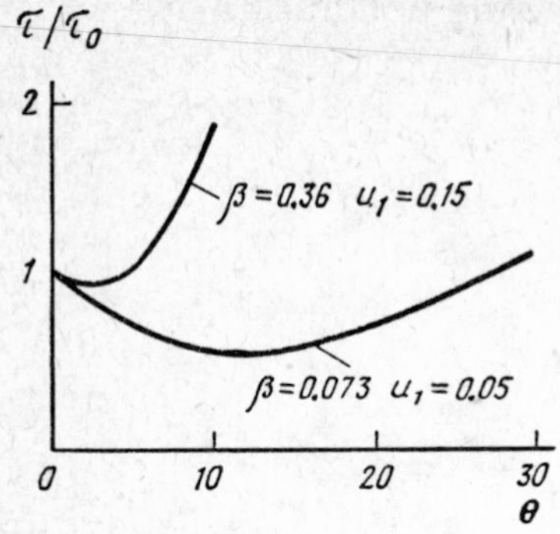

FIGURE 1.2.

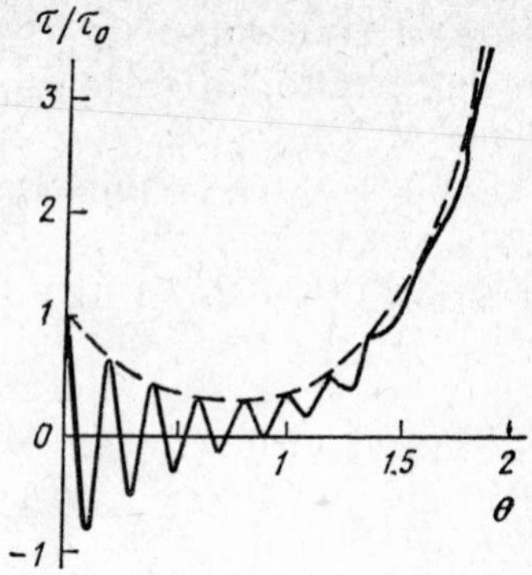

FIGURE 1.3.

2. If $\mathscr{D}=0$, k_2 is expressed in terms of β and u_1 while a relationship exists between u_1 and β. In this case

$$A_1 = 4\,\frac{u_1(1+u_1)}{(1+3u_1)^2}\,\tau_0,\quad A_2 = \frac{5u_1+2u_1+1}{(1+3u_1)^2}\,\tau_0,$$

$$A_3 = \frac{1-u_1^2}{2(1+3u_1)^2}\,\tau_0. \tag{1.19}$$

The condition $\dot{\tau}_0 = 0$ has the form

$$e^x = \frac{(1+u_1)^2}{8u_1}\,x+1,\quad x=\frac{\theta(1+3u_1)}{2}. \tag{1.20}$$

The solution has the same features as in the previous case.

3. The case $\mathscr{D}<0$. It should be noted that $k \gg 1$ for a metallic rod. For simplicity we introduce the notation

$$-\mathscr{D} = \omega^2 = k_2 - \frac{(1-u_1)^2}{4}, \tag{1.21}$$

$$\omega_1 = -E\lambda\omega. \tag{1.22}$$

The coefficients in equation (1.14) are given by

$$A_1 = \frac{u_1(1+u_1)}{2u_1(1+u_1)+k_2}\,\tau_0,$$

$$A_2 = \frac{u_1(1+u_1)+k_2}{2u_1(1+u_1)+k_2}\,\tau_0, \tag{1.23}$$

$$2\omega A_3 = \frac{(1+u_1)\,[u_1(1+u_1^2)+k_2]}{2u_1(1+u_1)+k_2}\,\tau_0.$$

We have here several distinct cases. For small k_1 (of the order of unity) the form of the dependence of τ on t does not differ in principle from that discussed above. With further increase the trigonometric terms become noticeable and at sufficiently large k_1 (of order 1,000 or more) the graph has the shape shown in Figure 1.3, which presents the dependence of τ/τ_0 on θ for $u_1 = 3$, $\beta = 0.75$ and $k_1 = 1{,}000$. The dashed line denotes evaluation by "amplitude." The latter case is of most interest from the practical point of view. Evidently, the condition $\dot{\tau} = 0$ possesses many roots. The simplest evaluation is θ_{max} for all θ satisfying the solution of the equation.

However, for sufficiently large k_1 it can be shown that θ_{max} lies in the region where $\tau \gg \tau_0$. Therefore another evaluation will be given in regions of large k_1 (of order 10,000 and more). Since in this case the condition $A_3 \ll A_2$ is valid,

$$\tau_1 = A_1 \exp(\theta u_1) + A_2 \exp\left(-\frac{1+u_1}{2}\theta\right) \tag{1.24}$$

is the lower limit of τ. The second term corresponds to the amplitude of oscillations. Therefore, after Shesterikov, the condition $\dot{\tau}_1 = 0$ will be referred to briefly as evaluation by amplitude. Subject to the condition $\dot{\tau}_1 = 0$, we derive from (1.24)

$$\theta = \frac{2}{1+3u_1} \ln \frac{\omega^2}{2u_1^2}. \tag{1.25}$$

This equation was derived on the assumption that $k_1 \gg u_1^3$. For comparison it should be noted that

$$\theta_{max} \approx \frac{2}{1+3u_1} \ln \frac{\omega^3}{u_1^2(1+u_1)}. \tag{1.26}$$

Further, for large k_1

$$u_1 \approx \frac{\beta}{1-\beta}, \quad \omega^2 \approx k_2.$$

Consider now the second limiting case of the initial conditions

$$\tau(0) = 0, \quad \dot{\tau}(0) = \dot{\tau}_0 \neq 0, \quad \ddot{\tau}(0) = 0,$$

the last of which results from condition (1.5).

1. If $\mathscr{D} > 0$, then

$$A_1 = \frac{1+u_1}{2(1+u_1)u_1+k_2}\tau_{00},$$
$$A_2 = \frac{1-u_1+2\sqrt{\mathscr{D}}}{2\sqrt{\mathscr{D}}\,[2\sqrt{\mathscr{D}}-1-3u_1]}\tau_{00}, \tag{1.27}$$
$$A_3 = \frac{1-u_1-2\sqrt{\mathscr{D}}}{2\sqrt{\mathscr{D}}\,[2\sqrt{\mathscr{D}}+1+3u_1]}\tau_{00}, \quad \left(\tau_{00} = \frac{\dot{\tau}_0}{-E\lambda}\right).$$

Here, when $\beta \ll 1$ the equation $\ddot{\tau} = 0$ can be satisfied. For large β, $\ddot{\tau} = 0$ can be regarded as defining the critical state.

2. If $\mathscr{D} = 0$, then

$$A_2 = -A_1 = \frac{4(1+u_1)}{(1+3u_1)^2}\tau_{00}, \quad A_3 = \frac{1-u_1}{1+3u_1}\tau_{00}, \tag{1.28}$$

and consequently the derivation of the critical state is analogous to the previous case.

3. If $\mathscr{D} < 0$, then

$$A_1 = -A_2 = \frac{1+u_1}{2u_1(1+u_1)+k_2}\tau_{00}.$$
$$A_3 = \frac{u_1^2-1+k_2}{2u_1(1+u_1)+k_2}\,\frac{\tau_{00}}{2\omega}, \tag{1.29}$$

so that, analogously to the problem of τ_0, the region of large k_1 is of most interest. The critical time is evaluated from the condition $\dot{\tau} = 0$ in the form

$$\theta = \frac{2}{1+3u_1}\ln\frac{\omega^2}{u_1(1+u_1)}. \tag{1.30}$$

If the estimate is made by amplitude, then, in contrast to the τ_0 problem,

$$A_2 \ll A_3. \tag{1.31}$$

Thus if τ is given by

$$\frac{\tau}{\tau_{00}} = (1+u_1)\exp(u_1\theta) + \frac{k_2}{\omega}\exp\left(-\frac{1+u_1}{2}\theta\right), \tag{1.32}$$

the condition $\dot{\tau} = 0$ yields the single root

$$\theta = \frac{2}{1+3u_1} \ln \frac{\omega}{2u_1}. \tag{1.33}$$

It can be easily demonstrated that θ determined by (1.33) is less than θ determined by (1.30).

Consider now the general case where τ_0 and τ_0 are given at the initial moment (note again that $\ddot{\tau}_0$ is not given but is derived from condition (1.5)). In view of the linearity of the equations for A_i their values are readily obtained by simple summation of two particular solutions selected from the three cases involving parameter $\mathscr{D}$.

A general investigation is unnecessary, as it differs little from previous studies. We shall dwell only on the case in which k_1 is sufficiently large; consequently $\mathscr{D} < 0$. Here it is possible to write expressions for A_i in which only the main terms are retained:

$$\begin{aligned} A_1 &= \frac{u_1(1+u_1)}{\omega^2}\tau_0 + \frac{1+u_1}{\omega^2}\tau_{00}, \\ A_2 &= \tau_0 - \frac{1+u_1}{\omega^2}\tau_{00}, \\ A_3 &= \frac{1+u_1}{2\omega}\tau_0 + \frac{\tau_{00}}{\omega}. \end{aligned} \tag{1.34}$$

Let us consider the possible variants.

If $\tau_0 \gg \tau_{00}$, the solution is valid when $\tau_{00} = 0$. If τ_0 is of the same order as τ_{00}, the solution is still valid when $\dot{\tau} = 0$, but a correction is applied to A_1. If $\omega\tau_{00}$ is of the same order as τ_{00}, then A_2 and A_3 are also of the same order and a solution is possible subject to the condition $\tau = 0$, since $\ddot{\tau}_{00}$ is fully determined. Finally, if $\tau_{00} \gg \omega\tau_0$, the solution is completely determined by the condition $\tau_0 = 0$.

The two cases $\dot{\tau}_0 = 0$ and $\tau_0 = 0$ lead to low values for (1.33) and (1.25), from which it is apparent that the minimum time is determined by relationship (1.33). Since consideration of the general case does not introduce a substantial error into the final result, the critical time is determined by the most disadvantageous relationship while it corresponds to (1.33). Consequently relationship (1.33) renders an estimate of the critical times. The very same result may be derived by using the changes in amplitude, determined by expression (1.34) for an arbitrary ratio of τ_0 to τ_{00}, and then determining the minimum value of θ for that ratio.

Thus the critical time for a rod with sufficiently large k_1 is determined as the time t_* which separates the region of decreasing amplitude of deflection from the region in which the amplitude increases:

$$t_* = \frac{1}{-E\lambda} \cdot \frac{2}{1+3u_1} \ln \frac{\omega}{u_1}. \tag{1.35}$$

For large k_1 we have the simple approximate relationship

$$u_1 = \frac{\beta}{1-\beta}, \quad \omega = \sqrt{k_1(1-\beta)},$$

so that (1.35) becomes

$$t_* = \frac{1}{-E\lambda} \cdot \frac{1-\beta}{1+2\beta} \ln \frac{k_1(1-\beta)^3}{4\beta^2}. \tag{1.36}$$

One important circumstance should be noted: the study reported here was carried out for a linearized problem. It can be applied successfully to cross-linked polymers, but for these the equation of state can be expressed with good approximation in the form

$$\dot{p} = -\lambda\sigma. \tag{1.37}$$

A simpler model of nonsteady-state creep is the linear visco-elastic body. Consider a rod made from a material for which the following relationship holds:

$$\dot{p} + Hp + \lambda\sigma = 0, \quad (\lambda < 0). \tag{1.38}$$

In this case equation (1.10) assumes the form

$$u^3 + u^2 + k_1(1-\beta)u - k_1(\beta - \gamma) = 0,$$
$$\left(\gamma = \frac{H}{H - E\lambda} < 1\right). \tag{1.39}$$

It is evident that here the stipulated region of parameter β is divided into two: one in which $\beta < \gamma$, when all the roots have negative real parts and the rod is always stable; and the other in which $\beta > \gamma$. In the latter case only the equation for determining u_1 is replaced, while the rest of the investigation is quite valid since u_2 and u_3 are expressed in terms of u_1 in (1.11).

For sufficiently large k_1 and when $\beta > \gamma$, u_1 can be given by the approximate expression

$$u_1 = \frac{\beta - \gamma}{1-\beta}. \tag{1.40}$$

Substitution in (1.33) yields the critical value t_*.

When H and λ depend on accumulated plastic strain, an investigation in general form is futile. The critical time can be estimated in the following manner. At times less than t_1, determined by the condition

$$\mu + \beta E\lambda - \beta\dot{\mu} = 0, \tag{1.41}$$

the rod is always stable according to the quasistatic criterion. At $t > t_1$, coefficients μ and λ change sufficiently slowly so that an evaluation can be obtained by substituting their average values.

Consider now several general problems dealing with buckling of plates under conditions of creep, where the stress-strain relation is taken from work-hardening theory /6/. Here the equations will be derived from stability criteria /5, 7, 8/. Possible initial deflections will also be studied.

The stress-strain relation here assumes the form

$$\begin{gathered} \dot{p}_{ij} = \frac{3}{2} g S_{ij}, \quad \dot{p}_i = g\sigma_i, \\ \sigma_i^2 = \frac{3}{2} S_{ij} S_{ij}, \quad p_{ij} = \varepsilon_{ij} - \frac{S_{ij}}{2G}, \quad \dot{p}_i^2 = \frac{2}{3} \dot{p}_{ij} \dot{p}_{ij}, \end{gathered} \tag{1.42}$$

where ε_{ij} is the strain tensor, p_{ij} the creep tensor, S_{ij} the stress deviator, g a function of p_i and σ_i, G the shear modulus. The material is taken as incompressible. Summation is over repeated indices.

The validity of Kirchhoff's hypothesis of linear normals is assumed, in which case

$$\delta\varepsilon_{11} = -z\frac{\partial^2 w}{\partial x^2}, \quad \delta\varepsilon_{22} = -z\frac{\partial^2 w}{\partial y^2}, \quad \delta\varepsilon_{12} = -z\frac{\partial^2 w}{\partial x \partial y}, \tag{1.43}$$

where w is the deflection in excess of the initial one; x and y are coordinates in the plane of the plate. Variation δ denotes the components which characterize the distortion. Relationships (1.42) yield expressions for the strain and stress variations:

$$\begin{gathered} \delta\dot{p}_i = a\delta p_i + (b+1) g\delta\sigma_i, \\ \delta\dot{\varepsilon}_{ij} = \frac{\delta \dot{S}_{ij}}{2G} + \frac{3}{2} g\delta S_{ij} + \frac{3}{2} g\sigma_{ij}^* b\delta\sigma_i + \frac{3}{2}\alpha_{ij}^* a\delta p_i \alpha_{ij}, \\ a = \sigma_i \frac{\partial g}{\partial p_i}, \quad b = \frac{\sigma_i}{g}\frac{\partial g}{\partial \sigma_i}, \quad \alpha_{ij}^* = \frac{S_{ij}}{\sigma_i}, \quad \alpha_{ij} = \frac{\sigma_{ij}}{\sigma_i}. \end{gathered} \tag{1.44}$$

By multiplying the second of equations (1.44) by $\dot{\alpha}_{ij}$, summing over i and j and substituting the first of equations (1.44), we obtain

$$\alpha^*_{ij}\delta\varepsilon_{ij} = \frac{\alpha^*_{ij}\delta S_{ij}}{2G} + \delta\dot{p}_i. \qquad (1.45)$$

Henceforth it should be remembered that the condition $\dot{\alpha}_{ij} = 0$ is fulfilled and corresponds to the condition of proportional stress. Then (1.45) can be integrated to give

$$\delta p_i = m - \frac{\delta\sigma_i}{E} \quad \left(m = \alpha^*_{ij}\delta\varepsilon_{ij},\ \delta\sigma_i = \frac{3}{2}\alpha^*_{ij}\delta S_{ij}\right). \qquad (1.46)$$

Hence from (1.46) and (1.44),

$$\delta\sigma_i = e^{-T}\int_0^t E(\dot{m} - am)\, e^T dt,\ T = \int [Eg(b+1) - a]\, dt. \qquad (1.47)$$

Substitution of δp_i and $\delta\sigma_i$ from (1.46) and (1.47) into the second equation of (1.44) yields an equation for δS_{ij}, from which we derive

$$\delta S_{ij} = 2G\delta\varepsilon_{ij} - \alpha^*_{ij}e^{-T}\int_0^t E^2 g(b+1)\, m e^T dt -$$
$$- e^{-R}\int_0^t [2G\delta\varepsilon_{ij} - \alpha^*_{ij} mE]\, Ege^R dt,\ R = \int Egdt. \qquad (1.48)$$

The following equilibrium equation holds for plates:

$$\frac{\partial^2 M}{\partial x^2} + 2\frac{\partial^2 M_{12}}{\partial x \partial y} + \frac{\partial^2 M_2}{\partial y^2} + 2h\sigma_i\Lambda(w + w_0) = 0,$$
$$M_1 = \int_{-h}^{h} (2\delta S_{11} + \delta S_{22})\, zdz,\ M_2 = \int_{-h}^{h} (2\delta S_{22} + \delta S_{11})\, zdz, \qquad (1.49)$$
$$\Lambda = \alpha_{11}\frac{\partial^2}{\partial x^2} + 2\alpha_{12}\frac{\partial^2}{\partial x \partial y} + \alpha_{22}\frac{\partial^2}{\partial y^2}.$$

If (1.48) is substituted in (1.49), we obtain the following integro-differential equation for the deflection w:

$$\nabla^2\nabla^2 w - \sigma_0\Lambda(w + w_0) - e^{-R}\int_0^t Eg\nabla^2\nabla^2 w e^R dt +$$
$$+ \frac{3}{4}e^{-R}\int_0^t Eg\Lambda\Lambda w e^R dt - \frac{3}{4}e^{-T}\int_0^t Eg(b+1)\,\Lambda\Lambda w e^T dt = 0,$$
$$\sigma_0 = \frac{9\sigma_i}{(2h)^2 E}. \qquad (1.50)$$

In the general case, when the time dependence of the coefficients is studied, conversion from the integrodifferential equation to a differential equation introduces second-order time derivatives into the latter.

When $\dot{\alpha}_{ij}^{*} \neq 0$, an integral equation can be derived from (1.44) for determining $\delta\sigma_i$ and cannot be solved in general form. By using this expression for determining $\delta\sigma_i^{*}$ in terms of $\delta\varepsilon_{ij}$, an integrodifferential equation for the deflection can be obtained with the aid of (1.49).

If several transverse loads act on the plate, equation (1.50) assumes the form

$$L(w) = \frac{q}{D}, \tag{1.51}$$

where L is the integrodifferential operator determined by the condition $L(w) = 0$ from (1.50), and D the cylindrical rigidity of the plate.

Equation (1.51) is necessary for studying the stability of plates by quasi-static criteria. According to Rabotnov /8/, it can be assumed that a plate without initial deflection is under the action of a load acting in the plane of the plate. During some finite time intervals a disturbing load acts on the plate. After removing this load the deflection of the plate can increase or diminish, depending on the time instant considered. Time can be considered as critical when

$$\dot{w} = 0. \tag{1.52}$$

Let us discuss several qualitative features of the investigation method observed in the case of uniformly compressed plates, in which case operators Λ and ∇^2 coincide. We introduce the variable

$$x = \int_0^t Eg\,dt.$$

Then (1.51) yields the equation

$$u - Se^{-x}\int_0^x e^{x}u\,dx - 3Se^{-(1+b)x-\alpha}x\int_0^x x^{\alpha}(1+b)\,e^{(1+b)x}u\,dx = k_0,$$

$$g \equiv A\sigma_i^{n-1}p_i^{-\alpha},\ k_0 = \beta u_0 + m_0,\ \beta = \frac{\sigma_i}{\sigma_E}, \tag{1.53}$$

$$4(1-\beta)S = 1,\ w(t, x, y) = u(t)\,\varphi(x, y),$$

where σ_E is the Euler critical force for an elastic plate, and $\varphi(x, y)$ a function satisfying the requirements of solution of the stability problem for an elastic plate. In order to simplify the investigation it is assumed that

$$w_0 = u_0\varphi, \ q = Dm_0\varphi.$$

In the general case equation (1.53) is reduced to a linear second-order differential equation with variable coefficients, converging to Whittaker's equation. Here only the qualitative features are outlined and the methods given of approximate treatment of the problem.

Consider the general case. When passing from (1.53) to the differential equation some relationship always links u and u'_x. In a general solution of a second-order differential equation this relationship imposes a limitation which permits the expression of one arbitrary constant in terms of the other. Consequently the general solution of homogeneous equation (1.53) possesses only one arbitrary constant and condition (1.52) ensures a unique solution.

Equation (1.53) cannot be solved in the general case, so two approximate evaluations will be given.

In the first case $\beta \to 1$, therefore the value of x at which the critical state sets in is small and the second term in (1.53) can be neglected. Indeed, if u'_x is evaluated at the initial moment, neglecting the second term with respect to the third is equivalent to neglecting unity compared with $3n/\alpha$. Thus the equation governing u reduces to

$$u'_x + \left[1 + b - \frac{3}{4}\frac{1+b}{1-b} + \frac{\alpha}{x}\right]u = \frac{k_0}{1-\beta}\left(1 + b + \frac{\alpha}{x}\right). \quad (1.54)$$

Hence

$$u = e^{kx}x^{-\alpha}\int_0^x \frac{k_0}{1-\beta}\left(1 + b + \frac{\alpha}{\xi}\right)e^{-k\xi}\,\xi d\xi + u(0),$$

$$k = \frac{4\beta - 1}{4(\beta - 1)}. \quad (1.55)$$

When studying the stability by the quasi-static criterion we have $k_0 = m_0 \neq 0$ in the interval $[x_1, x_2]$, and $k_0 = 0$ when $x > x_2$, where x_2 can be arbitrarily small. Consequently, when $x > x_2$ the integral in (1.55) is constant and the condition $\dot{w} = 0$, in analogy to $u'_x = 0$, assumes the form

$$k - \frac{\alpha}{x} = 0 \ \text{or} \ p_l = \frac{\alpha}{n}\frac{4\beta}{4\beta - 1}(1 - \beta)\varepsilon_E. \quad (1.56)$$

It follows from (1.56) that $p_i = 0$ only for $\beta = 1$, as for a rod.

In the second case $\beta \to 0$, where the value of x at which the critical state sets in cannot be considered small. For evaluating the second term we observe that

$$e^{-x} \int_0^x e^{\xi} u d\xi \approx u_1, \tag{1.57}$$

which represents sufficiently correctly the actual state of affairs if u changes little. This approach leads to the equation

$$u'_x + \left[1 + b - 3\frac{1+b}{3-4\beta} + \frac{\alpha}{x}\right] u = \frac{4k_0}{3-4\beta}\left(1 + b + \frac{\alpha}{x}\right). \tag{1.58}$$

Hence

$$u = e^{k_1 x} x^{-\alpha} \int_0^x \frac{4k_0}{3-4\beta}\left[1 + b + \frac{\alpha}{\xi}\right] e^{-k_1 \xi} \xi d\xi + u(0),$$

$$k_1 = \frac{4\beta(1+\beta)}{3-4\beta}. \tag{1.59}$$

As in the first case, the critical state sets in when p_i is determined by the condition

$$k_1 - \frac{\alpha}{x} = 0, \text{ or } p_i = \frac{\alpha}{n}\left(\frac{3}{4} - \beta\right)\varepsilon_{E}. \tag{1.60}$$

Exact evaluation coincides practically with (1.56) for $\beta > \frac{3}{4}$, with (1.60) for $\beta < \frac{1}{4}$, and lies between (1.56) and (1.60) for $\frac{3}{4} > \beta > \frac{1}{4}$.

Consider now buckling of a plate having an initial distortion. It is readily shown that $\dot{w}(t \to 0) \to \infty$ at arbitrary β. Consequently the condition $\ddot{w} = 0$ is satisfied at $t \neq 0$ for $\beta < 1$. In this case all the above qualitative features are also valid. To simplify the solution we set $\alpha = 1$ and again deal with two cases.

In the first case $\beta \to 1$. On the basis of the previous assumptions we obtain from (1.55)

$$u = e^{kx} x^{-1} \int_0^x \frac{\beta u_0}{1-\beta}(n\xi + 1) e^{-k\xi} d\xi$$

or

$$\left[\frac{u(1-\beta)}{\beta u_0} + \frac{n}{k}\right]\frac{k}{n+k} = \frac{e^{kx} - 1}{kx}. \tag{1.61}$$

The critical condition $u''_{tt}=0$ yields for relationship (1.61)

$$kx \approx 1.36 \text{ or } p_i = 1.36 \frac{1}{n} \frac{4\beta}{4\beta - 1} (1 - \beta)\, \varepsilon_E. \tag{1.62}$$

In the second case $\beta \to 0$. Expression (1.59), as in the previous case, gives

$$p_i \approx 1.36 \frac{1}{n} \left(\frac{3}{4} - \beta\right) \varepsilon_E. \tag{1.63}$$

It is noteworthy that, in line with flow theory, the critical state for a plate is determined by two criteria, as for the state of a rod /5/.

The simpler cases of the boundary conditions and loading conditions have been considered, for which the form of buckling coincides with the form determined by the purely elastic problem. As an example, consider a rectangular, freely supported plate affecting the form of the buckling as dependent on the additional load. The shape of the buckling is determined by the condition of minimum critical time.

For plates compressed in one direction

$$\Lambda = \frac{\partial^2}{\partial x^2}, \quad \alpha_{11} = -1, \quad \alpha_{12} = \alpha_{22} = 0\,. \tag{1.64}$$

The deflection of a freely supported rectangular plate is given by

$$\begin{aligned} w &= a(t) \sin \frac{m_1 \pi x}{l_1} \sin \frac{m_2 \pi y}{l_2}, \\ w_0 &= a_0 \sin \frac{m_1 \pi x}{l_1} \sin \frac{m_2 \pi y}{l_2}. \end{aligned} \tag{1.65}$$

Substitution of (1.64) and (1.65) in (1.50) yields the equation

$$\begin{gathered} a - \beta_1 (a_1 + a_0) - (1 - S_1)\, e^{-R} \int_0^t Ega e^{R} dt - \\ - S_1 e^{-T} \int_0^t Eg (b + 1)\, a e^{T} dt = 0; \\ \pi^2 \left(\frac{m_1^2}{l_1^2} + \frac{m_2^2}{l_2^2}\right) \beta_1 = \frac{m_1^2}{l_1^2} \sigma_0, \quad S_1 = \frac{3}{4} \pi^2 \frac{m_1^2 \beta_1}{\sigma_0 l_1^2}. \end{gathered} \tag{1.66}$$

For hardening governed by a power law, equation (1.66) assumes the form

$$a - \beta_1(a_1 + a_0) - (1 - S_1)\, e^{-x} \int_0^x a e^x dx -$$

$$- S_1 e^{-nx} x^{-\alpha} \int_0^x x^\alpha n e^{nx} a dx = 0. \quad (1.67)$$

Consider here two limiting cases for which the critical state sets in at small and large x, corresponding respectively to loads close to the Euler critical load and close to zero.

F i r s t c a s e. Let x be small. Then

$$\int_0^x a e^x dx \approx 0$$

in which case (1.67) reduces to the form

$$a - \beta_1(a_1 + a_0) - S_1 e^{-nx} x^{-\alpha} \int_0^x x^\alpha n e^{nx} a dx = 0. \quad (1.68)$$

This yields the following equation for a:

$$a'_x(1 - \beta_1) + a\left[(1 - \beta_1)\left(n + \frac{\alpha}{x}\right) - S_1 n\right] = a_0\beta_1\left(n + \frac{\alpha}{x}\right). \quad (1.69)$$

In line with the quasi-static criterion the critical state sets in upon fulfillment of the condition

$$(1 - \beta_1)\left(n + \frac{\alpha}{x}\right) - S_1 n = 0. \quad (1.70)$$

Actually, it can be easily shown that for small x, less than the value of x_1 determined from (1.70), there exists a stable state, whereas for $x > x_1$ the state is unstable. This circumstance is readily verified for all other cases too.

From (1.70) we have

$$x = \frac{\alpha}{n} \frac{1}{\frac{S_1}{1 - \beta_1} - 1}, \quad \left(\beta_1 < 1, \ \frac{S_1}{1 - \beta_1} > 1\right). \quad (1.71)$$

With increasing m_2, parameters S_1 and β_1 decrease and consequently x increases. However, since m_2 only assumes integral positive values, minimum x is realized when $m_2=1$. Employing the condition $x'_{m_1}=0$ (1.71) yields

$$m=\frac{l_1}{l_2\sqrt{2\beta-1}}, \qquad \beta=\frac{\sigma_l}{\sigma_E}. \tag{1.72}$$

Consider now the criterion $\ddot{a}=0$. From (1.69) we obtain the following expression for a:

$$a=x^{-\alpha}e^{n_1x}a_1\int_0^x\left(n+\frac{\alpha}{x}\right)x^{\alpha}e^{-n_1x}dx,$$

$$n_1=n\left(\frac{S_1}{1-\beta_1}-1\right), \qquad a_1=\frac{\alpha_0\beta_1}{1-\beta_1}. \tag{1.73}$$

For integral α, a is readily found in finite form. Suppose $\alpha=1$. Then the following equation is derived with which to determine x from the condition $\ddot{a}=0$:

$$\left[\frac{e^{n_1x}-1}{x}\right]^{\cdot\cdot}=0, \tag{1.74}$$

and therefore

$$x=\frac{1.36}{n}\cdot\frac{1}{\dfrac{S_1}{1-\beta_1}-1}. \tag{1.75}$$

Expressions (1.71) and (1.75) differ only by a factor. Consequently in the present case the values of m_1 and m_2 coincide for both criteria.

S e c o n d c a s e. Let x be large. Then

$$e^{-x}\int_0^x ae^x dx\approx a$$

in which case (1.67) reduces to the form

$$(S_1-\beta_1)a-\beta_1a_0-S_1e^{-nx}x^{-\alpha}\int_0^x x^{\alpha}e^{x}nadx=0, \tag{1.76}$$

or, in differential equation form for a,

$$a'_x+a\left(\frac{\alpha}{x}-\frac{n\beta_1}{S_1-\beta_1}\right)=\frac{a_0\beta_1}{S_1-\beta_1}\left(n+\frac{\alpha}{x}\right). \tag{1.77}$$

In line with the quasi-static criterion the critical state is determined by the condition

$$x = \frac{\alpha}{n}\left(\frac{S_1}{\beta_1} - 1\right) \text{ or } x = \frac{\alpha}{n}\left[\frac{3}{4}\frac{\pi^2}{\sigma_0}\frac{m_1^2}{l_1^2} - 1\right]. \tag{1.78}$$

which yields $m_1 = 1$.

The moment at which $\ddot{a} = 0$ is found from equation (1.77):

$$a = \frac{a_0\beta_1}{S_1 - \beta_1} x^{-\alpha} e^{-n_2 x} \int_0^x \left(n + \frac{\alpha}{x}\right) x^{\alpha} e^{-n_2 x} dx, \tag{1.79}$$

$$n_2 = \frac{n\beta_1}{S_1 - \beta_1}.$$

Equation (1.79) is the same as (1.73), and consequently the results satisfying the quasi-static criterion and the condition $\ddot{a} = 0$ are identical.

Thus the shape of the buckling as dependent on the ratio of the applied and critical load determined by the elastic problem is the same for both criteria. Therefore the qualitative picture coincides with the results obtained for plates from the condition $\ddot{a} = 0$ using the deformation theory of Shesterikov /9/, who notes that, within the frame of linear deformation theory, an infinitesimal increase in deflection over a finite time is observed in the case of plates. Flow theory predicts no such result for plates.

Consider now Ivanov's method of determining the critical state by residual deflection /7/. It is based on the critical residual initial deflection. As for the criteria applied above, for the case in question the method of residual deflection gives a small quantitative deviation upon numerical computation, but nevertheless gives a qualitative rigorous picture. In addition, they are all characterized by the initial behavior of the element.

The method of residual deflection employing flow theory makes possible a very simplified investigation of the behavior of plates. In this case there is actually no need for additional hypotheses. Suppose, for example, a plate without initial deflection is subjected to stresses distributed over its surface. Let us assume that a definite system of small transverse loads acts on it, and is distributed with time in such a manner that the resulting deflection is maintained constant. The critical time is taken as the instant at which the rotating forces return to zero.

As an illustration we use the method of residual deflection to determine the critical state of a rectangular, freely supported plate compressed in one direction.

Assuming $u=u_0$ and setting the right-hand side equal to zero, equation (1.51) yields the following relationship for x_1:

$$1-(1-S_1)e^{-x_1}\int_0^{x_1} e^x dx-\beta_1-S_1 e^{-nx_1}x_1^{-\alpha}\int_0^{x_1} x^\alpha n e^{nx} dx=0. \qquad (1.80)$$

The investigation is carried out for $\alpha = 1$. In this case (1.80) reduces to the transcendental equation

$$\left(\frac{m_1^2}{l_1^2}+\frac{m_2^2}{l_2^2}\right)^2=\frac{3}{4}\frac{m_1^4}{l_1^4}+4\beta\frac{m_1^2}{l_1^2 l_2^2}e^{x_1}=$$

$$=\frac{e^{x_1}(1-e^{-nx_1})}{nx_1}\frac{3m_1^4}{4l_1^4},\quad \beta=\frac{\sigma_i}{\sigma_E}. \qquad (1.81)$$

It follows from the condition $\frac{\partial x_1}{\partial m_2}=0$ that $m_2=0$, and, since $m_2\to\infty$ when $x_1\to\infty$, for minimum x_1 at m_2 the value of m_2 must be minimum. Consequently the condition $m_2=1$ is fulfilled for any β, in which case (1.81) reduces to the following equation for x_1:

$$(m_0+1)^2=\frac{3}{4}m_0^2\left[1-\frac{e^{x_1}(1-e^{-nx_1})}{nx}\right]+4\beta m_0 e^{x_1},$$

$$m_0=\left(\frac{m_1 l_2}{l_1}\right)^2. \qquad (1.82)$$

The value of parameter m_0 (and consequently m_1) is determined by the condition $\frac{\partial x_1}{\partial m_1}=0$. Hence

$$m_0^2=\frac{4n\ln p}{n\ln p+3p(1-p^{-n})},\quad \beta=\frac{m_0+1}{2m_0 p}. \qquad (1.83)$$

Figure 1.4 presents the dependence of m_0 on β for n equal to 2, 3, 4 and 10. The condition $m_0=1$ corresponds to the elastic solution. A comparison of the results with those computed by Shesterikov's method /6/ shows that the shape of the curves $m_0\sim\beta$ coincides qualitatively with the shape of the graph of buckling vs. β, as determined by the quasi-static criterion and the condition $\ddot{a}=0$.

The stability problem of shells subject to creep was first formulated and solved by Hoff /10, 11/. He studied the loss of stability of a cylindrical shell during bending. This loss was ascribed to the effect on flexural rigidity exerted by flattening of the cross-section. We shall treat the problem here according to /12/.

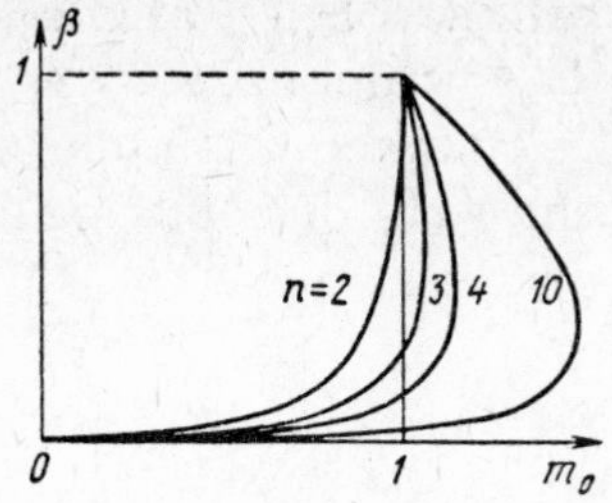

FIGURE 1.4.

Suppose R is the radius of the shell and the x axis points along the generatrix. Let angle φ denote the angular position of a point, v the displacement in the direction of the tangent to the directrix, and w the displacement perpendicular to the shell.

The condition that the tangential strain vanishes is

$$\frac{\partial v}{\partial \varphi} - w = 0.$$

This condition is satisfied by setting

$$w = c \cos 2\varphi, \quad v = \frac{c}{2} \sin 2\varphi. \tag{1.84}$$

Thus the circular cross-section is transformed into an elliptical one with semiaxes $R \pm c$. The change of curvature in the circumferential direction is

$$k_\varphi = \frac{1}{R^2}\left(\frac{\partial^2 w}{\partial \varphi^2} + \frac{\partial v}{\partial \varphi}\right) = -\frac{3c}{R^2} \cos 2\varphi. \tag{1.85}$$

The simplification used in treating the present problem is that the stress σ along the generatrix is assumed to depend only on the strain rate $\dot{e}$ in that direction, whereas the rate of change of curvature $\dot{k}_\varphi$ depends only on the transverse bending moment M_φ:

$$\dot{e} = \varepsilon_*\left(\frac{\sigma}{\sigma_*}\right)^n, \quad \dot{k}_\varphi = \varkappa_*\left(\frac{M_\varphi}{M_*}\right)^p. \tag{1.86}$$

This assumption is close to reality in the case of reinforced shells, when stringers take part in longitudinal strain and independently acting frames in transverse strain. Relationship (1.86) pertains to several reduced shells in which the rigidity of the reinforcement is included. When applying the first of these relationships it must be remembered that the stress σ is distributed over some reduced thickness $2h$.

Before deformation, the distance of the points of the middle surface of the shell from the axis of bending is $y=R\cos\varphi$, after deformation

$$y = R\cos\varphi - w\cos\varphi - v\sin\varphi,$$

or

$$y = R\cos\varphi\left[1 - \frac{c}{R}\cos^2\varphi\right].$$

If k denotes the change in the curvature of the shell axis caused by the bending moment M, then

$$e = ky = kR\cos\varphi\left[1 - \frac{c}{R}\cos^2\varphi\right]. \tag{1.87}$$

When determining the condition of shell equilibrium, we first investigate possible displacements. Only such parameters c are varied which preserve the invariability of the value of moment M. The equilibrium equation is expressed in the form

$$h\int_0^{\pi/2}\sigma\delta e d\varphi + 2\int_0^{\pi/4} M_\varphi \delta k_\varphi d\varphi = 0. \tag{1.88}$$

Here e and k_φ are given by formulas (1.87) and (1.88), since σ and M_φ must be determined from (1.86). Parameters c and k must be computed, as well as their derivatives $\dot{c}$ and $\dot{k}$. The second equation is obtained by equating the moment of the stress σ in the cross-section to the constant additional moment M:

$$M = 4hR\int_0^{\pi/2}\sigma y d\varphi. \tag{1.89}$$

The computation of the unknown functions $k(t)$ and $c(t)$ leads to two differential equations:

$$\dot{k} = \frac{\varepsilon_*}{R}\left(\frac{M}{hR^2\sigma_*}\right)^n\left[\frac{I_{1n}}{1 - \frac{n+1}{n}\frac{c}{R}\left(1+\frac{z}{n+1}\right)\frac{I_{3n}}{I_{1n}}}\right]^n, \tag{1.90}$$

$$\dot{c} = \varkappa_* R^2\frac{1}{3}\left(\frac{M_k}{M_*}\right)^p\left[\frac{I_{3n}}{3I_{1n}I_{1p}}\,\frac{1 - \frac{c}{nR}(1+z)\frac{I_{5n}}{I_{3n}}}{1 - \frac{n+1}{n}\frac{c}{R}\left(1+\frac{Z}{n+1}\right)\frac{I_{3n}}{I_{1n}}}\right]^p. \tag{1.91}$$

Here

$$z = \frac{\dot{kc}}{kc},\ I_{kn} = 4\int_0^{\pi/2} (\cos\varphi)^{\frac{kn+1}{n}}\, d\varphi.$$

System (1.90) and (1.91) can be integrated numerically. Determination of the critical time, i. e., the time at which the rate of flattening is infinitely large, is not related to the specified initial flattening. Indeed, system (1.90)–(1.91) possesses the following solution satisfying the initial conditions $k(0)=c(0)=0$:

$$c = c_0 t^{p+1} + \ldots,\qquad k = k_0 t + \ldots$$

It is readily shown that the equation of axisymmetrical bending of a cylindrical shell with arbitrary initial force is applicable to the problem of axisymmetrical loss of stability, and consequently this class of problems can be investigated. The reader is referred to other work on the stability of plates and shells of polymeric material /13–17/.

§2. FORMULATION AND SOLUTION OF THE QUASI-STATIC PROBLEM OF THE STABILITY OF ELEMENTS MADE FROM LAYERED VISCOELASTIC MATERIAL

The problem of local surface buckling of compressed elements of layered material was formulated and solved by Bolotin and Sinitsyn /18/. This solution will now be examined.

Consider a body consisting of alternating layers of reinforcement and matrix, whose deformation is described by a system of kinematic and static hypotheses /19, 20/. Assuming that the reinforcing layer is prepared from ideal elastic orthotropic material, the deformation of the matrix layer is described by the linear viscoelastic law in the form

$$P_1(p) S_{jk} = P_2(p) e_{jk};\ P_3(p) S = P_4(p) e, \tag{2.1}$$

where S_{jk} and e_{jk} are the stress and strain deviators, S and e the first invariants of the stress and strain tensors, $p=\partial/\partial t$ the operator of differentiation with respect to time, and $P_j(p)$ linear operators with constant coefficients.

The operator expressions for the shear modulus and bulk modulus can be expressed in the form

$$G''(p) = G_0'' \prod_{j=1}^{M} \frac{p+\lambda_j}{p+\mu_j}; \; K''(p) = K_0 \prod_{j=1}^{Q} \frac{p+\delta_j}{p+\gamma_j}. \tag{2.2}$$

Here G_0'', K_0'' are the instantaneous shear and bulk moduli, and λ_j, μ_j, δ_j, γ_j are positive constants. Functions $G''(p)$ and $K''(p)$ are monotonically increasing functions of the variable $p > 0$ with singularities on the negative semiaxis.

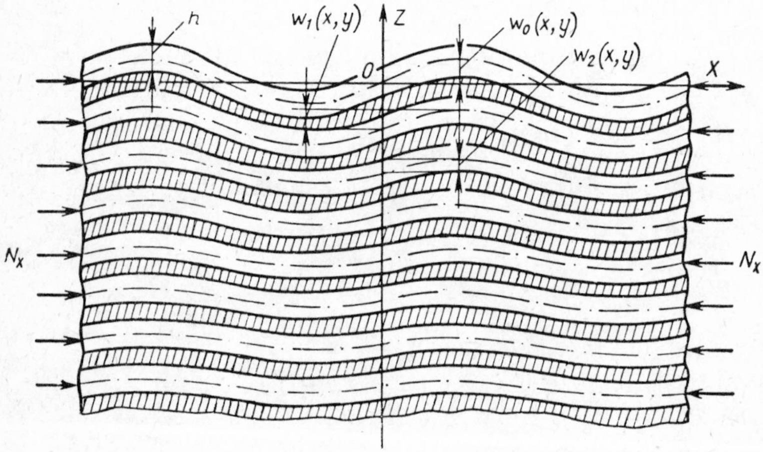

FIGURE 1.5.

Suppose the reinforced layer possesses a small initial deflection. For $t < 0$ the body is free of load. At $t = 0$ a constant load is applied to the reinforcing layer and acts in its plane. The problem is to determine how the additional normal deflection varies with time. The solution describing local (surface) buckling is also of interest. If the thickness of the layers and the depth to which significant buckling extends is small in comparison with the transverse dimensions of the body, then the body can henceforth be replaced by a half-space (Figure 1.5). In addition, the problem may be treated in a quasi-static formulation.

We first turn to the solution of the corresponding elastic problem. The normal displacements of the reinforcing layers $w\ (x,\ y)$ satisfy the equations /20/

$$D_{11}\frac{\partial^4 w_\alpha}{\partial x^4}+2D_{12}\frac{\partial^4 w_\alpha}{\partial x^2\partial y^2}+D_{22}\frac{\partial^4 w_\alpha}{\partial y^4}-\frac{E_3''}{s}(w_{\alpha+1}-2w_\alpha+w_{\alpha-1})-$$
$$-\frac{G''r^2}{4s}(\nabla^2 w_{\alpha+1}+2\nabla^2 w_\alpha+\nabla^2 w_{\alpha-1})+ \qquad (2.3)$$
$$+N_x\frac{\partial^2(w_\alpha+w^0)}{\partial x^2}+N_y\frac{\partial^2(w_\alpha+w^0)}{\partial y^2}=0 \quad (\alpha=1,2\ldots,).$$

For the surface layer ($\alpha = 0$) this equation reduces to

$$D_{11}\frac{\partial^4 w_0}{\partial x^4}+2D_{12}\frac{\partial^4 w_0}{\partial x^2\partial y^2}+D_{22}\frac{\partial^4 w_0}{\partial y^4}-\frac{E_3''}{s}(w_1-w_0)-$$
$$-\frac{G''r^2}{4s}(\nabla^2 w_1+\nabla^2 w_0)+N_x\frac{\partial^2(w_0+w^0)}{\partial x^2}+N_y\frac{\partial^2(w_0+w^0)}{\partial y^2}=0. \qquad (2.4)$$

Here we have introduced the following notation: D_{11}, D_{12} and D_{22} are the flexural rigidities of the reinforcing layers; E_{11}', E_{22}', G_{12}', ν_{12}' and ν_{21}' are the elastic constants of the reinforcing layers; N_x, N_y are the tangential forces distributed uniformly over the thickness of the reinforcing layer; $w^0(x, y)$ is the initial distortion of the reinforcing layers; $E_3''=2(1-\nu'')G''/(1-2\nu'')$ is the equivalent transverse modulus of elasticity of the matrix; G'' and ν'' are respectively the shear modulus and Poisson ratio of the matrix; h and s are the thicknesses of the reinforcing layer and matrix, respectively; $r=h+s$, ∇^2 is the Laplace operator in the x, y plane.

The initial distortion is specified in the form

$$w^0(x, y)=W^{(0)}\sin k_1x\sin k_2y, \qquad (2.5)$$

where $W^{(0)}$ is a constant, and k_1 and k_2 are wave numbers. The solution of differential-difference equations (2.3) with boundary conditions (2.4) is taken in the form

$$w_\alpha(x, y)=W_\alpha\sin k_1x\sin k_2y, \qquad (2.6)$$

where W_α are undetermined coefficients. Substitution of expressions (2.5), (2.6) in (2.3), (2.4) yields the difference equations

$$\overline{D}W_\alpha-\frac{E_3''}{s}(W_{\alpha+1}-2W_\alpha+W_{\alpha-1})+$$
$$+\frac{aG''}{4}(W_{\alpha+1}+2W_\alpha+W_{\alpha-1})=\overline{N}(W_\alpha+W^{(0)}), \quad (\alpha=1,2,\ldots,) \qquad (2.7)$$

with boundary conditions $\overline{D} = D_{11}k_1^4 + 2D_{12}k_1^2k_2^2 + D_{22}k_2^4$,

$$\overline{D}W_0 - \frac{E_3''}{s}(W_1 - W_0) + \frac{aG''}{4}(W_1 + W_0) = \overline{N}(W_0 + W^{(0)}). \quad (2.8)$$

Here

$$a = \frac{r^2}{s}(k_1^2 + k_2^2);\ \overline{N} = N_x k_1^2 + N_y k_2^2.$$

The solution of difference equations (2.7) with exponential damping into the interior of the multilayer medium is

$$W_\alpha = C\exp(-\alpha\eta) + \frac{\overline{N}W^{(0)}}{D + aG'' - \overline{N}}, \quad (2.9)$$

where C is a constant, $\eta > 0$ is the characteristic exponent, and $\eta = \ln[\theta + (\theta^2 - 1)^{1/2}]$.

We introduce the following notation:

$$\theta = \frac{\overline{D} - \overline{N} + G''(b + a)}{bG''},\ b = \frac{4(1 - \nu'')}{s(1 - 2\nu'')} - \frac{a}{2}.$$

For wave numbers of interest $b > a/2$. If a solution of (2.9) exists, it is essential that the load parameter $\overline{N}$ is less than the critical buckling load parameter $\overline{N} < \overline{N}_2$, where $\overline{N}_2 = \overline{D} + aG''$. Constant C is found from boundary condition (2.8):

$$C = \frac{a\overline{N}W^{(0)}T(\overline{N})}{2(a + b)(\overline{N}_1 - \overline{N})(\overline{N}_2 - \overline{N})}. \quad (2.10)$$

Here we have introduced the following symbols (quantity N_1 denotes the critical surface buckling parameter):

$$\overline{N}_1 = \overline{D} + a\left(\frac{b + \frac{a}{2}}{b + a}\right)G'',\ T(\overline{N}) = (\overline{N}_3 - \overline{N})^{1/2}(\overline{N}_2 - \overline{N})^{1/2} - $$
$$- \overline{D} + \overline{N},\ \overline{N}_3 = \overline{D} + (2b + a)G''. \quad (2.11)$$

With allowance for (2.9) and (2.10), the solution of differential-difference equations (2.3) with boundary conditions (2.4) has the form

$$w_\alpha = \frac{\overline{N}W^{(0)}}{\overline{N}_2 - \overline{N}}\left[1 + \frac{aT(\overline{N})\exp(-\alpha\eta)}{2(a + b)(\overline{N}_1 - \overline{N})}\right]\sin k_1x \sin k_2y\ (\alpha = 0, 1, 2, \ldots,). \quad (2.12)$$

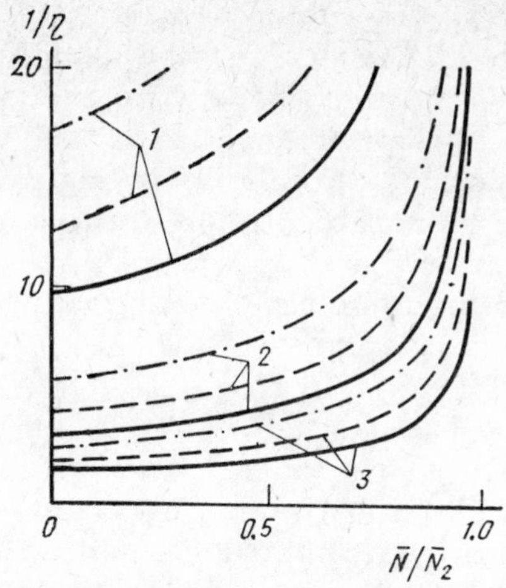

FIGURE 1.6.

Quantity $1/\eta$, which characterizes the number of layers over whose total thickness significant buckling takes place, increases with increasing compressive load, buckling wavelength, and Poisson ratio of the matrix layers. Figure 1.6 shows the change in layer thickness of the half-space into which substantial buckling propagates as a function of the compressive force, buckling wavelength and Poisson ratio of the matrix. The key to the figure is:

$$kr = 0.1\,(1);\ 0.2\,(2);\ 0.3\,(3);\ \nu'' = 0.3\,(—);\ 0.4\,(— — —);\ 0.45\,(—\cdot—).$$

We now examine the problem in which the matrix is assumed to be a viscoelastic material. Variation in the Poisson ratio of the matrix during creep is neglected. According to the correspondence principle /21/ the elastic constants in the solution of the elastic problem (2.12) are replaced by the viscoelastic operators (2.2) and apply to the result obtained using an inverse Laplace-Carson transform (parameter p is regarded as a Laplace-Carson transform parameter). The result of the substitution is denoted by $w^*_\alpha(x, y, p)$.

The asymptotic behavior of function $w_\alpha(x, y, p)$ is examined now. The behavior of function $w_\alpha(x, y, p)$ at large times t is determined by the singular points of the transform $w^*_\alpha(x, y, p)$ with maximum real part.

The critical surface buckling parameters determined by relationship (2.11) with shear moduli G_0'' and G_∞'' correspond to the instantaneous and long-time critical surface buckling parameters ($\bar{N}_1^0$, $\bar{N}_1^\infty$), respectively. For load parameters less than the critical surface buckling parameters, the singular points of the transform $w_\alpha^*(x, y, p)$ lie in the left-hand half-plane Re$p < 0$. In this case, as $t \to \infty$, the deflections of the reinforcing layers tend to a finite value determined from the solution of the corresponding problem, in which the matrix material is regarded as elastic with shear modulus equal to the long-time shear modulus of the viscoelastic matrix layers:

$$w_\alpha(x, y, t) \approx w_\alpha^*(x, y, 0).$$

For load parameters lying between the instantaneous and long-time critical load parameters of surface buckling, the singular points of the transform $w_\alpha^*(x, y, p)$ with maximum real part are simple poles p'_α. The asymptotic representation of function $w_\alpha(x, y, t)$ has the form /22/

$$w_\alpha(x, y, t) \approx \operatorname*{Res}_{p \to p'_\alpha} \left[\frac{w_\alpha^*(x, y, p)}{p} \exp(pt) \right].$$

The deflections of the reinforcing layer increase in time (following an exponential law) without limit.

The transform $w_\alpha^*(x, y, p)$ has a simple zero pole for a load parameter equal to the long-time critical load parameter of surface buckling. The inverse transform $w_\alpha(x, y, t)$ possesses a linear asymptote.

For a load parameter equal to the instantaneous critical surface buckling parameters, functions w_α^* are not Laplace-Carson transforms of any function. From the mechanical point of view this means that instantaneous buckling of the reinforcing layers takes place at load parameters not less than the instantaneous critical surface buckling parameters.

Consider the computations of Bolotin and Sinitsyn /18/ for the case when the matrix material is a standard viscoelastic body with a viscoelastic shear operator of the type

$$G''(p) = \frac{G''_\infty + \tau'' G''_0 p}{1 + \tau'' p}$$

(τ'' is the relaxation time of the matrix material, G''_0 and G''_∞ are the instantaneous and long-time shear moduli of matrix material relaxation, respectively). For load parameters $\bar{N} \neq \bar{N}_1^\infty$ the function of buckling of the surface layer assumes the form

$$w_0\left(x, y, \frac{t}{\tau''}\right) = \frac{\overline{N}W^{(0)}}{\overline{N}_2^0 - \overline{N}} \left\{\varphi_1\left(\frac{t}{\tau''}\right) + \right.$$

$$+ \frac{a}{2(a+b)(\overline{N}_1^0 - \overline{N})} [(\overline{N}_2^0 - \overline{N})^{1/2} (\overline{N}_3^0 - \overline{N})^{1/2} \varphi_2\left(\frac{t}{\tau''}\right) -$$

$$\left. - (\overline{D} - \overline{N}) \varphi_3\left(\frac{t}{\tau''}\right)]\right\} \sin k_1 x \sin k_2 y,$$

$$\varphi_1(t) = \frac{1}{\alpha_2} [1 - (1 - \alpha_2) \exp(-\alpha_2 t)],$$

$$\varphi_2(t) = \varphi(t) + \frac{\alpha_3}{\alpha_1} \int_0^t \varphi(z)\, dz +$$

$$+ \left(1 + \alpha_3 - \alpha_1 - \frac{\alpha_3}{\alpha_1}\right) e^{-\alpha_1 t} \int_0^t e^{\alpha_1 z} \varphi(z)\, dz, \tag{2.13}$$

$$\varphi_3(t) = \frac{1}{\alpha_1 \alpha_2} + \sum_{k=1}^{2} \frac{(1 - \alpha_k)^2 \exp(-\alpha_k t)}{\alpha_k (2\alpha_k - \alpha_1 - \alpha_2)},$$

$$\varphi(t) = \exp[-(\alpha_2 + \alpha_3) t] I_0 \left[\frac{(\alpha_3 - \alpha_2) t}{2}\right];$$

$$\alpha_1 = \frac{\overline{N}_1^\infty - \overline{N}}{\overline{N}_1^0 - \overline{N}}; \quad \alpha_2 = \frac{\overline{N}_2^\infty - \overline{N}}{\overline{N}_2^0 - \overline{N}}; \quad \alpha_3 = \frac{\overline{N}_3^\infty - \overline{N}}{\overline{N}_3^0 - \overline{N}}.$$

Equation (2.13) remains valid for a load parameter $\overline{N} = \overline{N}_1^\infty$, in which case functions $\varphi_2(t)$ and $\varphi_3(t)$ are given by

$$\varphi_2(t) = \varphi(t) + [1 + \alpha_3(1 + t)] \int_0^t \varphi(z)\, dz - \alpha_3 \int_0^t z\varphi(z)\, dz,$$

$$\varphi_3(t) = \frac{2\alpha_2 - 1}{\alpha_2^2} + \frac{t}{\alpha_2} + \frac{(1 - \alpha_2)^2}{\alpha_2^2} \exp(-\alpha_2 t). \tag{2.14}$$

The following characteristics of the isotropic reinforcing and matrix layers were taken in the calculations: $E' = 7.65 \cdot 10^5$ kg/cm^2; $\nu' = 0.25$; $G_0'' = 2.55 \cdot 10^4$ kg/cm^2; $G_\infty'' = 1.53 \cdot 10^2$ kg/cm^2; $\nu'' = 0.3$; $h = 0.04$ cm; $s = 0.02$ cm. The wave numbers and tangential stresses are given by $k_1 = k_2 = 6.28$ cm^{-1}; $N_x = N_y = N$. The long-time and instantaneous critical surface buckling load are $N_0 = 48 \cdot 10^2$ kg/cm, $N_\infty = 3.65 \cdot 10^2$ kg/cm, respectively.

The computation results are presented in Figure 1.7, which shows buckling of the half-space surface layer. Curves 1 to 5 are constructed for the following loads: 1 — $N = -2\, N_\infty$; 2 — $0.6\, N_\infty$; 3 — $0.8\, N_\infty$; 4 — N_∞; 5 — $1.1\, N_\infty$. Curves 1'–5' correspond to the buckling of a half-space under the same loads, but disregarding surface effects.

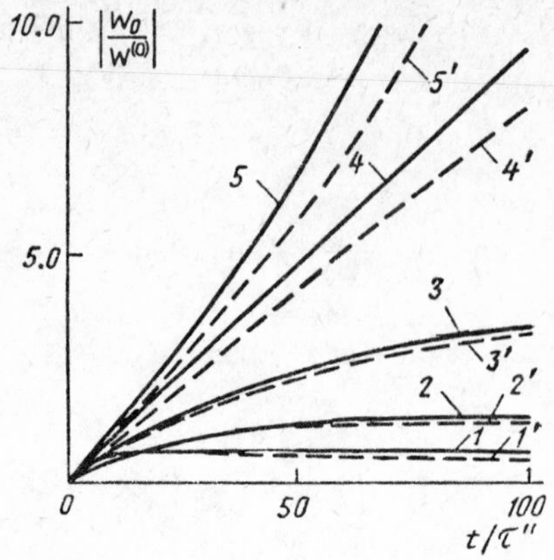

FIGURE 1.7.

Bolotin and Sinitsyn /18/ reached the following conclusions:

1. If the compressive stresses of the reinforcing layers do not exceed a certain critical value which, for sufficiently large wavelengths, is of the order of the long-time shear modulus of the matrix material, the surface buckling deformation attains stability close to the value determined for an elastic reinforced half-space with long-time moduli of elasticity.

2. If the compressive stresses in the reinforcing layer exceed a certain "long-time" critical value, the surface buckling deformations increase with time according to a near-exponential law until the conditions governing the applicability of linear theory are disturbed. The deformation increases with increasing compressive forces and buckling wavelengths.

3. The thickness of the half-space layer to which significant buckling extends increases with increase in the compressive forces, the buckling wavelength and the Poisson ratio of the matrix material.

§3. STABILITY OF PLATES MADE FROM GLASS-REINFORCED PLASTICS

In practice glass-reinforced plastics are often used with cross-reinforcement and with perpendicular positioned reinforcement elements as well as materials with diagonal reinforcement. Such glass-reinforced plastics are orthotropic materials /16/.

The hereditary creep law for an anisotropic linear body can be expressed in the form /23, 24/

$$\varepsilon_x = \bar{E}_1^{-1}(\sigma_x - \bar{\nu}_1\sigma_y),\ \varepsilon_y = \bar{E}_2^{-1}(\sigma_y - \bar{\nu}_2\sigma_x),\ \varepsilon_{xy} = \bar{G}^{-1}\sigma_{xy},$$
$$\bar{E}_1\bar{\nu}_2 = \bar{E}_2\bar{\nu}_1.$$

Here $\bar{E}_1, \bar{E}_2, \bar{\nu}_1, \bar{\nu}_2, \bar{G}$ are essentially Volterra operators, corresponding to the moduli of elasticity along the principal directions x and y, the Poisson ratios and the shear modulus. For example, if $f(t)$ is some function of time, then /25/

$$\bar{G}f(t) = G_0\left[f(t) - \int_0^t G(t-\tau)\, f(\tau)\, d\tau\right] = G_0(1 - \bar{G}^*)\, f(t).$$

Henceforth, on the basis of /25/ and experimentally determined data (for example, /26/), operators $\bar{E}^*, \ldots, \bar{G}^*$ will be taken as the Rabotnov operators determined by

$$\bar{\mathit{Э}}^*_\alpha(\beta)\, f(t) = \int_0^t (t-\tau)^\alpha \sum_{n=1}^{\infty} \frac{\beta^n (t-\tau)^{n(1+\alpha)}}{\Gamma[(n+1)(1+\alpha)]} f(\tau)\, d\tau, \qquad (3.1)$$

where parameters β are essentially negative quantities.

Consider a thin rectangular orthotropic plate of glass-reinforced plastic and supported on all four sides. Suppose a uniformly distributed compressive load of intensity p is applied to two opposite sides /25/. The x, y axes are chosen in the middle plane of the plate along two perpendicular sides of length a and b, respectively (Figure 1.8). The planes of elastic symmetry are parallel to the edges of the plate. The stress acts in the xy plane along the x axis. The validity of the hypothesis of non-deforming normals is assumed to extend with sufficient accuracy also to the case of bent plates made from glass-reinforced plastics, in which case one may neglect the influence of shear between the layers on the rigidity parameters.

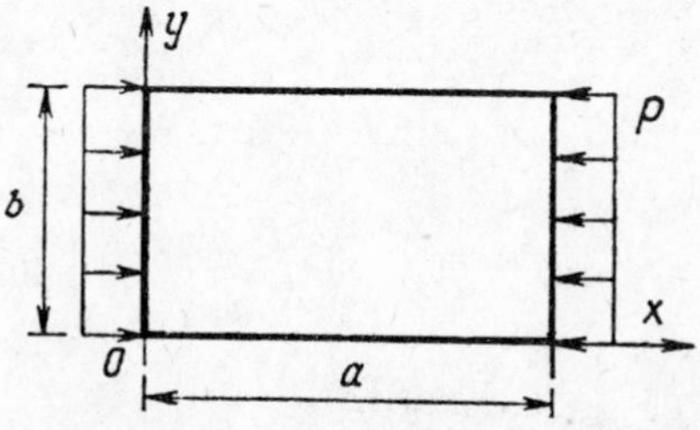

FIGURE 1.8.

In the presence of an initial deflection w_0 the equation of the curved surface of elastic orthotropic plates under the conditions formulated above is

$$D_1 \frac{\partial^4 w}{\partial x^4} + 2(D_1\nu_2 + D_3)\frac{\partial^4 w}{\partial x^2 \partial y^2} + D_2 \frac{\partial^4 w}{\partial y^4} + p\frac{\partial^2 (w + w_0)}{\partial x^2} = 0, \quad (3.2)$$

where w is the deflection of plates, D_1 and D_2 the flexural rigidities, and D_3 the torsional rigidity.

Employing the Volterra principle and the Rabotnov method, one can derive from (3.2) an equation for orthotropic plates of linear hereditary material in the form

$$\overline{D}_1 \frac{\partial^4 w}{\partial x^4} + 2(\overline{D}_1 \nu_2 + \overline{D}_3)\frac{\partial^4 w}{\partial x^2 \partial y^2} + \overline{D}_2 \frac{\partial^4 w}{\partial y^4} + p\frac{\partial^2 (w + w_0)}{\partial x^2} = 0, \quad (3.3)$$

where $\overline{D}_1$, $\overline{D}_2$ and $\overline{D}_3$ are linear viscoelastic operators related to operators $\overline{E}_1, \ldots, \overline{G}$ by the relationships

$$\overline{D}_1 = \frac{\overline{E}_1 h^3}{12(1 - \nu_1\nu_2)}, \quad \overline{D}_2 = \frac{\overline{E}_2 h^3}{12(1 - \nu_1\nu_2)}, \quad \overline{D}_3 = \frac{\overline{G} h^3}{12},$$

h being the plate thickness. Henceforth the Poisson ratios will be assumed constant and equal to ν_1 and ν_2, since the introduction of operators $\overline{\nu}_1$ and $\overline{\nu}_2$ considerably complicates the problem without contributing substantially to the accuracy of its solution.

Suppose the initial deflection w_0 is given by

$$w_0 = A^0_{mn} \sin\frac{m\pi x}{a} \sin\frac{n\pi y}{b} \quad (3.4)$$

(m and n are essentially integers).

The solution for w is

$$w = A_{mn}(t) \sin\frac{m\pi x}{a} \sin\frac{n\pi y}{b}. \quad (3.5)$$

Substitution of (3.4) and (3.5) in (3.3) yields

$$\frac{\pi^2}{b^2}\left[\left(\frac{m}{c}\right)^2 \overline{D}_1 + 2n^2(\nu_2 \overline{D}_1 + \overline{D}_3) + n^4\left(\frac{c}{m}\right)^2 \overline{D}_2\right] A_{mn}(t) =$$
$$= p[A_{mn}(t) + A^0_{mn}], \quad c = \frac{a}{b}. \quad (3.6)$$

It is evident from equation (3.6) that the minimum value of the critical force is obtained when $n = 1$. Therefore we limit ourselves to this case.

The operators $\overline{D}_1, \overline{D}_2, \overline{D}_3$ are proportional to $\overline{E}_1, \overline{E}_2, \overline{G}$, the hereditary part of which (as mentioned above) is the operator $\overline{Э}_\alpha^*(\beta)$ determined from relationship (3.1). Thus the operators D_i ($i = 1, 2, 3$) assume the form

$$D_i = \overline{D}_i^0 [1 + \varkappa_i \overline{Э}_\alpha^* (\beta_i)]. \tag{3.7}$$

Quantity D_i^0 is the rigidity related to the elastic deformations; they are constant numbers. Substituting the $\overline{D}_i$ in equation (3.6) by their values given by (3.7), we obtain

$$\left[1 - \frac{\pi^2}{b^2 (p_0 - p)} \sum_{i=1}^{3} \lambda_i \varkappa_i D_i^0 \overline{Э}_\alpha^* (\beta_i)\right] A_{mn}(t) = \frac{p A_{mn}^0}{p_0 - p}, \tag{3.8}$$

where

$$p_0 = \frac{\pi^2}{b^2} [\lambda_1 D_1^0 + \lambda_2 D_2^0 + \lambda_3 D_3^0],\ \lambda_1 = \left(\frac{m}{c}\right)^2 + 2\nu_2,$$

$$\lambda_2 = \left(\frac{c}{m}\right)^2,\ \lambda_3 = 4.$$

Multiplication of both sides of equation (3.8) by an operator which is the reciprocal of the operator in square brackets on the right-hand side yields, in accordance with the algebraic rules pertaining to operators $\overline{Э}_\alpha^*$, /12/

$$A_{mn}(t) = \left[1 + \sum_{s=1}^{3} \chi_s \overline{Э}_\alpha^* (r_s)\right] \frac{A_{mn}^0 p}{p_0 - p} =$$

$$= \frac{A_{mn}^0 p}{p_0 - p} \left[1 + \sum_{s=1}^{3} \chi_s \overline{Э}_\alpha^* (r_s)\right] \cdot 1. \tag{3.9}$$

Quantities r_s are the roots of the equation

$$r^3 + g_2 r^2 + g_1 r + g_0 = 0, \tag{3.10}$$

where

$$g_0 = -\beta_1 \beta_2 \beta_3 \left[1 + \frac{\pi^2}{b^2 (p_0 - p)} \sum_{i=1}^{3} \lambda_i \frac{\varkappa_i}{\beta_i} D_i^0\right],$$

$$g_1 = \beta_1\beta_2 + \beta_2\beta_3 + \beta_3\beta_1 +$$

$$+ \frac{\pi^2}{b^2(p_0 - p)} [\lambda_1\varkappa_1 D_1^0(\beta_2 + \beta_3) + \lambda_2\varkappa_2 D_2^0(\beta_3 + \beta_1) + \lambda_3\varkappa_3 D_3^0(\beta_1 + \beta_2)], \quad (3.11)$$

$$g_2 = -\sum_{i=1}^{3} \beta_i - \frac{\pi^2}{b^2(p_0 - p)} \sum_{i=1}^{3} \lambda_i \varkappa_i D_i^0.$$

Coefficients χ_s are found by solving the system of three linear equations

$$1 + \sum_{s=1}^{3} \frac{\chi_s}{\beta_i - r_s} = 0, \quad i = 1, 2, 3. \quad (3.12)$$

Computation of functions $A_{mn}(t)$ from (3.9) for small t does not introduce serious errors, since in that case the right-hand side of (3.1) converges rapidly.

However, for large t this series converges very slowly and it is then advantageous to use the asymptotic approximation proposed by Rozovskii:

$$\bar{\partial}^*_\alpha(b)\cdot 1 \approx = -\frac{1}{\beta}\{1 - \exp[(1+\alpha)^{1+\alpha}\beta t^{1+\alpha}]\}, \quad (3.13)$$

or by Annin:

$$\bar{\partial}^*_\alpha(\beta)\cdot 1 \approx -\frac{1}{\beta} - t^{1+\alpha} \sum_{n=2}^{\infty} \frac{(\beta t^{1-\alpha})^{-n}}{\Gamma[\alpha + 2 - n(1+\alpha)]}$$

(Γ is the gamma-function).

In line with the known definitions of stability /12, 27/, we shall regard as absolute stability that state in which the deflection A_{mn} retains a finite value for any value of t, and as absolute instability that state in which for some t the deflection tends to infinity. Relationships (3.9)–(3.11) yield the critical value of the load p (denoted by p^*) for which, when $p < p^*$, the state of the plate is absolutely stable, but when $p \geqslant p^*$ it is absolutely unstable.

It is perfectly clear that $p^* < p_0$, since if the load p_0 had been applied to the plate, it would have lost stability immediately at time $t=0$. It thus follows from equation (3.9) that $A_{mn}(t)$ is infinite only when for some time t at least one of the functions $\bar{\partial}^*_\alpha(r_s)\cdot 1$ becomes infinite. It is known that $\bar{\partial}^*_\alpha(r_s)\cdot 1$ is essentially monotonically increasing, and always remains finite at finite times and approaches a definite limit (equal to $-\frac{1}{r_s}$ if $r_s < 0$) when $t \to \infty$. If $r_s \geqslant 0$, then $\bar{\partial}^*_\alpha(r_s)\cdot 1 \to \infty$ when $t \to \infty$; in this case the deflection $A_{mn}(t) \to \infty$ when $t \to \infty$.

Thus the condition of absolute stability may be stated as follows: all parameters r_s of the integral operator with fractional-exponential kernel $\bar{\mathcal{E}}^*_\alpha(r_s)$ given by (3.9) and (3.10) must be less than zero.

It is advisable to select for the critical load p^* a quantity p for which at least one $r_s = 0$ $(s = 1, 2, 3)$. For all $r_s < 0$ we obtain a finite deflection $A_{mn}(t)$. When $r_s \geqslant 0$, the deflection is infinitely greater. If at least one $r_s = 0$, then g_0 also equals zero and the corresponding value p^* of the critical load is obtained by equating to zero the right-hand side of the first of equations (3.11). If we substitute for p_0 its value, we obtain

$$p^* = \frac{\pi^2}{b^2}\left[\lambda_1\left(1-\frac{\varkappa_1}{\beta_1}\right)D_1^0 + \lambda_2\left(1-\frac{\varkappa_2}{\beta_2}\right)D_2^0 + \lambda_3\left(1-\frac{\varkappa_3}{\beta_3}\right)D_3^0\right]. \quad (3.14)$$

Expression (3.14) determines the value of the critical forces. When $p<p^*$ the plate is absolutely stable, and when $p \geqslant p^*$ it is absolutely unstable.

The value of m (denoted by m_2) which gives the lowest critical load is found in a similar way to that of an elastic plate /28/; in the corresponding formula in /28/ D_i ($i = 1, 2, 3$) is replaced by $D_i^0\left(1-\frac{\varkappa_i}{\beta_i}\right)$.

It is noteworthy that the condition of limiting stability (at $t \to \infty$) in the form of equation (3.14) is derived by applying the ideas of Krush /29/ on a steady-state elastic-hereditary medium. By setting $\varkappa_1 = \varkappa_2 = 0$ in equation (3.14) we obtain the critical force for a plate of glass-reinforced plastic for which creep develops only with respect to shear strain ε_{12}. The behavior of such plates has been studied by Bryzgalin /30/ whose results are less general than those reported here, because he assumed that there was no creep in directions 1 and 2 and limited his analysis to infinitely large times ($t \to \infty$).

The above discussion of possible infinite growth of A_{mn}, although following the classical approach, is nevertheless formal in character. For a real plate the deflection cannot be infinite. Further, in some cases even larger loads can act on the plate than those determined by (3.14). Such a plate, even if it is not absolutely stable in the sense discussed here, can withstand a load $p>p^*$ for a sufficiently long time, while preserving small deflections, and only at $t \to \infty$ does the deflection tend to infinity.

In connection with the account of the critical state, it is advantageous to choose a state for which A_{mn} possesses some finite values. Justification for such an approach is given elsewhere /12, 27/, although this approach is less rigorous than the classical one.

It is apparently best to select as critical state one for which the initial deflection A_{mn}^0 is increased k times. Thus k is determined by the relationship

$$k = \frac{A_{mn}(t)}{A_{mn}^0}.$$

Here k can be considered independent of the dimensions of the plate, since thinner plates of large dimensions in plan tolerate large transverse deformations but usually also have a large initial deflection. The actual values of k will be fixed in dependence on the type of structure and the work conditions of the plate, i. e., the tolerance of initial inaccuracies and the magnitude of the deflection.

In this connection (3.9) can be proposed as an equation for determining the critical load for a certain time of load action, or conversely, the critical time for a certain applied load. For the region in which the approximate Rozovskii equation (3.13) is valid the relation between quantities k, p and t consistent with equations (3.9) and (3.13) can be expressed in the form

$$k \approx \frac{p}{p_0 - p}\left\{1 - \sum_{s=1}^{3} \frac{\chi_s}{r_s}\left[1 - e^{(1+\alpha)^{1+\alpha}}\, r_s t^{1+\alpha}\right]\right\}. \qquad (3.15)$$

In accordance with the above, if k has some critical value k^* determined, say, by the specifications of the geometrical shape of the plate in the undeformed state and when undergoing the permissible deflections, then a relationship of type (3.15) links the critical load p^* and the critical time t^*.

Quantities r_s and χ_s are determined by solving the cubic equation (3.10) and system (3.12). However, these equations contain the undefined quantity m. Hence it is not possible to find in general the roots of equation (3.10) and (3.12) in an analytically acceptable form. It can be shown that the largest "dangerous" value of m at which, for some p, the lowest critical times are obtained lies within a denumerable set bounded by m_1 and m_2, so that $m \in [m_1, m_2]$.

Quantity m_2 was determined above; m_1 is determined as for elastic plates with rigidities equal to D_1^0 and D_2^0. If the ratio of the sides is $c > 3$, then with sufficient accuracy we may set $c/m = 1$. If $c \leqslant 3$, then for a given p it is necessary to solve (3.11), (3.12) and (3.15) for all $m \in [m_1, m_2]$. A set of times is obtained, the minimum of which is taken as the critical time. The determination of the critical load p^* for the given "resource" of working plates follows a similar procedure.

The stability of plates made from glass-reinforced plastics connected to an elastic base was treated by Pelekh et al. /31/.

§4. STABILITY OF ORTHOTROPIC VISCOELASTIC SHELLS

Boltzmann adjusted his theories in the light of test results and reached two main conclusions: (1) the stress depends not only on the strain at a given instant, but also on previous strains, the the effect of the latter diminishing with time; (2) the law of independence of action is applicable to elastic forces.

On the basis of these hypotheses, the time-dependent stress-strain relations proposed by Boltzmann assume the form

$$\begin{gathered}\varepsilon(t)=\frac{\sigma(t)}{E}+\frac{1}{E}\int_0^t K(t-s)\,\sigma(s)\,ds,\\ \sigma(t)=E\,\varepsilon(t)-E\int_0^t \Gamma(t-s)\,\varepsilon(s)\,ds.\end{gathered}\tag{4.1}$$

At the beginning of the present century Volterra developed the theory of integral equations from which, in particular, follows the relationship between the kernel K and resolvent Γ:

$$K(t)-\Gamma(t)=\int_0^t \Gamma(t-s)\,K(s)\,ds.\tag{4.2}$$

Certain nonlinear effects of creep for an incompressible material can be described by means of the equations

$$\begin{gathered}\varepsilon(t)=\psi(\sigma)+\int_0^t K(t-s)\,\psi[\sigma(s)]\,ds,\\ \varphi(\varepsilon)=\sigma(t)+\int_0^t K(t-s)\,\sigma(s)\,ds,\end{gathered}\tag{4.3}$$

where function $\psi(\sigma)$ is constructed from the similarity condition of the creep curves, whereas function $\varphi(\varepsilon)$ is constructed from the similarity condition of the isochronic curves characterizing strain upon rapid loading.

For the construction of a theory for plates and shells with rheonomic material properties, linear Boltzmann-Volterra theory in the form (4.1) and (4.2) is chosen as the physical law. Then kernel K can be chosen either with a singularity at $t=0$, or in the form of the sums of several kernels $D(t, \alpha)$ /32/, reflecting the beginning of the process and regulating K so that the relationship $\sigma\sim\varepsilon\sim t$ is expressed in the form

$$\sigma(t)=E\left[\varepsilon(t)-\lambda\int_0^t D(t-s)\,\varepsilon(s)\,ds-\int_0^t K_1(t-s)\,\varepsilon(s)\,ds\right].$$

If, for the material under investigation, the temperature displacement $a_T(T)=t/t_L$ is known, where t is the instant of observation and t_L some reduced or "local" time, the basis of the hereditary theory is valid for any temperature in a region where the temperature-time analogy is applicable. This can be expressed by replacing time t by t_L /34, 35/. For example, in the linear case

$$E\varepsilon=\int_0^{t_L} K_T(t_L-s_L)\,d\sigma(s_L);\quad K_T(x)=\int_0^x K(x)\,dx.$$

Since glass-fiber-reinforced plastics, which generally possess orthotropic properties, are widely used in the manufacture of plates and shells, the equations of shell theory are set up as applied to flexible (i.e., with geometric nonlinearity taken into account) orthotropic shallow shells whose material possesses linear heredity /35/. We assume that the hypothesis of linear normals is applicable to glass-fiber-reinforced plates and shells. In addition we assume that the stresses acting normal to the middle surface are negligible in comparison with other components, and that orthotropy is maintained during the entire deformation process.

We choose an $(x,\ y,\ z)$ coordinate system with the ox and oy axes in the directions of the warp and weft, and the oz axis normal to the $(x,\ y)$ coordinate surface. Strains of the middle layer of the shell and the curvature satisfy the following expressions in terms of displacements of the middle layer $u_0,\ v_0,\ w$:

$$\begin{aligned}
e_{11}^0&=\frac{\partial u_0}{\partial x}+\frac{1}{2}\left(\frac{\partial w}{\partial x}\right)^2-k_1w, & \varkappa_x&=-\frac{\partial^2 w}{\partial x^2},\\
e_{22}^0&=\frac{\partial v_0}{\partial y}+\frac{1}{2}\left(\frac{\partial w}{\partial y}\right)^2-k_2w, & \varkappa_y&=-\frac{\partial^2 w}{\partial y^2},\\
e_{12}^0&=\frac{\partial u_0}{\partial y}+\frac{\partial v_0}{\partial x}+\frac{\partial w}{\partial x}\cdot\frac{\partial w}{\partial y}, & \varkappa_{xy}&=-\frac{\partial^2 w}{\partial x\partial y}.
\end{aligned}\tag{4.4}$$

By virtue of the Kirchhoff hypothesis, the displacements and deformations in a layer located distance z from the middle surface are given by

$$\begin{gathered}
u=u_0-z\frac{\partial w}{\partial x},\quad v=v_0-z\frac{\partial w}{\partial y},\\
e_{11}=e_{11}^0-z\frac{\partial^2 w}{\partial x^2},\quad e_{22}=e_{22}^0-z\frac{\partial^2 w}{\partial y^2},\quad e_{12}=e_{12}^0-2z\frac{\partial^2 w}{\partial x\partial x}.
\end{gathered}\tag{4.5}$$

The stress-strain relations for orthotropic materials are written in the form /36/

$$
\begin{aligned}
\sigma_{11} &= B_{11}e_{11} - \int_0^t R'_{11}(t-\tau)\, e_{11}(\tau)\, d\tau + B_{12}\, e_{22} - \\
&\quad - \int_0^t R'_{12}(t-\tau)\, e_{22}(\tau)\, d\tau, \\
\sigma_{22} &= B_{21}\, e_{11} - \int_0^t R'_{21}(t-\tau)\, e_{11}(\tau)\, d\tau + B_{22}\, e_{22} - \\
&\quad - \int_0^t R'_{22}(t-\tau)\, e_{22}(\tau)\, d\tau, \\
\sigma_{12} &= 2Be_{12} - 2\int_0^t R'(t-\tau)\, e_{12}(\tau)\, d\tau.
\end{aligned} \tag{4.6}
$$

Here

$$
\begin{gathered}
B_{11} = \frac{E_1}{1-\nu_1\nu_2}, \quad B_{12} = B_{21} = \frac{\nu_1 E_2}{1-\nu_1\nu_2} = \frac{\nu_2 E_1}{1-\nu_1\nu_2}, \quad B_{22} = \frac{E_2}{1-\nu_1\nu_2}, \\
2B = G = \frac{E_{\pi/4}}{2(1+\nu_{\pi/4})}, \quad \nu_1 = \nu_{21} = \left|\frac{e_{22}}{e_{11}}\right|, \quad \nu_2 = \nu_{12} = \left|\frac{e_{11}}{e_{22}}\right|
\end{gathered} \tag{4.7}
$$

are components of the tensor of the moduli of elastic anisotropy, and the Poisson ratios in tension along the warp and the weft:

$$
R'_{11} = B_{11}R_{11}(t), \; R'_{22} = B_{22}R_{22}(t), \; R'_{12} = B_{12}R_{12}(t), \; R' = BR \tag{4.8}
$$

are the components of the tensor of relaxation kernels.

The forces acting on unit width of the cross-section of the shell element are

$$
T_k = \int_{-\frac{h}{2}}^{+\frac{h}{2}} \sigma_{kk}\, dz, \; M_k = \int_{-\frac{h}{2}}^{+\frac{h}{2}} \sigma_{kk}\, z dz, \; \widetilde{S} = \widetilde{S}_1 = \widetilde{S}_2 = \int_{-\frac{h}{2}}^{+\frac{h}{2}} \sigma_{12}\, dz,
$$

$$
H = H_1 = H_2 = \int_{-\frac{h}{2}}^{+\frac{h}{2}} \sigma_{12} z\, dz,
$$

while the stresses σ_{mn} are given by (4.6). Substitution of expressions (4.4), (4.6) and (4.8) yields

$$\begin{aligned} T_1 &= hB_{11}(e_{11}^0 - I_{11}e_{11}^0) + hB_{12}(e_{22}^0 - I_{12}e_{22}^0), \\ T_2 &= hB_{12}(e_{11}^0 - I_{12}e_{11}^0) + hB_{22}(e_{22}^0 - I_{22}e_{22}^0), \\ \widetilde{S} &= 2hB(e_{12}^0 - Ie_{12}^0), \end{aligned} \tag{4.9}$$

where

$$I_{ij}e_{lk}^0 = \int_0^t R_{ij}(t-\tau)\,e_{lk}^0(\tau)\,d\tau.$$

Application of Laplace transforms enables (4.9) to assume the form

$$T_1^* = hB_{11}^* e_{11}^{0*} + hB_{12}^* e_{22}^{0*};\quad T_2^* = hB_{12}^* e_{11}^{0*} + hB_{22}^* e_{22}^{0*}.$$

$$\widetilde{S}^* = 2hB^* e_{12}^{0*}. \tag{4.10}$$

where

$$B_{ij}^* = B_{ij}(1 - R_{ij}^*),\quad R_{ij}^* = \int_0^\infty R_{ij}(t)\,e^{-pt}\,dt.$$

Hence

$$e_{11}^{0*} = \frac{1}{h}\,\frac{T_1^* B_{22}^* - T_2^* B_{12}^*}{B_{11}^* B_{22}^* - B_{12}^* B_{21}^*},\qquad e_{22}^{0*} = \frac{1}{h}\,\frac{B_{11}^* T_2^* - B_{21}^* T_1^*}{B_{11}^* B_{22}^* - B_{12}^* B_{21}^*},$$

$$e_{12}^{0*} = \frac{\widetilde{S}^*}{2hB^*}.$$

Consider the identity

$$\begin{aligned} &\frac{\partial^2}{\partial y^2}[2B^*(B_{22}^* T_1^* - B_{12}^* T_2^*)] + \frac{\partial^2}{\partial x^2}[2B^*(B_{11}^* T_2^* - B_{21}^* T_1^*) - \\ &- \frac{\partial^2}{\partial x\,\partial y}[B_{11}^* B_{22}^* - B_{12}^* B_{21}^*]\widetilde{S}^* = 2hB^*(B_{11}^* B_{22}^* - B_{12}^* B_{21}^*) \times \\ &\times \left[\frac{\partial^2}{\partial y^2}(e_{11}^{0*}) + \frac{\partial^2}{\partial x^2}(e_{22}^{0*}) - \frac{\partial^2}{\partial x\,\partial y}(e_{12}^{0*})\right], \end{aligned} \tag{4.11}$$

into which we introduce the above expressions for e_{ij}^{0*}. With certain simplifications we introduce the stress function φ satisfying

$$\frac{\partial^2\varphi}{\partial y^2} = \frac{1}{h}T_1,\quad \frac{\partial^2\varphi}{\partial x^2} = \frac{1}{h}T_2,\quad \frac{\partial^2\varphi}{\partial x\,\partial y} = -\frac{1}{h}\widetilde{S},$$

where application of Laplace transforms yields

$$T_1^* = h\frac{\partial^2 \varphi^*}{\partial y^2},\quad T_2^* = h\frac{\partial^2 \varphi^*}{\partial x^2},\quad \widetilde{S}^* = -h\frac{\partial^2 \varphi^*}{\partial x\,\partial y}.$$

As a result we obtain in operator form the continuity equation for an orthotropic flexible shell whose material possesses linear hereditary properties:

$$\begin{aligned}B_{11}^*\frac{\partial^4 \varphi^*}{\partial x^4} &+ \frac{1}{2B^*}(B_{11}^* B_{22}^* - B_{12}^* B_{21}^* - 4B^* B_{12}^*)\frac{\partial^4 \varphi^*}{\partial x^2\,\partial y^2} + \\ &+ B_{22}^*\frac{\partial^4 \varphi^*}{\partial y^4} = (B_{11}^* B_{22}^* - B_{12}^* B_{12}^*)\left\{\left[\left(\frac{\partial^2 w}{\partial x \partial y}\right)^2\right]^* - \right. \\ &\left. -\left(\frac{\partial^2 w}{\partial x^2}\,\frac{\partial^2 w}{\partial y^2}\right)^* - k_1\frac{\partial^2 w^*}{\partial y^2} - k_2\frac{\partial^2 w^*}{\partial x^2}\right\}.\end{aligned} \tag{4.12}$$

The right-hand side of this equation contains the nonlinear terms $\left[\left(\frac{\partial^2 w}{\partial x\,\partial y}\right)^2\right]^*, \ldots$. Henceforth we assume that the deflection can be expressed in the form $w(x, y, t) = w(x, y)\,w_1(t)$, where function $w_1(t)$, its derivatives and their squares can be operated on by Laplace transforms.

With the aid of (4.6), the expressions for the moments have the form

$$\begin{aligned}M_1 &= \int_{-\frac{h}{2}}^{+\frac{h}{2}} \sigma_{11} z\,dz = -\frac{h^3}{12}\left\{B_{11}\left[\frac{\partial^2 w}{\partial x^2} - \int_0^t R_{11}(t-\tau)\frac{\partial^2 w}{\partial x^2}\,d\tau\right] + \right. \\ &\left. + B_{12}\left[\frac{\partial^2 w}{\partial y^2} - \int_0^t R_{12}(t-\tau)\frac{\partial^2 w}{\partial y^2}\,d\tau\right)\right\}, \\ M_2 &= -\frac{h^3}{12}\left\{B_{21}\left[\frac{\partial^2 w}{\partial x^2} - \int_0^t R_{21}(t-\tau)\frac{\partial^2 w}{\partial x^2}\,d\tau\right] + \right. \\ &\left. + B_{22}\left[\frac{\partial^2 w}{\partial y^2} - \int_0^t R_{22}(t-\tau)\frac{\partial^2 w}{\partial y^2}\,d\tau\right]\right\}, \\ H &= -\frac{h^3}{12}B\left[\frac{\partial^2 w}{\partial x\,\partial y} - \int_0^t R(t-\tau)\frac{\partial^2 w}{\partial x\,\partial y}\,d\tau\right].\end{aligned} \tag{4.13}$$

Introducing M_1, M_2, H and T_1, T_2, $\widetilde{S}$ into the equation of shell equilibrium gives

$$\frac{\partial^2 M_1}{\partial x^2} + 2\frac{\partial^2 H}{\partial x\,\partial y} + \frac{\partial^2 M_2}{\partial y^2} + T_1\left(k_1 + \frac{\partial^2 w}{\partial x^2}\right) + + T_2\left(k_2 + \frac{\partial^2 w}{\partial y^2}\right) + 2\widetilde{S}\frac{\partial^2 w}{\partial x\,\partial y} + q = 0$$

and application of Laplace transforms results in the following equilibrium equation for a flexible orthotropic shell made from material with linear hereditary properties:

$$B_{11}^{*}\frac{\partial^4 w^*}{\partial x^4} + 2\left(B_{12}^{*} + 4B^*\right)\frac{\partial^4 w^*}{\partial x^2\,\partial y^2} + B_{22}^{*}\frac{\partial^4 w^*}{\partial y^4} - -\frac{12}{h^2}\left(k_2\frac{\partial^2 \varphi^*}{\partial x^2} + k_1\frac{\partial^2 \varphi^*}{\partial y^2}\right) - \frac{12}{h^2}\left[\left(\frac{\partial^2 \varphi}{\partial x^2}\,\frac{\partial^2 w}{\partial y^2}\right)^* + +\left(\frac{\partial^2 \varphi}{\partial y^2}\,\frac{\partial^2 w}{\partial x^2}\right)^* - 2\left(\frac{\partial^2 \varphi}{\partial x\,\partial y}\,\frac{\partial^2 w}{\partial x\,\partial y}\right)^*\right] - \frac{12}{h^3}q^* = 0. \quad (4.14)$$

Here $B_{ij}^{*} = B_{ij}(1 - R_{ij}^{*})$ is a known function of p.

In addition

$$M_1^* = -\frac{h^3}{12}\left(B_{11}^{*}\frac{\partial^2 w^*}{\partial x^2} + B_{12}^{*}\frac{\partial^2 w^*}{\partial y^2}\right),$$
$$M_2^* = -\frac{h^3}{12}\left(B_{21}^{*}\frac{\partial^2 w^*}{\partial x^2} + B_{22}^{*}\frac{\partial^2 w^*}{\partial y^2}\right), \quad (4.15)$$
$$H^* = -\frac{h^3}{3}B^*\frac{\partial^2 w^*}{\partial x \partial y}.$$

Thus we have the two resolvents (4.12) and (4.14) for the unknown stress $\varphi(x, y, t)$ and deflection $w(x, y, t)$. Note that two types of terms are contained in (4.12) and (4.14). For the type $B_{11}^{*}\frac{\partial^4 w^*}{\partial x^4}$, the coefficients B_{ij}^{*} are known functions of complex parameter p and the transform of the unknown functions enters linearly. For the type $\left(\frac{\partial^2 \varphi}{\partial x^2}\,\frac{\partial^2 w}{\partial y^2}\right)^*$, essential because of the method proposed, w is regarded as a known function of coordinates and time, specified to within undetermined constants. Consequently, the product under consideration is linear in the unknown function φ.

To explain the method we present one possible approximate solution of system of equations (4.12) and (4.14). Consider an orthotropic plate that is rectangular in the plan or a slightly curved panel of glass-fiber-reinforced plastic for which the known stress relaxation curves in tensile test pieces are presentable, for example, in the form

$$\sigma(t) = \sigma_0 [1 - \gamma(1 - e^{-\alpha t})]. \quad (4.16)$$

The relaxation kernel is evidently

$$R = \gamma\alpha e^{-\alpha t} \quad (0 < \gamma < 1, \ 0 < \alpha < 1), \quad (4.17)$$

where quantities α and γ depend on the orientation of the test piece.

The transform of the kernel has the form

$$R^* = \frac{\gamma\alpha}{p + \alpha}. \quad (4.18)$$

Furthermore, for simplicity we assume that

$$B^*_{ik} = B_{ik}(1 - R^*) \quad (4.19)$$

and that the deflection function is

$$w(x, y, t) = w_0(x, y) w_1(t), \quad (4.20)$$

where $w_0(x, y)$ is the elastic solution, while function $w_1(t)$ is chosen to within undetermined parameters λ and μ in the form

$$w_1(t) = \lambda - \mu e^{-\alpha t}; \ \lambda - \mu = 1. \quad (4.21)$$

The stress function φ is sought in the form

$$\varphi(x, y, t) = \varphi_0(x, y) \varphi_1(t), \quad (4.22)$$

where $\varphi_0(x, y)$ is the elastic solution, while $\varphi_1(t)$ must be determined for a given form of function $w_1(t)$.

The Laplace transform of $w_1(t)$ is

$$w_1^*(p) = \frac{\lambda}{p} - \frac{\mu}{p + \alpha}. \quad (4.23)$$

Substitution of expressions (4.19), (4.20) and (4.22) into continuity equation (4.12) gives

$$\varphi_1^* = \varkappa_1 \mathscr{E}(1 - R^*) w_1^* + n_1 \mathscr{E}(1 - R^*)(w_1^2)^*. \quad (4.24)$$

Here

$$\varkappa_1 = -\frac{\nabla_k^2 w_0}{\nabla^2\nabla^2\widetilde{\varphi}_0} = \frac{-\left(k_1 \dfrac{\partial^2 w_0}{\partial y^2} + k_2 \dfrac{\partial^2 w_0}{\partial x^2}\right)}{B_{11}\dfrac{\partial^4\varphi_0}{\partial x^4} + C\dfrac{\partial^4\varphi_0}{\partial x^2 \partial y^2} + B_{22}\dfrac{\partial^4\varphi_0}{\partial y^4}},$$

$$C = \frac{1}{2B}(\mathcal{E} - 4BB_{12}) \quad \mathcal{E} = B_{11}B_{22} - B_{12}^2,$$

$$n_1 = \frac{N_0}{\nabla^2\nabla^2\widetilde{\varphi}_0} = \frac{\left(\dfrac{\partial^2 w_0}{\partial x \partial y}\right)^2 - \dfrac{\partial^2 w_0}{\partial x^2}\dfrac{\partial^2 w_0}{\partial y^2}}{\nabla^2\nabla^2\widetilde{\varphi}_0}.$$

If we substitute expressions (4.18) and (4.23) into (4.24) and make use of the identity

$$\frac{1}{(p+k\alpha)(p+m\alpha)} = \frac{1}{(m-k)\alpha(p+k\alpha)} - \frac{1}{(m-k)\alpha(p+m\alpha)},$$

we obtain

$$\varphi_1^* = \frac{A_1}{p} + \frac{A_2}{p+\alpha} + \frac{A_3}{p+2\alpha} + \frac{A_4}{(p+\alpha)^2}. \tag{4.25}$$

Inversion of (4.25) yields

$$\varphi_1 = A_1 + A_2 e^{-\alpha t} + A_3 e^{-2\alpha t} + A_4 t e^{-\alpha t}, \tag{4.26}$$

where

$$\begin{gathered} A_1 = \mathcal{E}(1-\gamma)(\lambda\varkappa_1 + \lambda^2 n_1), \; A_2 = n_1\mathcal{E}(\nu\lambda^2 - 2\lambda\mu - \gamma\mu^2) - \\ -\varkappa_1\mathcal{E}(\mu - \lambda\gamma), \; A_3 = n_1\mathcal{E}\mu^2(1+\nu), \\ A_4 = \mathcal{E}\gamma\alpha(\varkappa_1\mu + 2n_1\lambda\mu). \end{gathered} \tag{4.27}$$

The unknown parameters λ and μ are determined by substituting expressions (4.20) and (4.22) into equilibrium equation (4.14) with allowance for (4.21) and (4.26). Hence

$$\frac{K_1}{p} + \frac{K_2}{p+\alpha} + \frac{K_3}{p+2\alpha} + \frac{K_4}{p+3\alpha} + \frac{K_5}{(p+\alpha)^2} + \frac{K_6}{(p+2\alpha)} = 0,$$

which, after inversion, gives the relationship between the load and deflection in the form

$$K_1 + K_2 e^{-\alpha t} + K_3 e^{-2\alpha t} + K_4 e^{-3\alpha t} + K_5 t e^{-\alpha t} + K_6 t e^{-2\alpha t} = 0. \tag{4.28}$$

Here

$$K_1=\nabla^2\nabla^2\widetilde{w}_0\lambda(1-\gamma)-\frac{12}{h^2}\nabla_k^2\varphi_0A_1-\frac{12}{h^2}M_0\lambda A_1-\frac{12}{h^3}q(t),$$

$$K_2=-\nabla^2\nabla^2\widetilde{w}_0(\mu-\lambda\gamma)-\frac{12}{h^2}\nabla_k^2\varphi_0A_2-\frac{12}{h^2}M_0(\lambda A_2-\mu A_1),$$

$$K_3=-\frac{12}{h^2}\nabla_k^2\varphi_0A_3-\frac{12}{h^2}M_0(\lambda A_3-\mu A_2),\ K_4=\frac{12}{h^2}M_0\mu A_3,$$

$$K_5=\nabla^2\nabla^2\widetilde{w}_0\gamma\alpha\mu-\frac{12}{h^2}\nabla_k^2\varphi A_4-\frac{12}{h^2}\lambda A_4M_0,\ K_6=\frac{12}{h^2}M_0\mu A_4.$$

From equation (4.28) we obtain

$$\begin{aligned}K_1+K_2+K_3+K_4=0\ \text{for}\ t=0,\\ K_1=0\ \text{for}\ t=\infty.\end{aligned}\tag{4.29}$$

In order to determine λ we substitute A_1 as given by relationship (4.27) in (4.29). Thus, for example, if $q=q_0=\text{const}$,

$$\lambda^3-(\varkappa_2-\varkappa_1)\lambda^2-\left(\frac{h^2}{12\mathcal{E}}\frac{m_1}{n_1}+\varkappa_1\varkappa_2\right)\lambda+\frac{q_0m}{h(1-\gamma)}=0.\tag{4.30}$$

Here

$$\varkappa_1=\frac{\nabla_k^2w_0}{N_0},\quad \varkappa_2=\frac{\nabla_k^2\varphi}{M_0},\quad m_1=\frac{\nabla^2\nabla^2\widetilde{w}_0}{M_0},\quad n_1=\frac{N_0}{\nabla^2\nabla^2\widetilde{\varphi}_0},$$

$$m=\frac{\nabla^2\nabla^2\widetilde{\varphi}_0}{\mathcal{E}N_0M_0},\quad M_0=\frac{\partial^2\varphi_0}{\partial x^2}\frac{\partial^2w_0}{\partial y^2}+\frac{\partial^2\varphi_0}{\partial y^2}\frac{\partial^2w_0}{\partial x^2}-2\frac{\partial^2w_0}{\partial x\partial y}\frac{\partial^2\varphi_0}{\partial x\partial y}.$$

The solution of equation (4.30) for a square plate made from orthotropic polyester glass-fiber-reinforced plastic with hinged support, with components of the tensor of the moduli of elasticity B_{ij}, given by

$$B_{11}=1.49\cdot10^5\ \text{kg/cm}^2,\ B_{22}=1.143\cdot10^5\ \text{kg/cm}^2,$$
$$B_{12}=B_{21}=0.18\cdot10^5\ \text{kg/cm}^2,\ B=0.13\cdot10^5\ \text{kg/cm}^2,$$

yields one real root $\lambda=1.21$, which agrees well with experimental creep data for a square plate with hinged edge support ($\lambda=1.19$).

When solving shell stability problems, it is advantageous to select function $w_1(t)$ in the form

$$w_1(t)=\lambda-\mu e^{-\alpha t}-\beta\vartheta(t-t_{\text{cr}}),$$

where

$$\vartheta = \begin{vmatrix} 0, & t < t_{cr}, \\ 1, & t = t_{cr}. \end{vmatrix}$$

Parameter β is found from the condition that the deflection "jump" in the viscoelastic problem equals the deflection "jump" in the elastic problem, since it is reasonable to assume that creep does not develop during the corresponding time.

We present the results of the problem of the stability of a circular cylindrical shell of PN-1 and T-1 polyester glass-fiber-reinforced plastic subjected to axial compression. Here, the warp and weft are directed along the generatrix and directrix, respectively.

Creep and relaxation tests showed that we can set

$$\gamma_{11} = \gamma_{22} = \frac{1}{6}, \ \alpha_{11} = \alpha_{12} = \alpha_{22} = 0.5, \ \gamma_{12} = \mu_1\gamma_{11}, \ \gamma = 3\gamma_{11},$$

where μ_1 has the order of magnitude of the Poisson ratio and is to be determined (from the condition at $t = \infty$ we obtain $\mu_1 = 0.12$). The elastic solution is found by the Ritz method, while the viscoelastic solution is found by the method presented above.

It follows from the solution for a constant load that the critical loads do not vary in comparison with the elastic loads, whereas the critical deflections increase. For a time-varying load the critical load is reduced, but the deflections increase in comparison with the elastic values. Thus $\widehat{P}_{\mathrm{u.el}} = 0.558$; $\widehat{P}_{\mathrm{u.red}} = 0.483$; $\widehat{P}_{\mathrm{l.el}} = 0.171$; $\widehat{P}_{\mathrm{l.red}} = 0.137$. Note that the values of the "upper" and "lower" critical loads depend essentially on the rate of loading (as the rate increases, the "upper" critical load increases).

Note further an important aspect which can be used with success: if we know the region of the temperatures within which the temperature-time analogy $T \sim t$ holds, i. e., if the temperature shift $a_T(T) = t/t_L$ is constructed for the material specified, then for any temperature T_k in this region the solution is obtained by simple substitution of time t by local time $t_L = a_T t$, where T_k is the "working" temperature of the shell.

§5. DYNAMIC STABILITY OF GLASS-REINFORCED PLASTIC SHELLS

The dynamic stability of a circular-cylindrical glass-reinforced-plastic shell subject to external transverse pressure was first investigated by Vol'mir and Smetanina /37/. An account of their investigation will now be given.

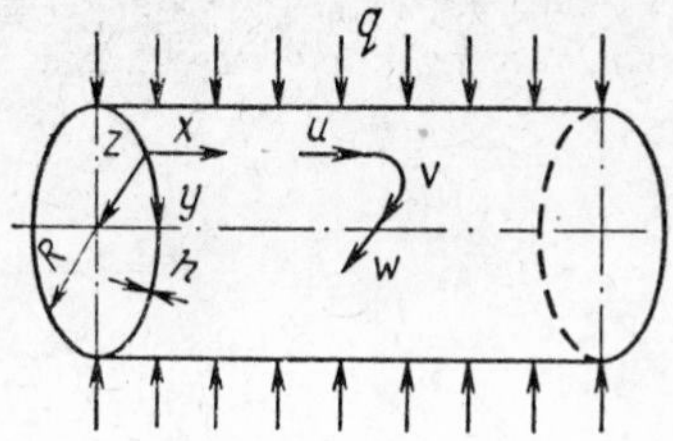

FIGURE 1.9.

Consider a closed circular-cylindrical glass-reinforced-plastic shell of radius R, length L and thickness h under the dynamic action of an external normal pressure, distributed uniformly over its lateral surface and varying with time according to the law $q=q\ (t)$ (Figure 1.9). Such a loading is characteristic of airframes and in ship-building. Vessels in the chemical industry are also frequently subjected to external overpressure.

The problem of the stability of the closed circular-cylindrical shell will be treated in the nonlinear formulation /37/. It is assumed that the end faces of the shells are hinged on frames, points of which may experience certain radial displacements, the frames themselves remaining circular. The scatter of the experimental values of the critical loads depends primarily on initial irregularities in the shape of the shell; therefore we study the behavior of shells with an initial deflection.

We assume that the cylindrical glass-reinforced-plastic shell is orthotropic and that the principal directions of rigidity coincide with the generatrix of the cylinder and the arc of the cross-section. The elastic properties of orthotropic shells are characterized by moduli E_1 and E_2 in the x and y directions, shear modulus G and Poisson ratio ν_1 (note that $E_2\nu_1=E_1\nu_2$). The coordinate system is selected so that its origin lies on the middle surface and the x, y, and z axes coincide with the generatrix, the arc of the cross section and the inner normal, respectively. The corresponding displacements of points on the middle surface are u, v, and w.

We write the differential equations of nonlinear theory of flat shells with allowance for initial irregularities and supplement them with an inertial term corresponding to w. Inertial terms corresponding to displacements u and v will be disregarded. Thus we will not investigate at present elastic wave propagation in the middle surface. The equation of motion of a shell is therefore

$$\frac{D_1\partial^4(w-w_0)}{h\partial x^4}+\frac{2D_3\partial^4(w-w_0)}{h\partial x^2\partial y^2}+\frac{D_2\partial^4(w-w_0)}{h\partial y^4}=$$
$$=\frac{\partial^2 w}{\partial x^2}\frac{\partial^2\Phi}{\partial y^2}+\frac{\partial^2 w}{\partial y^2}\frac{\partial^2\Phi}{\partial x^2}-2\frac{\partial^2 w}{\partial x\partial y}\frac{\partial^2\Phi}{\partial x\partial y}+ \tag{5.1}$$
$$+\frac{1}{R}\frac{\partial^2\Phi}{\partial x^2}+\frac{q}{h}-\frac{\gamma}{g}\frac{\partial^2 w}{\partial t^2}.$$

Here w and w_0 are the total and initial deflections, Φ the stress function, γ the specific weight of the shell material, D_1 and D_2 the flexural rigidities in the axial and annular directions, D_3 the reduced rigidity and D_G the torsional rigidity:

$$D_1=\frac{E_1h^3}{12(1-\nu_1\nu_2)},\quad D_2=\frac{E_2h^3}{12(1-\nu_1\nu_2)},\quad D_3=D_1\nu_2+2D_G,\quad D_G=\frac{Gh^3}{12}.$$

The equation of strain compatibility assumes the form

$$\delta_2\frac{\partial^4\Phi}{\partial x^4}+2\delta_3\frac{\partial^4\Phi}{\partial x^2\partial y^2}+\delta_1\frac{\partial^4\Phi}{\partial y^4}=\frac{\partial^2 w}{\partial x^2}\frac{\partial^2 w}{\partial y^2}-$$
$$-\left(\frac{\partial^2 w}{\partial x\partial y}\right)^2-\frac{\partial^2 w_0}{\partial x^2}\frac{\partial^2 w_0}{\partial y^2}+\left(\frac{\partial^2 w_0}{\partial x\partial y}\right)^2-\frac{1}{R}\frac{\partial^2(w-w_0)}{\partial x^2}, \tag{5.2}$$

where

$$\delta_1=\frac{1}{E_1},\quad \delta_2=\frac{1}{E_2},\quad 2\delta_3=\frac{1}{G}-\frac{2\nu_1}{E_1}.$$

The boundary conditions for deflection w are $w=0$, $\frac{\partial^2 w}{\partial x^2}=0$ at $x=0,\ L$.

The authors adopted the method of solution employed previously for metallic isotropic shells /38/. Approximate expressions for the total and initial deflections are selected in the form

$$w=f(\sin\alpha x\sin\beta y+\psi\sin^2\alpha x+\varphi), \tag{5.3}$$
$$w_0=f_0(\sin\alpha x\sin\beta y+\psi\sin^2\alpha x+\varphi), \tag{5.4}$$

where $\alpha=m\pi/R$ and $\beta=n/R$; m is the number of half-waves along the shell generatrix and n the number of circumferential waves. We assume that the initial waviness, characterized by parameters ψ and φ, is "in resonance" with the waviness of the shell during strain, and that the only parameter given in advance is quantity f_0. This assumption slightly intensifies the effect of the initial irregularities.

Under external pressure a shell buckles along the generatrix in a single half-wave. Therefore we shall henceforth assume that

$m = 1$. Expressions (5.3) and (5.4) are substituted in the right-hand side of (5.1). Integration of the resulting equation yields the stress function in the form

$$\Phi = C_1 \cos 2\alpha x + C_2 \cos 2\beta y + C_3 \sin 3\alpha x \sin \beta y + \\ + C_4 \sin \alpha x \sin \beta y - \frac{qR}{2h} x^2. \tag{5.5}$$

Here

$$C_1 = B_1 (f^2 - f_0^2) + B_5 (f - f_0) \psi, \; C_2 = B_2 (f^2 - f_0^2),$$
$$C_3 = B_3 (f^2 - f_0^2) \psi, \; C_4 = B_4 (f - f_0) - B_6 (f^2 - f_0^2) \psi,$$
$$B_1 = \frac{\beta^2 E_2}{32\alpha^2}, \; B_3 = \frac{\alpha^2\beta^2}{81 \frac{\alpha^4}{E_2} + 9\alpha^2\beta^2 \left(\frac{1}{G} - \frac{2\nu_1}{E_1}\right) + \frac{\beta^4}{E_1}},$$
$$B_2 = \frac{\alpha^2 E_1}{32\beta^3}, \; B_4 = \frac{\alpha^2}{R\left[\frac{\alpha^4}{E_2} + \alpha^2\beta^2 \left(\frac{1}{G} - \frac{2\nu_1}{E_1}\right) + \frac{\beta^4}{E_1}\right]},$$
$$B_5 = -\frac{E_2}{8R\alpha^2}, \; B_6 = \frac{\alpha^2\beta^2}{\frac{\alpha^4}{E_2} + \left(\frac{1}{G} - \frac{2\nu_1}{E_1}\right)\alpha^2\beta^2 + \frac{\beta^4}{E_1}}.$$

The last term in expression (5.5) corresponds to the stresses in the middle surface determined from membrane theory.

For known Φ and w one can determine the stresses in the middle surface:

$$\sigma_x = \frac{\partial^2 \Phi}{\partial y^2}, \; \sigma_y = \frac{\partial^2 \Phi}{\partial x^2}, \; \tau = -\frac{\partial^2 \Phi}{\partial x \partial y} \tag{5.6}$$

and hence strains $\varepsilon_x, \varepsilon_y$ and ε_z.

Displacement v must satisfy the closure condition

$$\int^{2\pi R} \frac{\partial v}{\partial y} dy = 0. \tag{5.7}$$

Comparison of these expressions for ε_y in terms of displacements, on the one hand, and in terms of function Φ, on the other hand, yields

$$\frac{\partial v}{\partial y} = \frac{1}{E_2}\left(\frac{\partial^2 \Phi}{\partial x^2} - \nu_2 \frac{\partial^2 \Phi}{\partial y^2}\right) - \frac{1}{2}\left(\frac{\partial w}{\partial y}\right)^2 + \frac{1}{2}\left(\frac{\partial w_0}{\partial y}\right)^2 + \frac{w - w_0}{R}. \tag{5.8}$$

With the aid of (5.3), (5.4) and (5.8) we obtain

$$\varphi = \frac{qR^2}{E_2 h(f-f_0)} + \frac{f+f_0}{8} R\beta^2 - \frac{\psi}{2}. \tag{5.9}$$

Thus parameter φ is expressed in terms of f and ψ.

In order to find the relationship between the deflection parameters and the time-varying load, we consider a Lagrange equation of type

$$\frac{\partial}{\partial t}\left(\frac{\partial \hat{T}}{\partial \dot{\hat{q}}_j}\right) - \frac{\partial \hat{T}}{\partial \hat{q}_j} + \hat{Q}_j = 0. \tag{5.10}$$

As generalized coordinates we select deflection parameters $\hat{q}_1 = \zeta_1$ and $\hat{q}_2 = \zeta_2$, and as generalized forces $\hat{Q}_1 = \partial\hat{Э}/\partial\zeta_1$ and $\hat{Q}_2 = \partial\hat{Э}/\partial\zeta_2$. Here we have introduced dimensionless parameters

$$\zeta_1 = \frac{f-f_0}{h};\ \zeta_2 = \frac{(f-f_0)\psi}{h};\ \hat{Э} = Э\frac{4R}{\pi L h^3\sqrt{E_1E_2}};\ \hat{q} = \frac{q}{\sqrt{E_1E_2}}\left(\frac{R}{h}\right)^2.$$

The kinetic energy T of the system is given by

$$T = \frac{1}{2}\int_0^L\int_0^{2\pi R} \frac{\gamma h}{g}\left(\frac{\partial w}{\partial t}\right)^2 dxdy \tag{5.11}$$

in dimensionless form $\hat{T} = T\dfrac{4R}{\pi L h^3\sqrt{E_1E_2}}$. The total potential energy of the system $Э$ equals the sum of the potential strain energy of the middle surface and the potential flexural energy, less the work done by normal pressure forces. Hence

$$\begin{aligned}\hat{Q}_1 &= \frac{\eta(\xi^4+\Delta^2)\zeta_1(\zeta_1+2\zeta_0)}{16\Delta} + \frac{(\lambda_1+\lambda_2)\Delta\xi^4\eta(\zeta_1+2\zeta_0)\zeta_2^2}{\zeta_1+\zeta_0} - \\ &\quad - \frac{\zeta_2\Delta}{4}(1+8\xi^4\lambda_2) + \frac{\Delta\xi^4\lambda_2\zeta_1}{\eta(\zeta_1+\zeta_0)} - \hat{q} + \frac{\eta\vartheta\zeta_1\lambda_3}{\zeta_1+\zeta_0},\\ \hat{Q}_2 &= 2\zeta_2\Delta\xi^4\eta^2(\zeta_1+2\zeta_0)^2(\lambda_1+\lambda_2) - \frac{\Delta\eta\zeta_1}{4}(\zeta_1+2\zeta_0)(1+8\xi\lambda_2) + \\ &\quad + \zeta_2\Delta + 16\vartheta\Omega\zeta_2\xi^4\eta^2,\end{aligned} \tag{5.13}$$

where

$$\zeta_0 = \frac{f_0}{h},\ \xi = \frac{\pi R}{nL},\ \delta = \frac{Rh}{L^2},\ \eta = \frac{n^2h}{R}.$$

$$\Delta = \sqrt{\frac{E_1}{E_2}},\ \omega = \frac{\sqrt{E_1E_2}}{G},\ \theta = \frac{G}{\sqrt{E_1E_2}},\ \Omega = \frac{E_1}{\sqrt{E_1E_2}},$$

$$\vartheta = \frac{1}{12(1-\nu_1\nu_2)},\ \lambda_1 = \frac{1}{81\xi^4 + 9\xi^2(\omega - 2\nu_1\Delta)\Delta + \Delta^2},$$

$$\lambda_2 = \frac{1}{\xi^4 + \xi^2\Delta(\omega - 2\nu_1\Delta) + \Delta^2},\ \lambda_3 = \xi^4\Omega + \left(2\nu_2\Omega + \frac{\theta}{3\vartheta}\right)\xi^2 + \Delta.$$

Henceforth we assume that pressure q varies with time according to the law $q=ct$, and further that the shell buckles on the ascending branch of the pressure pulse. We introduce the dimensionless time parameter

$$\hat{t}=\frac{ctR^2}{h^2\hat{q}_B\sqrt{E_1E_2}}=\frac{\hat{q}}{\hat{q}_B}. \tag{5.14}$$

The first of equations (5.10) yields

$$\frac{d^2\zeta_1}{d\hat{t}^2}+\frac{\eta^2(\zeta_1+\zeta_0)}{4+\eta^2(\zeta_1+\zeta_0)^2}\left(\frac{d\zeta_1}{d\hat{t}}\right)^2-\frac{4S_1(\zeta_1+\zeta_0)}{4+\eta^2(\zeta_1+\zeta_0)^2}\left\{\hat{t}-\right.$$
$$-\frac{\eta(\xi^4+\Delta^2)\zeta_1(\zeta_1+\zeta_0)}{16\Delta\hat{q}_B}-\frac{(\lambda_1+\lambda_2)\Delta\xi^4\eta(\zeta_1+2\zeta_0)\zeta_2^2}{\hat{q}_B(\zeta_1+\zeta_0)}+$$
$$\left.+\frac{\Delta(1+8\xi^4\lambda_2)\zeta_2}{4\hat{q}_B}-\frac{\zeta_1}{\zeta_1+\zeta_0}\right\}=0, \tag{5.15}$$

where

$$S_1=(E_1E_2)^{3/2}\eta\hat{q}_B^3\left(\frac{1}{cR}\right)^2\left(\frac{h}{R}\right)^4\frac{g}{\gamma}.$$

The second of equations (5.10) yields

$$\frac{d^2\zeta_2}{d\hat{t}^2}+\frac{S_1}{\eta\hat{q}_B^3}\left\{2\zeta_2\Delta\xi^4\eta^2(\zeta_1+2\zeta_0)^2(\lambda_1+\lambda_2)-\right.$$
$$\left.-\frac{\Delta\eta\zeta_1}{4}(\zeta_1+2\zeta_0)(1+8\xi^4\lambda_2)+\zeta_2\Delta+16\vartheta\Omega\zeta_2\xi^4\eta^2\right\}=0. \tag{5.16}$$

Equations (5.15) and (5.16) were integrated by the Runge-Kutta method on a BESM-2M digital computer using the following initial data:

$$\zeta=\zeta_0,\quad \frac{d\zeta_1}{d\hat{t}}=0,\quad \frac{d\zeta_2}{d\hat{t}}=0 \text{ at } \hat{t}=0. \tag{5.17}$$

In the computation we employed various values of ν_1, ν_2, E_1 and E_2 (corresponding to different grades of glass-reinforced plastic) and the following shell parameters: $L/R=2.6$, 3.5 and $h/R=2/143$ for the case $\zeta_0=0.001$.

The $\zeta_1=\zeta_1(\hat{t}')$ curves in Figure 1.10 have been constructed for shells with $L/R=2.6$, $h/R=2/143$, $E_1/E_2=2$ and loading rate $c=2{,}000$ atm/sec at various numbers of revolutions n. Evidently, the curve with $n=7$ leaves the axis of abscissas first. It can be assumed that at the specified loading rate and selected initial deflection buckling of the actual shells will be accompanied by the formation of seven circumferential depressions instead of the five or six observed under static loading. A rapid increase in deflections occurs for parameter $\hat{t}'$ between 2.7 and 3.9. Thus the critical pressure is here approximately three times the upper critical load.

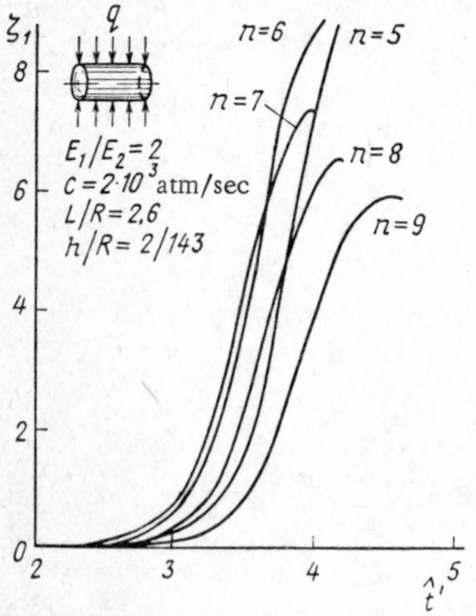

FIGURE 1.10.

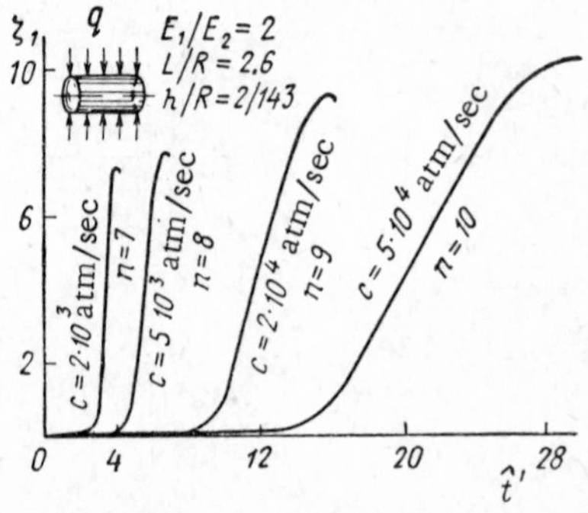

FIGURE 1.11.

Curves $\zeta_1 = \zeta_1(\hat{t}')$ in Figures 1.11 and 1.12 present the relationship between the total deflection and the loading times at rates $c = 0.2 \cdot 10^4$, $c = 0.5 \cdot 10^4$, $c = 2 \cdot 10^4$, $c = 5 \cdot 10^4$ atm/sec for $E_1/E_2 = 2$ and $E_1/E_2 = 5$, respectively. The figures denote the wave numbers n at which the rapid increase in deflection corresponds to the smallest parameter $\hat{t}'$. Clearly the dynamic effect is manifested by the consequent increase in wave number and the considerable growth of critical pressure.

Figure 1.13 shows curves $\zeta_1 = \zeta_1(\hat{t}')$ for various ratios E_1/E_2 at loading rate $c = 5 \cdot 10^3$ atm/sec. The first curve on the left shows the relationship $\zeta_1 = \zeta_1(\hat{t}')$ for isotropic shells, the other curves for shells with various degrees of anisotropy. As the latter increases, the entire curve is displaced to the right in the direction of large $\hat{t}'$.

The curves in Figure 1.14 illustrate the relationship between the dynamic coefficient and the loading rate ε (atm/sec) for various ratios E_1/E_2 when $E_1 \gtrsim E_2$. The graphs show that coefficient k_d increases with increasing loading rate and degree of anisotropy.

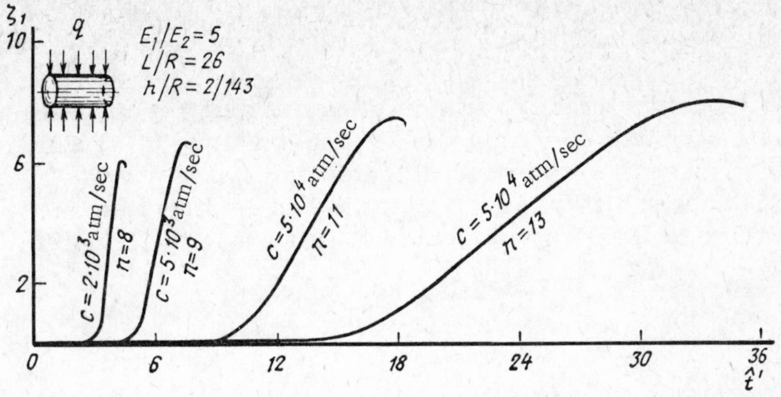

FIGURE 1.12.

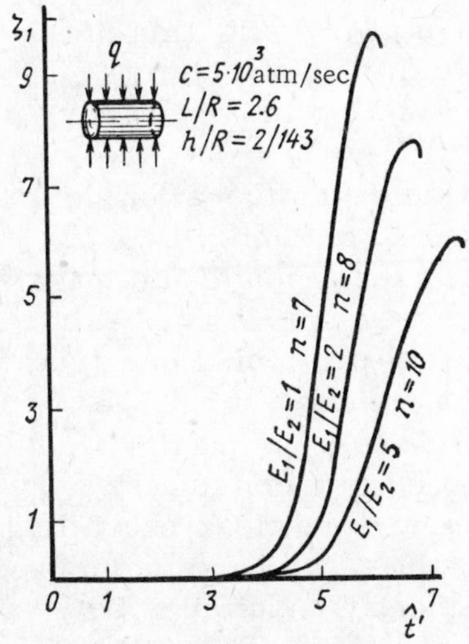

FIGURE 1.13.

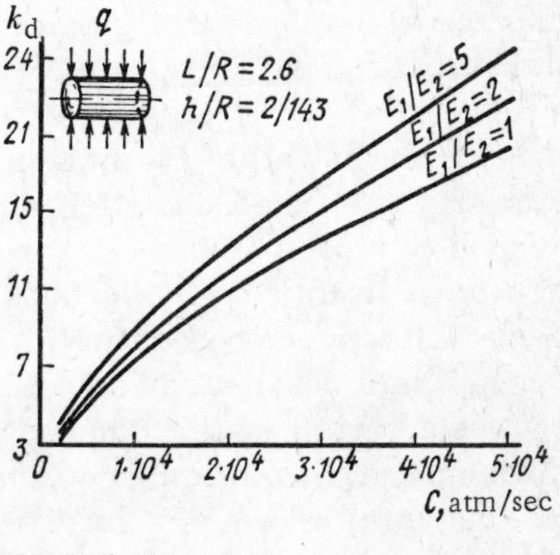

FIGURE 1.14.

Thus a numerical solution of the problem for some parameters L/R and h/R at specific loading rates yielded a relationship between the deflection and time parameters, characterizing the behavior of the shell. Dynamic buckling is treated elsewhere /37/ as a process in which the shell snaps into a new equilibrium state.

The effect of the dynamic property is expressed as an increase in the circumferential wave number. The wave number increases with loading rate. This indicates a transition to higher buckling modes. As the loading rate increases, the value of the critical load increases too. At the selected shell parameters the wave number

n increases from 4–6 to 10–12 and the critical load exceeds the upper critical pressure under static loading by a factor of three or more.

As the degree of anisotropy increases the $\zeta_1=\zeta_1(\hat{t}')$ curves are shifted to the right in the direction of larger values of t', which indicates an increase in the coefficients of dynamic overload for orthotropic shells. It is assumed that the fiber direction corresponding to the larger modulus E_1 lies along the length of the shell.

§6. EXPERIMENTAL INVESTIGATION OF STABILITY OF THIN-WALLED GLASS-REINFORCED-PLASTIC ELEMENTS

The test design, and method of experimental investigation of the strength and stability of thin-walled glass-reinforced-plastic elements is of great practical interest, and is also important for theoretical solutions.

We regard as the most successful solution of this question the one developed by Antipov et al. /39/, presented below.

Antipov et al. /39/ noted that, as a rule, experimental investigations of strength and deformation properties are carried out either on specially prepared samples not related to a particular construction, or on samples from a composition of a construction. The authors believe that both methods entail serious inaccuracies.

A specially prepared sample, not connected to a construction, does not permit reproduction of all the special conditions prevailing during preparation of the construction. On the other hand, samples taken directly from a construction are frequently unsuitable for preparing test-pieces. From this point of view it is especially difficult to study the properties of glass-fiber-reinforced plastics with samples cut from shells, in view of their curvature.

The structure of glass-fiber-reinforced plastics is generally constructed symmetrical relative to three mutually perpendicular planes (axes), i. e., with accuracy sufficient for practical purposes glass-fiber-reinforced plastics can be regarded as orthotropic material. The thickness of a layer of reinforcing material is generally small in comparison with the thickness of the construction. Therefore one can consider, with a high degree of approximation, glass-reinforced plastics to be homogeneous material. In conformity with a homogeneous orthotropic material, the solution of many important problems requires data on five elastic constants:

modulus of normal elasticity in the plane of layering in the direction of the principal axes of symmetry (E_1 and E_2), shear modulus of the material in the plane of layering (G), and Poisson ratios ν_1 and ν_2.

Bearing in mind the relationship $E_1\nu_2=E_2\nu_1$, four independent elastic constants must be determined.

Antipov et al. /39/ developed a method for investigating cylindrical shells which calls for the prior determination of the modulus of normal elasticity E_2 (in the tangential direction), the normal elasticity modulus (in the direction of the axis), Poisson ratio ν_1 (under the action of a force along the shell axis) and shear modulus G.

The normal elasticity modulus is determined from measurements of the deflection while testing the shell under the action of lateral compression distributed evenly over the length of the generatrix (Figure 1.15). Compression of the shell can be effected with any testing apparatus by means of which the load can be fixed to within 1% in accordance with given degrees of shell loading. The latter are chosen so that their number is not less than four or five, while the stress on the shell under maximum load does not exceed by 30% the corresponding yield value of the glass-fiber-reinforced plastic. For determining E_2 we measure the change in the length of two mutually perpendicular shell diameters (in the direction of, and perpendicular to, the force) at two of its cross-sections, distance 50–100 mm from the end-faces of the shell.

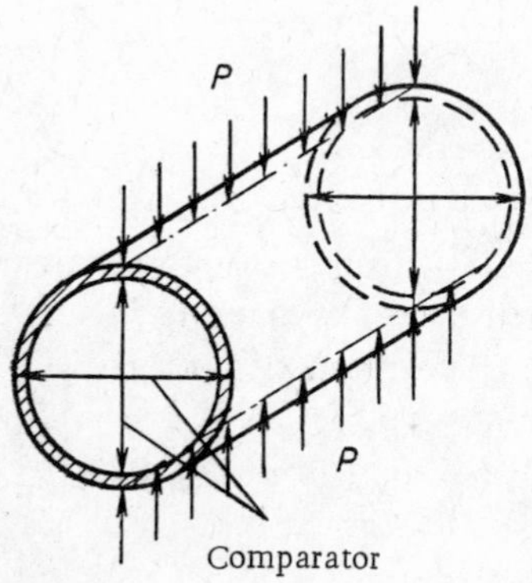

FIGURE 1.15.

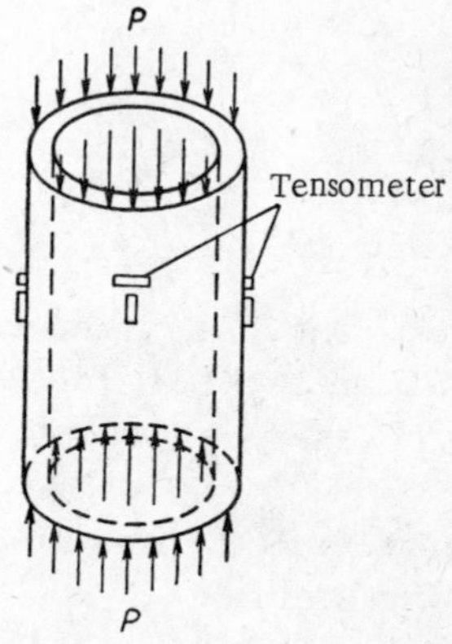

FIGURE 1.16.

The elasticity modulus is computed by the formulas

$$E_2 = 0.223\,\frac{\Delta P}{Lf}\left(\frac{D_m}{h}\right)^3, \tag{6.1}$$

$$E_2 = 0.206\,\frac{\Delta P}{Lf_1}\left(\frac{D_m}{h}\right)^3, \tag{6.2}$$

where L is the shell length, D_m the mean diameter of the middle surface of the shell, h the shell thickness, ΔP the increase in the compressive force acting on the shell, f the change in the vertical shell diameter caused by change in load ΔP, and f_1 the change in horizontal shell diameter.

Experiments /39/ have shown that the values of the elasticity modulus computed by (6.1) and (6.2) differ little from one another. However, for thin shells ($R/h \geqslant 30$) (6.1) gives results which are 10–12% lower than the values of E_2 determined by (6.2). This can be explained by the effect of local shell bending in the region of the applied load.

The values of the modulus of normal elasticity E_1 and Poisson ratio ν_1 are determined by measuring the fiber strains of the shell compressed axially (Figure 1.16). Shell loading is affected by a press in four or five steps, at each of which measurements are carried out. An I4-10 comparator with dial indicators and ~300 mm base (not larger than ⅔ of the shell) and wire tensometers with 20 mm base are used to measure strain. The load is chosen so that the maximum stress on the shell does not exceed 30% of the ultimate strength and is definitely not less than ten times the marginal shell stability:

$$\sigma = \frac{P}{\pi D_m h} \leqslant 0.3\sigma_{com}, \tag{6.3}$$

$$P \leqslant 0.36\sqrt{E_1 E_2}\,h^2, \tag{6.4}$$

where E_1 and E_2 are the values of the elasticity modulus determined by tests on flat test pieces and σ_{com} the compressive strength of the glass-fiber-reinforced plastic in the direction of the shell axis.

The elasticity modulus E_1 and Poisson ratio ν_1 are computed by the formulas

$$E_1 = \frac{\Delta P}{\pi D_m h \varepsilon_1}, \tag{6.5}$$

$$\nu_1 = \frac{\varepsilon_2}{\varepsilon_1}, \tag{6.6}$$

where ε_t is the increment in the relative strain along the tangential direction during change of load ΔP, and ε_l the increment in the relative strain along the axial direction under the same conditions.

The shear modulus is determined by measuring the angular strain of the shell upon twisting with the aid of a special device. The loading and strain setup is shown in Figure 1.17. The load-step conditions are chosen as in the previous case. The torque and angle of torsion are measured.

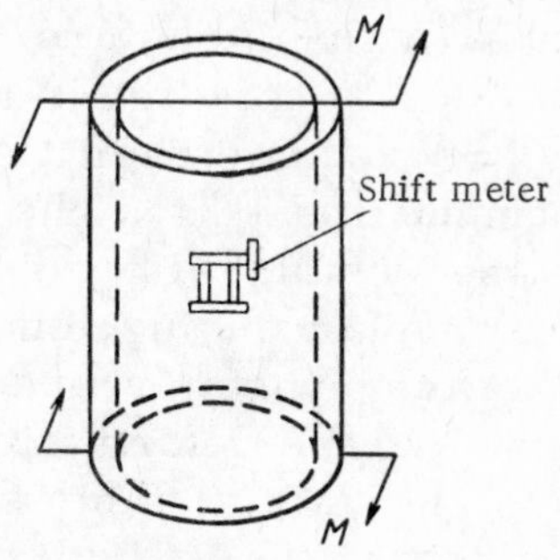

FIGURE 1.17.

The shear modulus is computed by the relationship

$$G = \frac{Ml}{I_p \varphi}, \tag{6.7}$$

where M is the torque, l the length of the base on which the angle of torsion is determined, φ the angle of torsion and I_p the polar moment of inertia of the cross-section

$$I_p = \frac{\pi (D^4 - d^4)}{32}.$$

Here D and d are the external and internal shell diameters, respectively.

The angle of torsion is determined by the magnitude of the displacement of one base cross-section relative to another: $\varphi = r/z$, where z is the displacement of one base cross-section relative to another, and r the radius of the device by means of which the displacement is measured.

Only after carrying out all the above measurements is the shell subjected to tests in an autoclave in order to study its strength or stability under the action of hydrostatic pressure on all its sides.

Such a procedure allows one to also study features of the structure of glass-fiber-reinforced plastics composing the shells with respect to the glass content, the influence of technological factors, and so on.

The specific features of glass-fiber-reinforced plastics impose definite limitations on the conditions under which experiments can be conducted in an autoclave. For example, in view of the prevailing elastic and Mackian-elastic deformations in the deformation process of a glass-fiber-reinforced plastic shell and the related possibility that the structure is damaged even when it fully regains its original shape after load removal, one can draw no conclusions on the damage to the structure from its shape after the test. Hence, in order to completely represent the working features of the structure we require facilities to photograph it or observe it visually throughout the test. The ambient temperature strongly influences the results of tests on glass-fiber-reinforced plastics, in particular during long-time or cyclic loading. The shell can be very unstable under considerable temperature fluctuations during the deformation test. Hence measures must be taken to maintain a stable specified temperature in the autoclave during the test.

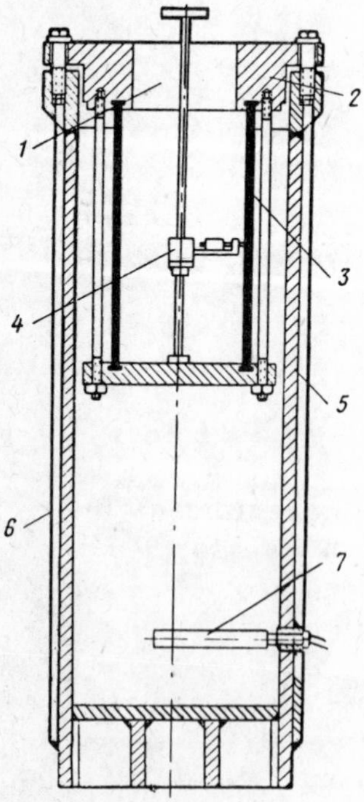

FIGURE 1.18.

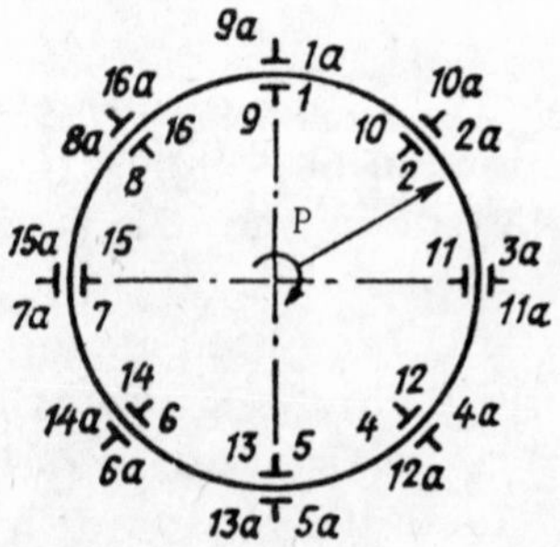

FIGURE 1.19.

A diagram of the autoclave (equipped to meet all the above-mentioned requirements) and model is shown in Figure 1.18 with the following notation: 1 is the window for observing the shell and recording the profilograph readings, 2 the lid, 3 the test shell, 4 the profilograph, 5 the body of the autoclave, 6 the thermal insulation, and 7 the automatic heater.

During shell testing in the autoclave we can make a second (control) determination of the elasticity modulus E_2 (in the tangential direction). For this purpose eight longitudinal strain gages are attached to the circumference of the shell in tangential directions (on both surfaces of the shell).

The elasticity modulus is computed using the relationship

$$E_2 = \frac{\Delta p R_{\text{m}}}{\Delta \varepsilon_2 h} (1 - 0.5\nu_2),$$

where Δp is the change in the value of the external pressure, $\Delta\varepsilon_2$ the deformation increment in the tangential direction for pressure change Δp ($\Delta\varepsilon_2$ is computed as the arithmetic mean of the strain-gage readings), ν_2 the Poisson ratio determined by tests on samples of the material or from the relationship $\nu_2 = \nu_1 E_2 / E_1$.

For a better check on the data obtained it is desirable to conduct measurements at two or three cross-sections along the shell length.

When the shell is investigated in the autoclave for strength and stability, the fibrous deformations are measured using a wire strain gage and the shell shape using a special profilograph, by means of which the shell displacements can be measured at 16 points of its perimeter. A typical instrumental setup is shown in Figure 1.19, where T denotes the strain gages (Nos. 9–19 and 9a–16a are fixed along the shell axis), and P the profilograph. A deformed shell surface at various load stages, determined by the profilograph, is shown in Figure 1.20, where the solid curve corresponds to short-time loading and the dashed curve corresponds to the shell being maintained at a pressure of 75 kg/cm^2 for 10 days. Further, the tests can be filmed, since the inner shell surface can be observed through the window in the lid of the autoclave. The measurements and film record enable one to obtain a complete picture of the shell behavior throughout the test.

Since the material characteristics are determined immediately, agreement between theoretical and experimental deformations and critical and destructive loads is shown to be very satisfactory. For example, data are cited in Table 1.1 concerning tests on a series of shells prepared by winding, using glass-fiber-reinforced plastics on an epoxy resin base. The shell was reinforced in the tangential direction by wound threads and in the axial direction by a cord-fabric ply. The ratio of the layers reinforced by wire and fabric was close to 2 : 1, but with quite a large deviation. The critical load of the shell was computed by the formula

$$p_{cr} = \frac{E_2}{4(1-\nu_2\nu_1)}\left(\frac{h}{R_{cr}}\right)^3 \frac{1}{3(0.5\alpha^2+n^2-1)}\left[\frac{E_1}{E_2}\alpha^4 + \right.$$
$$+ 2\left(\frac{E_1}{E_2}\nu_2 + \frac{2G}{E_2}\right)\alpha^2(n^2-1) + (n^2-1)^2 +$$
$$\left. + \frac{12R_{cp}}{h^2}\cdot\frac{\alpha^4}{\alpha^4 + \frac{E_2}{G}\alpha^2 n^2 + \frac{E_2}{E_1}n^4}\right],$$

where $\alpha = \frac{\pi R_m}{L}$, and n is the wave number of loss of stability.

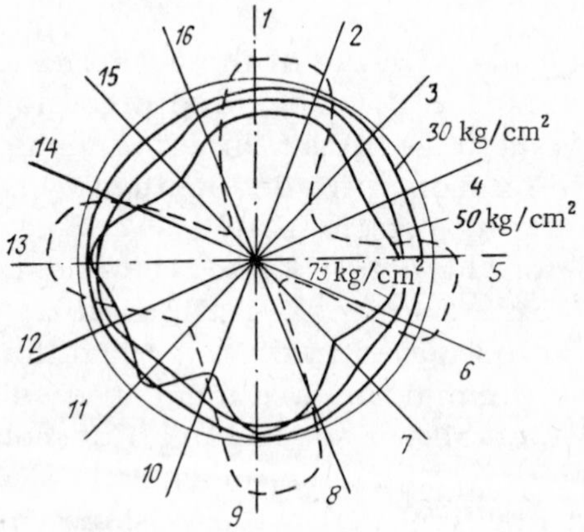

FIGURE 1.20.

It can be seen from Table 1.1 that the deviation between theoretical and experimental critical pressures does not exceed 18%. In all cases the experimental values are higher than the theoretical.

The elasticity and strength characteristics depend considerably not only on the reinforcing scheme, but also on the relative content of reinforcing material in the plastic. It is therefore mandatory during shell tests to check the actual ratio between the glass and resin in the plastic and the actual reinforcing scheme. This is done by cutting 50 × 50 mm test-pieces from undamaged parts of the shell. The thickness of the test-pieces is measured. Then the piece is weighed, the resin burned and the test-piece weighed once more. The reinforcing layers with different orientation of the reinforcing fibers are computed. However, for simplicity one may limit computation of the reinforcing layers and measure the sample thickness, while the ratio between glass and resin is determined from these data by existing nomographs.

TABLE 1.1. Test results on a series of glass-fiber-reinforced plastic shells

Number of reinforcing layers		Ratio of the number of reinforcing threads		Number of layers per 1 cm thickness	Elastic characteristics			Critical load			
in the axial direction	in the tangential direction	in the axial direction	in the tangential direction		E_1, kg/cm²	E_2, kg/cm²	G, kg/cm²	ν_1	q_{cal}, kg/cm²	q_{exp}, kg/cm²	q_{exp}/q_{cal}
11	26	1.0	2.35	44	$1.90 \cdot 10^5$	$2.70 \cdot 10^5$	$0.40 \cdot 10^5$	0.10	65.5	77.5	1.18
12	28	1.0	2.30	40	$1.75 \cdot 10^5$	$2.45 \cdot 10^5$	$0.39 \cdot 10^5$	0.08	82.5	90.0	1.09
12	30	1.0	2.50	44	$1.53 \cdot 10^5$	$3.00 \cdot 10^5$	$0.40 \cdot 10^5$	0.08	88.5	100.4	1.13
12	32	1.0	2.70	44	$1.58 \cdot 10^5$	$3.00 \cdot 10^5$	$0.40 \cdot 10^5$	0.07	99.0	110.0	1.11
4	14	1.0	3.50	46	$1.60 \cdot 10^5$	$3.00 \cdot 10^5$	$0.41 \cdot 10^5$	0.07	12.2	14.5	1.18

If it is not possible to conduct preliminary measurements of the elastic characteristics directly within the structure, it is absolutely necessary to determine the actual glass and resin content after carrying out autoclave tests and make corresponding corrections in the theoretical elastic and strength characteristics of the glass-fiber-reinforced plastic.

In connection with conducting experiments with long-time and cyclic loading, Antipov et al. /39/ noted that in this case it is particularly important to maintain a constant temperature throughout the test. Therefore the autoclave heater must be provided with suitable instruments for automatically maintaining a constant temperature. The maintenance of a constant specified pressure is achieved by full hermetic sealing of the structure and the autoclave itself. Slight pressure drops due to damage in the tested structure (and inevitable leaks) are compensated by periodic connection to a pump, to ensure automatic maintenance of the specified pressure level.

Measurements during investigations of shells subject to cyclic loading are conducted in the same manner for single short-time loading. It is advantageous to use only mechanical devices during long-time experiments. (Fibrous deformations are measured by a Huggenberger extensometer, the shift under compression by means of a dial indicator, and the shape of the deformed shell surface by a profilograph.)

Many shells of inner diameter 300 mm, thickness 3 to 15 mm and length 150 to 600 mm have been tested by the method outlined by Antipov et al. /39/. In all cases the experimental results indicated the reliability of their method.

Gumenyuk and Kravchuk /40/ conducted experimental investigations on the stability of cylindrical shells subjected to axial compressive forces. Their experimental results are discussed below.

Three types of shells were prepared (by winding) for the experiments (Figure 1.21, Table 1.2). The reinforcing filler was glass fiber No. 10 or glass fabric AST (b)-C_2, the matrix EFB-4 composition containing 70 weight-parts ED-6 epoxy resin, 30 weight-parts bakelite varnish, and 4 weight-parts BF-4 glue.

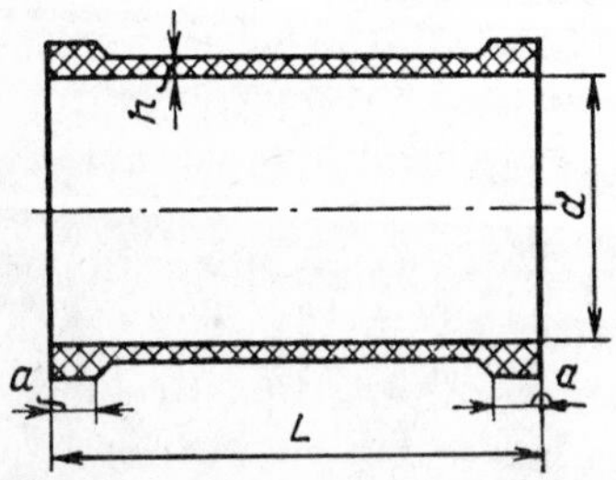

FIGURE 1.21.

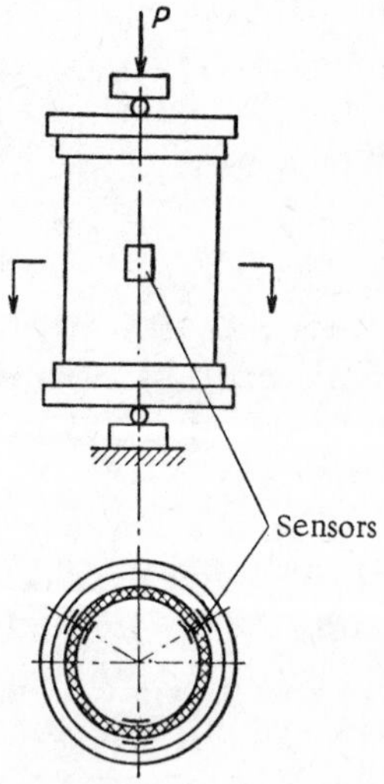

FIGURE 1.22.

The transverse layer of cylindrical shells is prepared by winding glass fibers around rigid mandrels.

For obtaining longitudinal layers for shells of type A and C (see Table 1.2) a layer of thread is wound on an auxiliary mandrel, which is then cut along the forming mandrel and applied to the main mandrel. The longitudinal layer of shell type B is prepared from glass fabric ASTT (b)-S_2.

TABLE 1.2

Shell type	Structure	Inner shell diameter d, mm	Shell length L, mm	Dimension of end-face thickening a, mm	Number of shells tested
A	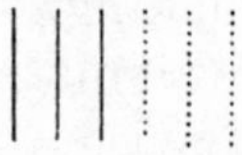	76 186 322	200 300 720	20 20 40	7 3 3
C	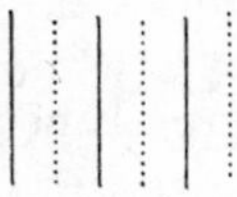	76 187 322 300	200 300 720 600	20 20 40 40	9 18 8 3
B		76	200	20	3
				Total :	54

 longitudinal layer—laminated glass-giber sheet ring layers—winding  glass fabric

Upon separation of the material into layers, places spoilt by locally badly stacked threads were discarded. The initial deflection was not measured, since the internal shell surface is an exact replica of the external surface of the mandrel.

Tests on shells under axial compression were made with the RN-30 universal testing machine with a maximum force of 30,000 kg. The shell deformations were recorded with an ARD-100 strain gage.

The shell used was loaded via a spherical support and steel discs (Figure 1.22). Strain indicators were fixed to the inside and outside wall at an angle of 120°, to secure the axial application of the load with respect to the shell. The deformation was measured up to a load equaling, for example, $0.5P_{cr}$. The shell was subjected to tests when the difference in the readings of the strain gages was less than 10%.

During the tests, some of the relatively thick shells with parameter $R/h = 20-30$ broke with layer displacement but without hollows forming. The results of these tests are not included in Table 1.2. Shells whose value R/h lies between 30 and 70 lost stability with the formation of characteristic rhombus-shaped hollows, after which the material started to crack and layer displacement was observed. Upon further increase in parameter

R/h from 70 to 150 stability loss was accompanied by the formation of rhombic hollows and breaking of the material into layers. Sometimes this layer formation would be insignificant, and after load removal the shell would recover its initial cylindrical shape, but upon repeated loading loss of stability of this shell would start at a markedly lower load than under primary loading. Shells with parameter $R/h = 150-200$ lost stability upon the formation of rhombic hollows, which were completely smoothed down after load removal. For repeated loading the critical load of such a shell remained unchanged.

It can be concluded from shell deformation measurements that under short-time tests glass-fiber-reinforced plastics behave as an elastic material, to which Hooke's law applies.

The mechanical material characteristics are determined by tests on flat plates possessing the same structure and prepared by the same technology as the shells. The values of E_1^{com}, E_2^{com}, E_1^{ben}, E_2^{ben}, ν_1 and ν_2 are determined from the experimental data on the test-pieces (subscript 1 refers to the direction along the shell and subscript 2 to the annular direction).

The flexural elasticity modulus E^{ben} is determined by tests on samples subject to transverse bending for $h/l = 1/10$ and modulus of elasticity E^{com} with compression of samples. The shear modulus is computed by the formula

$$G = \frac{E_{45}}{2(1+\nu_{45})}. \tag{6.8}$$

Experimental results for test pieces of shells and plates are given in Table 1.3. (The values for shells are given in the numerator of the fractions, and for plates in the denominator.) The results of tests on I1-I13 shells are taken from work by Ivanov /41/.

In order to determine the limit of errors in the experimental value of the critical stress with some given probability, we must know the theoretical distribution, found by using the obtained experimental recurrence frequency of the critical stresses. Since shells with different rigidity and geometry characteristics were tested, a dimensionless parameter was used:

$$\rho = \frac{\hat{\sigma}_{cr}^{E}}{n\hat{\sigma}_{cr}^{T}}, \tag{6.9}$$

where $\hat{\sigma}_{cr}^{E}$ is the dimensionless critical stress, given by

$$\hat{\sigma}_{red}^{E} = \frac{\sigma_{cr}^{E} R}{E_{red} h}, \tag{6.10}$$

E_{red} is the reduced modulus of elasticity, given by

$$E_{red} = \sqrt{E_1^{com} E_2^{ben}}, \tag{6.11}$$

$\hat{\sigma}_{cr}^{T}$ is computed by a formula cited in /42/. For the case satisfying $\frac{D_1}{D_2} = \frac{\delta_1}{\delta_2}$, this formula assumes the form

$$\hat{\sigma}_{cr}^{T} = \frac{1}{\sqrt{3(1-\nu_1\nu_2)}} \sqrt{\frac{1+\nu_2\sqrt{\frac{E_1^{com}}{E_2^{com}}} + \frac{2G}{E_{red}}\sqrt{\frac{E_1^{com}}{E_1^{ben}}}(1-\nu_1\nu_2)}{1-\nu_2\sqrt{\frac{E_1^{com}}{E_2^{com}}} + \frac{E_{red}}{2G}\sqrt{\frac{E_2^{com}}{E_2^{red}}}}}, \tag{6.12}$$

$n = \frac{\Sigma \hat{\sigma}_{cr}^{T}}{\Sigma \hat{\sigma}_{cr}^{E}}$. For the conducted computation $n = 0.52$.

It can be seen from Table 1.3 that ρ lies between 0.57 and 1.59. The values of the empirically obtained frequencies are shown in the form of a histogram (Figure 1.23). The skewness A and kurtosis $Э$ of the distribution ($A = 0.183$, $Э = -0.73$) have been computed in line with /43/. The obtained values of A and $Э$ and the nature of the histogram permit acceptance of the normal distribution law as the theoretical one.

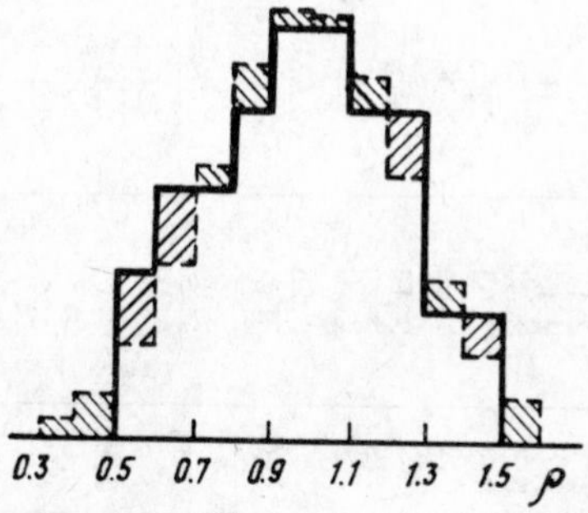

FIGURE 1.23.

The Kolmogorov criteria /43/ have been applied to evaluate the agreement between the theoretical and experimental distribution laws. Accordingly, for the case under consideration the criterion is $p(\lambda) \approx 1$, which indicates good agreement between the chosen theoretical distribution and the empirical one.

Similar histograms for metallic shells, discussed elsewhere /44/, differ qualitatively from histograms for shells made from glass-fiber-reinforced plastics. This difference can be explained

TABLE 1.3

Serial No.	Shell	R, mm	h, mm	Compression: $E_1^{com}\cdot10^{-5}$, kg/cm^2	Compression: $E_2^{com}\cdot10^{-5}$, kg/cm^2	Bending: $E_1^{ben}\cdot10^{-5}$, kg/cm^2	Bending: $E_2^{ben}\cdot10^{-5}$, kg/cm^2	$G\cdot10^{-5}$, kg/cm^2	ν_1	$\hat{\sigma}^E_{cr}$	ρ
1	A7	38.4	0.9	2.1	2.1	1.72	1.72	0.35	0.2	0.181	0.862
2	A8	38.6	1.0	2.1	2.1	1.72	1.72	0.35	0.2	0.136	0.646
3	A9	38.6	0.95	2.1	2.1	1.72	1.72	0.35	0.2	0.124	0.592
4	A17	94.0	1.02	2.1	2.1	1.72	1.72	0.35	0.2	0.164	0.780
5	A18	94.0	1.1	2.1	2.1	1.72	1.72	0.35	0.2	0.122	0.575
6	A19	94.0	1.0	2.1	2.1	1.72	1.72	0.35	0.2	0.136	0.644
7	26 (A)	161.5	0.95	2.63	2.63	1.92	1.92	0.48	0.22	0.242	1.04
8	27 (A)	161.4	0.9	2.63	2.63	1.92	1.92	0.48	0.22	0.278	1.19
9	28 (A)	161.4	0.9	2.63	2.63	1.92	1.92	0.48	0.22	0.226	0.965
10	C3	94.5	1.9	$\frac{2.16}{2.10}$	2.16	1.72	1.72	0.35	$\frac{0.2}{0.18}$	0.225	1.06
11	C5	94.3	1.75	$\frac{2.28}{2.10}$	$\frac{2.28}{2.10}$	1.72	1.72	0.35	$\frac{0.2}{0.16}$	0.248	1.18
12	C7	94.5	2.14	$\frac{2.02}{2.10}$	$\frac{2.02}{2.10}$	1.72	1.72	0.35	$\frac{0.2}{0.19}$	0.192	0.914
13	C33	38.4	0.86	2.1	2.1	1.72	1.72	0.35	0.2	0.165	0.790
14	C34	38.4	0.92	2.1	2.1	1.72	1.72	0.35	0.2	0.178	0.848
15	C35	38.5	1.05	2.1	2.1	1.72	1.72	0.35	0.2	0.189	0.887
16	IC	150.5	1.0	$\frac{2.34}{2.10}$	$\frac{2.34}{2.10}$	1.72	1.72	0.35	0.2	0.196	0.928
17	2C	150.5	1.0	$\frac{2.47}{2.10}$	$\frac{2.47}{2.10}$	1.72	1.72	0.35	0.2	0.315	1.49
18	5C	150.5	1.0	$\frac{2.18}{2.10}$	$\frac{2.18}{2.10}$	1.72	1.72	0.35	0.2	0.125	0.595

TABLE 1.3 (continued)

Serial No.	Shell	R, mm	h, mm	Compression		Bending		$G\cdot 10^{-5}$, kg/cm^2	ν_1	$\hat{\sigma}^E_{cr}$	ρ
				$E_1^{com}\cdot 10^{-5}$, kg/cm^2	$E_2^{com}\cdot 10^{-5}$, kg/cm^2	$E_1^{ben}\cdot 10^{-5}$, kg/cm^2	$E_2^{ben}\cdot 10^{-5}$, kg/cm^2				
19	12C	161.5	1.05	$\frac{2.54}{2.63}$	$\frac{2.54}{2.63}$	$\frac{2.02}{1.92}$	$\frac{2.02}{1.92}$	0.48	0.22	0.288	1.24
20	13C	161.5	0.95	$\frac{2.53}{2.63}$	$\frac{2.53}{2.63}$	$\frac{1.92}{1.92}$	$\frac{1.92}{1.92}$	0.48	0.22	0.3	1.28
21	14C	161.4	0.9	$\frac{2.37}{2.63}$	$\frac{2.37}{2.63}$	$\frac{2.26}{2.63}$	$\frac{2.26}{2.63}$	0.48	0.22	0.315	1.35
22	15C	161.6	1.1	2.63	2.63	1.92	1.92	0.48	0.22	0.241	1.14
23	16C	161.6	1.1	$\frac{2.41}{2.63}$	$\frac{2.41}{2.63}$	$\frac{1.85}{1.92}$	$\frac{1.85}{1.92}$	0.48	0.22	0.215	1.01
24	C23	93.8	0.68	2.15	2.87	2.1	2.84	0.42	0.14	0.204	1.05
25	C24	93.8	0.7	2.15	2.87	2.1	2.84	0.42	0.14	0.22	1.09
26	C26	94.0	1.02	2.15	2.87	2.1	2.84	0.42	0.14	0.236	1.22
27	17C	161.3	0.55	1.62	2.52	1.28	2.48	0.32	0.14	0.139	0.678
28	18C	161.4	0.8	1.41	2.52	1.28	2.3	0.32	0.14	0.15	0.732
29	19C	161.4	0.75	$\frac{1.88}{1.41}$	2.52	1.28	2.41	0.32	0.14	0,146	0.710
30	C28	94.3	1.56	1.52	3.85	1.39	3.62	0.444	0.07	0.112	0.570
31	C29	94.0	1.1	1.52	3.85	1.39	3.62	0.44	0.07	0.158	0.802
32	C30	94.0	0.96	1.52	3.85	1.39	3.62	0.44	0.07	0.218	1.11
33	A2	38.4	0.66	2.52	1.41	2.3	1.28	0.32	0.25	0.199	0.968
34	A3	38.4	0.67	2.52	1.41	2.3	1.28	0.32	0.25	0.178	0.863
35	A4	38.4	0.67	2.52	1.41	2.3	1.28	0.32	0.25	0.202	0.978
36	C1	38.8	1.2	2.52	1.41	2.3	1.28	0.32	0.25	0.218	1.06
37	C2	38.8	1.52	2.52	1.41	2.3	1.28	0.32	0.25	0.183	0.895

TABLE 1.3 (continued)

Serial No.	Shell	R, mm	h, mm	Compression		Bending		$G\cdot 10^{-5}$, kg/cm^2	ν_1	$\hat{\sigma}^E_{cr}$	ρ
				$E_1^{com}\cdot 10^{-5}$, kg/cm^2	$E_2^{com}\cdot 10^{-5}$, kg/cm^2	$E_1^{ben}\cdot 10^{-5}$, kg/cm^2	$E_2^{ben}\cdot 10^{-5}$, kg/cm^2				
38	C8	39.0	1.6	2.52	1.41	2.3	1.28	0.32	0.25	0.238	0.673
39	C9	94.5	2.02	2.87	2.15	2.84	2.1	0.42	0.2	0.234	1.19
40	C10	94.5	1.99	$\frac{2.78}{2.87}$	2.15	2.84	2.1	0.42	0.2	0.212	1.09
41	C11	94.5	1.71	$\frac{2.75}{2.87}$	2.15	2.84	2.1	0.42	0.2	0.244	1.25
42	C19	94.0	0.87	2.87	2.15	2.84	2.1	0.42	0.2	0.245	1.26
43	C20	93.9	0.77	2.87	2.15	2.84	2.1	0.42	0.2	0.127	0.658
44	C21	93.8	0.72	2.87	2.15	2.84	2.1	0.42	0.2	0.187	0.962
45	C5	38.8	1.41	3.25	0.91	3.1	0.85	0.35	0.3	0.165	0.785
46	C4	38.4	0.79	3.25	0.91	3.1	0.85	0.35	0.3	0.143	0.642
47	C6	38.5	0.74	3.25	0.91	3.1	0.85	0.35	0.3	0.19	0.865
48	C12	94.2	1.35	$\frac{2.82}{3.85}$	1.52	3.62	1.39	0.44	0.18	0.243	1.24
49	C13	94.1	1.26	$\frac{2.97}{3.85}$	1.52	3.62	1.39	0.44	0.18	0.225	1.14
50	C14	94.2	1.49	$\frac{3.64}{3.85}$	1.52	3.62	1.39	0.44	0.18	0.182	0.925
51	C32	38.6	0.89	3.25	0.91	3.1	0.85	0.35	0.3	0.157	0.716
52	C1	38.5	0.76	1.35	1.93	1.15	1.86	0.38	0.12	0.208	1.02
53	C2	38.4	0.72	1.35	1.93	1.15	1.65	0.38	0.12	0.193	0.957
54	B3	38.4	0.84	1.35	1.93	1.15	1.65	0.38	0.12	0.205	1.02
55	I1			2.8	0.7				0.25	0.209	0.914

TABLE 1.3 (continued)

Serial No.	Shell	R, mm	h, mm	Compression		Bending		$G\cdot10^{-5}$, kg/cm²	ν_1	$\hat{\sigma}^E_{cr}$	ρ
				$E_1^{com}\cdot10^{-5}$, kg/cm²	$E_2^{com}\cdot10^{-5}$, kg/cm²	$E_1^{ben}\cdot10^{-5}$, kg/cm²	$E_2^{ben}\cdot10^{-5}$, kg/cm²				
56	I2			2.0	2.0				0.08	0.154	0.826
57	I3			0.7	2.8				0.063	0.281	0.990
58	I4			$\frac{2.9}{2.9}$	$\frac{0.89}{0.60}$				$\frac{0.29}{0.17}$	0.316	1.44
59	I5			$\frac{2.3}{2.1}$	$\frac{1.5}{1.5}$				$\frac{0.13}{0.11}$	0.264	1.32
60	I6			$\frac{1.5}{1.5}$	$\frac{2.3}{2.1}$				$\frac{0.088}{0.080}$	0.246	1.24
61	I7			0.89	2.9				0.09	0.305	1.32
62	I8			$\frac{2.8}{2.45}$	$\frac{0.80}{0.75}$				$\frac{0.26}{0.30}$	0.256	1.14
63	I9			1.8	1.8				0.08	0.2	1.04
64	I10			$\frac{0.89}{0.80}$	$\frac{2.9}{2.8}$				$\frac{0.092}{0.066}$	0.26	1.19
65	I11			3.0	0.8				0.20	0.352	1.59
66	I12			2.9	0.9				0.30	0.308	1.41
67	I13			1.9	1.9				0.10	0.234	1.21

by the fact that a condition for a deviation of experimental values of the critical stresses in the case of metallic shells is the presence of initial irregularities in the shape of the shell, while in the case of shells made from glass-fiber-reinforced plastics deviations of the same stresses are caused by a marked degree of random deviation in the mechanical properties of the shell material, heterogeneity in material structure, etc. This substantial difference between shells made from glass-fiber-reinforced plastics and metallic shells, connected with the different physical nature of the shell material, is reflected in the types of histogram.

On the basis of the obtained normal distribution law, the confidence limit of calculations was determined for shells of glass-fiber-reinforced plastics according to formula (6.12), with confidence coefficient $p = 0.95$. Hence $\hat{\sigma}^{E}_{cr} = \hat{\sigma}^{T}_{cr} n\ (1 \pm 0.410)$.

The experimental investigation led Gumenyuk and Kravchuk /40/ to the following conclusions.

1. Under short-time loading at normal temperatures glass-fiber-reinforced plastics behave as elastic materials, conforming well with Hooke's law.

2. The form of loss of stability (displacement or formation of hollows) depends on the ratio R/h.

3. The ratio G/E_{red} is the main factor determining the critical stress in glass-fiber-reinforced plastics.

4. Both metallic shells and glass-fiber-reinforced plastic shells are very sensitive to various defects in their preparation. Therefore, the experimental critical stresses are much lower than the theoretical values. However, in contrast to metallic shells initial irregularities in shape are much less significant in glass-fiber-reinforced plastic shells, which explains the difference in the statistical distribution laws.

§7. WAVE PROPAGATION IN A VISCOELASTO-PLASTIC MEDIUM

It is known that under conditions of dynamic action a material behaves differently than under static loading /45, 46/. Hence stress analysis of structural elements and of the structure as a whole is important in order to evaluate the dynamic action, or, at least, to evaluate the dynamic effects.

Here we draw attention once more to possible formulations and methods of solving dynamic problems for media possessing viscoelastoplastic properties. The problem of Sokolovskii /47–49/, who treated wave propagation in rods without hardening, is now discussed.

Consider first the following relations between stress σ (or τ) and strain ε (or γ):

$$E\frac{d\varepsilon}{dt}=\frac{d\sigma}{dt} \quad \text{when } |\sigma|\leqslant\sigma_s, \tag{7.1}$$

$$E\frac{d\varepsilon}{dt}=\frac{d\sigma}{dt}+\varkappa kf(|\sigma|-\sigma_s) \quad \text{when } |\sigma|\geqslant\sigma_s,$$

where

$$f(0)=0,\quad f'(z)>0,\quad \varkappa=\operatorname{sign}\sigma. \tag{7.2}$$

Here k is a physical constant with dimension of reciprocal time, $f(z)$ an experimentally determined function, t time, E the elasticity modulus, and σ_s the yield stress.

We deal now with the wave process due to oscillations of a rod with variable cross-section. The displacement equation assumes the form

$$\frac{\partial}{\partial x}(\sigma F)=\rho_0 F\frac{\partial^2 u}{\partial t^2}, \tag{7.3}$$

where ρ_0 is the density of the rod material and u the displacement; an alternate form of the equation is

$$\frac{\partial\sigma}{\partial x}+\frac{F'}{F}\sigma=\rho_0\frac{\partial v}{\partial t},\quad v=\frac{\partial u}{\partial t}. \tag{7.4}$$

No body force is included here. Such a term would present no difficulties, and its inclusion causes only insignificant complications of the basic equation.

Relationships (7.1) and (7.2) yield

$$E\frac{\partial v}{\partial x}=\frac{\partial\sigma}{\partial t}+\varkappa k\Phi(|\sigma|-\sigma_s), \tag{7.5}$$

where function Φ is defined as follows:

$$\Phi(z)=0 \qquad (z\leqslant 0),$$

$$\Phi(z)=f(z) \qquad (z\geqslant 0).$$

System of equations (7.4) and (7.5) is used to determine stress σ and velocity $v=\frac{\partial u}{\partial t}$. The strain $\varepsilon=\frac{\partial u}{\partial x}$ is determined by (7.5) after transformation into the form

$$E\frac{\partial \varepsilon}{\partial t} = \frac{\partial \sigma}{\partial t} + \varkappa k \Phi(|\sigma| - \sigma_s), \tag{7.5a}$$

$$\left(\frac{\partial \varepsilon}{\partial t} = \frac{\partial v}{\partial x}\right).$$

With known methods, equations (7.4) and (7.5) lead to one second-order hyperbolic differential equation possessing the following family of characteristics:

$$x = \pm a_0 t + \text{const}, \tag{7.6}$$

$$a_0 d\sigma \mp E dv + \left\{a_0 \sigma \frac{F'}{F} \pm \varkappa k \Phi(|\sigma| - \sigma_s)\right\} dx = 0.$$

The displacement of the cross-section of the rod, satisfying equations (7.4) and (7.5), is determined in some region of change in t and x and the continuous first-order derivatives are wavelike. The point dividing two waves displaced over a period of time along the rod is called the front. The values of σ and v at the front are continuous, but their derivatives are discontinuous. The waves at the front of which σ and v are discontinuous are termed shock waves. It follows from (7.6) that in the case under consideration the rate of wave propagation is constant and equals a_0 (especially in the case of shock waves).

Continuity of displacement u upon passage through the wave $x = \pm a_0 t +$ const implies that

$$du = v dt + \varepsilon dx = (v \pm a_0 \varepsilon) dt = 0,$$

in which case

$$[v] \pm a_0 [\varepsilon] = 0, \tag{7.7}$$

where the brackets denote discontinuities of the relevant quantities. On the other hand, condition (7.6) on the lines $x = \pm a_0 t +$ const yields correspondingly

$$a_0 [\sigma] \mp E [v] = 0. \tag{7.8}$$

At the cross-section $x = l$, where a jumpwise variation in area F occurs, the force and velocity must be continuous

$$[\sigma F] = 0, \qquad [v] = 0. \tag{7.9}$$

In terms of dimensionless quantities

$$\tau = kt, \quad \xi = k\frac{x}{a_0}, \quad \delta = k\frac{d}{a_0}, \quad \lambda = k\frac{l}{a_0},$$

$$\bar{u} = \varkappa\frac{k\bar{u}}{a_0\varepsilon_s}, \quad \bar{v} = \varkappa\frac{v}{a_0\varepsilon_s}, \quad \bar{\sigma} = \frac{|\sigma|}{\sigma_s}, \quad \bar{\varepsilon} = \varkappa\frac{\varepsilon}{\varepsilon_s},$$

$$f(\zeta) = \frac{1}{\sigma_s}f(z), \quad \zeta = \frac{z}{\sigma_s}, \quad \Omega = \frac{a_0}{k}\frac{F'}{F}$$

(d is a characteristic dimension), equations (7.4) and (7.5) and relationships (7.5a), (7.6), (7.7), (7.8) and (7.9) reduce to the form

$$\frac{\partial\bar{v}}{\partial\tau} = \frac{\partial\bar{\sigma}}{\partial\xi} + \Omega\bar{\sigma}, \tag{7.10}$$

$$\frac{\partial\bar{v}}{\partial\xi} = \frac{\partial\bar{\sigma}}{\partial\tau} + \varphi(\bar{\sigma}-1), \tag{7.11}$$

$$\frac{\partial\bar{\varepsilon}}{\partial\tau} = \frac{\partial\bar{\sigma}}{\partial\tau} + \varphi(\bar{\sigma}-1), \tag{7.12}$$

$$\xi = \pm\tau + \text{const}, \quad d\bar{\sigma} \mp d\bar{v} + \{\Omega\bar{\sigma} \pm \varphi(\bar{\sigma}-1)\}\,d\xi = 0, \tag{7.13}$$

$$[\bar{\varepsilon}] \pm [\bar{v}] = 0, \quad [\bar{v}] \pm [\bar{\sigma}] = 0 \tag{7.14}$$

$$\text{for } \xi = \pm\tau + \text{const}; \quad [\bar{v}] = 0 \text{ for } \xi = \lambda. \tag{7.15}$$

Here $\varphi(\zeta) \equiv 0$, $(\zeta \leqslant 0)$; $\varphi(\zeta) \equiv f(\zeta)$ $(\zeta \geqslant 0)$. The first equation of (7.13) determines the distribution laws governing wave fronts and the reflected waves, displaced correspondingly to the side of increased or decreased ξ. The second equation of (7.13) states the laws of change in stress σ and velocity v along these fronts.

Suppose at time $\tau = 0$ an instantaneous stress $\bar{\sigma}_0$ is applied to the end of the rod $\xi = 0$, which corresponds to a deformation $\bar{\varepsilon}_0 = \bar{\sigma}_0$ and a velocity $\bar{v}_0 = -\bar{\sigma}_0$. The change in stress at the leading front $\xi = \tau$ propagating in the undeformed part of the rod is readily determined. Taking into account that at the front $\xi = \tau$, $\bar{\sigma} = \bar{\varepsilon} = -\bar{v}$, equation (7.13) assumes the form

$$2\frac{d\bar{\sigma}}{d\xi} + \Omega\bar{\sigma} + \varphi(\bar{\sigma}-1) = 0, \tag{7.16}$$

where $\varphi(\bar{\sigma}-1) \equiv 0$ when $\bar{\sigma} \leqslant 1$.

For cylindrical rods $\Omega \equiv 0$, and the integral of (7.16) satisfying the boundary condition is

$$\bar{\sigma} = \bar{\sigma}_0 \quad (\bar{\sigma} \leqslant 1),$$

$$\bar{\sigma} = \frac{\xi}{2} + \int\limits_{\bar{\sigma}_0-1}^{\bar{\sigma}-1} \frac{d\xi}{f(\xi)} \quad (\bar{\sigma} \geqslant 1).$$

For $f(\zeta)\equiv\zeta$, $f(\zeta)\equiv\zeta^{\mu}$, $f(\zeta)\equiv \operatorname{sh}\frac{\zeta}{\mu}$, relationship (7.17) becomes correspondingly

$$\bar\sigma = 1+(\bar\sigma_0-1)\exp\left(-\frac{\xi}{2}\right),$$

$$\sigma = 1+\left[(\bar\sigma_0-1)^{1-\mu}-(1-\mu)\frac{\xi}{2}\right]^{\frac{1}{1-\mu}}, \qquad (7.17')$$

$$\bar\sigma = 1+2\mu\,\operatorname{arcth}\left[\exp\left(-\frac{\xi}{2\mu}\right)\operatorname{th}\left(\frac{\bar\sigma_0-1}{2\mu}\right)\right].$$

Finally, it should be mentioned that (7.17) is valid only when $\bar\sigma_0>1$, i. e., when the stress applied to the end-face of the rod exceeds the value σ_s.

For a finite rod, when $\Omega=\frac{2}{\xi+\delta}$, equation (7.16) when $f(\zeta)=\zeta$ is also readily integrated:

$$\bar\sigma=\bar\sigma_0\frac{\delta}{\delta+\xi}\qquad (\bar\sigma\leqslant 1),$$

$$\bar\sigma = 1+\frac{2}{\xi+\delta}\left(\exp\frac{\gamma-\xi}{2}-1\right)\qquad(\bar\sigma\geqslant 1),$$

$$\gamma = 2\ln\left[1+(\bar\sigma_0-1)\frac{\delta}{2}\right].$$

Suppose at time $\tau=\tau_0$ a new jumpwise variation in stress occurs at the end-face of the rod $\xi=0$. At this moment a new discontinuity front $\xi=\tau-\tau_0$ is formed. We denote by $+$, $-$, 0 the parameters corresponding to the left and right of the discontinuity and at the section $\xi=0$. Since at the new discontinuity front $[\bar\sigma]=[\bar\varepsilon]=-[\bar v]$, equation (7.13) yields the variation in stress on the line $\xi=\tau-\tau_0$ (at which, for the initial time, $[\bar\sigma]=[\bar\varepsilon_0]=-[\bar v_0]$).
Then

$$\frac{d\bar\sigma^+}{d\xi}-\frac{d\bar v^+}{d\xi}+\Omega\bar\sigma^+ +\varphi(\bar\sigma^+-1)=0,$$

or

$$2\frac{d\bar\sigma^+}{d\xi}+\Omega\bar\sigma^+ +\varphi(\bar\sigma^+-1)=\frac{d\bar\sigma^-}{d\xi}+\frac{d\bar v^-}{d\xi}.$$

For the two most interesting variants the last equation becomes

$$2\frac{d\bar\sigma^+}{d\xi}+\Omega\bar\sigma^+ = \frac{d\bar\sigma^-}{d\xi}+\frac{d\bar v^-}{d\xi}\qquad(\bar\sigma^+\leqslant 1,\ \bar\sigma^-\geqslant 1), \qquad (7.18)$$

$$2\frac{d\sigma^+}{d\xi}+\Omega\bar\sigma^+ + f(\bar\sigma^+-1)=\frac{d\bar\sigma^-}{d\xi}+\frac{d\bar v^-}{d\xi}\qquad(\bar\sigma^+\geqslant 1,\ \bar\sigma^-\leqslant 1);$$

for the two remaining variants analogous considerations can be applied.

For a cylindrical rod equation (7.18) can be integrated and, after satisfying the boundary conditions at $\xi = 0$, gives

$$2(\bar{\sigma}^+ - \bar{\sigma}_0) = (\bar{\sigma}^- - \bar{\sigma}_0) + (\bar{v}^- - \bar{v}_0) \quad (\bar{\sigma}^+ \leqslant 1,\ \bar{\sigma}^- \geqslant 1).$$

The solution of equation (7.19) for $f(\xi) \equiv \xi$ and $\bar{\sigma}^+ = \text{const}$, $\bar{v}^- = \text{const}$ is

$$\bar{\sigma}^+ = 1 + (\bar{\sigma}_0 - 1)\exp\left(-\frac{\xi}{2}\right) \quad (\bar{\sigma}^+ \geqslant 1,\ \bar{\sigma}^- \leqslant 1).$$

Similarly one determines the change in the parameters at the wave front reflected either from the end-face of the rod, or from the section $\xi = \lambda$ at which there occurs a jumpwise variation in the cross-section.

Later, we shall require formulas which determine the change in deformation at the leading wave front $\xi = \tau$ and at the cross-section $\xi = \text{const}$. With the aid of (7.5) and (7.13) we obtain

$$\bar{\varepsilon} = \bar{\sigma}(\tau, \xi) + \int_{\xi}^{\tau} \varphi[\bar{\sigma}(z, \xi) - 1]\, dz, \tag{7.20}$$

$$\bar{\varepsilon} = \bar{\sigma} \quad (\xi \leqslant \tau \leqslant \tau(\xi)),\ \bar{\varepsilon} = \bar{\sigma}(\tau, \xi) + \int_{\tau(\xi)}^{\tau} f[\bar{\sigma}(z, \xi) - 1]\, dz \quad (\tau > \tau(\xi)), \tag{7.21}$$

$$\bar{\varepsilon} = \bar{\sigma}(\tau, \xi) + \int_{\xi}^{\tau} f[\bar{\sigma}(z, \xi) - 1]\, dz \quad (\xi \leqslant \tau \leqslant \tau(\xi)), \tag{7.22}$$

$$\bar{\varepsilon} = \bar{\sigma}(\tau, \xi) + \bar{\varepsilon}_r(\xi) \quad (\tau > \tau(\xi)),\ \bar{\varepsilon}_r(\xi) = \int_{\xi}^{\tau(\xi)} f[\bar{\sigma}(z, \xi) - 1]\, dz.$$

Relationship (7.20) holds when, between time $\tau = \xi$ and time $\tau = \tau(\xi)$, $\bar{\sigma} \leqslant 1$ and at time $\tau = \tau(\xi)$, $\bar{\sigma} > 1$. Relationship (7.21) is valid if $\bar{\sigma} \geqslant 1$ for $\xi \leqslant \tau \leqslant \tau(\xi)$, and $\sigma \leqslant 1$ for $\tau \geqslant \tau(\xi)$.

Consider now four basic problems of viscoelastoplastic wave propagation in rods. The solutions of these problems were derived /47/ using finite-difference equations, replacing system (7.13).

F i r s t p r o b l e m. Let a force $p(\tau)$ act on the end $\xi < 0$ of a semi-infinite cylindrical rod according to the rule

$$\bar{\sigma}=p \quad (0 \leqslant \tau \leqslant \tau_0), \ \bar{\sigma}=0 \quad (\tau_0 < \tau \leqslant \infty).$$

Assume that $f(\zeta) \equiv \zeta$.

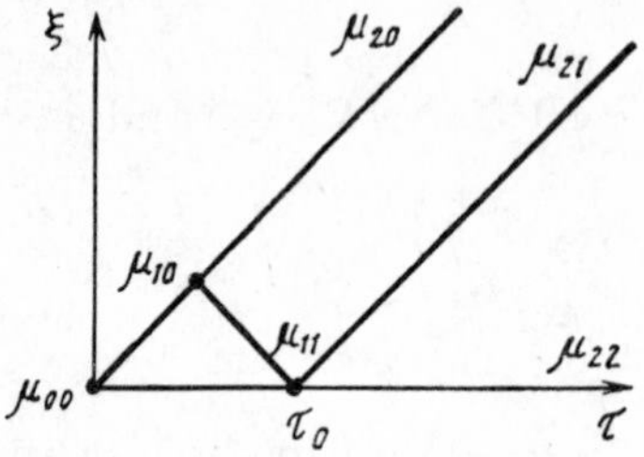

FIGURE 1.24.

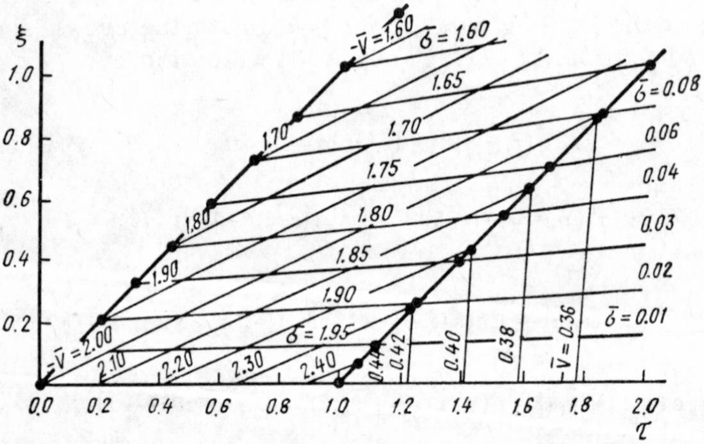

FIGURE 1.25.

According to (7.20), at the end-face of the rod

$$\begin{aligned} \bar{\varepsilon} &= p+(p-1)\,\tau \quad (0 \leqslant \tau \leqslant \tau_0), \\ \bar{\varepsilon} &= (p-1)\,\tau_0 \quad (\tau_0 \leqslant \tau \leqslant \infty). \end{aligned} \tag{7.23}$$

At the leading front $\xi=\tau$ ($\mu_{00}\mu_{20}$ in Figure 1.24) the values of stresses, strains and velocities are derived from (7.17'):

$$\bar{\sigma}=\bar{\varepsilon}=-\bar{v}=1+(p-1)\exp\left(-\frac{\xi}{2}\right). \tag{7.24}$$

The characteristics $\xi=\tau$ and $\xi=\tau-\tau_0$ in the plane ξ, τ (Figure 1.24) represent waves with strong discontinuity. In the region $\mu_{20}\mu_{10}\mu_{00}\mu_{11}\mu_{21}$ bounded by these characteristics and the abscissa axis $\xi=0$, the stress ($\bar{\sigma}>1$) and the velocity are found by a graphoanalytical construction of the solution of (7.10) and (7.11), starting with the triangle $\mu_{00}\mu_{10}\mu_{11}$ and then with the half-strip $\mu_{20}\mu_{10}\mu_{11}\mu_{21}$. Here the boundary conditions are (7.18) and (7.19). Strain ε is determined by (7.21):

$$\bar{\varepsilon}=\bar{\sigma}(\tau, \xi)+\int_{\xi}^{\tau}\bar{\sigma}(z, \xi)\,dz+\xi-\tau.$$

At the corner $\mu_{21}\mu_{11}\mu_{22}$ between the characteristics $\xi=\tau-\tau_0$ and the end-face of the rod the stress ($\bar{\sigma}<1$) and velocities are determined by applying the boundary conditions at $\xi=\tau-\tau_0$ and $\xi=0$. Here the strain $\bar{\varepsilon}$ is given by

$$\bar{\varepsilon}=\bar{\sigma}(\tau, \xi)+\bar{\varepsilon}_r.$$

The results of numerical computation of the problem at hand for $p=2$, $\tau_0=1$ are shown in Figure 1.25. Lines of constant stress $\bar{\sigma}=\text{const}$ and velocities $\bar{v}=\text{const}$ are plotted in the plane ξ, τ. In Figure 1.26 the graphs of the stress-strain relations at the cross-sections $\xi=0$, 0.2, 0.4, 0.6, 0.8, 1 for $\bar{\sigma}\geqslant 1$ are constructed.

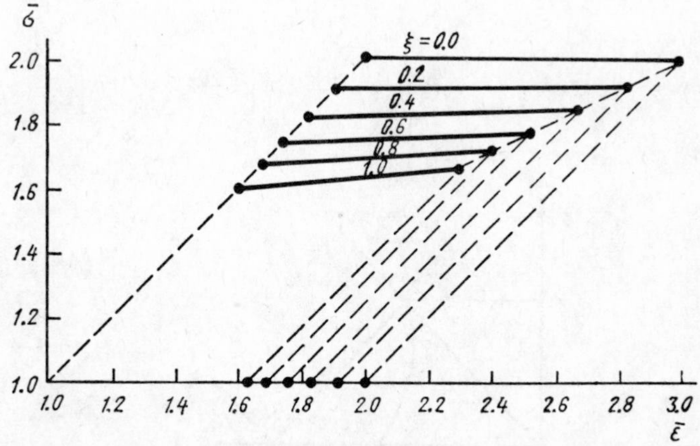

FIGURE 1.26.

Second problem. At the end $\xi = 0$ of a semi-infinite conical rod there acts a stress

$$\bar{\sigma} = p\left(1 - \frac{\tau}{\tau_0}\right) \quad (0 \leqslant \tau \leqslant \tau_0),$$
$$\bar{\sigma} = 0 \quad (\tau_0 < \tau \leqslant \infty). \tag{7.25}$$

Assuming $f(\zeta) \equiv \zeta$, we study the wave propagation process in this case. At the cross-section $\xi = 0$ the strain is determined by (7.21), in which case

$$\bar{\varepsilon} = p\left(1 - \frac{\tau}{\tau_0}\right) - \tau + p\tau\left(1 - \frac{\tau}{2\tau_0}\right) \quad (0 \leqslant \tau \leqslant \tau_*),$$
$$\bar{\varepsilon} = p\left(1 - \frac{\tau}{\tau_0}\right) + p\,\frac{\tau_*^2}{2\tau_0} \quad (\tau_* \leqslant \tau \leqslant \tau_0), \tag{7.26}$$
$$\bar{\varepsilon} = p\,\frac{\tau_*^2}{2\tau_0} \quad (\tau_0 \leqslant \tau \leqslant \infty),$$

where

$$\tau_* = \frac{p-1}{p}\,\tau_0.$$

In a wave with a strong discontinuity $\xi = \tau$ ($\mu_{00}\mu_{20}$ in Figure 1.27), the stresses, strains, and velocities are given by

$$\bar{\sigma} = \bar{\varepsilon} = -\bar{v} = 1 + \frac{2}{\xi + \delta}\left(\exp\frac{\gamma - \xi}{2} - 1\right) \quad (0 \leqslant \xi \leqslant \gamma),$$
$$\bar{\sigma} = \bar{\varepsilon} = -\bar{v} = \frac{\gamma + \delta}{\xi + \delta} \quad (\xi \geqslant \gamma),\ \gamma = 2\ln\left[1 + \frac{p-1}{2}\,\delta\right]. \tag{7.27}$$

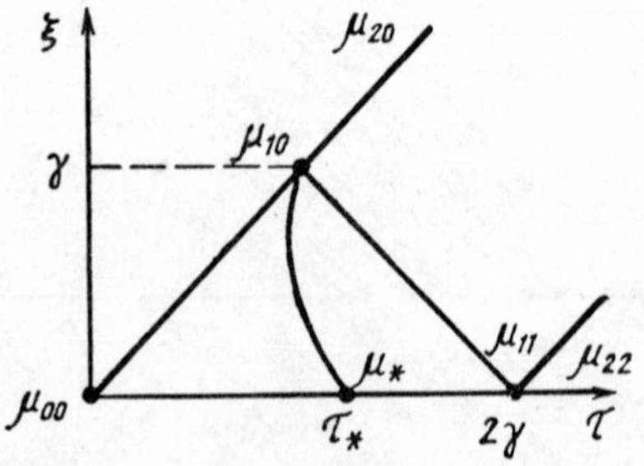

FIGURE 1.27.

The displacement region in the plane ξ, τ is shown in Figure 1.27. The points μ_{10} and μ_* have coordinates $\tau=\xi=\gamma_*$ and $\tau=\tau_*$, $\xi=0$. At some neighboring corner $\mu_{10}\mu_{00}\mu_*$ bounded by the curve $\xi=\xi(\tau)$ passing through the points μ_{10} and μ_*, $\bar{\sigma}>1$. Therefore, when computing the velocity and stress fields in this region one must apply the corresponding conditions on the characteristics for the case $\bar{\sigma}\geqslant 1$. In this case the strain is

$$\bar{\varepsilon} = \bar{\sigma}(\tau, \xi) + \int_{\xi}^{\tau} \bar{\sigma}(z, \xi)\, dz + \xi - \tau. \qquad (7.28)$$

Evidently, in the subsequent region $\mu_{20}\mu_{10}\mu_*\mu_{22}$ the stress $\bar{\sigma}\geqslant 1$.

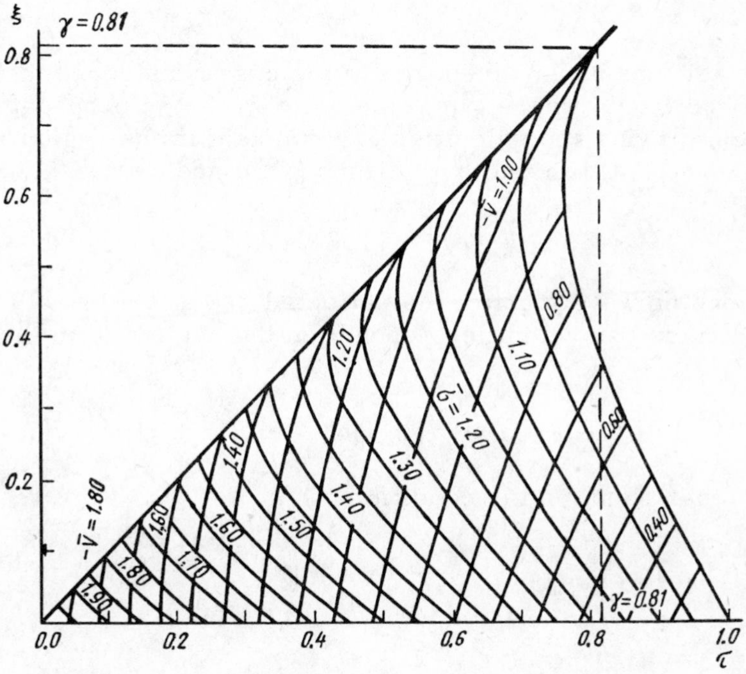

FIGURE 1.28.

The numerical solution of the problem considered for $p=2$, $\tau_0=1$ is illustrated in Figures 1.28 and 1.29. In the plane ξ, τ, lines of equal stress and velocity are plotted (Figure 1.28), and the stress-strain relation for $\bar{\sigma}\geqslant 1$ is presented at different cross-sections of the rod (Figure 1.29).

T h i r d p r o b l e m. Suppose a stress $\bar{\sigma}=p$ acts on the end $\xi=0$ of a cylindrical rod of length l, where $1<2p<2$. The other end of the rod is clamped. As in the two preceding problems we assume $f(\xi)\equiv\xi$.

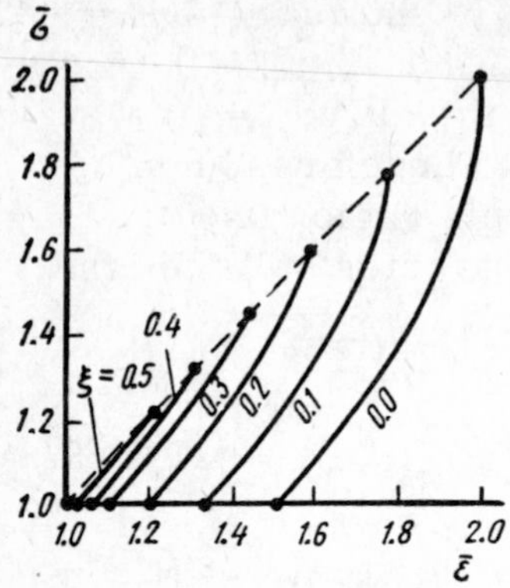

FIGURE 1.29.

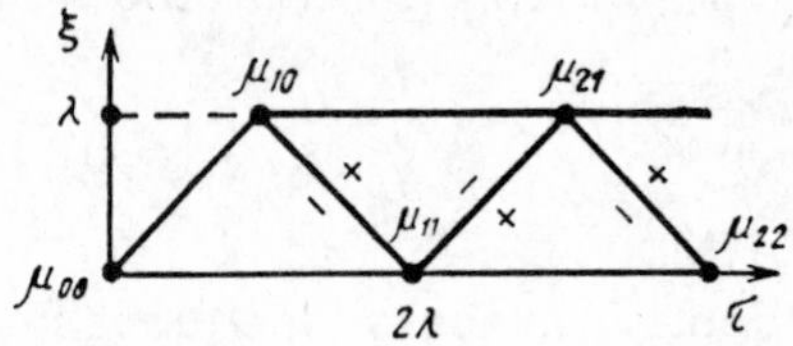

FIGURE 1.30.

It can readily be ascertained that in the case considered the end-face of the rod $\xi = 0$, where $\bar{\varepsilon}=p$, an elastic wave $\xi=\tau$ propagates, the stresses, strains and velocities are constant in the region $\mu_{10}\mu_{00}\mu_{11}$ (Figure 1.30) limited by the lines $\xi = 0$ and $\xi=\tau$:

$$\bar{\sigma} = \bar{\varepsilon} = -\bar{v} = p. \tag{7.29}$$

On the leading wave front of the reflected waves $\xi=2\lambda-\tau$, the stresses, strains and velocities depend, on the one hand, on the condition

$$[\bar{\sigma}] = [\bar{\varepsilon}] = [\bar{v}], \tag{7.30}$$

and on the other hand, on the condition

$$\frac{d\bar{\sigma}}{d\xi} + \frac{d\bar{v}}{d\xi} - \bar{\sigma} + 1 = 0.$$

Hence

$$\bar{\sigma} = \bar{\varepsilon}, \ \bar{\sigma} = \bar{v} + 2p, \tag{7.31}$$

$$2\frac{d\bar{v}}{d\xi} - \bar{v} + 1 - 2p = 0, \tag{7.32}$$

in which case

$$\bar{v} = 1 - 2p + (2p - 1)\exp\left(\frac{\xi - \lambda}{2}\right), \tag{7.33}$$

$$\bar{\sigma} = 1 + (2p - 1)\exp\left(\frac{\xi - \lambda}{2}\right). \tag{7.34}$$

In the triangle $\mu_{10}\mu_{11}\mu_{21}$ bounded by the characteristics $\xi = 2\lambda - \tau$, $\xi = \tau - 2\lambda$ and the straight line $\xi = \lambda$, the stress $\bar{\sigma} > 1$. Computation of the velocities and stresses in this region is conducted numerically. The strain $\bar{\varepsilon}$ is determined by (7.21) which, in the present case, assumes the form

$$\bar{\varepsilon} = \bar{\sigma}(\tau, \xi) + \int_{2\lambda-\xi}^{\tau} \sigma(z, \xi)\, d\xi - (\tau + \xi) + 2\lambda.$$

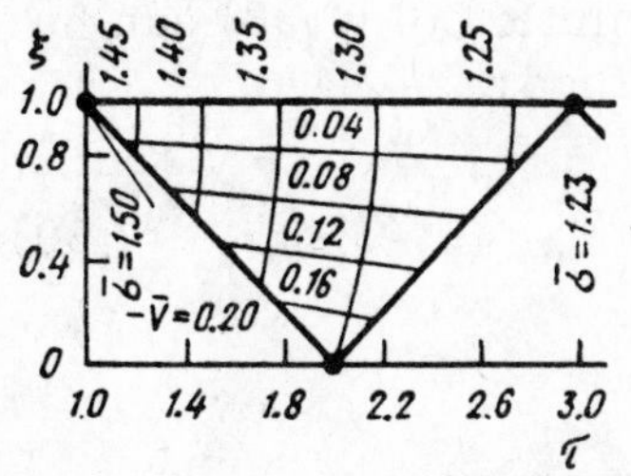

FIGURE 1.31.

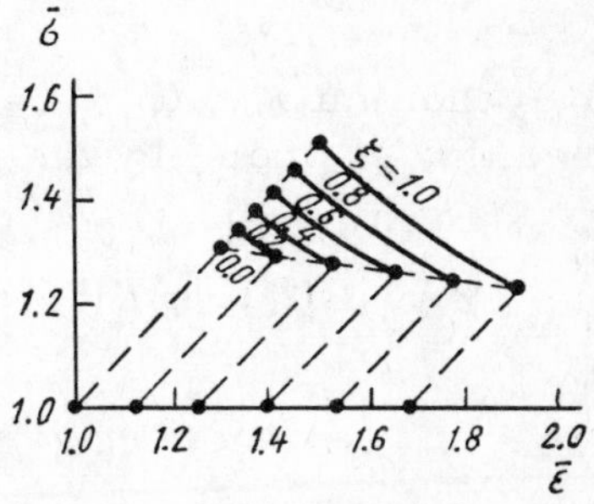

FIGURE 1.32.

The results of computations pertaining to the case considered for $\lambda = 1$, $p = 0.75$ are shown in Figures 1.31 and 1.32. Lines of constant velocity and stress are plotted in the plane ξ, τ (Figure 1.31). The stress-strain relation is illustrated for $\bar{\sigma} \geqslant 1$ at different cross-sections of the rod (Figure 1.32). Corresponding problems under different boundary conditions for $\xi = \lambda$ can be treated similarly.

Fourth problem. Consider a semi-infinite rod moving with constant velocity v_0 in the direction of the negative $0x$ axis. At time $t = 0$ it strikes an immobile wall. The velocity v_0 is assumed to be so large that the stress at the instant of impact exceeds the yield stress σ_s. It can readily be shown that the latter condition is fulfilled if $v_0 > v_s = \sigma_s / \rho_0 a_0$. Wave propagation features in this case were studied for $\varphi(z) \equiv z$ /50/. Assuming $\bar{\xi} = \frac{1}{4}(\xi + \tau)$, $\eta = \frac{1}{4}(\tau - \xi)$, we discuss here the conditions on characteristics (7.13), as in paper /50/:

$$d(\sigma + \rho_0 a_0 v) + 2\varkappa \max[0, |\sigma| - \sigma_s]\, d\eta \text{ for } \bar{\xi} = \text{const},$$
$$d(\sigma - \rho_0 a_0 v) + 2\varkappa \max[0, |\sigma| - \sigma_s]\, d\bar{\xi} \text{ for } \eta = \text{const}. \tag{7.35}$$

The velocity v and stress σ are given by

$$v = \frac{a_0}{4}(\chi_{\bar{\xi}} - \chi_\eta) \exp[-(\bar{\xi} + \eta)], \tag{7.36}$$

$$\sigma - \varkappa\sigma_s = \frac{E}{4}(\chi_{\bar{\xi}} - \chi_\eta - 2\chi) \exp[-(\bar{\xi} + \eta)], \tag{7.37}$$

in terms of function $\chi(\bar{\xi}, \eta)$, satisfying the equation

$$\chi''_{\bar{\xi}\eta} = \chi \tag{7.38}$$

and the condition $\chi(0, 0) = 0$. A general solution of (7.38) can be obtained, for example, by the Riemann method:

$$\chi = \int_0^{\bar{\xi}} I_0(2i\sqrt{y\eta})\, f'(\bar{\xi} - y)\, dy + \int_0^{\eta} I_0(2i\sqrt{\bar{\xi} y}\, g'(\eta - y)\, dy, \tag{7.39}$$

where

$$\chi(\bar{\xi}, 0) = f(\bar{\xi}), \quad \chi(0, \eta) = g(\eta).$$

Allowing for the fact that $\sigma_0 = -\rho_0 a_0 v_0$, in our case (7.37) becomes

$$\sigma_s + \sigma(\bar{\xi}, 0) = -\rho_0 a_0 (v_0 - v_s) \exp(-\bar{\xi})], \tag{7.40}$$

The law of velocity change can be obtained similarly:

$$v(\bar{\xi}, 0) = (v_0 - v_s)[-1 + \exp(-\bar{\xi})], \tag{7.41}$$

from which it is evident that when $x \to \infty$, the velocity of the particles on the leading front of a wave with a strong discontinuity tends to the value $v_0 - v_s$ (it vanishes at $x = 0$).

In order to obtain the variation in velocity and stress for all regions of a front with a strong discontinuity $\eta = 0$, we must find the form of functions $f(\bar{\xi})$ and $g(\eta)$ in (7.39) from condition (7.40) or (7.41) and the boundary condition

$$\frac{\partial^2 u}{\partial x^2} = ReS\frac{\partial u}{\partial t} - \frac{1}{x}\frac{\partial u}{\partial x} + \frac{S}{x}, \tag{7.42}$$

where Re and S are the Reynolds and Saint-Venant numbers.

Thus

$$f'(0)-g'(0)+\int_0^{\bar{\xi}}[f''(\bar{\xi})-f(\bar{\xi})]\,d\bar{\xi}=\frac{4(v_0-v_s)}{a_0}[1-\exp\bar{\xi}], \qquad (7.43)$$

$$f'(0)+g'(0)+\int_0^{\bar{\xi}}[f(\bar{\xi})-2f'(\bar{\xi})+f''(\bar{\xi})]\,d\bar{\xi}=-\frac{4(v_0-v_s)}{a_0}, \qquad (7.43')$$

$$z'(0)I_0(2i\bar{\xi})+\int_0^{\bar{\xi}}I_0(2i\sqrt{\bar{\xi}y})\,[z''(\bar{\xi}-y)-z(\bar{\xi}-y)]\,dy=0 \qquad (7.43'')$$

$$(z=f-g).$$

System of equations (7.43) has the solution

$$f(y)=g(y)=-\frac{2(v_0-v_s)}{a_0}\,y\exp y, \qquad (7.44)$$

therefore

$$-\frac{v}{v_0-v_s}=1-I_0(2i\sqrt{\bar{\xi}\eta})\exp[-(\bar{\xi}+\eta)]-$$

$$-2\exp(-\bar{\xi})\int_0^{\eta}[I_0(2i\sqrt{\bar{\xi}y})\exp(-y)]\,dy, \qquad (7.45)$$

$$-\frac{\sigma+\sigma_s}{\rho_0a_0(v_0-v_s)}=I_0(2i\sqrt{\bar{\xi}\eta})\exp[-(\bar{\xi}+\eta)].$$

It follows from (7.45) that in every cross-section x of the rod the value v decreases monotonically to zero, decreasing with $t^{-1/2}$ at large times.

For cross-sections satisfying the condition $\rho_0a_0x/2\mu\leqslant 2$ the stress decreases monotonically to $-\sigma_s$ with increasing t. At $\rho_0a_0x/2\mu\geqslant 2$ it increases slightly at first. In both cases, at large times the value of $\sigma+\sigma_s$ decreases with $t^{-1/2}$.

The propagation of the residual strain $\tilde{\varepsilon}=\varepsilon-\sigma/E$ is found by integrating the relationship $\frac{d\tilde{\varepsilon}}{dt}=\frac{\sigma+\sigma_s}{\mu}$. It should be noted that the limiting impulse of the rod is

$$I(t)=\sigma_st+\rho_0a_0(v_0-v_s)\int_0^tI_0\left(i\frac{Ez}{2\mu}\right)\exp\left(-\frac{Ez}{2\mu}\right)dz. \qquad (7.46)$$

The problem of a rod of finite length can be treated similarly.

The above theory cannot always be applied to polymeric material, as the latter displays relaxation and viscous properties independent of the stress level. Moreover, because of the viscous properties "delayed yield" is observed, which will be examined in the following section.

§8. PROPAGATION OF PERTURBATION WAVES IN A LONG POLYMERIC ROD

Delayed yield in a polymeric material gives rise to a region of plastic overload. Elastic overstresses occur in an elastoplastic medium. In a medium displaying viscoelastic properties, viscoelastic overstresses occur under stresses which are less than the dynamic yield stress. On the basis of these concepts, Kokoshvili /51a/ concluded that the state of a polymeric rod is determined by two deformation stages: (a) a viscoelastic stage manifested as an elastic overstress at a time less than the yield delay time τ_s, and (b) a viscoplastic stage occurring at a time greater than the yield delay time, provided the static yield stress σ_s has been reached.

In a first approximation the viscoelastic stage can be described by the equations of a standard linear solid:

$$E\dot{\varepsilon}+\frac{E_\infty}{\tau_1}\varepsilon=\dot{\sigma}+\frac{\sigma}{\tau_1}, \qquad (8.1)$$

where E is the instantaneous elasticity modulus, E_∞ the long-time elasticity modulus, τ_1 the relaxation time coefficient of the viscoelastic stage, σ the stress acting along the x axis, and ε the strain in the same direction.

In order to describe the viscoplastic stage we take the relationship between stress and strain rate in the form of two equivalent relationships: for a nonlinear relaxation function $\Phi(\sigma-\sigma_s)$ and constant viscosity η:

$$\eta\dot{\varepsilon}^p=\Phi(\sigma-\sigma_s), \qquad (8.2)$$

for a linear function $\Phi(\sigma-\sigma_s)$ and stress-dependent viscosity $\eta(\sigma)$,

$$\eta(\sigma)\dot{\varepsilon}^p=(\sigma-\sigma_s). \qquad (8.3)$$

Kokoshvili assumed that parameters σ and ε, together with their first and second derivatives with respect to t and x, do not possess a discontinuity at stress $\sigma=\sigma_s$ and that the relaxation time does not change abruptly. Allowing for the relaxation nature, Kokoshvili introduced a hypothesis about the relationship between the relaxation times of the viscoelastic and viscoplastic stages in the form

$$\tau_2 = \frac{\tau_1}{1 - \frac{\tau_s}{\tau_0}}, \tag{8.4}$$

where τ_s is the yield delay time for arbitrary dynamic loading and τ_0 the maximum yield delay time in static tests.

If the yield delay time is taken as

$$\tau_s = \tau_0\, e^{-\frac{1}{m}\frac{\sigma-\sigma_s}{\sigma_s}},$$

the relaxation time for the viscoplastic stage is

$$\tau_2 = \frac{1}{1 - e^{-\frac{1}{m}\frac{\sigma-\sigma_s}{\sigma_s}}}. \tag{8.5}$$

If the viscosities η and $\eta(\sigma)$ are given by

$$\eta = E\tau_1, \quad \eta(\sigma) = E\tau_2 = \frac{E\tau_1}{1 - e^{-\frac{1}{m}\frac{\sigma-\sigma_s}{\sigma_s}}}$$

and $\dot{\varepsilon}^p$ is eliminated from relationships (8.2) and (8.3), we obtain

$$\Phi(\sigma-\sigma_s) = (\sigma-\sigma_s)\left(1 - e^{-\frac{1}{m}\frac{\sigma-\sigma_s}{\sigma_s}}\right) = (\sigma-\sigma_s)\left(1 - \frac{\tau_s}{\tau_0}\right), \tag{8.6}$$

where m is a physical constant.

The rate influence function $\Phi(\sigma-\sigma_s)$, obtained on the basis of hypothesis (8.4), is meaningful only in relation to a dynamic law of deformation.

The equation of state in the viscoplastic stage can be derived if the strain rate of a viscoelastic-viscoplastic body is composed of the strain rates of the viscoelastic and viscoplastic stages:

$$E\ddot{\varepsilon} + \frac{E_\infty}{\tau_1}\dot{\varepsilon} - \frac{\dot{\Phi}}{\tau_1} - \frac{E_\infty}{E\tau_1^2}\Phi = \ddot{\sigma} + \frac{\dot{\sigma}}{\tau_1}. \tag{8.7}$$

In order to allow for the yield delay effect, we must introduce time-dependent conditions. The body is then described by the following system of equations:

$$E\dot{\varepsilon} + \frac{E_\infty}{\tau_1}\varepsilon = \dot{\sigma} + \frac{\sigma}{\tau_1}$$

when

$$0 \leqslant \sigma \leqslant \infty,\ 0 \leqslant t \leqslant \tau_s;\ \sigma \leqslant \sigma_s,\ \tau_s < t \leqslant \infty;$$

$$E\ddot{\varepsilon} + \frac{E_\infty}{\tau_1}\dot{\varepsilon} - \frac{\dot{\Phi}}{\tau_1} - \frac{E_\infty}{E\tau_1^2}\Phi = \frac{\dot{\sigma}}{\tau_1} + \ddot{\sigma} \qquad (8.8)$$

when

$$\sigma \geqslant \sigma_s,\ t \geqslant \tau_s.$$

The formulation and solution of the wave propagation problem in a long viscoelastoplastic rod with allowance for delayed yield was given by Kokoshvili /51a/. The solution is based on the physical relationship described by system (8.8).

Following /51a/, as basic assumption we postulate that the plane sections remain plane during the displacements, that the stresses and strains are distributed uniformly over the cross-section, and that there are no displacements in a direction perpendicular to the x axis of the rod. The stress-strain curve and all the rheological characteristics have been determined from dynamic loading experiments. Unloading is not examined.

Suppose a perturbation is applied to the end-face of a semi-infinite rod, as result of which the end-face moves such that, at $x = 0$, $\varepsilon = Wt^2$.

As initial condition, it is assumed that there are no displacements and stresses at $t = 0$.

The second equation of system (8.8) can be simplified by linearizing $\Phi(\sigma-\sigma_s)$ in the form

$$\Phi(\sigma-\sigma_s) = \Phi_i(\sigma-\sigma_s) + (\sigma-\sigma_i)R_i, \qquad (8.9)$$

where $\Phi_i(\sigma-\sigma_s)$ and σ_i correspond to the points of intersection of straight lines with constant slope R_i approximating function $\Phi(\sigma-\sigma_s)$ in the i-th segment of the approximation. Determination of the strains reduces to the solution of equations (8.10) and (8.11), obtained by eliminating parameters σ and $\dot{\sigma}$ from system of equations (8.8) and the equation of motion with the aid of (8.9):

$$\frac{E}{\rho}\frac{\partial^3\varepsilon}{\partial x^2\,\partial t} + \frac{E_\infty}{\rho\tau_1}\frac{\partial^2\varepsilon}{\partial x^2} = \frac{\partial^3\varepsilon}{\partial t^3} + \frac{1}{\tau_1}\frac{\partial^2\varepsilon}{\partial t^2}$$

when

$$0 \leqslant \sigma \leqslant \infty,\ 0 \leqslant t \leqslant \tau_s;\ \sigma \leqslant \sigma_s,\ \tau_s < t \leqslant \infty;$$

$$\frac{E}{\rho}\frac{\partial^3\varepsilon}{\partial x^2\,\partial t} + \frac{E_\infty}{\rho\tau_1}\frac{\partial^2\varepsilon}{\partial x^2} - \frac{R_i}{\tau_1}\frac{\partial^2\varepsilon}{\partial t^2} - \frac{E_\infty}{E\tau_1^2}R_i\frac{\partial\varepsilon}{\partial t} =$$

$$= \frac{\partial^3\varepsilon}{\partial t^3} + \frac{1}{\tau_1}\frac{\partial^2\varepsilon}{\partial t^2} \qquad (8.10)$$

when

$$\sigma \geqslant \sigma_s, \; t \geqslant \tau_s.$$

In terms of the following dimensionless variables and notation:

$$\frac{E}{\rho} = c_0^2, \; \frac{E_\infty}{\rho} = c_\alpha^2, \; \frac{E_\infty}{E} = \alpha, \; \tilde{x} = \frac{x}{b},$$

$$\tilde{t} = \frac{tc_0}{b}, \; \tilde{W} = W\tau_1^2, \; \tilde{\sigma} = \frac{\sigma}{\rho c_0^2}, \quad \beta = \frac{b}{c_0\tau_1},$$

$$R_i + 1 = k_i, \quad R_i\alpha = r_i,$$

where b is a constant with the dimension of length, system (8.10) reduces to the form

$$\frac{\partial^3 \tilde{\varepsilon}}{\partial \tilde{x}^2 \, \partial \tilde{t}} + \beta\alpha \frac{\partial^2 \tilde{\varepsilon}}{\partial \tilde{x}^2} = \frac{\partial^3 \tilde{\varepsilon}}{\partial \tilde{t}^3} + \beta \frac{\partial^2 \tilde{\varepsilon}}{\partial \tilde{t}^2}$$

when

$$0 \leqslant \tilde{t} \leqslant \tilde{\tau}_s, \; 0 \leqslant \tilde{\sigma} \leqslant \infty; \;\; \tilde{\tau}_s \leqslant \tilde{t} \leqslant \infty, \; \tilde{\sigma} \leqslant \tilde{\sigma}_s; \tag{8.11}$$

$$\frac{\partial^3 \tilde{\varepsilon}}{\partial \tilde{x}^2 \, \partial \tilde{t}} + \beta\alpha \frac{\partial^2 \tilde{\varepsilon}}{\partial \tilde{x}^2} = \frac{\partial^3 \tilde{\varepsilon}}{\partial \tilde{t}^3} + \beta k_i \frac{\partial^2 \tilde{\varepsilon}}{\partial \tilde{t}^2} + \beta^2 r_i \frac{\partial \tilde{\varepsilon}}{\partial \tilde{t}}$$

when

$$\tilde{\sigma} \geqslant \tilde{\sigma}_s, \; \tilde{t} \geqslant \tilde{\tau}_s. \tag{8.12}$$

In accordance with the time-dependent conditions, Kokoshvili /51a/ solved the problem in three stages.

F i r s t S t a g e. Asymptotic solution of equation (8.11) for $0 \leqslant t \leqslant \tau_s$. Application to equation (8.11) of a Laplace transform with respect to variable t, subject to the above-mentioned initial conditions, yields take ordinary differential equation

$$\frac{d^2 \bar{\varepsilon}}{dx^2} = \frac{s^2 (s+\beta)}{s + \alpha\beta} \bar{\varepsilon}. \tag{8.13}$$

The sign ~ has been omitted; the bar indicates a Laplace transform with parameter s.

The solution of equation (8.13) which vanishes as $x \to \infty$ is

$$\bar{\varepsilon} = C \exp\left(-s \sqrt{\frac{s+\beta}{s+\alpha\beta}}\, x\right). \tag{8.14}$$

The constant of integration is determined from the boundary condition. If the value of constant C is substituted in the transform of the solution, we obtain

$$\bar{\varepsilon} = 2\beta^2 \frac{W}{s^3} \exp\left(-s\sqrt{\frac{s+\beta}{s+\alpha\beta}}\,x\right). \tag{8.15}$$

The inverse transform of the solution is difficult to derive. However, we can obtain an asymptotic solution by series expansion in the small parameter $\beta = \frac{b}{c_0\tau_1}$, which is the ratio of the time taken by an elastic wave to reach the rod coordinate b to the relaxation time τ_1. The resulting solution gives the relationship at times less than the relaxation time (neglecting terms containing higher powers of the small parameter is equivalent to neglecting the same power of the ratio t/τ_1).

Series expansion in the small parameter yields a relationship possessing the inverse transform

$$\varepsilon = \beta^2 W\left[(t-x)^2 + 2\beta^2\delta x\,\frac{(t-x)^3}{3} + \ldots\right] e^{-\frac{1-\alpha}{2}\beta x}. \tag{8.16}$$

In terms of dimensional variables

$$\varepsilon = W\left[\left(t-\frac{x}{c_0}\right)^2 + 2\delta\,\frac{x}{c_0\tau_1}\,\frac{\left(t-\frac{x}{c_0}\right)^3}{3} + \ldots\right] e^{-\frac{1-\alpha}{2}\frac{x}{c_0\tau_1}},$$

where

$$\delta = \frac{1+2\alpha-3\alpha^2}{8}. \tag{8.17}$$

This solution describes the excitation of motion, determining deformation close to the leading wave front. The solution shows that in viscoelastic wave propagation the leading front carries a deformation which is $\sim e^{-\frac{1-\alpha}{2}\frac{x}{c_0\tau_1}}$ times smaller than in an elastic rod. (The solution for an elastic rod is derived from (8.17) by setting $\tau_1 = \infty$.)

When $\tau_1 \leqslant \tau_s$ and the wave front is not a shock front, the solution for times close to τ_s can be obtained by neglecting the deformation distributed in the rod as a result of the excitation of motion at time $t = t_0 \leqslant \tau_1$. The wave front carrying this deformation will be taken as the leading front. The solution for the deformations will have a form analogous to (8.17). The parameters are

$$\beta^* = \frac{b}{c_0^* \tau_1}, \qquad \alpha^* = \frac{c_\alpha^2}{(c_0^*)^2},$$

where c_0^* is the rate of propagation of the deformation $\varepsilon(x, t_0)$. The stresses are found from the equation of state on the characteristics $dx = 0$.

Second Stage. Asymptotic solution of equation (8.11) when $0 \leqslant \sigma \leqslant \sigma_s$, $\tau_1 \leqslant t \leqslant \infty$. When $\tau_1 \ll \tau_s$, the solution close to the limit of the viscoplastic state (at times close to τ_s) can be obtained by applying the method of steepest descents.

Application to equation (8.11) of a complex Laplace transform with respect to the variable t, and subject to the previous initial conditions, results in a differential equation different from (8.13), because parameter s is a complex quantity. The inverse transform of the solution of this equation yields

$$\varepsilon = \frac{2\beta^2 W}{\pi i} \int_{-i\infty}^{+i\infty} \frac{ds}{s^3} \exp\left[s\left(t - \sqrt{\frac{s+\beta}{s+\alpha\beta}}\, x\right)\right]. \tag{8.18}$$

Solution (8.18) can be expressed in another form, by fixing the ratio of the velocity of the leading wave front to the elastic wave velocity ($x = c_* t$):

$$\varepsilon = \frac{2\beta^2 W}{\pi i} \int_{-i\infty}^{+i\infty} \frac{ds}{s^3} \exp\left[st\left(1 - c_* \sqrt{\frac{s+\beta}{s+\alpha\beta}}\right)\right],$$

$$\widetilde{c}_* = \frac{c_*}{c_0}. \tag{8.19}$$

For brevity, we write (8.19) in the form

$$\varepsilon = \frac{2\beta^2 W}{\pi i} \int_{-i\infty}^{+i\infty} e^{tf(s)} F(s)\, ds. \tag{8.20}$$

The integral can be represented asymptotically by the method of steepest descents and its modifications. The saddle point s_0 of function $f(s)$ is determined by the equation $\frac{\partial f}{\partial s} = 0$. When the parameter c_* changes, function $f(s)$ may have a saddle point located close to the pole s_i. In this case the asymptotic representation of the integral assumes the form

$$\varepsilon \approx \frac{2\beta^2 W}{\sqrt{\pi}} F(s_0)(s_i - s_0) \exp\left[f(s_0)\, t + t\, \frac{f''(s_0)}{2} \cdot (s_i - s_0)^2\right] \operatorname{erf} \sqrt{\frac{f''(s_0)}{2}}\, t\,(s_i - s_0). \tag{8.21}$$

When the saddle point passes through the pole ($c_* = c_i$), function ε changes sign and experiences a jump equal in magnitude to the residue at the pole, ε varying continuously:

$$\varepsilon \approx \frac{2\beta^2 W}{\sqrt{\pi}} F(s_0)(s_i - s_0) \exp\left[f(s_0)t + t\frac{f''(s_0)}{2}(s_i - s_0)^2\right]$$

$$\cdot \operatorname{erf}\sqrt{\frac{f''(s_0)}{2}t}\,(s_i - s_0) + E\left(t - \frac{x}{c_i}\right)\operatorname{res}\left[F(s_i)e^{tf(s_i)}\right]. \qquad (8.22)$$

When the saddle point is remote from the neighborhood of the pole, the ordinary method of steepest descents is used:

$$\varepsilon \approx \frac{2\beta^2 W F(s_0) e^{tf(s_0)}}{\sqrt{2\pi t f''(s_0)}} + E\left(t - \frac{x}{c_i}\right)\operatorname{res}\left[F(s_i)e^{tf(s_i)}\right]. \qquad (8.23)$$

The solutions for the stresses have an analogous form.

Third Stage. Asymptotic solution of equation (8.12) when $\sigma \geqslant \sigma_s$, $t \geqslant \tau_s$. The above solutions, plotted on the x—t plane in the form of lines of equal stresses and strains, are respectively limited by the boundary of the viscoplastic state, which can be constructed by starting from the stress-dependence of the yield delay time:

$$\tau_s = \tau_0 e^{-\frac{1}{m}\frac{\sigma - \sigma_s}{\sigma_s}}. \qquad (8.24)$$

On each of the lines σ = const ($\sigma \geqslant \sigma_s$) there is a yield delay time given by (8.24). The geometric locus of points corresponding to the yield delay time for constant stress is the boundary of the viscoplastic state.

In order to solve equation (8.12) using Laplace transforms, one must approximate function $\Phi(\sigma - \sigma_s)$ by an approximation linear over several segments in the interval $\Delta\sigma \to 0$. The lines of equal stress for σ = const were constructed with the same interval. The i-th segment in the approximation corresponds to a definite value of the slope R_i. Assuming that the stress does not vary continuously but with a jump $\Delta\sigma$ on transition from line σ_i to line σ_{i+1}, we have regions of constant stresses, L_i and L_{i+1}.

When solving the problem in the viscoplastic stage it is assumed that the stress and strain are continuous on crossing the line τ_s.

Starting from the condition of stress continuity, we can extend the region of constant stresses to the right of the line τ_s in the neighborhood of points not far removed from the boundary. Since the equations of state change on transition to the viscoplastic stage, the line σ_i = const to the right of the boundary will not satisfy the relationship $\sigma(x, t) = \sigma_i$ = const derived from the line σ_i to the left of the boundary. The problem reduces to finding the line $\sigma(x, t)=\sigma_i$ to the right of the boundary, in the region of constant stress.

Equation (8.12) is linear on the lines σ_i = const. Moreover, if the approximation extends over the interval $\Delta\sigma\to 0$, then in the present case too parameter β is small.

By using the method of a small parameter, it is possible to obtain an approximate analytical description of the line in the neighborhood of the end of the previously constructed curve σ_i = const. The method of successive adjustments enables the curve σ_i to be constructed up to the inequality $x \geqslant c_* t$, which is realized at the line σ_i = const on which the solutions are meaningless.

Thus these solutions are represented by lines σ, ε = const which are solutions of piecewise-linear equations with the adjusted solutions of the previous linear equations as initial conditions. The solution for the deformations in the region of the constructed lines is obtained similarly.

In accordance with the method of solution we transfer the coordinate origin in the x—t plane to the point $A(x_0, t_0)$, from which the solution is begun. Here, in applying Laplace transforms it is necessary to take into account the initial conditions

$$\varepsilon(x, t_0), \quad \frac{\partial\varepsilon(x, t_0)}{\partial t}, \quad \frac{\partial^2\varepsilon(x, t_0)}{\partial t^2}, \quad \frac{\partial^2\varepsilon(x, t_0)}{\partial x^2}.$$

Since the solution is obtained in the region σ_i = const, these conditions are simplified:

$$\varepsilon_i(x_0, t_0), \quad \frac{\partial\varepsilon_i(x_0, t_0)}{\partial t}, \quad \frac{\partial^2\varepsilon_i(x_0, t_0)}{\partial t^2}, \quad \frac{\partial^2\varepsilon_i(x_0, t_0)}{\partial x^2}.$$

We introduce the following notation:

$$\tilde{x}=\frac{x-x_0}{b}, \quad \tilde{t}=\frac{t-t_0}{b}c_*, \quad \beta=\frac{b}{c_*\tau_1}, \quad \alpha=\frac{c_\alpha^2}{c_*^2},$$

where c_* is the rate of stress propagation in a section of the rod with coordinate x_0 at time t_0.

Application of Laplace transforms to equation (8.12) with allowance for the initial conditions yields

$$(s+\beta\alpha)\frac{d^2\bar{\varepsilon}_i}{dx^2}=\bar{\varepsilon}_i(s^3+k_i\beta s^2+\beta^2 r_i s)-s^2\varepsilon_i(x_0, t_0)-sP_{0i}-m_{0i}, \quad (8.25)$$

where

$$P_{0i} = \beta k_i \varepsilon_i (x_0, t_0) + \frac{\partial \varepsilon_i (x_0, t_0)}{\partial t}.$$

$$m_{0i} = \frac{\partial^2 \varepsilon_i (x_0, t_0)}{\partial t^2} + \beta k_i \frac{\partial \varepsilon_i (x_0, t_0)}{\partial t} + \beta^2 r_i \varepsilon_i (x_0 \; t_0) - \frac{\partial^2 \varepsilon_i (x_0, t_0)}{\partial x^2}.$$

The general solution of equation (8.25) for a semi-infinite rod has the form

$$\bar{\varepsilon}_i = C \exp\left(-\sqrt{\frac{s^3 + \beta k_i s^2 + \beta^2 r_i s}{s + \alpha\beta}} x\right) + \frac{s^2 \varepsilon_i (x_0, t_0) + sP_{0i} + m_{0i}}{s^3 + \beta s^2 k_i + \beta^2 r_i s}. \qquad (8.26)$$

The constant of integration is determined from the boundary condition at the beginning of the adjustment: when $x = 0$, $\varepsilon = \varepsilon_i (x_0, t_0)$; $\bar{\varepsilon} = \frac{\varepsilon_i (x_0, t_0)}{s}$. After substituting the constant c the transform of the solution becomes

$$\bar{\varepsilon}_i = \left[\frac{\varepsilon_i (x_0, t_0)}{s} - \frac{s^2 \varepsilon_i (x_0, t_0) + sP_{0i} + m_{0i}}{s^3 + \beta s^2 k_i + \beta^2 r_i s} \right] \cdot$$

$$\cdot \exp\left(-\sqrt{\frac{s^3 + \beta k_i s^2 + \beta^2 r_i s}{s + \alpha\beta}} x\right) + \frac{s^2 \varepsilon_i (x_0, t_0) + sP_{0i} + m_{0i}}{s^3 + \beta k_i s^2 + \beta^2 r_i s}. \qquad (8.27)$$

Expanding the fractional-rational function in simple fractions and the exponent in series form with respect to the small parameter, we obtain the relationship

$$\frac{s^2 \varepsilon_i (x_0, t_0) + sP_{0i} + m_{0i}}{s (s^2 + \beta k_i s + \beta^2 r_i)} = \frac{s^2 \varepsilon_i (x_0, t_0) + sP_{0i} + m_{0i}}{s (s + \beta h)(s + \beta g)} = \frac{A_i}{s + \beta g} +$$

$$+ \frac{B_i}{s + \beta h} + \frac{C_i}{s}, \quad \exp\left(-\sqrt{\frac{s^3 + \beta k_1 s^2 + \beta^2 r_i s}{s + \alpha\beta}} x\right) \approx$$

$$\approx e^{-sx} e^{-\lambda_i \beta x} \left(1 - \beta^2 D_i \frac{x}{s}\right), \qquad (8.28)$$

where $g = \frac{1}{2} (k_i - \sqrt{k_i^2 - 4r_i}), \qquad h = \frac{1}{2} (k_i + \sqrt{k_i^2 - 4r_i}),$

$$A_i = \varepsilon_i (x_0, t_0) - \frac{P_{0i} - \beta \varepsilon_i (x_0, t_0) h - \frac{m_{0i}}{\beta g}}{\beta (g - h)},$$

$$B_i = \frac{1}{\beta (g - h)} \left(P_{0i} - \frac{m_{0i}}{\beta h} - \varepsilon_i (x_0, t_0) h\beta\right), \quad C_i = \frac{m_{0i}}{\beta^2 gh},$$

$$A_i + B_i + C_i = \varepsilon_i (x_0, t_0),$$

$$\lambda_i = \frac{1}{2} (g + h - \alpha), \qquad D_i = \frac{1}{8} [(g - h)^2 + 2\alpha (g + h) - 3\alpha^2]. \qquad (8.29)$$

Substitution of the expansions and inversion of the transform yields an approximate analytical description of the line ε_i = const in the i-th approximation segment:

$$\varepsilon_i(x_0, t_0) - e^{-\beta\lambda_i x}\{\varepsilon_i(x_0, t_0) - (A_i\theta_1 + B_i\theta_2 + C_i) + \beta x D_i \cdot$$
$$\cdot\left[\frac{A_i}{g}(1-\theta_1) + \frac{B_i}{h}(1-\theta_2) + C_i\beta(t-x)\right]\Big\} -$$
$$-(A_i e^{-\beta g t} + B_i e^{-\beta h t} + C_i) = 0,$$

where

$$\theta_1 = e^{-\beta g(t-x)}, \qquad \theta_2 = e^{-\beta h(t-x)}.$$

A similar expression is obtained for the line σ_i = const on the i-th segment of approximation.

Finally, we outline a general scheme for numerical solution of the problem, which is carried out in the following sequence.

1. Construction of the solution in the viscoelastic stage. When $\tau_l \leqslant \tau_s$, the construction is based on (8.17). The stress is found from the equation of state. When $\tau_l \ll \tau_s$, the solution close to the boundary τ_s is constructed using (8.21)–(8.23), for which we require the relationship $f(s_0)$. Rays are drawn from the coordinate origin in the x—t plane. In order to find the solution at a required point of the x—t plane we fix the parameter $0 \leqslant c_* \leqslant 1$ at that point and determine the proximity of the saddle point to the pole $s_i - s_0 \leqslant \beta$.

2. The solution in the viscoplastic stage is preceded by approximation of function $\Phi(\sigma - \sigma_s)$ and evaluation of parameters R_i. Construction of the solution is begun from the boundary τ_s. The values of c_*, P_{0i}, m_{0i}, $\varepsilon(x_0, t_0)$, g, h are found at the end of the previously constructed line σ_i = const. From a relationship analogous to (8.30) we find the analytical description of the line in a region not far removed from the beginning of the construction, which is drawn to intersect the boundary of this region (the circle $r = \Delta\sigma/2$). The remaining segments of the curves σ_i = const are constructed in the same way.

The lines of constant strain are constructed similarly, with the sole difference that in this case parameter R_i along the curve ε_i = const changes on transition from one stress level to another. The constructions are terminated at $x \geqslant c_* t$.

Kokoshvili /51b/ carried out an experimental investigation of the propagation of perturbation waves in a long polyethylene rod. He used a high-speed motion-picture camera to record the wave process, which enabled him to find the regularities of the dynamic deformations. As a result he established the presence of two deformation stages of the polyethylene rod. He derived quantitative values of the material characteristics for the given dynamic load regularity, and established relationships between the rate of wave propagation and the change in material properties of the sample upon deformation.

The latest experimental investigations of Kokoshvili /51b/ enabled him to reach the following conclusions. 1. The rate of propagation of the leading front in the polyethylene rod is independent of the previous stress. 2. The Boltzmann-Volterra linear elastoplastic laws of deformation, constructed by starting from data on the modulus of elasticity and phase-shift angle over a broad frequency range and characterized by a broad range of relaxation times of polymers, give a satisfactory description of wave propagation in a long polyethylene rod with insignificant previous stress. 3. In the case of previous stress resulting in a deformation $\varepsilon \geqslant 2\%$, the wave propagation process in a polyethylene rod corresponds well to the behavior of models of a standard solid with unique relaxation time. 4. The influence of the velocity on the inclination of the $\sigma \sim \varepsilon$ curve with respect to the ε-axis is noticeable on the initial section of the line.

§9. STABILITY OF CYLINDRICAL SHELLS UNDER THERMAL SHOCK

Almost ideal elasticity is an important feature of the behavior of polymeric solids under short-time action /52/. This property appears during wave tests, in which two characteristic wave velocities are observed, namely the velocity of waves of volume deformation and shear waves. The bulk and shear moduli are determined simultaneously, and the Poisson ratio is close to that of an elastic body. The deformation rate at the fronts of these waves is very large, since the thickness of the fronts (which, from the standpoint of mechanics of continuous media, equals zero) is commensurable with molecular dimensions and since the time of jumpwise change in deformation and stress is markedly less than the minimum relaxation time of the structure /53/. The bulk modulus obtained from wave and from static tests are close to one another, but the values of the shear modulus differ by an order of magnitude /53/. This kind of consideration provides sufficient justification to apply extensively the formulations and methods of elasticity theory to the treatment of dynamic problems of polymer mechanics.

Vol'mir and Ponomarev /54/ have formulated and solved the problem of the stability of cylindrical shells under thermal shock, discussed below.

Consider a thin annular cylindrical shell of finite length subjected to an axisymmetric heat impulse at a zone located at one of the end-faces.

A portion of the shell length is subjected to dynamic compression as the heat flux propagates along the structure, and is especially strong in the case of a thermal shock. Under certain known conditions this gives rise to buckling in the compressed zone of the shell, accompanied by cracking. This phenomenon is described for structures. When treating the behavior of shells, inertial forces must be included in the fundamental equations, corresponding not only to deflection but also to displacements relative to the middle surface. Experience has shown such a problem to be very complex, so it is stipulated that the change in the thermoelastic deformation along the shell is independent of the deflection and is determined by the corresponding one-dimensional problem /55/. As regards buckling, it is assumed that the deflections formed thereby are equal for thick shells and are found by solving the geometrical nonlinear problem.

The displacement of points on the middle surface along the shell axis satisfy the differential equations /55/

$$\theta_{,t} - \varkappa\theta_{,xx} + \beta' u_{,xt} = 0, \tag{9.1}$$

$$u_{,xx} - \frac{1}{c^2} u_{,tt} - \alpha\theta_{,x} = 0 \tag{9.2}$$

while for large deflections /56/

$$\frac{D}{h} \nabla^2\nabla^2 (w - w_0) = L(w, \Phi) + \frac{1}{R} \Phi_{,xx} - \frac{\gamma}{g} w_{,tt}, \tag{9.3}$$

$$\frac{1}{E} \nabla^2\nabla^2 \Phi = -\frac{1}{2} [L(w, w) - L(w_0, w_0)] - \frac{1}{R} (w - w_0)_{,xx}, \tag{9.4}$$

where θ denotes temperature, $\varkappa$ the heat conductivity coefficient, β' a coefficient accounting for the inverse effect of elastic deformation, x, y coordinates measured along the generatrix and arc, t the time, u the displacement of points in the middle surface along the axis, α the coefficient of linear expansion, c the rate of propagation of longitudinal elastic waves in the material, w the total deflection, w_0 the initial deflection, Φ the stress function in the middle surface, R the radius of curvature of the middle surface, h the shell thickness, D the cylindrical rigidity, and γ the specific weight of the material. Suffixes denote differentiation with respect to the corresponding variable, ∇^2 is a Laplacian operator, and L some bilinear operator.

We assume that the shell is subjected to an initial deflection. The total and initial deflection are approximated by expressions of the type

$$w = f(\sin\alpha_0 x \sin\beta_0 y + \psi\sin^2\alpha_0 x + \varphi), \quad \alpha_0 = m\pi/l, \quad \beta_0 = n/R;$$

m is the wave number along the shell generatrix, n the wave number along the circumference, and l the length of the shell. Function Φ is found by substituting these expressions into the right-hand part of the equation (9.4) and integrating. Hence the term $(-py^2/2)$ is introduced into the expression for Φ, where $p=p(t)$ is the intensity of the compressive force in the selected shell cross-section, determined by the equation $p=E(\partial u/\partial x-\alpha\theta)$. The relationship between the shell deflection parameter and the time-dependent compressive force is best determined by applying the Bubnov-Galerkin method to equation (9.3). This approach yields a nonlinear ordinary second-order differential equation in f.

Consider the case of rapid local heating of one end-face, while the rest of the surface is thermally insulated. The solution is derived by integrating the following equations:

$$\overset{*}{\theta}_{,\tau} - d\overset{*}{\theta}_{,x^*x^*} + \alpha\beta' \overset{*}{u}_{,x^*\tau} = 0, \tag{9.5}$$

$$\overset{*}{u}_{,x^*x^*} - \overset{*}{u}_{,\tau\tau} - \overset{*}{\theta}_{,x^*} = 0, \tag{9.6}$$

$$\zeta_{,\tau\tau} - s\left\{\left[p^* - \frac{1}{16}\frac{(1+\rho^4)}{\rho^2}\eta(\zeta^2-\zeta_0^2)\right]\zeta - \frac{1}{12(1-\nu^2)}\frac{(1+\rho^2)^2}{\rho^2}\times\right.$$
$$\times\eta(\zeta+\zeta_0) - \psi^2\eta\rho^2\zeta(\zeta^2-\zeta_0^2)\left[\frac{1}{(1+\rho^2)^2}+\frac{1}{(1+9\rho^2)^2}\right]+$$
$$+\frac{1}{4\rho^2}\psi\zeta(\zeta-\zeta_0)\left[1+\frac{4\rho^2}{(1+\rho^2)^2}\right]+\psi\frac{\rho^2}{(1+\rho^2)^2}(\zeta^2-\zeta_0^2)-$$
$$\left.-\frac{\rho^2}{\eta(1+\rho^2)^2}(\zeta-\zeta_0)\right\} = 0. \tag{9.7}$$

Here, the following dimensionless parameters have been introduced: $x^* = x/l, \quad \tau = tc/l,$

$$\theta^* = \theta\alpha, \quad u^* = u/l, \quad \gamma^* = \gamma/i, \quad d = \varkappa/cl,$$
$$\lambda = l/i, \quad p^* = pR/Eh, \quad \zeta = f/h, \quad \zeta_0 = f_0/h,$$
$$\eta = n^2h/R, \quad \rho = m\pi R/nl, \quad s = (l/R)^2\eta\rho^2,$$

where $i=R/\sqrt{2}$ is the radius of inertia of the shell cross-section and λ characterizes the total flexibility of the structure. Conditionally, ψ satisfies the solution of the static problem for ideal shells.

Equations (9.5) and (9.6) were solved in implicit form by applying successively integral Fourier and Laplace transforms subject to the following boundary and initial conditions:

$$\theta^*_{,x^*} = u^* = 0 \quad \text{when } x^* = 0 \quad \text{and } x^* = 1;$$

$$u^* = u^*_{,\tau} = 0, \quad \theta^* = \frac{Qg}{c_\gamma \gamma}\,\delta(x^*) \quad \text{when } \tau = 0,$$

where Q is the supplied thermal energy, c_γ the specific heat of the material, and $\delta(x^*)$ the Dirac functions.

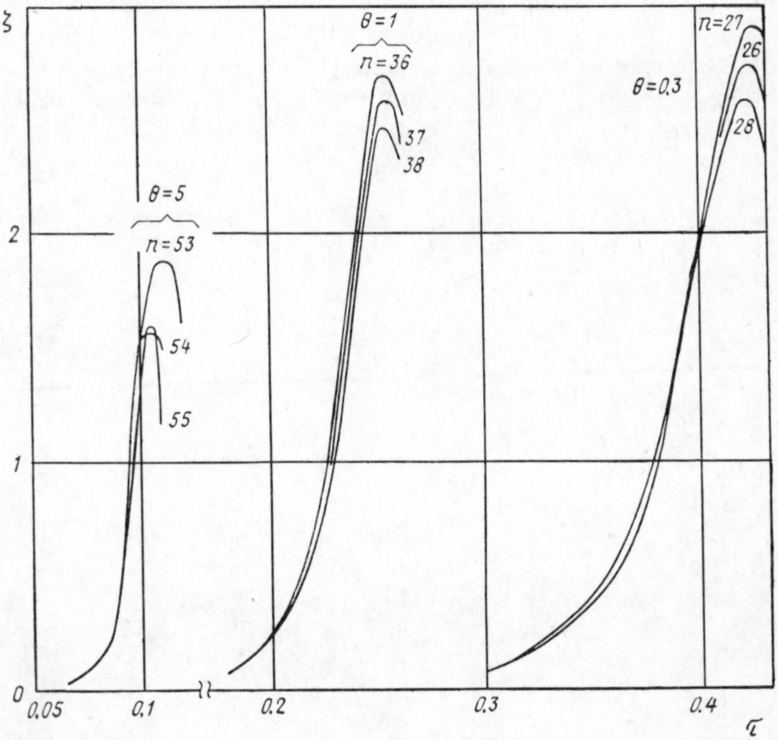

FIGURE 1.33.

Equation (9.7) was integrated by the Runge-Kutta method with the aid of a BESM-2M digital computer, with initial conditions $\zeta - \zeta_0 = \zeta_{,\tau} = 0$.

Solving the problem, the ratio between the maximum compressive force and the upper critical value (p^*/p^*), and the wave number at which rapid buckling sets in, were determined.

The computational results /54/ are illustrated in Figure 1.33 by graphs of the rate of increase in deflection ζ of the shell at the cross-section $x=l/2$ vs. dimensionless time τ for various thermal impulse parameters θ. They refer to a shell with ratio $R/h = 300$, amplitude of initial deflection $\zeta_0 = 0.001$, and wave formation parameters $\rho = 3$, $L/R = 3.75$. The time τ_{cr}, corresponding to the front of rapid increase in deflection, was taken conditionally as critical time. It can be seen that, when $\theta = 5$, the most probable form of shell buckling corresponds to the wave number $n = 54$, the critical time parameter being $\tau \approx 0.09$. Similar results for $\theta = 1$ and $\theta = 0.3$ are also presented.

Thus Vol'mir and Ponomarev developed a mathematical model for describing the buckling process of a cylindrical shell under thermal shock which can be successfully applied in polymer mechanics. Computation has shown that the effect of dynamic properties is especially apparent for thinner shells possessing substantial ratios R/h.

Chapter II

POLARIZATION-OPTICAL METHOD OF STRESS INVESTIGATION

Many important technological problems cannot yet be investigated theoretically, even in approximate formulation, owing to mathematical difficulties. On the other hand their solutions are now a necessity. Therefore many semiexperimental physicomechanical methods have been developed and have found extensive application. Of these, the polarization-optical method of stress investigation is nowadays the most effective.

This chapter gives a systematic account of the main achievements of photoplasticity and photocreep as applied to stress investigations in structural polymers and other materials.

§1. INTRODUCTORY REMARKS

The polarization-optical method is an experimental method for investigating the stress-strain state of machine and structural parts subjected to various forces and temperatures.

Investigation by this method is conducted using prototypes prepared from optically transparent materials, or by means of thin plates of optically active materials fixed to the surface of the actual parts. One studies the optical effects in the optically active material under load during the passage of polarized light. Conversion of optical effects into mechanical values (stresses and strains) is realized by computation based on laws correlating the optical and mechanical quantities. The laws themselves depend on the optical and mechanical properties of the materials and the deformation conditions. In addition, investigation via models involves the conversion of the stresses in the models to actual stresses.

From the beginning of the 20th century (when the polarization-optical method was first proposed) to the 1950s, the method developed essentially as applied to the study of stresses under elastic deformations (photoelastic method).

Many investigations have shown unquestionably that the photoelastic method has advantages over other experimental methods, since it enables one to obtain a general picture of the stress distribution and investigate any state of stress. It is especially useful for investigating stress concentrations and for selecting the optimum shape and dimensions of machine and structural components during their design.

This method is an effective tool in the hands of engineers in assessing the strength of machines and structures subject to strains in the elastic range, thanks to the possibility of a quantitative study of the stress field, visualization, and the reliability of the results obtained for relatively low demands as to means and time.

In the last decade scientists in various countries have tried to use the polarization-optical method in solving problems of plasticity, creep, viscoelasticity, in the investigation of the state of anisotropic bodies, etc.

Here the choice of two basically different approaches has been shown, namely the use of a photoelastic covering and the application of model materials.

Photoelastic covering enables one to investigate stress-strain states at the immediate surface of a part made from the structural material under elastic and elastoplastic deformations. This approach involves measuring the optical effects in the layers of transparent, optically active materials fixed to the surface of the part. Consequently it is essential that the optically active covering undergoes elastic deformations independently of the deformations of the part being investigated.

As regards model materials, investigation of the stress-strain distribution in machine or structural parts is carried out on geometrically similar models or on models subject to a similar load. The models are made of transparent polymeric or transparent crystalline materials possessing the necessary complex physicochemical and mechanical properties.

Henceforth the polarization-optical method of investigating the stress-strain state of bodies subject to elastoplastic strain or creep, and of viscoelastic or anisotropic bodies by means of model materials will be referred to, respectively, as the photoelastic method, the photocreep method, the photoviscoelastic method, and the photoelastic method for anisotropic bodies.

Nowadays, photoelastic covering is a very successful technique. An account of the main achievements and a systematic summary of the results obtained by this method has been given elsewhere /1/. A review of applications of this method to solving engineering problems of forming metals under pressure is given by Vorontsov and Polukhin /2/.

Polarization-optical methods of studying the stress state under viscoplastic strain or creep with the aid of model materials are treated only in individual publications and is mentioned in few monographs. Therefore, in the present chapter we shall try to give a systematic summary of the main achievements and potential of photoplastic and photocreep methods. In addition we shall discuss several problems and possibilities of the photoelastic method for anisotropic bodies.

These methods are based on the same optical phenomena: light polarization and the effect of induced birefringence of light. The optical effects in model materials are investigated by means of polariscopes. The underlying principles of polarization-optical methods and polariscope optics are satisfactorily described elsewhere /3–5/.

§2. RELATIONSHIP BETWEEN OPTICAL EFFECTS AND MECHANICAL VALUES IN POLYMERIC MATERIALS UNDER SIMPLE LOADING

The polarization-optical method of stress investigation makes use of two physical phenomena arising in strain of polymeric materials: the pseudo-optic effect related to variation in dielectric constant, and the double refraction of polarized light. The dependence of the refractive index and the difference in velocity of polarized light rays after passing through a deformed medium on the mechanical quantities is established during the study of these methods.

A linear relationship is usually established in the region of elastic strain between the dielectric constant, and either stress or strain /6, 7/. Filon and Jessop /4/ established a linear equation for the difference in optical path which contains both stress and strain. To such an equation corresponds a linear dependence of dielectric constant on both mechanical quantities. Experiments have shown that this equation is not valid for a number of materials.

In his investigation of the pseudo-optical properties of linear viscoelastic materials, the behavior of which is described by a four-element model, Midlin /8/ also established a linear relationship between the difference in optical path and the mechanical quantities. Bugakov /9/ has shown that in the case of simple loading of polymers undergoing small inelastic strain, the relationship between dielectric constant and mechanical quantities can be described with sufficient accuracy by a tensor linear equation.

It is known /6/ that the dielectric constant of a medium is characterized by the symmetric dielectric constant tensor $\varkappa_{ij}$. When establishing the relationship between the dielectric constant ($\varkappa_{ij}$), stress (σ_{ij}) and strain (ε_{ij}) tensors it is convenient not to introduce beforehand the rheological equation of the medium but to regard σ_{ij} and ε_{ij} as independent, i. e., to assume that the change in the components of tensor $\varkappa_{ij}$ upon strain of polymers depends on the components of both (σ_{ij} and ε_{ij}) tensors.

Consider the static processes of the strain of homogeneous, initially isotropic polymeric materials when the deviator components vary in proportion to one parameter, but the principal directions remain unchanged /10/. In general, the strains are assumed small in the sense of the mechanics of deformable materials. For constant directions of the stress tensor σ_{ij}, the principal directions of the strain tensor ε_{ij} of an isotropic material are also constant and coincide with the principal directions of tensor σ_{ij}. Consequently, in a body deformed in this manner there is one system of preferred directions. Indeed, the principal directions of the dielectric constant tensor coincide with this system.

Under these conditions, the equation relating the dielectric constant to mechanical quantities can be derived similarly to the equations of plasticity theory /12/. It is assumed that for simple loading the relationship linking the deviators of dielectric constant $\widetilde{\varkappa}_{ij}=\varkappa_{ij}-{}^1/_3\,\varkappa_{nn}\delta_{ij}$, stress $\widetilde{\sigma}_{ij}=\sigma_{ij}-{}^1/_3\,\sigma_{nn}\delta_{ij}$ and strain $\widetilde{\varepsilon}_{ij}=\varepsilon_{ij}-{}^1/_3\,\varepsilon_{nn}\delta_{ij}$ have the form

$$\widetilde{\varkappa}_{ij}=\widetilde{\varkappa}_{ij}(\widetilde{\sigma}_{mn},\widetilde{\varepsilon}_{mn},T,H,\omega) \qquad (2.1)$$
$$(i,j,m,n=1,2,3),$$

where T is temperature, H the second invariant of the strain rate deviator, and ω the frequency of waves passing through the medium. Quantities T, H and ω can be regarded as external parameters determining the state of the polymer /9/.

If the components $\widetilde{\varkappa}_{ij}$ are continuous functions, then their approximating by polynomials and subsequent substitution by means of the Hamilton-Cayley identity yield the general relationship between dielectric constant and mechanical quantities:

$$\widetilde{\varkappa}_{ij}=\psi_1\widetilde{\sigma}_{ij}+\psi_2\widetilde{\varepsilon}_{ij}+\psi_3\left(\widetilde{\sigma}_{in}\widetilde{\sigma}_{nj}-\frac{1}{3}\widetilde{\sigma}^2\delta_{ij}\right)+$$
$$+\psi_4\left(\widetilde{\varepsilon}_{in}\widetilde{\varepsilon}_{nj}-\frac{1}{3}\widetilde{\varepsilon}^2\delta_{ij}\right)+\psi_5\left[\widetilde{\sigma}_{in}\widetilde{\varepsilon}_{nj}+\widetilde{\varepsilon}_{im}\widetilde{\sigma}_{mj}-\right.$$
$$\left.-\frac{2}{3}(\widetilde{\sigma}_{ij}\widetilde{\varepsilon}_{ij}\delta_{ij})\right]+\psi_6\left[\widetilde{\sigma}_{im}\widetilde{\varepsilon}_{mn}-\frac{1}{3}\widetilde{\sigma}_{ij}\widetilde{\varepsilon}^2+\widetilde{\varepsilon}_{im}\widetilde{\sigma}_{mn}\widetilde{\sigma}_{nj}-\frac{1}{3}\widetilde{\varepsilon}_{ij}\widetilde{\sigma}^2\right], \qquad (2.2)$$

where $\tilde{\sigma}^2=\tilde{\sigma}_{ij}\tilde{\sigma}_{ij}$, $\tilde{\varepsilon}^2=\tilde{\varepsilon}_{ij}\tilde{\varepsilon}_{ij}$, $\psi_1, \psi_2, \ldots, \psi_6$ are scalar quantities, functions of the invariants of the mechanical quantities, as well as of temperature, strain rate and wave frequency.

For simple stress processes, equation (2.2) can be simplified using a postulate analogous to Il'yushin's isotropy postulate /11, 12/. Consider first a given stress tensor $\sigma_{ij}=\sigma_{ij}(t)$ and strain tensor $\varepsilon_{ij}=\varepsilon_{ij}(t)$ at some time, and consequently with given tensor and deviator invariants. Suppose further that the external parameters of temperature, strain rate and wave frequency are known. Then, in the case of simple loading in the region of small strains, the dielectric constant deviator $\tilde{\varkappa}_{ij}$ at time t is determined by the values of the stress deviator $\tilde{\sigma}_{ij}$ and strain deviator $\tilde{\varepsilon}_{ij}$ corresponding to the preceding instants of time. Thus their linear functions contain coefficients depending on the first and second invariants of σ_{ij}, ε_{ij} in the interval $[t_0, t]$, the times within this interval, and also parameters T, H, ω.

Consequently, the relationship between the dielectric constant and mechanical quantities in polymers under simple loading is

$$\tilde{\varkappa}_{ij} = \psi_1\tilde{\sigma}_{ij} + \psi_2\tilde{\varepsilon}_{ij}. \tag{2.3}$$

Coefficients ψ_1 and ψ_2 depend on the physical properties of the medium and must be determined experimentally. This involves measurement of the variation in dielectric constant with strain. However, since this variation is small and measurement of the dielectric constant is associated with experimental difficulties, the polarization-optical method used to study the pseudo-optical properties of polymers is based on the effect of the birefringence of polarized light in a deformable medium.

The equations of electrodynamics enable us to convert from dielectric to optical quantities. We direct the x_3 axis of a Cartesian system of coordinates (x_1, x_2, x_3) along the wave normal of plane monochromatic waves. In the case of normal incidence of monochromatic waves on a plane-layered anisotropic nonconducting medium, the electrodynamic equation assumes the form /13/

$$\frac{d^2E_j}{dx_3^2} + \frac{\omega^2}{c^2}D_j = 0 \quad (j = 1, 2), \tag{2.4}$$

where E_j is the vector component of the electric intensity along the axes of a rectangular coordinate system, D_j the vector components of electromagnetic induction, ω the angular frequency, and c the velocity of light in vacuo. Vectors $\overline{E}$ and $\overline{D}$ in an anisotropic medium are related by

$$D_i = \sum_{j=1}^{2} \varkappa_{ij} E_j \quad (i = 1, 2), \tag{2.5}$$

where $\varkappa_{ij}$ is the dielectric constant tensor.

We denote by $\varkappa_1$ and $\varkappa_2$ the quasi-principal values of tensor $\varkappa_{ij}$ in the plane of the wave front (in the plane x_1x_2). Since the wave normal coincides with one of the principal directions of tensor $\varkappa_{ij}$, $\varkappa_1$ and $\varkappa_2$ are the principal values of this tensor. In general, the quasi-principal direction of the dielectric constant tensor coincides with the direction of the wave normal with some angle φ. In a homogeneous medium the wave tensor $\varkappa_{ij}$ along the wave normal is constant, and consequently angle φ is constant.

The expression for the tensor components $\varkappa_{ij}$ in the plane of the wave front in terms of the quasi-principal values $\varkappa_1$ and $\varkappa_2$ is /7/

$$\begin{aligned} \varkappa_{11} &= \frac{\varkappa_1 + \varkappa_2}{2} + \frac{\varkappa_1 - \varkappa_2}{2} \cos 2\varphi, \\ \varkappa_{22} &= \frac{\varkappa_1 + \varkappa_2}{2} - \frac{\varkappa_1 - \varkappa_2}{2} \cos 2\varphi, \\ \varkappa_{12} &= \varkappa_{21} = \frac{\varkappa_1 - \varkappa_2}{2} \sin 2\varphi, \end{aligned} \tag{2.6}$$

and that for the components of vector E_j in terms of its components in the quasi-principal directions E_j' is

$$E_1 = E_1' \cos\varphi - E_2' \sin\varphi, \quad E_2 = E_1' \sin\varphi + E_2' \cos\varphi \tag{2.7}$$

If the quasi-principal directions are selected as those of the coordinate axes, equation (2.4), with the aid of (2.5), (2.6) and (2.7), assumes the form /14/

$$\frac{d^2 E_j'}{dx_3^2} + \frac{\omega^2}{c^2} \varkappa_j E_j' = 0 \quad (j = 1, 2). \tag{2.8}$$

The solution of this equation is

$$E_j'(x_3) = E_{0j} e^{\pm i \frac{\omega}{c} \sqrt{\varkappa_j} x_3}, \tag{2.9}$$

where E_{0j} is a constant of integration.

When linearly polarized light is incident on the surface of a medium at $x_3 = 0$, constant E_{0j} denotes the amplitude of the oscillations of the incident light. It follows from relationship (2.9) that in a homogeneous medium two independent, mutually perpendicular, linearly polarized oscillations with constant amplitude propagate. The phase difference Δ of these oscillations accumulated along the path of the wave front $x_3=h$ is given by

$$\Delta = \frac{\omega}{c} h(\sqrt{\varkappa_1} - \sqrt{\varkappa_2}). \tag{2.10}$$

Since the change in dielectric constant of the medium caused by the deformation is small,

$$\sqrt{\varkappa_1} - \sqrt{\varkappa_2} \approx \frac{1}{2\sqrt{\varkappa_0}} (\varkappa_1 - \varkappa_2),$$

where $\varkappa_0$ is the dielectric constant of the medium in the undeformed state. Equation (2.10) then becomes

$$\Delta = \frac{\pi h}{\lambda \sqrt{\varkappa_0}} (\varkappa_1 - \varkappa_2).$$

For the quasi-principal value of the tensor components $\varkappa_{ij}$, σ_{ij} and ε_{ij} equation (2.3) yields

$$\varkappa_1 - \varkappa_2 = \psi_1 (\sigma_1 - \sigma_2) + \psi_2 (\varepsilon_1 - \varepsilon_2). \tag{2.11}$$

Hence the relationship between the optical phase difference and the mechanical quantities assumes the form

$$\Delta = \frac{\pi h}{\lambda \sqrt{\varkappa_0}} \{\psi_1 (\sigma_1 - \sigma_2) + \psi_2 (\varepsilon_1 - \varepsilon_2)\}.$$

Accordingly, the optical path difference

$$\delta = \Delta \frac{\lambda}{2\pi}$$

becomes

$$\delta = \frac{h}{2n_0} [\psi_1 (\sigma_1 - \sigma_2) + \psi_2 (\varepsilon_1 - \varepsilon_2)], \tag{2.12}$$

where $n_0 = \sqrt{\varkappa_0}$ is the refractive index of the medium in the undeformed state.

The experimental investigation of the double refraction of a series of polymeric materials has shown that the relationship between the optical effects and mechanical quantities pertaining to these materials is described with sufficient accuracy by an equation like (2.12).

The pseudo-optical properties of polymers can be divided into four groups, according to the values and signs of coefficients ψ_1

and ψ_2 /9/: 1) $\psi_1 = 0$, 2) $\psi_2 = 0$, 3) $\psi_1\psi_2 > 0$, 4) $\psi_1\psi_2 < 0$. Thus in the case of the deformation of amorphous polymers in the Mackian-elastic state, birefringence depends on the stress but is independent of strain, and consequently for such materials coefficient ψ_2 equals zero. For crystalline polymers (polyethylene, nylon, etc.) coefficient ψ_1 equals zero and the birefringence depends on the strain.

§3. FEATURES OF THE PHOTOPLASTIC METHOD

The physical principles of the photoplastic method and the formal statement of the problem are identical with those of the photoelastic method. These methods are based on the phenomenon of light polarization and induced birefringence of light arising in transparent polymeric materials during their deformation. The application of these methods involves the solution of two problems: the stress-strain state of the models and their design, i. e., the transfer of model measurement data to parts of structural materials which are geometrically similar and under similar loading conditions.

However, a formal transfer of the means and methods developed for photoelasticity to the investigation of elastoplastic deformations is in general impossible, due to the difference in the laws describing the optical and mechanical behavior of the prototype materials under elastic and elastoplastic strain. Thus new experimental methods and the development of special computing methods must be formulated for photoplasticity, so rendering the latter an independent method.

The features of the photoplastic method become apparent when solving the two above-mentioned problems.

Consider the first problem, the stress-strain state of the models.

In the range of elastic strain the mechanical behavior of the model material can be described by a generalized Hooke's law, which for an isotropic material contains two constants, the Young modulus E and Poisson ratio ν. The optical behavior of the model material can also be described by a linear law, relating the optical path difference to the stress and containing a single constant, namely the optical constant of the material (the value of the band $\sigma_0^{1.0}$). The existence of a completely defined linear dependence of the optical path difference (order of magnitude of the interference bands) on stress permits one in photoelasticity to draw conclusions on the nature of the stress distribution from the picture of one band, while the universal validity of this dependence permits one to develop a general method of solving problems of photoplasticity irrespective of the model material.

The photoplastic method is intended for solving problems of the stress state of models subject to the condition that the stress exceeds the elastic limit.

The laws describing the mechanical behavior of materials under nonelastic strain have many forms, depending on the deformed material. The relationship between the stress and strain tensors reduces to a tensor linear equation with coefficients which are functions of time-invariants of the mechanical quantities only under simple loading /10/. In this case the relationship between the components of the stress and strain tensors reduces to some finite, but essentially nonlinear dependence. The relationships between the optical effects and mechanical quantities under nonelastic strain have many forms, depending on the molecular structure of the polymeric material and the strain conditions.

It was mentioned earlier that for nonelastic strain under simple loading, the majority of polymeric materials known to be optically isotropic under natural conditions display a tensor linear dependence of dielectric constant on mechanical quantities. In the case of a two-dimensional problem this results in a relationship between optical and mechanical quantities in the form of equation (2.12). Since coefficients ψ_1 and ψ_2 differ in magnitude and sign for each material or group of materials, it is obviously necessary to develop for each group of materials its own method of determining the stress-strain state of the models for known optical path differences.

It is also evident that one equation like (2.12) is insufficient for determining the stress state of models under inelastic strain from known optical path differences. For a two-dimensional problem it is first of all necessary to have one additional relationship between stress and optical effects. The method of establishing such a relationship and its form are determined by the material properties. For instance, in the case of celluloid such a relationship is obtained by considering the dispersion properties of birefringence of light appearing at some given strain. However, such properties have not been observed with other familiar materials. Hence for these the additional relationships are determined by other considerations.

The particular features of the photoplastic method also manifest themselves in the requirements of the model materials. These requirements depend on the aim of the experiment. If the problem is limited to determining stresses and strains, then, in addition to the usual properties (such as transparency, homogeneity, absence of initial double refraction of light) the model materials must fulfill the following requirements: (a) they must display a sufficiently large double refraction effect related to mechanical properties by a completely determined law; (b) they must have an elastic range and a defined yield point; it is desirable that the beginning of plastic strain can be fixed by a clear optical effect which is independent of the dependence of the optical path differences on the mechanical properties; (c) they must undergo sufficient plastic flow before failure.

At present, there exists a limited number of optically active polymers which can be used when solving photoplastic problems. Not all of them completely fulfill the above-mentioned requirements. The properties of some materials will be examined below.

Determination of the components of the stress and strain state under elastoplastic strain is complicated by the fact that practically all synthetic resins display creep at room temperature. Consequently the stress-strain curves, and also the form of the relationship between the optical and mechanical quantities depend on the rate of loading and on the way in which the calibration is carried out.

It is therefore important in photoplastic investigations that tests with calibration samples and models are conducted with the same loading program. In addition, it is necessary when choosing the loading program to eliminate or take into account as far as possible errors and inaccuracies caused by creep. Relevant experiments in different countries are discussed.

The second problem of the photoplastic method, the design of models, can be solved with two aims: (a) analyzing the stress-strain distribution in plastically deformed solids composed of structural materials; (b) studying the plastic strain and physical phenomena accompanying plastic flow (mechanism of flow and destruction, fatigue and hardening, relaxation, etc.). They differ from one another in physical properties, contents and methods involved in solving each of them. In order to solve the problem with models, similarity as regards the mechanical, rheological and structural properties of the model and actual materials is required, in addition to similarity as regards forces and geometry.

Polymeric materials are used as model materials in the photoplastic method. Parts of machines and structures can be made from metal or other structural materials. It is known that the strain mechanism of polymers differs from that of polycrystalline materials, in particular that of metals.

There are three different types of polymer strain: reversible (elastic) strain involving changes in interatomic distances, Mackian-elastic strain developing with time and involving bending of the bonds of the molecular chains, and irreversible flow strain. In the case of metals one distinguishes only between two types of strain: reversible elastic and irreversible plastic strain.

Hence it is evident that one cannot model all the phenomena accompanying the plastic strain of a real body by means of any polymeric material whose structural and rheological properties differ from those of the prototype material. One can only talk about modeling a phenomenon which does not involve completely identical strain mechanisms. Such a situation pertains to the first group of problems of photoplasticity (phenomenological photoplasticity), i.e., problems of determining stresses, strains and regions of plasticity in bodies subjected to elastoplastic strain.

In the present case fulfillment of the similarity requirement concerning plastic strain of the photoplastic and natural materials is not necessary; similarity in the equations relating the tensors of stress, strain and strain rate is sufficient. In particular, plastic changes in shape can be investigated even on nonlinear elastic, optically active material under active loading conditions.

In analogy with metals we shall henceforth represent polymer strain as sums of elastic and plastic components. The presence of a plastic strain will be determined by means of a particular optical effect appearing at a certain strain value. Evidently this division is frequently conditional, as the plastic strain of a polymeric material determined in this manner is not completely irreversible but may change with time. However, such a division of plastic materials is acceptable for our purpose, in in the sense that the condition of plasticity and the equations relating the stress and strain tensors under simple monotonic loading can be expressed in the same form for polymeric materials and for metals.

The problem of modeling the stress-strain state of metallic bodies by means of polymeric material has not been solved for the case of compound loading. However, it has been shown /15/ that if the condition of simple loading is fulfilled, it is possible to model the elastoplastic strain state by means of polymeric materials whose rheological properties are described by sufficiently general equations. In this case conversion of the model results to metal and complying with the similarity condition as regards forces and geometry, imply that the model and the metal must satisfy at least three conditions: (1) the stress-strain curves of the model and metal must be similar, (2) the plasticity conditions must be identical for both materials, and (3) the Poisson ratios of the model and the metal must be equal.

It is evident that in order to fulfill these conditions it is necessary in each case to have available optically active polymeric materials with different mechanical properties so that, depending on the properties of the prototype material, the corresponding material can be chosen for the models.

Thus the application of polarization-optical methods to the study of stress-strain states of bodies subject to elastoplastic strain involves a series of special features and difficulties in comparison with photoelastic methods, as regards both model design problems and converting the results to full scale.

Nevertheless, investigations conducted in various countries have shown that with proper experimental design and allowance for the particular behavior of polymeric materials under nonelastic strain, the photoplastic method can be applied successfully to the solution of elastoplastic problems and yields not only qualitative but also quantitative results.

Various polymeric materials are used as material for models, such as nylon, styrene, polyethylene, celluloid, polycarbonates (Macrolon). Most of the work has been based on the application of celluloid.

Celluloid $C_6HN_3O_{11}$ is a linear polymer which is obtained from a solution of nitrocellulose in a mixture of alcohol and ether after treating this solution with camphor. The camphor content enables the celluloid to soften quickly upon heating and makes it viscous. The nitrocellulose fibers make it elastic and strong. Celluloid is transparent and isotropic.

For more than 30 years (since 1906) celluloid has been regarded as the main material for models in photoelasticity, and replaced the use of glass. Scientists were attracted by its high optical sensitivity in comparison with glass (about 5 times greater), the ease of its mechanical processing, and the ease in gluing by means of acetone, so allowing the preparation of complex models. Later, celluloid was replaced by other materials which comply better with the basic requirements demanded of materials to be used in photoelastic models.

An important reason for rejecting celluloid as modeling material in photoelasticity is its mechanical and optical creep at room temperature. In addition, at strains exceeding 1 or 2% the relationship between the stress and strain of celluloid is nonlinear. Unloading is accompanied by the disappearance of elastic reversible strains and the fixing of residual strains. This is exactly the reason for the renewed "discovery" of celluloid in connection with widespread work on photoplasticity and photocreep.

In the last 10–15 years scientists in various countries have continued to study the optical and mechanical properties of celluloid in connection with the problem of photoplasticity. These resulted in the development of various methods of determining the stress-strain state of celluloid models under elastoplastic strain. Before discussing the methods, we shall examine calibration tests in photoplasticity, the required samples and instruments, and also some optical and mechanical properties of celluloid.

§4. CALIBRATION TESTS AND METHODS, SAMPLES AND INSTRUMENTS

Calibration tests on samples and models must be conducted following an identical program, owing to the time-dependence of the properties of celluloid and other polymeric materials as a result of creep.

Several test programs have been proposed: (a) at constant strain rate /16–21/, (b) at constant difference in the principal stresses /22–25/, (c) at constant increase in loading rate /26–28/. In the last case the load is applied so that, for a given time interval $\Delta t = t_1 - t_2$, the increase in strain results not only from increased load, but also from creep of the sample due to the action of forces applied during time t_1.

Calibration tests aim at establishing the dependence of stress on strain, and the dependence of optical effects on the mechanical quantities under a complex state of stress. For this purpose it suffices to conduct two types of calibration test using one of the above-mentioned programs, namely uniaxial tension-compression of plane samples and tests with thin-walled tubes subjected to an axial force, torque, and internal pressure. As an example of a method of conducting a calibration test, we consider tests with constant loading rate.

Tubes of transparent celluloid are not manufactured in the Soviet Union. Therefore, a method for preparing tubes from celluloid sheets was developed in the laboratory of the Scientific Research Institute of Mechanics of Moscow State University. For this, depending on the dimensions of the tube desired, a blank of celluloid foil was wrapped around a mandrel, inserted in an aluminum tube, heated in a water bath to 80°, and then slowly cooled to room temperature. This caused annealing of the celluloid and the blank assumed the shape of a tube. The ends of the blank were then glued with a glue prepared from acetone by dissolving it in celluloid shavings. The tubes were then reduced on a special mandrel. The edges were glued together overlapping in a seam 4–5 mm wide, the edges of the blanks being prepared beforehand so that the seam thickness equaled the thickness of the glued foils.

The tubes were prepared from foils 0.5 mm thick. In order to make the tubes sufficiently strong, two blanks were selected, one of which was wrapped around the mandrel and glued as described above, while the second was glued on its surface. Its edges were also glued by the above method. Thereby a tube was obtained with a wall thickness of about 1 mm. After gluing, the tubes were kept on the mandrel for 12–14 days and then tested.

Two types of tests were carried out: 1) of the simultaneous action of an axial force L and internal pressure p ($L \sim p$ tests), and 2) of the simultaneous action of an axial force L and torque M ($M \sim L$ tests). In the first type of tests, tubes of the following dimensions were used: inner diameter $d = 60 \pm 0.4$ mm, gage length $l = 160$ mm, wall thickness $h = 1 \pm 0.02$ mm.

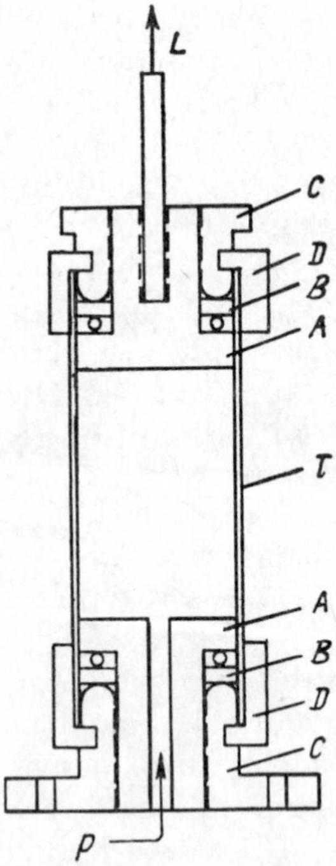

FIGURE 2.1.

The tubes with constant loading rate were tested in the following manner (Figure 2.1). The tube T was mounted on the lower flange A, rigidly fixed to the loading frame. Rubber gasket B and sliding nut C prevent liquid escaping from the tube under applied internal pressure. The tube was fixed by clamps D. The internal pressure was applied by means of glycerine pumped through an opening in the lower flange. A suspension rod was screwed in the upper flange, also provided with a gasket and sliding nut. The axial tensile stress L was applied by means of a lever through the rod. A tank was attached to the lever, and loading was effected with water at some previously determined rate. A device for photographing $L-p$ tests is shown in Figure 2.2.

FIGURE 2.2.

The following quantities were measured in each test.

1. The axial elongation Δl by means of two telescopic microscopes, provided with an eyepiece with micrometer mechanisms (one division = 0.0167 mm) and objectives with focal length $F = 240$ mm. Two marks were made to mark the gage length of the tube at the upper and lower points. The motion of these marks was recorded as a function of the loading. The instantaneous elongation was computed from the difference in the microscope readings with an absolute error of ±0.03 mm, or a relative error for a gage length $l = 80$ mm.

2. The radial elongation Δr by means of indicators with 0.01 mm divisions. The indicators were fixed on clamp D at the upper part of the tube.

3. The optical path difference δ for two monochromatic light sources with wavelengths $\lambda = 435.8$ mμ and $\lambda = 690.7$ mμ by means of a Babinet-Soleil compensator to within ± 5 mμ. The monochromatic light was obtained by separating the corresponding waves from the spectrum of a DPSh-250 mercury lamp using glass, FS-7 and ZhS-12 color filters for λ_{vio}, and KS-17 and ZS-7 color filters for λ_{red}, or corresponding interference color filters.

For tests involving the combined action of axial force L and torque M, tubes possessing the following dimensions were used: inner diameter $d = 35 \pm 0.05$ mm, wall thickness $h = 1 \pm 0.02$ mm, gage length $l = 130$ mm.

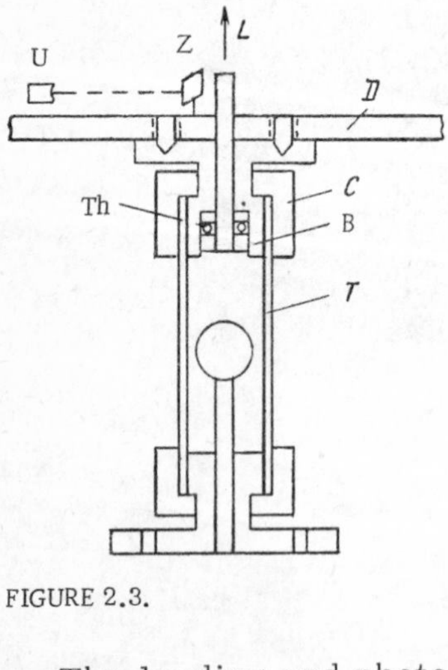

FIGURE 2.3.

FIGURE 2.4.

The loading and photographing devices are shown in Figures 2.3 and 2.4. The tube was fixed to a loading frame, and loading with an axial force L realized as in the previous case. For twisting the tube, a thrust bearing Th was installed between the head of the lever and flange B. A duralumin disk D of 300 mm diameter was fixed to the upper part of the flange. Ropes were attached to the disc and loading effected with water fed at a predetermined rate to a tank suspended on the ropes. An optical system for measuring the angle of torsion of the tube was mounted on the disk.

In each test, the applied forces were introduced at some recorded instant and the following values measured.

1. The axial elongation Δl of the tube on an 80-mm base, as outlined above.

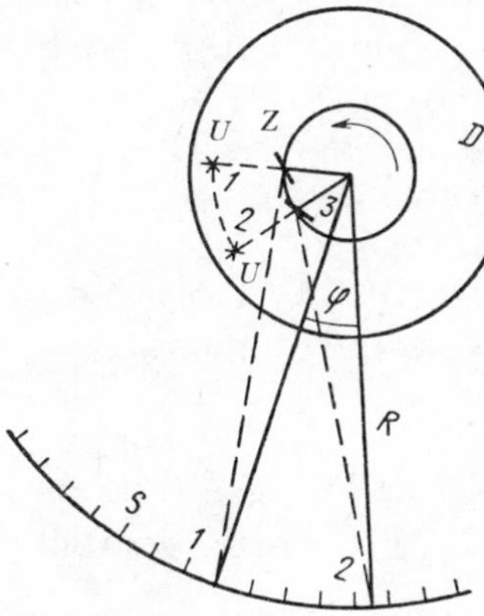

FIGURE 2.5.

2. The angle of torsion φ of the tube by means of an optical system, shown in Figure 2.5. Light from source U was transmitted to the mirror Z, and then reflected back through a system of lenses and a narrow slit to fall on the curved scale S. The light source and mirror were joined rigidly, so the angle of incidence does not change with rotation of the mirror. The angle of torsion, determined by the displacement of the ray on the scale, is $\varphi=S/R$, where S is the ray displacement on the scale and R the distance from the tube center to the scale. In the experiment described $R = 1{,}500$ mm. Readings on the scale were to within 1 mm.

3. The optical path difference δ for λ_{vio} and λ_{red} by means of the Babinet-Soleil compensator. During tube torsion, the points of incidence and emergence of the light transmitted normal to the generatrix determine the difference in the direction of the principal stresses. Therefore, the polarizer was placed inside the tube and optical measurements were carried out only in one wall of the tube.

The direction of the polarization plane of the polarizer was fixed beforehand according to the assumed inclination angle of the principal stresses. This is possible, since in the expression for the inclination angle of the principal stresses $\tan 2\alpha = 2M/rL$ it is evident that if M/L = const, the inclination angle is also constant. Tests on tubes have yielded the following quantities: a) order of the interference bands $m_{vio} = \frac{\sigma_{vio}}{\lambda_{vio}}$, $m_{red} = \frac{\delta_{red}}{\lambda_{red}}$, and their difference $m_{vio} - m_{red}$; b) dispersion of birefringence by the formula $D = 1 - \frac{m_{vio}\lambda_{vio}}{m_{red}\lambda_{red}}$; c) principal stresses σ_1 and σ_2, and their difference $\sigma_1 - \sigma_2$; d) stress intensity $\sigma_u = \sqrt{(\sigma_1 - \sigma_2)^2 + \sigma_1\sigma_2}$ and strain intensity $\varepsilon_u = \sqrt{(\varepsilon_1 - \varepsilon_2)^2 + \varepsilon_1\varepsilon_2}$ with allowance for incompressibility.

The tests were conducted under simple loading conditions. One test was carried out on each tube during which the ratios L/p and L/M at any instant remained constant, and consequently, also the ratio between the principal stresses. The latter ratio varied from test to test, but the rate of change in stress intensity was constant (6 kg/cm² per minute) for all tests. In both the $L \sim p$ and $M \sim L$ tests, 3 or 4 tubes were tested for each ratio of the principal stresses. Sufficiently good agreement was obtained between the experimental results.

Jira /19/ conducted tests on tubes subjected to axial tension and internal pressure for different ratios of the principal stresses, but for constant rate of increase in the octahedral shear strain γ_0 = 0.00183 per minute.

Frocht et al. /22–24/ conducted tests on tubes subjected to axial tension and internal pressure, and also to axial tension and torsion, for a constant difference in principal stresses ($\sigma_1 - \sigma_2 = k$).

With a view to investigating the effect of the loading rate on the optical and mechanical properties of celluloid, and also to comparing experimental results pertaining to uniaxial and complex states of stress, tests were conducted on plane samples subject to uniaxial tension with different loading rates /26–28/. In these tests, as in tests on tubes, the load was fixed at some time and the longitudinal elongation measured by means of a telescopic microscope. The optical path difference for the two above-mentioned wavelengths was also measured.

The tests were carried out on samples 1 mm and 4.5 mm thick. The 1-mm-thick samples were prepared in the same way as the tubes, by gluing celluloid films of thickness 0.5 mm. The loading rate of these samples equaled the loading rate of the tubes (6 kg/cm² per minute). The optical path difference was measured by a Babinet-Soleil compensator.

The tests for different loading rates were carried out on samples which were 4–5 mm thick. The optical path difference (order of the interference band) of the samples was measured by photoelectric polarization apparatus developed at the laboratory of the

Scientific Research Institute of Mechanics of Moscow State University /29/. This apparatus permitted simultaneous recordings of the change in intensity of monochromatic rays of different wavelengths passing through a given point of the model. Hence

$$I_{vio} = I_{0vio} \sin^2 \alpha \sin^2 m_{vio}\pi, \quad I_{red} = I_{0red} \sin^2 \alpha \sin^2 m_{red}\pi, \tag{4.1}$$

where α is the angle between the direction of the polarization plane and the principal stress; I_{0vio} and I_{0red} are the maximum values of the light intensity determined for $\alpha = \frac{\pi}{4}$, $m = \frac{1}{2}$.

Equations (4.1) suffice for determining the optical path difference and angle of inclination of the principal stresses at any point of the model /30/. In a state of uniaxial stress, when the directions of the principal stresses, and consequently angle α, are known beforehand, the optical path difference is determined immediately by equations (4.1) from known values of I_{vio}, I_{0vio}, I_{red} I_{0red}. In a state of nonhomogeneous stress in the model, equations (4.1) also suffice for determining δ and α for materials which do not display dispersion of birefringence of light, or if the model possesses constant values over the entire strain range.

Thus when $\delta_{vio} = \delta_{red}$ or $\delta_{red} = \delta_{vio}(1-D)$, if the material displays a constant, predetermined dispersion of birefringence of light D, equations (4.1) yield

$$\frac{I_{vio}}{I_{red}} = \frac{I_{0vio}}{I_{0red}} \frac{\sin^2 \frac{\delta_{vio}}{\lambda_{vio}}\pi}{\sin^2 \frac{\delta_{vio}(1-D)\pi}{\lambda_{red}}}. \tag{4.2}$$

If δ_{vio}, and hence δ_{red}, are determined from this equation, α is found from either of equations (4.1).

Suppose the model material displays dispersion of birefringence of light, the value of which is a function of the deformation. Then, when determining the optical path difference and angle of inclination of the principal stresses at points of the model, one must measure I_{vio} and I_{red} at the points specified for two values of angle α (α_1 and $\alpha_2 = \alpha_1 + \alpha_0$, where α_0 is known beforehand).

The photoelectric polarization apparatus (shown in Figure 2.6) consists of the following parts: (a) circular polariscope including light source (1), condenser (2), polarizer (3), quarter-wave plate (4), analyzer (5); (b) optical system (6) splitting into two the of light rays emerging from the polariscope; (c) a set of interference light filters (7); (d) two photomultiplers (8): an FEU-35 for the violet region of the spectrum and an FEU-27 for the red region of the spectrum; (e) a recording device in the form of either a recording microampere millivoltmeter or an oscillograph (9); (f) the power supply unit for the photomultiplier. The instrument is designed to work with transmitted and reflected light.

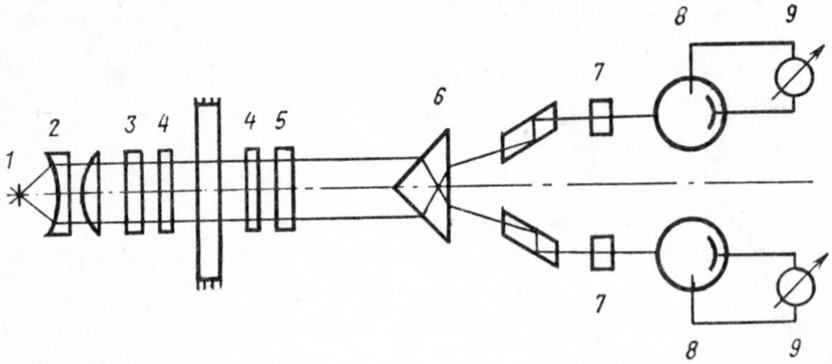

FIGURE 2.6.

§5. OPTICAL PROPERTIES OF CELLULOID. DISPERSION OF BIREFRINGENCE

Figure 2.7 illustrates the dependence of the optical path difference δ on the deformation ε, obtained from tests with uniaxial tension of plane samples under two different loading rates. The following facts can be seen from the figure: (a) the optical path difference is determined not only by the strain, but also by the loading rate, i.e., for the same strain the optical path difference possesses different values at different loading rates; (b) optical path differences measured at λ_{vio} and λ_{red} ($\lambda_{red} > \lambda_{vio}$) are independent of loading rate, and are almost identical up to some strain (δ_{vio} is slightly larger than δ_{red}); with further increase in strain they differ, δ_{red} being larger than δ_{vio}, i.e., anomalous dispersion of birefringence appears; (c) the strain at which appears anomalous dispersion of birefringence is independent of the loading rate.

Creep tests have also shown that, independent of the stress level, dispersion appears at the same same strain. This fact indicates that dispersion of birefringence is independent of creep. Hence it is natural to assume that the appearance of dispersion of birefringence coincides with the onset of plastic strain in celluloid. This conclusion has been confirmed by direct experiments with load removal from celluloid. The strain for which the first residual strain appears is identical with the strain on the $\delta \sim \varepsilon$ curve at which the anomalous dispersion of birefringence appears.

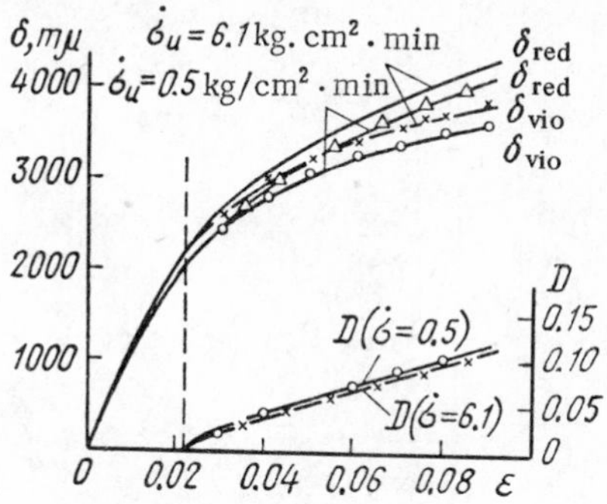

FIGURE 2.7.

The phenomenon of dispersion of birefringence in celluloid was first described by Ambronn /31/ in 1911, and later confirmed by Raumspeck /32/ in 1924. They observed that anomalous dispersion of birefringence appears at a stress exceeding the elastic limit of celluloid. This phenomenon had not been applied for a long time, and only in 1954 did Mönch /16/ propose the application of dispersion as a special optical effect in solving problems of photoplasticity. He suggested that the dispersion D be determined by the expression

$$D = \frac{(m\lambda)_{\text{red}} - (m\lambda)_{\text{vio}}}{(m\lambda)_{\text{red}}}, \tag{5.1}$$

where $m\lambda = \delta$.

From this expression it follows that in the range of elastic strain $D \leqslant 0$, but in the range of plastic strain $D > 0$. The boundary of the range of plastic strain is determined as the geometrical locus of the point at which $D = 0$.

The fact that the dispersion does not depend on the thickness of the material is an important property of expression (5.1). However, the value of the dispersion computed by this equation depends on the loading rate (Figure 2.7). It is true that this dependence is slight. When the loading rate changes by a factor of 10–15, the dispersion at the same strain differs by 3–4%.

TABLE 2.1. $\frac{\sigma_2}{\sigma_1} = 0.235$

ε_u	0.01	0.02	0.022	0.0242	0.0264	0.030	0.0356	0.0450	0.0594	0.0682	0.0814	0.0985	0.110
δ_{vio}, mμ	450	810	870	872	1002	1081	1164	1220	12.81	1303	1321	1335	1340
δ_{red}, mμ	445	805	870	877	1015	1098	1202	1285	1381	1423	1478	1540	1570
D	—	—	0	0.0057	0.0128	0.0154	0.0399	0.0505	0.0720	0.0843	0.106	0.133	0.146
$\frac{\varepsilon_u}{\varepsilon_s}$	—	—	1	1.1	1.2	1.36	1.62	2.05	2.70	3.10	3.70	4.48	5.0
$\frac{\sigma_u}{\sigma_s}$	—	—	1	1.04	1.09	1.13	1.16	1.19	1.23	1.24	1.26	1.27	1.275

TABLE 2.2 $\frac{\sigma_2}{\sigma_1} = 0.5$

ε_u	0.01	0.020	0.0220	0.0246	0.0257	0.0275	0.0319	0.0462	0.0528	0.0671	0.0836	0.118
δ_{vio}, mμ	260	490	540	584	610	636	693	763	789	828	880	941
δ_{red}, mμ	260	485	540	588	617	646	712	801	843	905	988	1126
D	—	—	0	0.00680	0.0113	0.0154	0.0266	0.0474	0.0640	0.0850	0.1109	0.164
$\frac{\varepsilon_u}{\varepsilon_s}$	—	—	1	1.12	1.17	1.25	1.45	2.10	2.40	3.05	3.8	5.36
$\frac{\sigma_u}{\sigma_s}$	—	—	1	1.05	1.07	1.09	1.14	1.19	1.21	1.24	1.26	1.28

TABLE 2.3. $\frac{\sigma_2}{\sigma_1} = 0.672$

ε_u	0.010	0.020	0.0220	0.0242	0.0254	0.0280	0.0330	0.040	0.0554	0.0836	0.0968
δ_{vio}, mμ	160	310	340	374	397	422	453	479	509	558	580
δ_{red}, mμ	160	305	340	376	401	428	466	502	548	626	672
D	—	—	0	0.0053	0.010	0.014	0.0278	0.0458	0.0711	0.105	0.137
$\frac{\varepsilon_u}{\varepsilon_s}$	—	—	1	1.1	1.2	1.27	1.5	1.82	2.52	3.8	4.6
$\frac{\sigma_u}{\sigma_s}$	—	—	1	1.04	1.07	1.11	1.15	1.18	1.22	1.26	1.27

Expression (5.1) is not the only one for dispersion; other expressions exist, such as

$$D^* = \frac{(m\lambda)_{\text{red}} - (m\lambda)_{\text{vio}}}{\lambda_{\text{red}}}. \tag{5.2}$$

The value D^* computed by this expression is independent of the loading rate /33/.

We resort to tests on thin-walled tubes in order to study the variation in dispersion D under complex stress states. The results of $p \sim L$ tests with the three principal stress ratios $\frac{\sigma_2}{\sigma_1} = 0.235, 0.5$ and 0.672 are given in Tables 2.1, 2.2, and 2.3.

The dispersion of the birefringence, which is independent of the ratio of the principal stresses, evidently appears at the same strain intensity ε_u. It follows, in particular, that the mechanical conditions for the appearance of plastic strain in celluloid can be expressed in the form $\varepsilon_u = \varepsilon_s$, where ε_s is the yield stress according to the strains. The value of ε_s can be determined from $\delta \sim \varepsilon$ curves from uniaxial tensile tests.

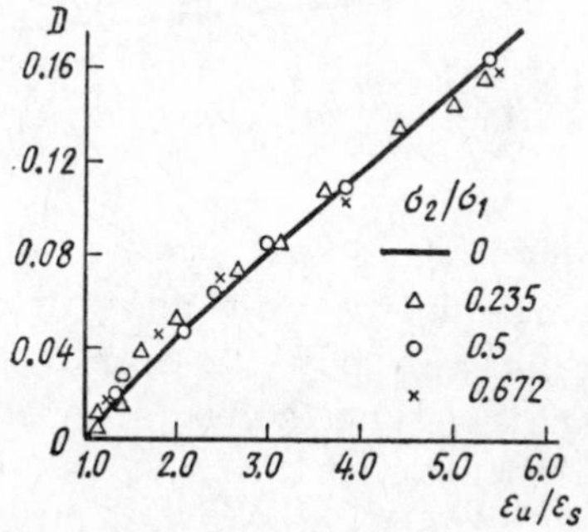

FIGURE 2.8.

Within the region of plastic strain the dispersion of birefringence is a measure of the strain intensity. Figure 2.8 shows the $\frac{\varepsilon_u}{\varepsilon_s} \sim D$ dependence for various ratios of the principal stresses. It can be seen that for all ratios of the principal stresses the $\frac{\varepsilon_u}{\varepsilon_s} \sim D$ curve can be approximated by the function

$$\frac{\varepsilon_u}{\varepsilon_s} = 1 + \eta(D). \tag{5.3}$$

Here $\eta(D)$ is the dispersion function, equal to zero when $D \leqslant 0$. The form of the function is determined by tests involving uniaxial tension.

Experiments with tubes subjected to axial tension and torque at various ratios of the principal stresses, but under the condition $\sigma_1+\sigma_2>0$, have also shown that the dispersion of birefringence for a fixed strain intensity is independent of the ratio of the principal stresses (Figure 2.9a and b), and that in the range of plastic strain the dispersion is a certain function of $\varepsilon_u/\varepsilon_s$, the form of the function being the same as in tests on tubes subjected to axial tension and internal pressure.

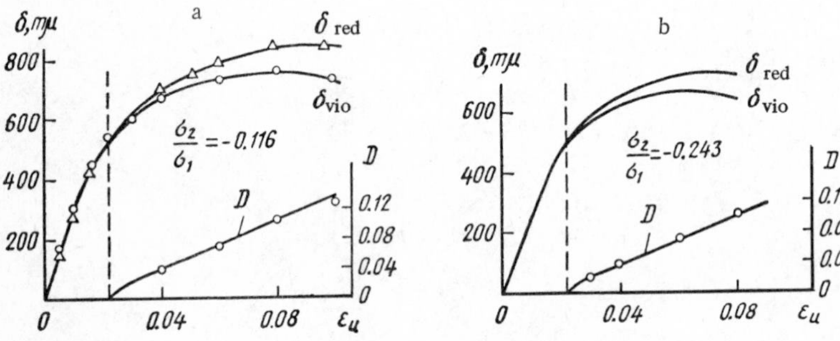

FIGURE 2.9.

Jira /19/ has also shown that for a state of plane stress, for which the first invariant of the stress tensor is positive $\sigma_1+\sigma_2>0$, the dispersion of birefringence has the same value for corresponding values of strain. The conclusion was reached by comparing results pertaining to tubes subjected to axial tension and internal pressure after tests on a broad ring under internal pressure.

Tests of uniaxial compression of plane samples of celluloid were conducted, in order to study the effect of the sign of the first invariant of the stress tensor on the dispersion of birefringence /33/. It was shown that upon compression, too, anomalous dispersion of the birefringence occurs for a certain strain which does not depend on the loading rate. However, at the same strain the dispersion D in compression is about one-third the value in tension.

Thus the relationship between dispersion and strain intensity differs in regions with positive and negative first invariants of the stress tensor. The form of this dependence is determined by tests with uniaxial tension and compression. This causes some inconvenience in solving actual problems, since it is necessary to determine beforehand the form of the stress state of the model. Nonetheless, in many cases this can be done either by starting from the mechanical approach to the problem, or from the elastic problem, since the relationship linking mechanical and optical quantities in the range of elastic strain coincides in tension and compression.

§6. SOME MECHANICAL PROPERTIES OF CELLULOID

The mechanical properties of celluloid under conditions of uniaxial and biaxial stress during different calibration tests have been investigated elsewhere /16–28, 33, 35–37/.

Tests with uniaxial tension for constant rate of loading will be examined first /26–28/. Figure 2.10 shows the $\sigma_u \sim \varepsilon_u$ curve derived from tests under uniaxial tension for loading rates between 0.104 and 48 kg/cm² per minute. Analysis of the experimental data lead to the following conclusions.

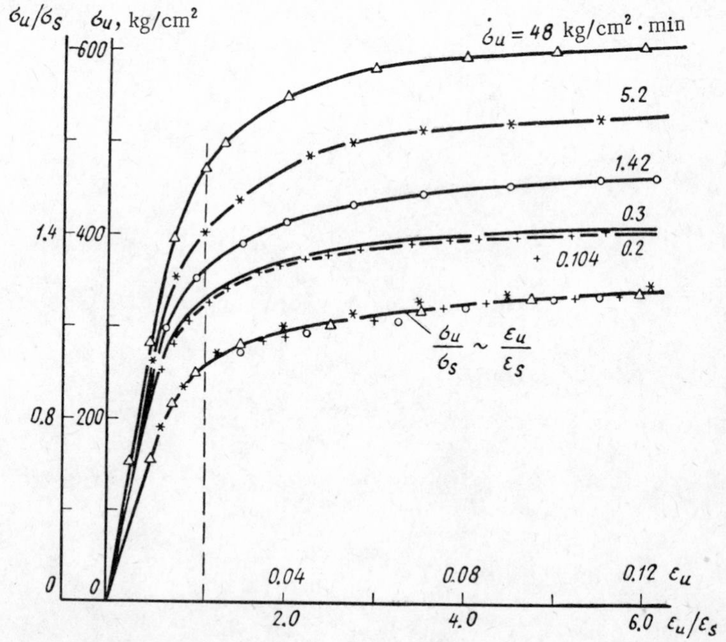

FIGURE 2.10.

1. The stress-strain curves obtained for different loading rates are similar.

2. There is a definite minimum loading rate at which or beneath which the $\sigma_u \sim \varepsilon_u$ curves coincide. The value $\dot{\sigma}_{um} = 0.2$ kg/cm^2 per minute can be selected as the minimum loading rate. In this case, the similarity condition of the $\sigma_u \sim \varepsilon_u$ curves can be expressed in the form

$$\sigma_u (\varepsilon_u, \dot{\sigma}_u) = \mu \sigma_{um} (\varepsilon_u), \tag{6.1}$$

where $\sigma_u(\varepsilon_u, \dot{\sigma}_u)$ is the stress at loading rate $\dot{\sigma}_u$, and $\sigma_{um}(\varepsilon_u)$ the stress for the same strain at minimum loading rate $\dot{\sigma}_{um}$; μ is the similarity factor of the curves, a function of the ratio of the loading rates $\mu = \mu(\dot{\sigma}_u / \dot{\sigma}_{um})$.

3. The stress-strain curves for different loading rates can be represented by a single curve with dimensionless coordinates $\sigma_u/\sigma_0 \sim \varepsilon_u/\varepsilon_0$, where σ_0 and ε_0 are characteristic quantities which, in particular, may coincide with the yield stress for stress σ_s and strain ε_s.

The values of σ_s and ε_s are determined by the properties of the dispersion of birefringence. It has been shown experimentally that the yield stress at strain ε_s is practically independent of the loading rate and amounts to about 2%. The yield stress at stress changes appreciably with changing loading rate /33/. The variation in the yield stress σ_s as a function of the rate $\dot{\sigma}_u$ is illustrated in Figure 2.11 in $\ln\dot{\sigma}_u \sim \ln\sigma_s$ coordinates. It is evident that with changing loading rate the $\sigma_s \sim \dot{\sigma}_u$ relationship can be expressed in the above-mentioned region in the form

$$\frac{\sigma_s^n}{\dot{\sigma}_u} = k \quad \text{for} \quad \dot{\sigma}_u > \dot{\sigma}_{um} \tag{6.2}$$

and

$$\sigma_s = \sigma_{sm} \quad \text{for} \quad \dot{\sigma}_u \leqslant \dot{\sigma}_{um}, \tag{6.3}$$

where n and k are constants.

The ratio of the yield stresses, $\frac{\sigma_s}{\sigma_{sm}}$, as a function of the ratio of the loading rates $\frac{\dot{\sigma}_u}{\dot{\sigma}_{um}}$ (Figure 2.12) satisfies the equations

$$\ln \frac{\dot{\sigma}_u}{\dot{\sigma}_{um}} = n \ln \frac{\sigma_s}{\sigma_{sm}},$$

or

$$\left(\frac{\sigma_s}{\sigma_{sm}}\right)^n = \frac{\dot{\sigma}_u}{\dot{\sigma}_{um}}. \tag{6.4}$$

Thus the similarity condition for the $\sigma_u \sim \varepsilon_u$ curves at different loading rates yields the single function

$$\frac{\sigma_u}{\sigma_0} = \Phi\left(\frac{\varepsilon_u}{\varepsilon_0}\right). \tag{6.5}$$

It is characteristic that this dependence remains unchanged in tension and compression /33/.

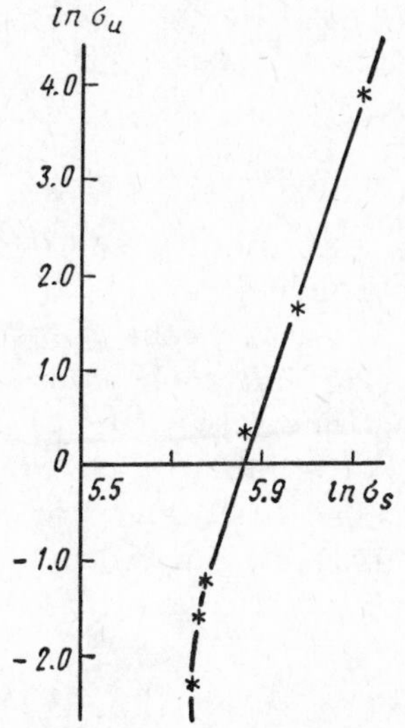

FIGURE 2.11.

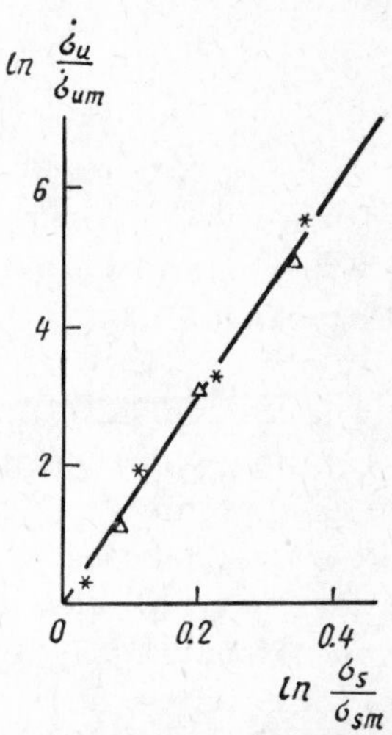

FIGURE 2.12.

Mönch, Jira and Loreck /16–20/ conducted tests under constant strain rate. The $\sigma \sim \varepsilon$ curves obtained from tests with uniaxial tension at different loading rates /20/ are shown in Figure 2.13. The form of the $\sigma \sim \varepsilon$ curves depends on the strain rate, and consequently the test duration time. A method for selecting a single $\sigma \sim \varepsilon$ curve for a certain test duration time from experimental results with uniaxial tension at constant loading rate has been proposed in /20/.

The following procedure has been suggested for constructing such a curve. Assume that the model is in a state of uniaxial stress, and that the strain rate is constant at each point but varies from point to point. Then each point can be assigned to a $\sigma \sim \varepsilon$

curve (dashed line in Figure 2.13) corresponding to its proper strain rate $\dot{\varepsilon}$. These curves can be obtained from uniaxial tensile tests.

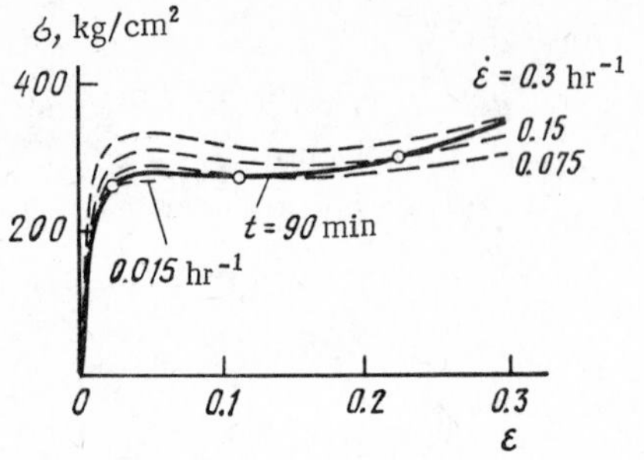

FIGURE 2.13.

At a definite time t after starting the loading, the stress at each point of the model can be determined by the corresponding $\sigma \sim \varepsilon$ curves. For example, at $t = 90$ min the stress attains the points indicated by circles in Figure 2.13. Assuming that such points are determined for an infinite number of calibration tests, a $\sigma \sim \varepsilon$ curve is obtained which describes the stress distribution of the model at loading time t. Such curves are called "effective" or "resultant" stress-strain curves. A limited number of calibration tests conducted at different loading rates is sufficient for the construction of such a curve in practice.

It is obvious that in a heterogeneous state of stress the strain rate varies from point to point and is generally not constant. Therefore, the actual effective $\sigma \sim \varepsilon$ curve does not coincide with the curve in homogeneous strain. It has been proposed that the tests be conducted under slow loading in order to decrease the errors caused by unequal strain rates. In this case the $\sigma \sim \varepsilon$ curves differ less from one another, and consequently the resulting curves constructed for different test durations are closer to one another.

Frocht and Thomson /22/ constructed $\sigma \sim \varepsilon$ curves from creep curves $\varepsilon \sim t$ obtained under different stress conditions, by determining their intersection with the straight lines $t = t_0$. Time t_0 was selected from $\delta \sim t$ curves as the time the sample is maintained under load, starting from which some optical path difference hardly varies. It was shown experimentally that $t_0 \geqslant 4$ hours.

Consider the properties of celluloid in a complex state of stress. We shall study, in particular, the conditions characterizing transition of the material from the elastic to the plastic state (plasticity condition), and the stress-strain relations.

The plasticity condition is determined when a certain critical value of various combinations of stresses or strains is attained. The form of the condition is determined experimentally for each material.

Two plasticity conditions are most widespread: the condition of constant maximum shearing stress (Tresca-Saint Venant condition) and the condition of constant stress intensity (Guber-Mises condition). We shall compare these plasticity conditions for the case of celluloid, in which case $L \sim p$ tests with thin-walled tubes suffice. We shall use the results of tests at constant loading rate. The experimental results are represented in the form of a relationship between $\frac{\sigma_1 - \sigma_3}{\sigma_s}$ (along the ordinate axis) and parameter $\mu_\sigma = \frac{2(\sigma_2 - \sigma_3)}{\sigma_1 - \sigma_3}$ (along the abscissa axis). Actually, the relationship linking $\frac{\sigma_1}{\sigma_2}$ and $\mu_\sigma = 2\sigma_2/\sigma_1 - 1$ is plotted and the stress σ_3 neglected.

The Tresca-Saint Venant condition $\tau_{max} = \sigma_s/2$ (σ_s being the yield stress in tension) shows that the $\frac{\sigma_2}{\sigma_s} \sim \mu_\sigma$ relationship is expressed in the form of a horizontal straight line /10/

$$\frac{\sigma_1}{\sigma_s} = 1, \tag{6.6}$$

while the Guber-Mises condition yields the curve

$$\frac{\sigma_1}{\sigma_s} = \frac{2}{\sqrt{3 + \mu^2}}. \tag{6.7}$$

In Figure 2.14, the theoretical curve is plotted as a solid line. The points represent experimental results for $\sigma_2/\sigma_1 = 0$, 0.235, 0.4, 0.5, 0.672, 0.822. The experimental points were obtained in the following manner. The value of the stress at which anomalous dispersion of birefringence appears was determined by uniaxial tensile tests of tubes. The stress value was taken as σ_s. Then the values of the principal stress σ_1 at the instant when anomalous dispersion of birefringence appears was determined by tests differing from simple tension. These values σ_1 were related to σ_s. All tests were carried out under the same rate of increase in stress intensity. The experimental points are close to the curve representing equation (6.7).

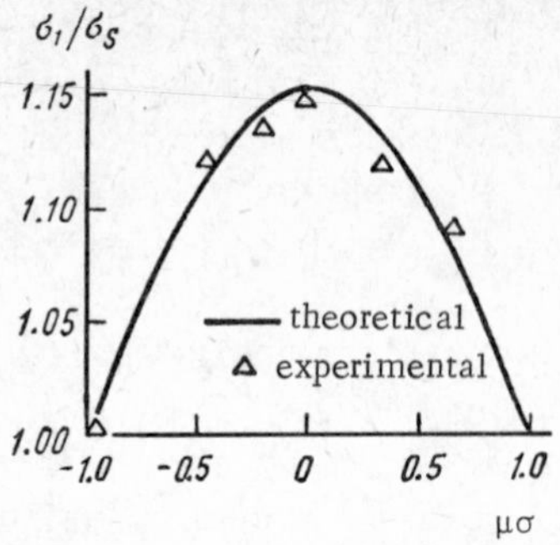

FIGURE 2.14.

Thus the plasticity condition for celluloid at a specified loading rate can be expressed in the form $\sigma_u=\sigma_s$.

Similar results were obtained from tests with constant strain rate. In order to investigate the plasticity condition for celluloid, Mönch and Jira /18/ compared stresses determined by the following tests: 1) for uniaxial tension; 2) from $p\sim L$ tests with tubes for $\sigma_2/\sigma_1 = 0.78$; 3) with a broad ring under internal pressure for $\sigma_2/\sigma_1 = -0.69$. The tests were conducted under simple loading conditions. The experimental data showed that the condition of constant intensity of shearing stresses may be selected as the plasticity condition for celluloid.

Let us consider possible stress-strain relations in the case of celluloid under constant loading (simple strain). We consider only processes of simple active strain, i.e., subject to the condition that the strain intensity does not diminish with time ($\dot{\varepsilon}_u>0$).

According to Il'yushin /11, 12/, when establishing the $\sigma\sim\varepsilon\sim t$ relationships for any initially isotropic medium its vector and scalar properties must be investigated. In the case of simple loading, the vector properties reduce to identical stress and strain tensor directions:

$$\frac{\tilde{\sigma}_{ij}}{\tilde{\sigma}}=\frac{\tilde{\varepsilon}_{ij}}{\tilde{\varepsilon}}, \tag{6.8}$$

and the scalar properties to the following relationship between the invariants:

$$\tilde{\sigma}=\Phi[\tilde{\varepsilon}(t),\ \theta(t),\ t]. \tag{6.9}$$

Here, $\tilde{\sigma}_{ij}=\sigma_{ij}-\sigma\delta_{ij}$ is the stress deviator, $\tilde{\sigma}=\sqrt{\tilde{\sigma}_{ij}\tilde{\sigma}_{ij}}$ the modulus of the stress deviator, $\tilde{\varepsilon}=\varepsilon_{ij}-\frac{1}{3}\theta\delta_{ij}$ the strain deviator, $\tilde{\varepsilon}=\sqrt{\tilde{\varepsilon}_{ij}\tilde{\varepsilon}_{ij}}$ the modulus of the strain deviator, and $\theta=\tilde{\varepsilon}_{ij}\delta_{ij}$ the first invariant of the strain tensor.

We shall now prove that relationships (6.8) and (6.9) are satisfied under simple loading of celluloid.

The stress and strain tensor directions are equal if the principal stress and strain axes coincide and the ratios of the principal tangential stresses to the corresponding principal displacements are constant for the specified body element /10/:

$$\frac{\tau_{12}}{\gamma_{12}}=\frac{\tau_{23}}{\gamma_{23}}=\frac{\tau_{31}}{\gamma_{31}}=\frac{\sigma_u}{3\varepsilon_u}, \qquad (6.10)$$

where $\tau_{12}=\frac{\sigma_1-\sigma_2}{2}$, $\gamma_{12}=\frac{\varepsilon_1-\varepsilon_2}{2}$, etc.

Under simple loading, the principal axes in a state of stress do not change direction relative to the body under study. Therefore the principal strain axes remain unchanged, and the stress and strain axes coincide according to the conditions of symmetry.

To verify the equality $\frac{\tau}{\gamma}=\frac{\sigma_u}{3\varepsilon_u}$, recourse is made to the $p\sim L$ tests with tubes. The results are illustrated in Figure 2.15, where the abscissa axis corresponds to the experiment duration and the ordinate axis to quantities γ/ε_u (points) and $3\tau/\sigma_u$ (solid lines) for various principal stress ratios. The γ/ε_u points lie with a sufficient degree of accuracy on the straight line $3\tau/\sigma_u$, so justifying equality (6.10). Hence the equality between the stress and strain tensor directions under simple loading of celluloid is justified.

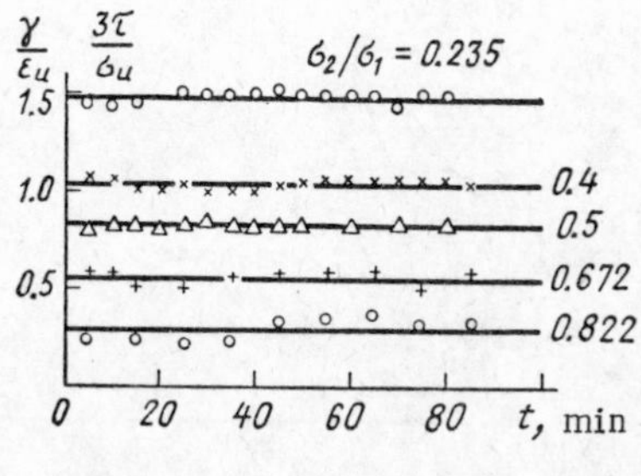

FIGURE 2.15.

When studying the relationship between the invariants, it is generally assumed that the bulk strain does not affect the relation linking the stress and strain deviators. Hence (6.9) assumes the form

$$\widetilde{\sigma} = \Phi[\widetilde{\varepsilon}(t), t]. \tag{6.11}$$

The introduction of the stress and strain tensors

$$\sigma_u = \sqrt{\frac{3}{2}}\,\widetilde{\sigma}, \quad \varepsilon_u = \sqrt{\frac{2}{3}}\,\widetilde{\varepsilon},$$

allows (6.11) to be expressed in the form

$$\sigma_u = \Phi[\varepsilon_u(t), t]. \tag{6.12}$$

The form of this relationship in the case of celluloid is derived from experimental data. The $\sigma_u \sim \varepsilon_u$ relationship constructed from $p \sim L$ tests on tubes is presented in Figure 2.16. The tests in uniaxial tension are illustrated by the solid curve. All tests were conducted for the same rate of increase in tensile-stress intensity. It is evident that for all tests the $\sigma_u \sim \varepsilon_u$ curves practically coincide (some divergence is observed only when the strain is large).

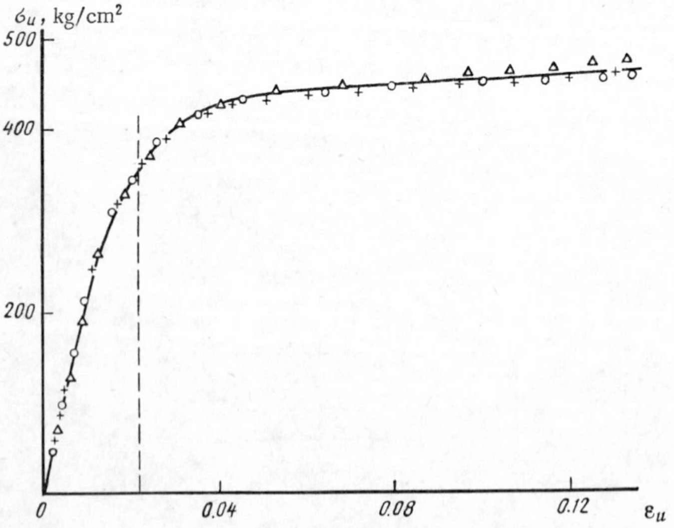

FIGURE 2.16.

Consequently, for specified loading rate and for states of stress in which the first invariants of the stress tensor are positive $\sigma_1+\sigma_2>0$, the intensity of the stress is a completely defined function of strain intensity. The form of this function does not change upon change in loading rate or in the sign of the first invariant of the stress tensor. It has been shown above, when analyzing the tests in uniaxial tension, that the stress-strain curves constructed in $\varepsilon_u/\sigma_0 \sim \varepsilon_u/\varepsilon_0$ coordinates coincide for different loading rates and also for different states of stress.

Comparison of these facts shows that under simple active strain of celluloid the relative stress intensity σ_u/σ_0 is a fully determined function which, independent of the form of the state of stress, is a function of the relative strain intensity $\varepsilon_u/\varepsilon_0$:

$$\frac{\sigma_u}{\sigma_0} = \Phi\left(\frac{\varepsilon_u}{\varepsilon_0}\right). \tag{6.13}$$

A relationship of type (6.9) is valid for the mean stress σ, as for any scalar:

$$\sigma = \sigma[\tilde{\varepsilon}(t), \theta(t), \tau]. \tag{6.14}$$

If it is assumed that the relationship between the spherical stress and strain tensors does not affect variations in the stress and strain deviators, and that this relationship is linear, then

$$\sigma = K(t)\theta(t), \tag{6.15}$$

where $K(t)$ is the bulk modulus of elasticity. In terms of relative coordinates $\bar{\sigma}=\sigma/\sigma_0$ and $\bar{K}=K/\sigma_0$, relationship (6.15) reduces to

$$\bar{\sigma} = \bar{K}\theta. \tag{6.16}$$

Since the volume change in plastic strain is small, relationship (6.16) satisfies the condition of incompressibility

$$\theta = \varepsilon_{ij}\delta_{ij} = 0. \tag{6.17}$$

Thus the principal laws governing strain of celluloid under simple loading are (6.8), (6.13) and (6.17).

Correlation of each component on the stress and strain tensor to σ_0 and ε_0, respectively, yields stresses expressed by strains in the form

$$\begin{aligned} \bar{\sigma}_{ij} - \bar{\sigma}\delta_{ij} &= \frac{2}{3}\,\frac{\bar{\sigma}_u}{\bar{\varepsilon}_u}\,\bar{\varepsilon}_{ij}, \\ \bar{\sigma}_u &= \Phi(\bar{\varepsilon}_u), \end{aligned} \tag{6.18}$$

where

$$\bar{\sigma}_{ij} = \frac{\sigma_{ij}}{\sigma_0}, \quad \bar{\varepsilon}_{ij} = \frac{\varepsilon_{ij}}{\varepsilon_0}.$$

It follows that the laws of strain for celluloid under simple loading, for relative stresses and strains, can be expressed in the form of laws of the strain theory of plasticity.

§7. RELATION BETWEEN STRESS AND OPTICAL EFFECTS IN CELLULOID

In order to solve photoplastic problems for models, we require the laws linking optical and mechanical quantities in the material of the model. It has been shown above that under simple loading the relationship between the optical path difference and mechanical quantities in polymeric materials satisfies (2.12).

A dependence of the optical path difference on stress alone is obtained, if the difference in principal strains is expressed in terms of stresses using deformation laws (6.18). However, one such equation is insufficient for determining stresses in models, since in addition to the principal stresses it must contain also the invariants of the stress tensor. Therefore other independent equations relating optical and mechanical quantities are required.

It has been shown that for celluloid in the range of plastic strain two independent relationships can be established between stresses and optical quantities. This permits one to determine the stress at any point inside the plastic range and also on its boundary. One of these relationships is readily found if one takes advantage of the properties of the dispersion of birefringence. In fact, it has been shown above that in the plastic range the dispersion of birefringence is a completely determined function of the strain intensity:

$$\frac{\varepsilon_u}{\varepsilon_s} = 1 + \eta(D).$$

A relationship between dispersion and stress intensity in the plastic range is also easily established. Figure 2.17 shows the $\sigma_u/\sigma_s \sim D$ relationship constructed from tests under uniaxial tension and from $p \sim L$ tests on tubes for various ratios of the principal stresses. Evidently, the relationship between σ_u/σ_s and D can be represented by the same function, independently of the ratio σ_2/σ_1 :

$$\frac{\sigma_u}{\sigma_s} = 1 + f(D). \qquad (7.1)$$

The form of $f(D)$ is determined by tests in uniaxial tension in regions where $\sigma_1+\sigma_2>0$, or by tests in uniaxial compression in regions where $\sigma_1+\sigma_2<0$. It is clear that (7.1) is valid only in the range of plastic strain of celluloid, since $f(D)$ is defined only for $D>0$.

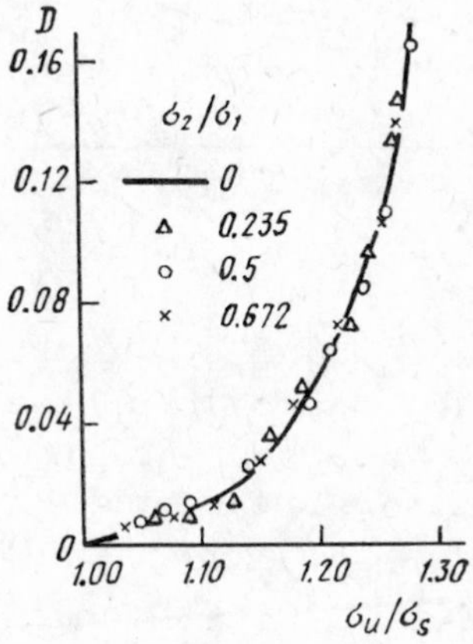

FIGURE 2.17.

Thus for celluloid, one of the relationships linking stresses and optical effects can be expressed in the form of (7.1).

For establishing a second relationship we consider the change in the interference band $m_{vio} - m_{red}$ as a function of the difference in principal stresses $\sigma_2 - \sigma_1$. The curves $m_{vio}\,(m_{red}) \sim (\sigma_1 - \sigma_2)$ and $(m_{vio} - m_{red}) \sim (\sigma_1 - \sigma_2)$ obtained from tests under two different loading rates are presented in Figure 2.18.

In the region of elastic strain the interference band $m_{vio} - m_{red}$ is proportional to the difference in principal stresses $(\sigma_1 - \sigma_2)$:

$$m_{vio} - m_{red} = Ah(\sigma_1 - \sigma_2), \qquad (7.2)$$

where A is a proportionality factor and h the thickness of the material. Quantity A is an optical constant of the material and is independent of the loading rate.

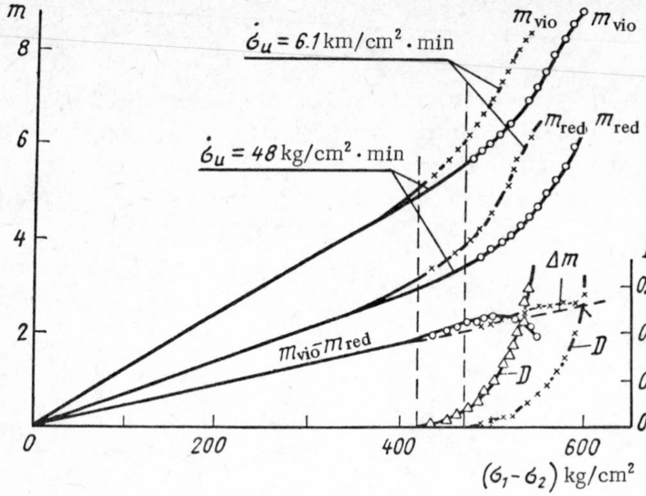

FIGURE 2.18.

Passing to the range of plastic strain (the boundary of the range being determined by the appearance of anomalous dispersion of birefringence), the difference in the bands diverges from the straight line (7.2). If this divergence is denoted by $|\Delta m_0|$, the formal equation assumes the form

$$m_{vio}-m_{red}=Ah(\sigma_1-\sigma_2)+|\Delta m_0|. \tag{7.3}$$

In order to apply this equation to actual computations, the deviation $|\Delta m_0|$ must be expressed in terms of measurable optical effects. It has been shown that $|\Delta m_0|$ is a completely determined function of the dispersion of birefringence, independent of the loading rate (Figure 2.19).

Let us represent the dependence $|\Delta m_0|\sim D$ for unit thickness of material in the form

$$\frac{|\Delta m_0|}{h}=D\psi(D). \tag{7.4}$$

Function $\psi(D)$ can be approximated by the linear-fractional relationship

$$\psi(D)=\frac{a+D}{h(c+kD)}, \tag{7.5}$$

where a, c and k are constants.

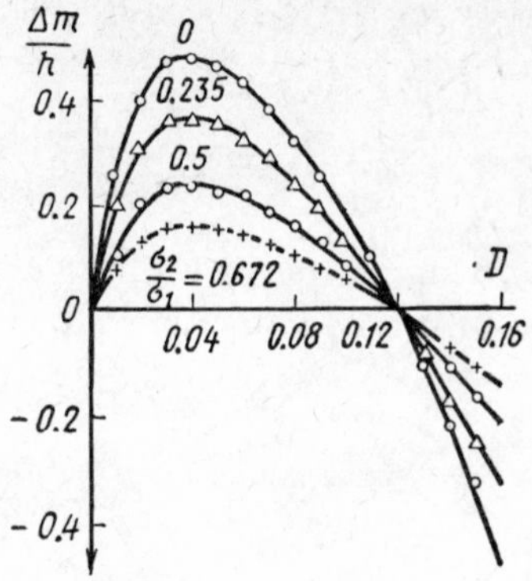

FIGURE 2.19.

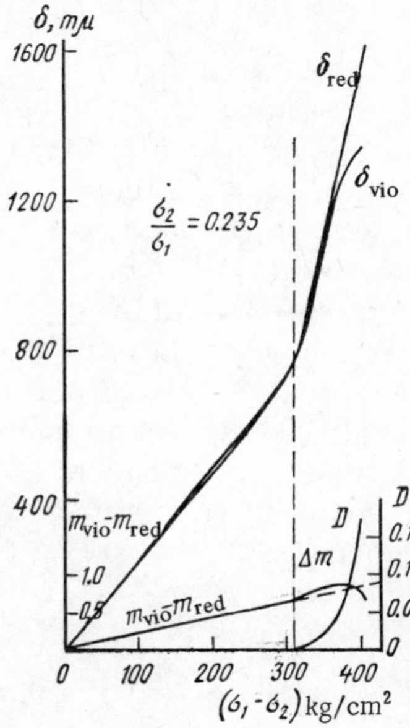

FIGURE 2.20a.

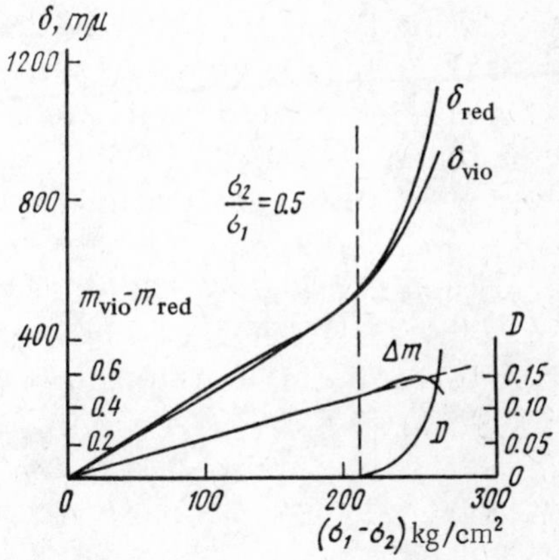

FIGURE 2.20b.

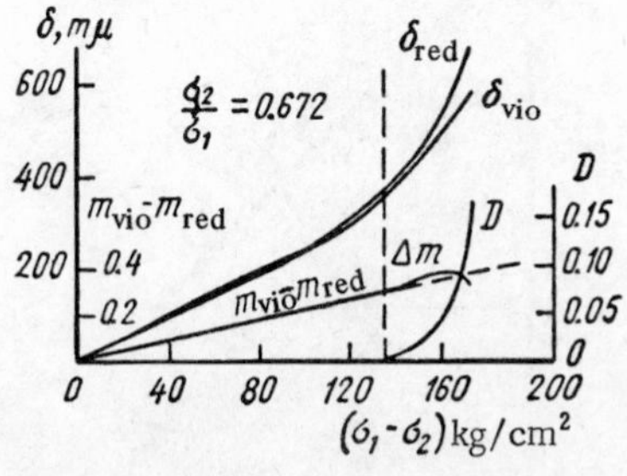

FIGURE 2.20c.

Application of the least squares method to this equation yields the following values for these latter constants:

$$a = -0.12, \quad c = 0.00855, \quad k = 0.176.$$

Substitution of corresponding values of $|\Delta m_0|$ into (7.3) results in a relationship between the principal stresses and measurable optical effects:

$$\sigma_1 - \sigma_2 = \frac{m_{vio} - m_{red}}{Ah} - \frac{D\psi(D)}{A}. \tag{7.6}$$

Consider now this dependence in a state of complex stress. For this we turn to tests on thin-walled tubes. Figure 2.20 shows the dependence of $\delta_{vio}(\delta_{red}) \sim (\sigma_1 - \sigma_2)$ and $(m_{vio} - m_{red}) \sim (\sigma_1 - \sigma_2)$ obtained for different ratios of the principal stresses.

It is evident that, as for uniaxial tension, in the region of elastic strain the difference in bands is proportional to the difference in principal stresses, the value of the proportionality factor A being independent of the ratio of the principal stresses. Upon passing to the region of plastic strain, the difference between the bands diverges from the straight line (7.2). The relationship between deviations $|\Delta m|$ and the dispersion of birefringence for $\sigma_2/\sigma_1 = 0.235,\ 0.5,\ 0.672$ is shown in Figure 2.19. The form of the relationship $\Delta m \sim D$ changes with the ratio of the principal stresses. However, for any value of the dispersion of birefringence D the value of deviation Δm for any ratio of the principal stresses can be expressed in terms of the deviation $|\Delta m_0|$ under uniaxial tension in the form (Figure 2.21)

$$|\Delta m| = |\Delta m_0| \left(1 - \frac{\sigma_2}{\sigma_1}\right). \tag{7.7}$$

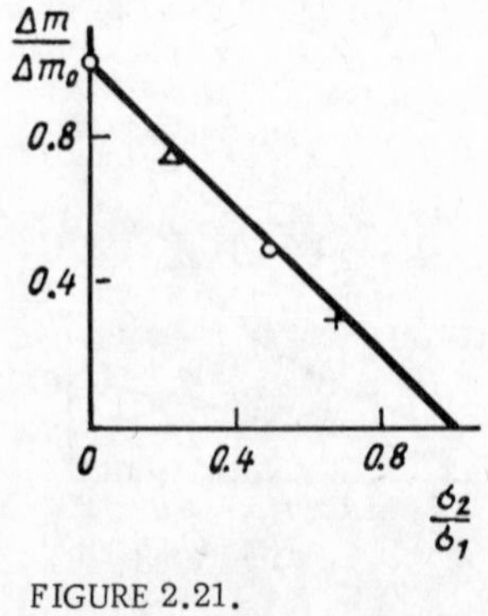

FIGURE 2.21.

Thus the second relationship between the principal stresses and optical effects for celluloid in a complex state of stress is

$$\sigma_1 - \sigma_2 = \frac{m_{\text{vio}} - m_{\text{red}}}{Ah} - \frac{D\psi(D)}{A}\left(1 - \frac{\sigma_2}{\sigma_1}\right). \tag{7.8}$$

It is important that factor A and function $\psi(D)$ are determined by tests for uniaxial state of stress. This relationship is valid only in the region where the first invariant of the stress tensor is positive $\sigma_1+\sigma_2 > 0$. Where $\sigma_1+\sigma_2 < 0$, the same form of the relationship could be accepted, but function $\psi(D)$ must be determined by tests with uniaxial compression. Factor A has the same value under tension and compression.

Suppose (7.8) assumes the form

$$m_{\text{vio}} - m_{\text{red}} = \left[Ah + \frac{D\psi(D)\,h}{\sigma_1}\right](\sigma_1 - \sigma_2) \tag{7.9}$$

and we consider the structure of the expression in square brackets. Here A is a material constant independent of the state of stress. In the case of planar state of stress (where $\sigma_3 = 0$), the principal stress σ_1 can be expressed in terms of parameter $\mu_\sigma = 2\frac{\sigma_2}{\sigma_1} - 1$ and the first invariant of the stress tensor I_1:

$$\sigma_1 = \frac{2I_1}{3+\mu_\sigma}. \tag{7.10}$$

It is known /34/ that parameter μ_σ is a function of the invariants of the stress deviator $\tilde{I}_2$ and $\tilde{I}_3$. However, since, as in the case of a planar state of stress, the third invariant of the deviator $\tilde{I}_3$ can be expressed in terms of the second invariant $\tilde{I}_2$ and the first invariant of the stress tensor I_1,

$$\tilde{I}_3 = \frac{1}{3} I_1 \tilde{I}_2 - \frac{1}{27} I_1^3, \tag{7.11}$$

μ_σ can be represented as a function of invariants I_1 and $\tilde{I}_2$.

The dispersion of birefringence D is a function of the stress intensity σ_u, i. e., it is also a function of invariant $\tilde{I}_2$. In addition, dispersion D is a function of wave frequency ω. Thus (7.9) assumes the form

$$m_{\text{vio}} - m_{\text{red}} = Ah(\sigma_1 - \sigma_2) + \Phi[I_1, \tilde{I}_2, \omega](\sigma_1 - \sigma_2). \tag{7.12}$$

Applying the law of the strain of celluloid under simple loading (6.18), and expressing the difference in principal stresses in terms of differences in the principal strains, (7.12) becomes

$$m_{\text{vio}} - m_{\text{red}} = Ah(\sigma_1 - \sigma_2) + \Psi[I_1, \tilde{I}_2, \omega]\,\varphi(\dot{\sigma}_u)(\varepsilon_1 - \varepsilon_2), \tag{7.13}$$

where $\varphi(\dot{\sigma}_u)$ is a function of the loading rate.

Comparison of this expression with (2.12) derived above for the relationship between optical and mechanical quantities under simple loading of polymers, shows that coefficient ψ_1 for celluloid does not depend on the invariants of the mechanical quantities and is a material constant, and that coefficient ψ_2 is a function of the invariants of the stress tensor, loading rate and wave frequency. Equation (7.13) confirms the validity of the hypothesis that a linear tensor relation exists between the dielectric constant and mechanical quantities under simple loading of polymers.

§8. DETERMINATION OF THE PRINCIPAL STRESSES AND COMPONENTS OF THE STRESS TENSOR IN THE PLASTIC RANGE

Equations (7.1) and (7.9), relating the principal stresses to the optical effects, are sufficient for determining the principal stresses in the plastic range. By expressing the stress intensity σ_u in terms of the principal stresses, $\sigma_u^2 = (\sigma_1 - \sigma_2)^2 + \sigma_1\sigma_2$, and setting $\sigma_s[1+f(D)] = M$, we obtain from equation (7.1)

$$\sigma_1 = \frac{\sigma_2}{2} + \sqrt{M^2 - \frac{3}{4}\sigma_2^2}. \tag{8.1}$$

Substitution of quantity σ_1 in (7.9) yields a fourth degree equation in σ_2:

$$\begin{aligned} &\sigma_2^4 + (m+k)\sigma_2^3 + (m^2 + k^2 - mk - 2M^2)\sigma_2^2 - \\ &- M^2(m+k)\sigma_2 + M^2[M^2 - (m-k)^2] = 0. \end{aligned} \tag{8.2}$$

The following notation is introduced for brevity:

$$m = \frac{m_{\text{vio}} - m_{\text{red}}}{Ah}, \quad k_D = \frac{D\psi(D)}{A}.$$

At some points of the model the equations for determining σ_1 and σ_2 are considerably simplified. Thus on the boundary of the range of plastic strain $(D = 0)$ the equation for determining the principal stresses assumes the form

$$\sigma_1 - \sigma_2 = \frac{m_{\text{vio}} - m_{\text{red}}}{Ah},$$
$$\sigma_1\sigma_2 = \sigma_s^2 - \frac{(m_{\text{vio}} - m_{\text{red}})^2}{A^2h^2}. \tag{8.3}$$

If the range of plastic strain extends into the load-free contours of the model, one of the principal stresses, σ_2 say, equals zero while σ_1 is given by

$$\sigma_1 = \frac{m_{\text{vio}} - m_{\text{red}}}{Ah} - \frac{D\psi(D)}{A},$$
$$\sigma_1 = \sigma_s[1 + f(D)]. \tag{8.4}$$

It is evident from (8.2), (8.3) and (8.4) that the expressions for the principal stresses contain the yield stress σ_s, the value of which depends on the rate of increase in stress intensity. For a heterogeneous stress state, the rate of increase in stress intensity at each point is generally different and hence the yield stress σ_s is a function of coordinates the form of which is initially unknown. This causes considerable difficulty in solving photoplasticity problems for models and also for translating the model results to metallic prototypes. However, it was mentioned above that under slow loading of celluloid at rates of increase in stress intensity of about 0.2 kg/cm^2 per minute the $\sigma \sim \varepsilon$ curves hardly vary and consequently the yield stress does not change either.

Hence it can be assumed with sufficient accuracy that for slow loading the yield stress assumes the same value at all points within the plastic range.

The numerical value of the yield stress at several points of the model can be determined at any instant. Thus at the boundary of the range of plastic strain the value of σ_s is determined by the known solution in the elastic range:

$$\sigma_s^2 = (\sigma_1\sigma_2)_{\text{yel}} + \frac{(m_{\text{vio}} - m_{\text{red}})^2}{A^2h^2}. \tag{8.5}$$

At the load-free contours of the model σ_1 can be determined from the first equation of (8.4). The second equation then gives

$$\sigma_s = \frac{\sigma_1}{1 + f(D)}. \tag{8.6}$$

If only one value of σ_s is known, its variation at any point in the plastic range can be evaluated.

In this context, the relative stress intensity is a known function of the coordinates:

$$\frac{\sigma_u}{\sigma_s} = \beta(x, y). \tag{8.7}$$

Moreover, the relationship $\sigma_s \sim \dot{\sigma}_u$ can be expressed in the form

$$\frac{\sigma_s^n}{\dot{\sigma}_u} = k, \quad \text{where } k = \frac{\sigma_{sm}^n}{\dot{\sigma}_{um}}. \tag{8.8}$$

If the expression $\dot{\sigma}_u = \beta\dot{\sigma}_s$ from (8.7) is introduced into (8.8), we obtain a differential equation for determining σ_s:

$$\frac{\dot{\sigma}_s}{\sigma_s^n} = \frac{1}{k\beta}. \tag{8.9}$$

Integration of this equation yields

$$\frac{1}{1-n}\,\sigma_s^{1-n} = \frac{t}{k\beta} + C. \tag{8.10}$$

On the assumption that at the loading instant $t = t_0$ the yield stress $\sigma_s = \sigma_{s0}$ is known, as well as the function $\beta = \beta_0$ at any point of the model, an equation can be derived from (8.10) for the yield stress at any point for a specified loading time:

$$\sigma_s^{n-1} = \frac{\sigma_{s0}^{n-1}}{1 + \frac{(n-1)\,\sigma_{s0}^{n-1}}{k}\left(\frac{1}{\beta_0} - \frac{1}{\beta}\right) t_0}. \tag{8.11}$$

Here, t_0 is the time of loading after the appearance of plastic strain in the model.

Once the principal stresses have been determined, it is possible to find the stress tensor components σ_{xx}, σ_{yy} and τ_{xy}. This is straightforward, if the angles of inclination of the principal stresses are known. In the range of elastic strain the angles of inclination of the principal stresses are determined by constructing the field of isoclines.

For simple monotonic loading and linear tensor relationships between the dielectric constant and the mechanical properties, the isocline measured by an optical method characterizes the directions of the principal stresses also in the range of plastic strain.

In fact, the direction of plane of polarization is determined by the quasi-principal directions of the dielectric constant tensor, but since under simple loading the stress and strain tensors remain unchanged during the loading process, the direction of the dielectric constant tensor also does not change and the quasi-principal directions of the tensors coincide.

For nonsimple stresses, when the directions of the stress and strain tensors vary with time during loading, it is not initially evident that the directions of the stress tensors coincide with those of the dielectric constant tensor. In other words, it is not evident beforehand that the isocline characterized by optical measurements is in this case the direction of the principal stresses or the direction of the principal strains. This problem is solved by tests under monotonic complex loading of celluloid tubes subjecting them to axial tension, internal pressure and torsion /25/. These tests have shown that, as in the elastic range, in the plastic range the isoclinic parameters determine the directions of the principal stresses.

But various difficulties are encountered in the actual construction of the isoclinic field in the range of plastic strain. During such a construction, loading can be varied so that the isoclinic field has a favorable appearance (by coloring the field of the model, small gradient of the bands, etc.). In the range of plastic strain we cannot vary the loading and must construct the isoclines with large band gradients, so blurring the isoclines and consequently making them badly visible. In addition, the time factor plays an important role. Therefore, a special method must be developed for their recording, in order to construct the isoclinic field both accurately and rapidly.

If isocline construction causes much difficulty, other methods can be used to determine the components of the stress tensor.

Suppose the principal stresses are known at an arbitrary point of the model. Then the sum of the principal stresses in the elastic and plastic ranges is known and hence also the sum of the normal components of the stress tensor:

$$\sigma_1 + \sigma_2 = \sigma_{xx} + \sigma_{yy} = \varphi(x, y). \tag{8.12}$$

Consider now the differential equations of equilibrium of the plane problem:

$$\frac{\partial \sigma_{xx}}{\partial x} + \frac{\partial \tau_{xy}}{\partial y} = 0,$$

$$\frac{\partial \tau_{xy}}{\partial x} + \frac{\partial \sigma_{yy}}{\partial y} = 0.$$

Differentiation of the first with respect to x, and the second with respect to y yields

$$\frac{\partial^2\sigma_{xx}}{\partial x^2} - \frac{\partial^2\sigma_{yy}}{\partial y^2} = 0. \tag{8.13}$$

Employing (8.12), we obtain

$$\frac{\partial^2\sigma_{xx}}{\partial x^2} + \frac{\partial^2\sigma_{xx}}{\partial y^2} = \frac{\partial^2\varphi}{\partial y^2}. \tag{8.14}$$

The equations involving σ_{yy} and τ_{xy} are obtained similarly:

$$\frac{\partial^2\sigma_{yy}}{\partial x^2} + \frac{\partial^2\sigma_{yy}}{\partial y^2} = \frac{\partial^2\varphi}{\partial x^2},$$

$$\frac{\partial^2\tau_{xy}}{\partial x^2} + \frac{\partial^2\tau_{xy}}{\partial y^2} = -\frac{\partial^2\varphi}{\partial x\partial y}. \tag{8.15}$$

Since the strains σ_{xx}, σ_{yy} and τ_{xy} are known in the elastic range close to the boundary of the range of plastic strain, and function $\varphi(x, y)$ is defined for the whole field of the model, equations (8.14) and (8.15) can be solved numerically.

§9. CHARACTERISTIC FEATURES OF PHOTOPLASTIC METHODS USING CELLULOID MODELS

Various techniques have been prepared for solving plane elasto-plastic problems with the aid of celluloid models. The techniques depend on the type of calibrating experiments, and the method of loading the models, and also on the particular relationships linking the mechanical and optical quantities. The details and possibilities of some of these models are examined below.

a) Constant rate of load increase

The main relationships pertaining to this method have already been described. The specific features of the method are as follows:

1. Loading of the models is effected continuously at a constant rate of load increase.

2. The anomalous dispersion of birefringence is used as the measure of plasticity. The geometric locus of points with zero dispersion is taken as the boundary of the range of plastic strain. Within the plastic range the dispersion of birefringence is a function of the strain intensity.

3. Two optical quantities are employed when determining the stress within the plastic range: dispersion of birefringence,

and the difference between the interference bands measured with two monochromatic light sources of different wavelength. This enables one to establish two independent relationships with which to determine the principal stresses. The coefficients and functions of dispersion entering these relationships are determined by experiments in uniaxial state of stress.

4. When determining the boundaries of the range of plastic strain and the principal stresses for a given load, it is sufficient to photograph two interference bands in the model with different monochromatic light sources. The adopted loading program makes it possible to obtain from the same model a series of pictures of interference bands for different degrees of loading.

5. The strain at an arbitrary point of the model is determined from known stresses by employing stress-strain relations. For celluloid, in the range of small strains and simple loading the relations satisfy the rules of the deformation theory of plasticity for relative stresses and strains.

6. The fundamental relations of this method of solving photoplastic problems are different in regions with positive and negative values of the first invariant of the stress tensor. The difference consists in different expressions for the functions of dispersion of birefringence entering these ratios. It is therefore necessary first to assess the form of the state of stress and then to choose the form of the relations.

7. The dependences of the optical effects on the mechanical quantities used in this method are derived for simple loading and under conditions of active strain. They can therefore be employed to solve plane elastoplastic problems only in the case of models in which each point is subjected to active loading.

Thus the photoplastic method for a constant rate of loading allows one to completely solve plane elastoplastic problems for models, i. e., to determine the boundary of the range of plastic strain and the stress and strain at any point of the model.

The problem of determining the stress in uniaxial state of stress is readily solved, in particular at the free boundaries of the model. Therefore this method is an effective means for investigating variations in the coefficients of stress concentration in elastoplastic strain and creep.

The question arises as to the accuracy of the method and the nature of possible errors. Excluding subjective errors, the photoplastic problem of determining the stress in uniaxial state and the boundaries of the range of plastic strain can be solved with the same degree of accuracy as photoelastic problems, since in this case it suffices to determine the order of the interference bands.

In the determination of stresses within the plastic range, errors may arise from the dependence of the yield stress of celluloid on the loading rate and from the impossibility of effecting accurately the loading program selected at all points of the model. These errors can be reduced by conducting the tests at low loading rates. Moreover, the relations between stress and strain and also between the mechanical quantities and optical effects employed in this method are correct only under conditions of simple monotonic loading. Although they can be applied to near-simple conditions, this may cause errors.

Thus errors may occur in solving photoplastic problems connected with material properties and with the loading program. Nevertheless, the examples described below show that the photoplastic method enables one to attain sufficient accuracy in comparison with computations and with other experimental techniques.

b) Constant strain rate

Photoplastic methods involving loading of models at constant strain rates are described elsewhere /16–21/. The principal features of this method are the following:

1. The dispersion of the birefringence is used as the measure of plasticity.

2. The curves used for computing the stress comprise: (a) the "effective" $\sigma \sim \varepsilon$ curve, constructed for a test duration determined by calibration test results at a constant strain rate; (b) the "effective" curve of optical path difference versus strain ($\delta \sim \varepsilon$), which is constructed like the $\sigma \sim \varepsilon$ curve; (c) the curve of dispersion of birefringence versus strain ($D \sim \varepsilon$).

3. The method is only applied when determining stresses and strains in uniaxial states of stress, in particular when determining the coefficients of stress concentration and the boundary of the range of plastic strain. For this, two photographs of the bands in the model with monochromatic light sources of different wavelengths are required for a given loading. Loading at constant strain rate permits one to obtain pictures of the bands at different loading levels with a single model. The stress is computed as follows: the dispersion of birefringence D and the variation in the bands along the inner cross-section of the model are determined from the picture of the interference bands. The strain is then determined by means of $\delta \sim \varepsilon$ calibration curves and the stress by means of $\sigma \sim \varepsilon$ curves.

Since the dispersion of birefringence and the order of the interference bands for a given strain have different values under tension and compression, the form of the state of stress must be evaluated when this method is used.

The principal errors likely to occur when this method is applied result from the fact that the corresponding $\sigma \sim \varepsilon$ and $\delta \sim \varepsilon$ curves are constructed on the basis of calibration tests at constant strain rate, while in the model the strain rate differs from point to point and is generally not constant. Hence the resulting curves give only an approximate description of the model behavior. It has been proposed that tests be conducted with slow loading in order to reduce the errors caused by unequal strain rate.

This method is employed to determine the coefficients of stress concentration for elastoplastic strain in plates with holes and recesses.

c) Loading at constant difference in the principal stresses

This method, which has been applied elsewhere /22–25/, possesses the following main features:

1. The samples and models are loaded for a definite period of time at a constant difference in the principal stresses (under constant load).

2. It is assumed that the optical path differences in the elastic and plastic regions are determined solely by the differences between the principal stresses. The $\delta \sim (\sigma_1 - \sigma_2)$ curves are constructed from $\delta \sim t$ creep curves for different stress levels when $t > 4$ hours.

3. A picture of the interference bands is required for determining the state of stress of the model. By means of the $\delta \sim (\sigma_1 - \sigma_2)$ calibration curve the difference between the principal stresses in the model is then found in addition to the isoclinic pattern, which determines the direction of the principal stresses. The stress distribution in the model is derived from these data by employing the differences between tangential stresses /3/.

On the strength of this method the following observations can be made:

1. The hypothesis, that the optical path difference in celluloid in the plastic region is determined only by the difference between the principal stresses, has not been confirmed by others /19/. This is apparently valid only for special stress patterns, in particular under the condition $\sigma_2 = \sigma_3$, or by replacing the intensity of tangential stresses by half the difference between the principal stresses /46/.

2. The selected loading program does not make it possible to investigate the stress distribution during the different stages of load increase in a single model. A separate model is required for each stress level.

3. This method can only be applied to strains which do not exceed the limit of elasticity by a factor of 3.5–4, since for large strains the $\delta \sim \varepsilon$ curves are no longer unique.

d) Javornicky /35–37/ also used celluloid in solving photoplastic problems. When determining the state of stress of the model he established the following relationships between the optical path difference and the mechanical quantities:

1) in a uniaxial state of stress

$$\delta = [c\sigma + k(\varepsilon - \varepsilon_e)]\,h, \tag{9.1}$$

2) in a planar state of stress

$$\delta = 2\,[c\tau_{max} + k(\gamma_{max} - \gamma_e)]\,h, \tag{9.2}$$

where c and k are constants, and ε_e and γ_e are strains at the elastic limit.

Relationships (9.1) and (9.2) contain stresses and strains, and therefore do not suffice for determining the state of stress of models from known optical effects. Additional relationships between the optical and mechanical quantities are necessary.

Javornicky proposed obtaining the additional relationships from the dependence of the optical path difference on the residual stress and strain upon load removal. However this approach is not very fruitful, since the residual strain and optical path difference in celluloid vary with time. It can also be readily shown that in the range of plastic strain relationships (9.1) and (9.2) are fulfilled only approximately. Since upon passing into the range of plastic strain the dispersion of birefringence appears in celluloid, we derive from (9.1) the optical path difference measured at λ_{vio} and and λ_{red}:

$$\begin{gathered}\delta_{vio} = ch\sigma + k_{vio}h(\varepsilon - \varepsilon_e),\\ \delta_{red} = ch\sigma + k_{red}h(\varepsilon - \varepsilon_e).\end{gathered} \tag{9.3}$$

Coefficient c has the same value in both equations, since δ_{vio} and δ_{red} practically coincide in the elastic range.

The dispersion of birefringence is given by

$$D^* = \frac{\delta_{red} - \delta_{vio}}{\lambda_{red}}.$$

Then

$$\delta_{red} - \delta_{vio} = (k_{red} - k_{vio})\,h\,(\varepsilon - \varepsilon_e) = D^*\lambda_{red}, \tag{9.4}$$

or

$$k_{red} - k_{vio} = \frac{D^*\lambda_{red}}{(\varepsilon - \varepsilon_e)\,h}. \tag{9.5}$$

Since the dispersion of birefringence D^* is a function of strain, $k_{red}-k_{vio}$ is also a function of strain, which confirms the hypothesis that coefficient k is also constant.

However, with the exception of the initial segment of the $D^{vio}\sim\varepsilon$ curve, the dispersion of birefringence can be represented approximately as a linear function of strain:

$$D^* \approx N(\varepsilon - \varepsilon_e). \tag{9.6}$$

Substitution of (9.6) into (9.5) yields $k_{red}-k_{vio}=N\lambda_{vio}/h=\text{const}$. Consequently, coefficient k in (9.1) is also a constant under these conditions.

In this case, the optical path difference for a uniaxial state of stress is

$$\delta = ch\sigma + N_1 hD^*, \tag{9.7}$$

where N_1 is a constant depending on the wavelength. This equality permits one to determine the stresses in the elastic and plastic ranges from known optical effects.

§10. EXAMPLES OF INVESTIGATING THE STATE OF STRESS IN CELLULOID MODELS

In order to illustrate the photoplastic method and explain the computation techniques, we consider some plane elastoplastic problems.

1. Extension of celluloid strips with semicircular notches. The model strips possessed the following dimensions: minimum cross-sectional width l = 30 mm, notch radius 15 mm, thickness 4.69 mm. Water was used to effect continuous uniform loading at a constant rate of load increase. The water feed rate was set beforehand and maintained constant throughout the test. In the example under consideration the rate of load increase was 1.45 kg per minute and the corresponding rate of nominal stress increase was 1.03 kg/cm^2 per minute.

After determined, generally arbitrary, time intervals the interference bands in the model were photographed simultaneously, with two monochromatic light sources of wavelengths λ_{vio} = 435.8 mμ and λ_{red} = 690.7 mμ supplying light.

Coefficient A and functions $f(D)$ and $\psi(D)$ in the fundamental photoplasticity equations (7.1) and (7.9) were determined for the uniaxial tension of plane samples prepared from the same grade of celluloid as the model. For the celluloid used, $A = 0.00106$ cm/kg, function $f(D)$ is shown in Figure 2.22, and function $\psi(D)$ is given by (7.5).

a) Determination of the coefficient of stress concentration. The coefficient of stress concentration α_k for different degrees of loading is defined as the ratio of the maximum stress on the notch contour σ_1 to the nominal stress:

$$\alpha_k = \frac{\sigma_1}{\sigma_n}. \tag{10.1}$$

In the elastic range the stress on the notch contour is given by

$$\sigma_1 = \frac{m_{\text{vio}} - m_{\text{red}}}{Ah}, \tag{10.2}$$

and in the plastic range by

$$\sigma_1 = \frac{m_{\text{vio}} - m_{\text{red}}}{Ah} - \frac{D\psi(D)}{A}. \tag{10.3}$$

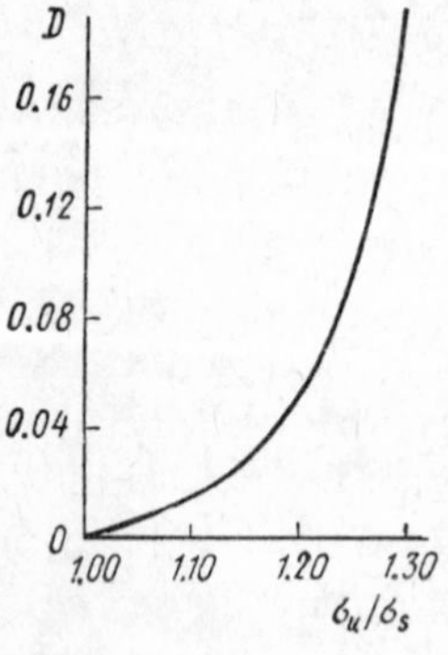

FIGURE 2.22.

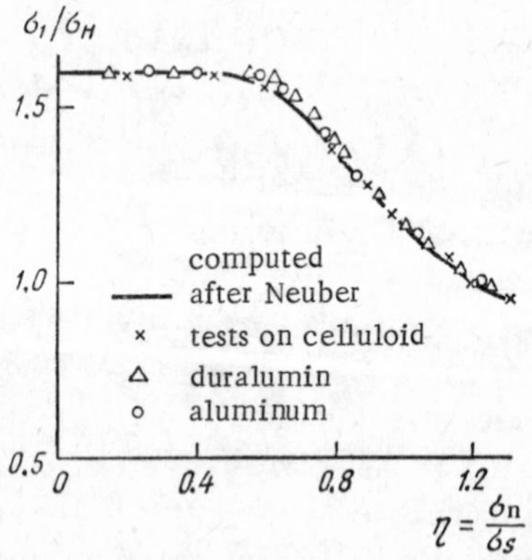

FIGURE 2.23.

The concentration coefficient α_k is plotted as a function of the loading parameter η in Figure 2.23. From the loading parameter η one can derive the ratio of the nominal stress σ_n to the yield stress σ_s. The yield stress σ_s for each degree of loading is given by

$$\sigma_s = \frac{\sigma_1}{1 + f(D)}. \tag{10.4}$$

As an example, consider the computations for several loading levels. When $\sigma_n = 358$ kg/cm² (the photograph of the interference bands is shown in Figure 2.24), on the notch contour $m_{vio} = 6.6$, $m_{red} = 4.4$, and dispersion $D = 0.0537$. Equation (7.5) yields $h\psi(D) = -3.7$, and it follows from (10.3) that $\sigma_1 = 461.3$ kg/cm². With the value $f(D) = 1.202$ determined from Figure 2.22, we derive from (10.4) that $\sigma_s = 383$ kg/cm². The concentration coefficient $\alpha_k = 1.28$ and the loading parameter $\eta = 0.935$.

When $\sigma_n = 480$ kg/cm² (the photograph of the interference bands is shown in Figure 2.25), on the recess contour $m_{vio} = 7.98$, $m_{red} = 5.6$, $D = 0.101$, $h\psi(D) = -0.722$, $\sigma_1 = 485.8$ kg/cm², $f(D) = 1.255$, $\sigma_s = 387$ kg/cm², $\alpha_k = 1.01$, and $\eta = 1.24$.

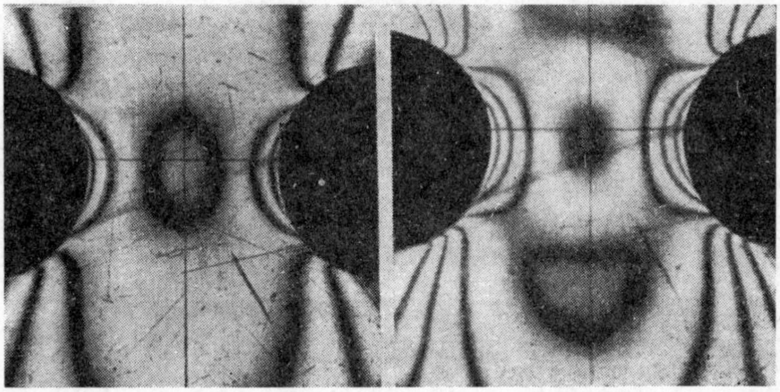

FIGURE 2.24.

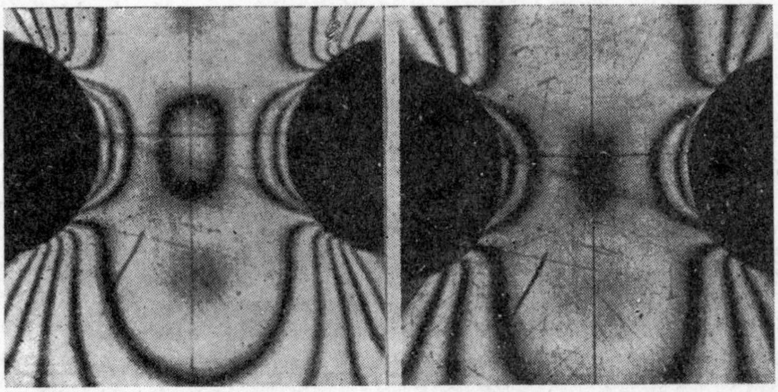

FIGURE 2.25.

The values of the coefficient of stress concentration α_k determined by the photoplastic method were compared with values computed by Neuber's method /38/. According to the latter method, the coefficient of stress concentration is determined by selecting on the continuation of the elastic part of the $\sigma \sim \varepsilon$ curve a fictitious maximum stress, equal to the product of the nominal stress and the concentration coefficient in the elastic range, $\sigma_f = \alpha_e \sigma_n$, and constructing the hyperbolic curve $\sigma_f \varepsilon$ const from the point obtained to the intersection with the $\sigma \sim \varepsilon$ curve. The ordinate of the point of intersection corresponds to the required value of the maximum stress σ_{max}.

An example of applying Neuber's method is illustrated in Figure 2.26 for the loading parameter $\eta = 1.24$. The $\sigma \sim \varepsilon$ curve for celluloid was chosen by the value of the yield stress σ_s on the notch contour. In the case specified $\sigma_n = 480$ kg/cm², the concentration coefficient in the elastic range $\alpha_e = 1.6$, and $\sigma_y = \alpha_e \sigma_n = 768$ kg/cm². This value of σ_f corresponds to strain $\varepsilon = 0.035$, so that $\sigma_f \varepsilon = 26.9$. Construction of the hyperbolic curve $\sigma_f \varepsilon = 26.9$ yields at the point of intersection of this hyperbola with the $\sigma \sim \varepsilon$ curve $\sigma = 4.79$, and consequently $\alpha_k = 0.998$. The value of α_k determined by the photoelastic method equals 1.01. Computed concentration coefficients are plotted in Figure 2.23 (solid line) and the crosses refer to values obtained by the photoplastic method.

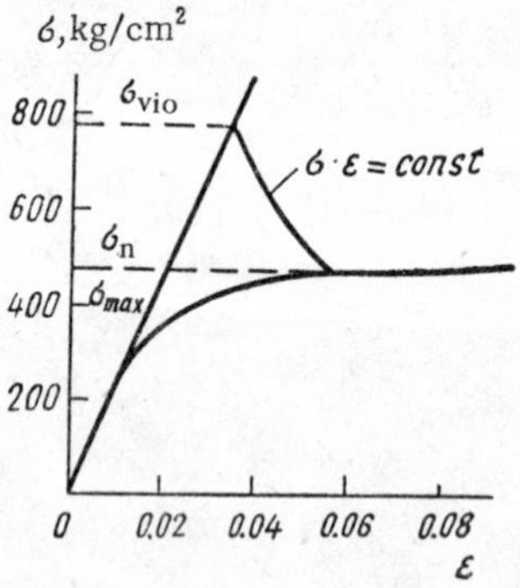

FIGURE 2.26.

The coefficients of stress concentration for the plates under consideration were also determined by the photoelastic cover method for duralumin /39/ and aluminum /20/. The results of these measurements are also illustrated in Figure 2.23, where △ refers to duralumin and O to aluminum. Evidently, the values of α_k computed for duralumin and aluminum are practically in agreement with the value computed for the celluloid model.

In the range of elastic and incipient plastic strain the agreement is practically almost complete. A certain divergence of the order of 3% is observed only in the transition segment. This is apparently connected with the fact that the $\frac{\sigma_u}{\sigma_s} \sim \frac{\varepsilon_u}{\varepsilon_s}$ curves for celluloid and duralumin, while differing from one another in the transition region, are in agreement in the range of plastic strain.

Hence the variation in the coefficients of stress concentration in the process of plastic strain, as determined by celluloid models, is in agreement with the variation in the effective stress coefficients of the actual structural members, if the $\frac{\sigma_u}{\sigma_s} \sim \frac{\varepsilon_u}{\varepsilon_s}$ curves of the material comprising the model and the actual member are similar.

b) Determination of the range of plastic strain.

The boundary of the range of plastic strain is readily determined by means of the photoplastic method, employing particular optical effects in the model material. It is important that the boundary of the range of plastic strain be determined independently of the problem of the stress-strain state of the model.

The boundary of the range of plastic strain in celluloid models is defined optically as the locus of points at which the anomalous dispersion of birefringence becomes zero:

$$D = 1 - \frac{m_{\text{vio}} \lambda_{\text{vio}}}{m_{\text{red}} \lambda_{\text{red}}} = 0.$$

Consequently, on the boundary of the range of plastic strain

$$m_{\text{vio}} = m_{\text{red}} \frac{\lambda_{\text{red}}}{\lambda_{\text{vio}}}. \qquad (10.5)$$

The boundary of plastic strain can be determined by calculating the dispersion of birefringence, involving simple but lengthy computation. However, one can employ approximate methods which reduce the amount of computations and are reasonably accurate.

In the elastic range close to the boundary of the range of plastic strain, $m_{\text{vio}} - m_{\text{red}} = Ah(\sigma_1 - \sigma_2)$. It is further known that the Huber-Mises ($\sigma_u = \sigma_s$) and Coulomb-St. Venant ($\tau_{\max} = \tau_s$) plasticity conditions differ little from one another. Therefore, assuming $\tau_{\max} \approx \frac{\sigma_1 - \sigma_2}{2}$, we find that the boundary of the range of plastic strain must approximately fulfill the condition $m_{\text{vio}} - m_{\text{red}} =$ const, or $m_{\text{vio}} = c_1$ and $m_{\text{red}} = c_2$, since (10.5) is valid near the boundary of plastic strain.

Therefore, when determining the boundary of the range of plastic strain, it is sufficient to find on the model only one point at which $D = 0$, and determine there the order of the bands m_{vio} and m_{red}. Hence the boundary of the range of plastic strain is derived as the locus of points at which $m_{vio}=c_1$ and $m_{red}=c_2$ subject to the condition $m_{vio}=m_{red}\lambda_{red}/\lambda_{vio}$. Figure 2.27 shows the extent of the range of plastic strain for a plate with semicircular notches. It is evident that the strain occurs initially at the two notches and then extends to the depth of the model. It is characteristic that, in addition to spreading of this zone, at a certain load plastic strain occurs on the central axis far from the notch. The two zones merge with increasing load.

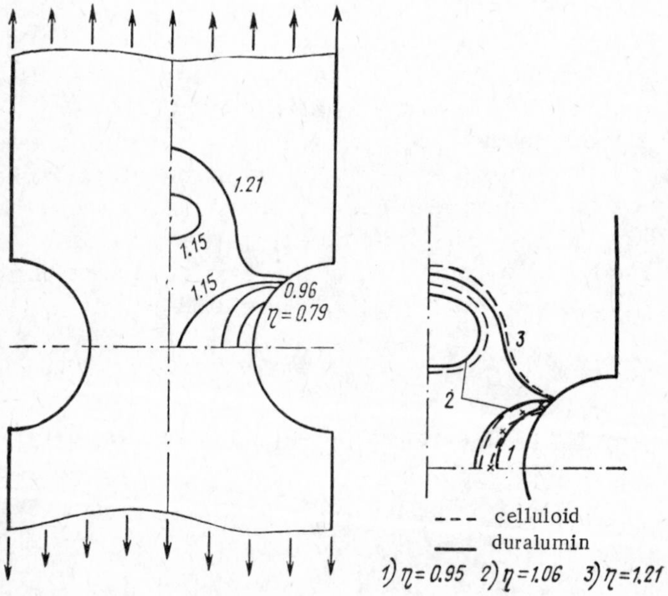

FIGURE 2.27a. FIGURE 2.27b.

The plastic strain of similar duralumin plates was determined for comparison. The boundary of the range of plastic strain for the duralumin plates was determined in the following manner. The principal strains were divided along the central horizontal cross-section of the plate by the known value of the difference between the principal strains $\varepsilon_1-\varepsilon_2$, determined by optical effects in photoelastic tests, and the value of the third principal strain ε_3, determined by the interferometer /40/.

The strain intensity was determined from the value of the principal strains. The order of the interference bands was determined at the point at which $\varepsilon_u = \varepsilon_s$. This value of the order of the bands was assumed to be constant on the boundary of the range of plastic strain throughout the plate.

The boundary of the range of plastic strain in celluloid (dashed lines) and in duralumin (solid lines) are shown in Figure 2.27b for load parameters $\eta = 0.95$, 1.06 and 1.21. Evidently, both the features and the dimensions of the plastic range are in sufficient agreement.

c) Determination of the principal stresses. As an example, we examine the principal stresses along the minimum cross-section for two loading levels: $\sigma_n = 358$ kg/cm^2 and $\sigma_n = 480$ kg/cm^2. In the first case the range of plastic strain occupies only part of the minimum cross-section and has an elastic core. In the second case the range of plastic strain includes the whole cross-section. A photograph of the interference bands in the model is shown in Figure 2.24 (for $\sigma_n =$ $= 358$ kg/cm^2) and Figure 2.25 (for $\sigma_n = 480$ kg/cm^2).

Consider first the stress when $\sigma_n = 358$ kg/cm^2. The order of the interference bands m_{vio} and m_{red}, their difference $m_{\text{vio}} - m_{\text{red}}$, and the dispersion of the birefringence D along the minimum cross-section are shown in Figure 2.28. Expressions (7.1) and (7.9) are used to determine the stresses. Since these expressions contain the yield stress, its variation must be determined along the cross-section. This can be done with the aid of (8.11) by substituting the following values corresponding to the given case: $\sigma_{s0} = 383$ kg/cm^2, $\sigma_{sm} = 325$ kg/cm^2, $\dot{\sigma}_{um} = 0.2$ kg/cm^2 per min, $= 1.202$, exponent $n = 15$, $t_0 = 117$ min. The exponent was derived from the relationship $\ln\dot{\sigma}_u/\dot{\sigma}_{um} \sim \ln\sigma_s/\sigma_{sm}$ (Figure 2.12). The value of t_0 was determined as the difference between the time of model loading $t_1 = 347$ min and the time $t_2 = 230$ min when plastic strain first occurred in the model.

We now find the value of the yield stress on the boundary of the range of plastic strain. Substitution of the above values into (8.11) yields $\sigma_s = 372$ kg/cm^2. The yield stress at the remaining points of the model cross-section is determined similarly. Calculations show that the yield stress changes along the cross-section by 3%. Therefore, when computing the stress the mean value of the yield stress over the section ($\sigma_s = 377$ kg/cm^2) can be taken.

The principal stresses at several points within the range of plastic strain are now derived. At a point whose distance from the contour is $x/l = 0.1$, $m_{\text{vio}} = 6.00$, $m_{\text{red}} = 3.95$, $\sigma_1 = 472$ kg/cm^2 and

$\sigma_2 = 42$ kg/cm^2. The stress at the boundary of the range of plastic strain is given by

$$\sigma_1 - \sigma_2 = \frac{m_{vio} - m_{red}}{Ah}, \quad (\sigma_1 - \sigma_2)^2 + \sigma_1\sigma_2 = \sigma_s^2.$$

Substitution of $m_{vio} = 4.5$ and $m_{red} = 2.84$ into this expression yields $\sigma_1 = 408.8$ kg/cm^2 and $\sigma_2 = 74.8$ kg/cm^2.

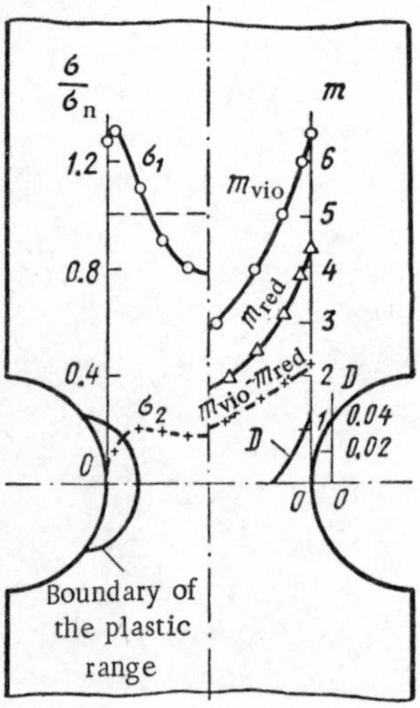

FIGURE 2.28.

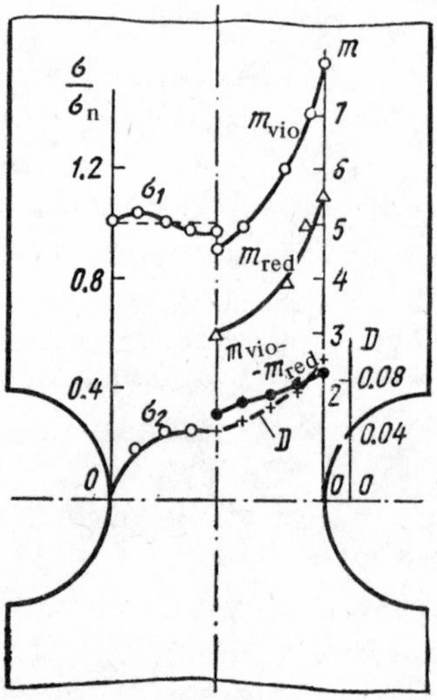

FIGURE 2.29.

In the elastic range the stresses are divided by the technique employing the difference between tangential stresses. A point on the boundary of the range of plastic strain is taken as the initial point of integration. The experimentally determined values of principal stresses σ_1 and σ_2 are shown in Figure 2.28.

Consider the stresses when $\sigma_n = 480$ kg/cm^2. The order of interference bands m_{vio} and m_{red}, their difference $m_{vio} - m_{red}$ and the dispersion of the birefringence are plotted in Figure 2.29. The dispersions differ from zero at all points and consequently the range of plastic strain contains the whole cross-section. The yield stress across the cross-section is ascertained as in the previous case. Thus on the contour of the notch $\sigma_s = 387$ kg/cm^2. At the center of the plate, where $m_{vio} = 4.6$, $m_{red} = 3.05$, $D = 0.0492$ and $\beta = 1.195$, we obtain $\sigma_s = 375$ kg/cm^2. Hence in the stress computation we select the mean value $\sigma_s = 377$ kg/cm^2.

The distribution of principal stresses σ_1 and σ_2 along the minimum cross-section of the plate at the loading level specified is given in Figure 2.29. The principal stress σ_1 changes little along the cross-section, its maximum value increasing with the distance from the notch.

2. Extension of a plate with a circular hole in which a disk is inserted. The plate has the following dimensions: length 60 mm, hole diameter 20 mm, thickness 3.65 mm.

In the absence of load the contour of the disk is in contact with that of the hole, but without pressure. When the plate is loaded the contact between the disk and hole disappears, with the exception of two small circular segments on the horizontal diameter of the disk. The surface of the hole at these parts of the contour experiences local normal pressure, causing compressive stress in the plate. Thus points lying both on the hole contour and on the horizontal diameter experience stresses of opposite sign, namely compressive radial stresses and tensile tangential stresses. Hence this problem illustrates the application of the fundamental relationships of photoplasticity to computing the state of stress in the case of principal stresses of opposite sign.

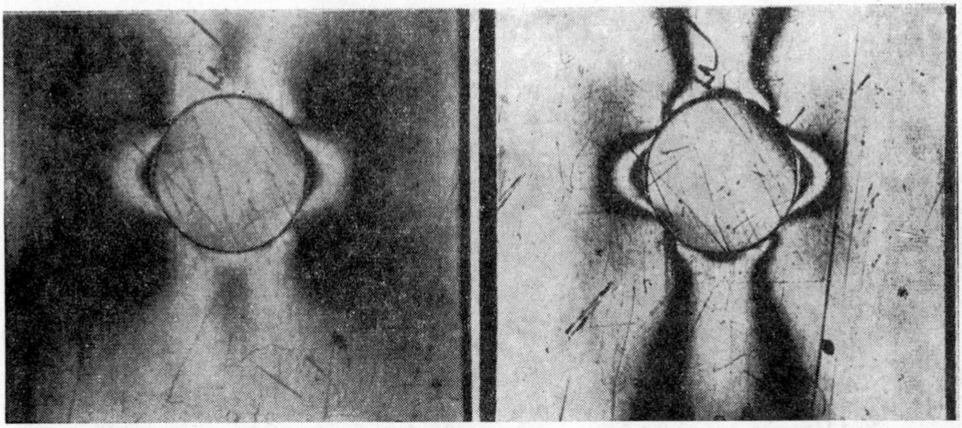

FIGURE 2.30.

Figure 2.30 presents a photograph of the bands of the model when $\sigma_n = 155$ kg/cm^2. The order of the bands and their difference along the horizontal diameter are plotted in Figure 2.31. Computations show that no points on the model possess anomalous dispersion of the birefringence, so it is in an elastic state. Figure 2.31 shows the distribution of the principal stresses along the horizontal diameter. The stresses were divided by the method of the difference between tangential stresses. It is seen that compressive stress appears on the contour of the hole and diminishes rapidly. Since the absolute value of the compressive stress is less than that of the tensile stress, the relationships of photoelasticity valid for $\sigma_1+\sigma_2>0$ can be applied to compute the stresses in the plastic range.

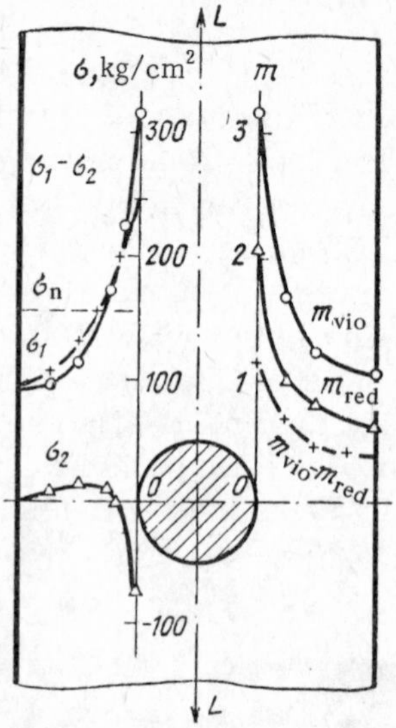

FIGURE 2.31.

Figure 2.32 is a photograph of the bands when $\sigma = 358$ kg/cm². The corresponding interference bands and dispersion D are plotted in Figure 2.33. Stress computation in the plastic range was carried out by means of (7.1) and (7.9). The stress in the elastic range was determined by the method of the difference between tangential stresses. The initial point of integration was selected on the free contour. The yield stress (~375 kg/cm²) was determined from the initial stress at the boundary of the plastic range. At the remaining points within the range of plastic strain the value of σ_s was determined from (8.11). For example, on the hole contour $D = 0.116$, $\beta = 1.264$, the stress was computed when $t_0 = 70$ min. Substitution of these values into (8.11) yields $\sigma_s = 360$ kg/cm² on the contour of the hole. The mean value $\sigma_s = 367$ kg/cm² was chosen for the stress computation.

The distribution of principal stresses along the central horizontal cross-section of the plate is shown in Figure 2.33. Residual compressive stress appears in the plate, the largest absolute value not being on the hole contour as in the elastic range, but some distance from the contour. The maximum value of the tensile stress with plastic strain is also displaced from the contour of the hole to the interior of the plate.

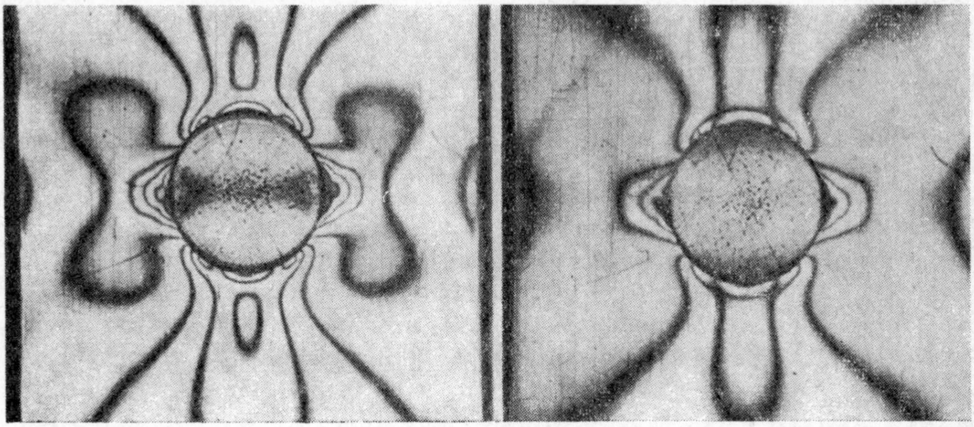

FIGURE 2.32.

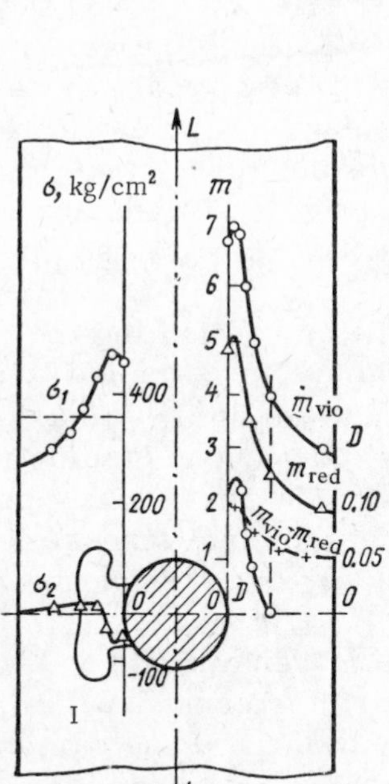

FIGURE 2.33.
(I denotes the boundary of the plastic range)

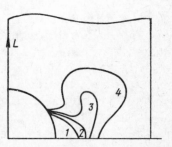

FIGURE 2.34.

Figure 2.34 shows the extent of the range of plastic strain under various loading conditions: 1) $\sigma_n = 240$ kg/cm^2; 2) $\sigma_n = 2$ $= 283$ kg/cm^2; c) $\sigma_n = 358$ kg/cm^2; 4) $\sigma_n = 370$ kg/cm^2.

§11. OPTICAL AND MECHANICAL PROPERTIES OF MACROLON AND ITS APPLICATION IN SOLVING PHOTOPLASTIC PROBLEMS

Macrolon, a polycarbonate resin, is obtained by the action of phosgene on diphenylpropane in an alkaline medium. This material belongs to the group of thermoplastic materials, but its structural changes are chemically hindered by relaxation processes which cause its properties to resemble those of rigid chain polymers. Because of its rigid molecular structure, Macrolon is dimensionally stable even at elevated temperatures. Shrinkage commences in Macrolon only at $T > 140$°C, i. e., at the glass point. The brittle point is below 100°. Macrolon is thermally stable (its melting point is 220–230° and its decomposition temperature is 310–340°). It has a high refractive index $n_D = 1.58$ and is partially crystalline.

Macrolon is a colorless transparent material displaying insignificant optical and mechanical relaxations and high optical sensitivity. For example, the mean value of the optical constant under stress in the elastic range at wavelength $\lambda_{\text{vio}} = 435.8$ mμ is $\sigma_0^{1.0} = 4.85$ kg/cm, which is half the corresponding figure for materials on the basis of epoxy resins. The optical constant for strain is $\varepsilon_0^{1.0} = 0.000317$ cm, which is also lower than in epoxy resins.

Two series of tests were conducted while investigating the optical properties of Macrolon: uniaxial tension of plane samples at different loading rates, and subjecting thin-walled tubes to axial tension and internal pressure. In all tests, continuous loading at a constant rate of load increase was applied. The tests with tubes were carried out for different ratios of the principal stresses, but the rate of increase in stress intensity for each test remained constant at 11 kg/cm^2 per min.

During each test the load was recorded at certain intervals of time, and the strain and order of the interference bands were measured. The longitudinal elongation of the plane samples and tubes was measured by means of two cathetometers using marks on the sample at the upper and lower points of the gage length. The change in the radii of the rubes was measured with an indicator with 0.01-mm divisions. The optical path difference for two monochromatic light sources of wavelengths

$\lambda_{vio} = 435.8$ mμ and $\lambda_{red} = 690.7$ mμ was measured with the above-mentioned photoelectric device.

We now examine several mechanical properties of Macrolon. Figure 2.35 shows the $\sigma_u \sim \varepsilon_u$ curve obtained from tests with uniaxial tension on plane samples at loading rates from 1.5 to 124 kg/cm² per min. Each curve was obtained by averaging the test results for 3 or 4 samples. The experimental results reveal the following facts:

1. The stress-strain curve of Macrolon depends on the loading rate, and in similar samples varies with changes in the rate.

2. There exists some minimum loading rate such that $\sigma_u \sim \varepsilon_u$ curves constructed for this or a lower rate practically coincide. Experimentation has yielded $\dot{\sigma}_{um} = 1.5$ kg/cm² per min for Macrolon. Hence the condition for similar $\sigma_u \sim \varepsilon_u$ curves can be expressed in the form

$$\sigma_u(\varepsilon_u, \dot{\sigma}_u) = \eta\left(\frac{\dot{\sigma}_u}{\dot{\sigma}_{um}}\right)\sigma_{um}(\varepsilon_u).$$

Since similar conditions hold for celluloid, it is apparently a general property of polymeric materials at constant increase in loading rate.

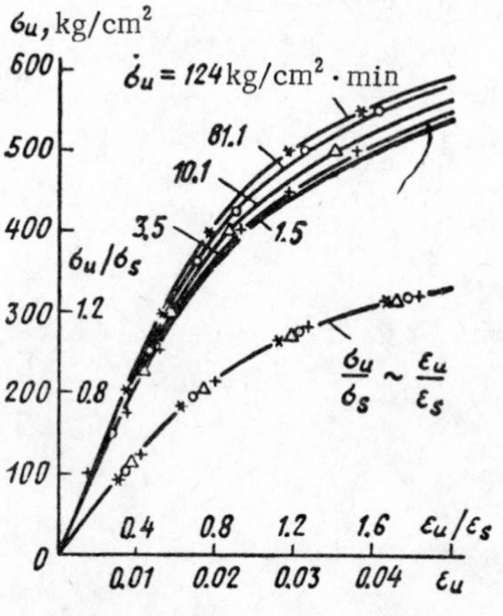

FIGURE 2.35.

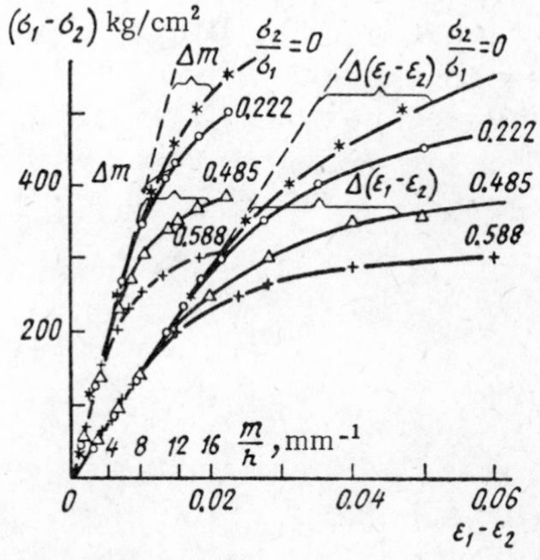

FIGURE 2.36.

3. It follows from the similarity condition that the $\sigma_u \sim \varepsilon_u$ curves for Macrolon subjected to different loading rates can be represented by a single curve in the dimensionless $\frac{\sigma_u}{\sigma_0} \sim \frac{\varepsilon_u}{\varepsilon_0}$ coordinates, where

σ_0 and ε_0 are characteristic stress and strain values, which, in particular, can coincide with the corresponding yield stress values σ_s and ε_s.

4. The yield stress σ_s depends on the loading rate, although this dependence is weaker than that for celluloid. Thus the yield stress of Macrolon varies by only 10 ~ 11% for loading rates varying by more than a factor of 80.

The properties of Macrolon in the general case of state of plane stress and possible forms of the stress-strain ratio under simple loading have been investigated by tests with thin-walled tubes subjected to axial tension and internal pressure. The tubes possessed the following dimensions: inner diameter 28 mm, wall thickness 0.5 mm, gage length 80 mm. The tests were conducted for the following principal stress ratios: $\sigma_2/\sigma_1 = 0.222$, 0.458 and 0.588.

The experimental data were studied similarly to those of the corresponding tests on celluloid tubes (§6), and indicated that the relationship between the relative stress and strain in Macrolon under simple loading assumes the form of an equation of the strain theory of plasticity /41/.

In order to establish a relationship between the optical and mechanical quantities in Macrolon, we consider the $(\sigma_1-\sigma_2)\sim(\varepsilon_1-\varepsilon_2)$ and $(\sigma_1-\sigma_2)\sim m$ curves (Figure 2.36), constructed for different ratios of the principal stresses. The $\sigma\sim m$ relationship is nonlinear in general, but at definite stress levels there are segments possessing proportionality. The limits of proportionality of the corresponding $(\sigma_1-\sigma_2)\sim(\varepsilon_1-\varepsilon_2)$ and $(\sigma_1-\sigma_2)\sim m$ curves coincide. In the proportionality range, independent of the ratio between the principal stresses, the following equations are valid:

$$\varepsilon_1-\varepsilon_2=\frac{1}{2G}(\sigma_1-\sigma_2), \tag{11.1}$$

$$m=\frac{h}{\sigma_0^{1.0}}(\sigma_1-\sigma_2), \tag{11.2}$$

where G is the shear modulus, $\sigma_0^{1.0}$ the optical constant under stress, and h the thickness of the material.

In the range of nonlinear dependence the following formal equations hold:

$$\varepsilon_1-\varepsilon_2=\frac{1}{2G}(\sigma_1-\sigma_2)+\Delta(\varepsilon_1-\varepsilon_2), \tag{11.3}$$

$$m=\frac{h}{\sigma_0^{1.0}}(\sigma_1-\sigma_2)+\Delta m, \tag{11.4}$$

where $\Delta(\varepsilon_1-\varepsilon_2)$ and Δm are the increase in the differences between the principal stresses and the order of the interference bands in comparison with their values determined by (11.1) and (11.2).

The relationship linking Δm and $\Delta(\varepsilon_1-\varepsilon_2)$ for the same principal stresses (Figure 2.37) can be expressed in the form

$$\Delta(\varepsilon_1-\varepsilon_2)=N\frac{\Delta m}{h}. \tag{11.5}$$

Here N is a proportionality factor, the value of which does not depend on the loading rate and the ratio of the principal stresses. Substituting in (11.3) quantity $\Delta(\varepsilon_1-\varepsilon_2)$ from (11.5) and allowing for (11.4), we obtain

$$m=Ah(\sigma_1-\sigma_2)+Bh(\varepsilon_1-\varepsilon_2), \tag{11.6}$$

where

$$A=\frac{2GN-\sigma_0^{1.0}}{2GN\sigma_0^{1.0}}, \qquad B=\frac{1}{N}.$$

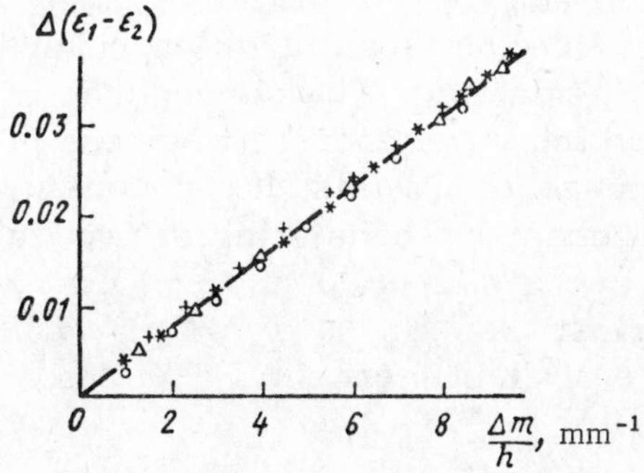

FIGURE 2.37.

Thus the linear dependence of the optical path difference on the difference between the principal stresses and the difference between the principal strains is valid also in the case of Macrolon.

However, equation (11.6) alone is insufficient for determining the stress-strain state of a model from a known optical path difference. In the plane problem one first requires a relationship between the optical and mechanical quantities. Thus a relationship can be derived by considering the dependence of the order of the interference bands on the difference between the principal strains.

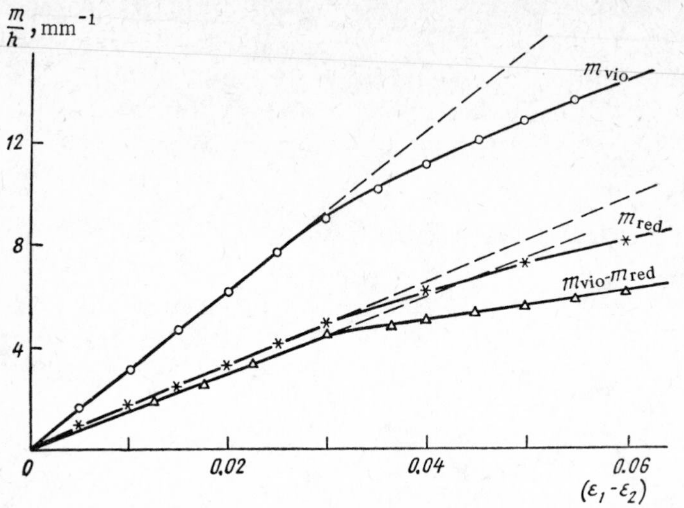

FIGURE 2.38.

The $m\sim(\varepsilon_1-\varepsilon_2)$ relationship is plotted in Figure 2.38, which illustrates that up to some strain the order of the bands is proportional to the difference between the principal strains. After exceeding this strain the $m\sim(\varepsilon_1-\varepsilon_2)$ relationship is generally nonlinear, although the $m_{vio}\sim(\varepsilon_1-\varepsilon_2)$ and $m_{red}\sim(\varepsilon_1-\varepsilon_2)$ curves deviate little from a straight line the slope of which differs from that of the above-mentioned segments. The dependence of the band difference m_{vio}-m_{red} on the difference between the principal strains $\varepsilon_1-\varepsilon_2$ in the whole range of strains under consideration can be approximated by a broken line consisting of two linear segments. The inflection point of the $(m_{vio}-m_{red})\sim(\varepsilon_1-\varepsilon_2)$ curve can be regarded as the beginning of plastic strain.

Thus, in the range of elastic strain

$$\varepsilon_1-\varepsilon_2=\frac{\varepsilon_{0el}}{h}(m_{vio}-m_{red}), \qquad (11.7)$$

where ε_{0el} is the difference between the bands of strain in the elastic range. In the plastic range

$$\varepsilon_1-\varepsilon_2=\frac{\varepsilon_{0pl}}{h}(m_{vio}-m_{red})+\left(\frac{\varepsilon_{0el}}{h}\,\frac{\varepsilon_{0pl}}{h}\right)(m_{vio}-m_{red})_s, \qquad (11.8)$$

where ε_{0pl} is the difference between the bands of strain in the plastic range, and $(m_{vio}-m_{red})_s$ is the difference between the bands on the boundary of the plastic range.

Coefficients ε_{0el} and ε_{0pl} are independent of the loading rate and the ratio between the principal stresses /41/, but depend only on the wavelength of the monochromatic light source used. For λ_{vio} and λ_{red} these coefficients are given by $\varepsilon_{0el} = 0.000720$ cm and $\varepsilon_{0pl} = 0.000904$ cm.

The difference between the bands $(m_{vio} - m_{red})_s$ at the boundary of the plastic range depends on the ratio between the principal stresses. Hence, quantity $(m_{vio} - m_{red})_s$ must be determined before using (11.8) in the calculation of the difference between the principal strains at an arbitrary point within the plastic range.

The $\frac{m_s^{vio}}{h} \sim \sigma_2/\sigma_1$ curve is plotted in Figure 2.39. When $\sigma_2/\sigma_1 = 0$, the value of m_s^{vio} equals the order of the bands at the boundary of the plastic range under uniaxial tension m_{s0}^{vio}. When $\sigma_2/\sigma_1 = 1$, $m_s^{vio} = 0$. For some arbitrary ratio between the principal stresses, m_s^{vio} assumes the form

$$m_s^{vio} = m_{s0}^{vio} f\left(\frac{\sigma_2}{\sigma_1}\right). \tag{11.9}$$

Function $f(\sigma_2/\sigma_1)$ must satisfy the conditions $f(0) = 1$ and $f(1) = 0$, which are fulfilled if we set $f(\sigma_2/\sigma_1)$

$$f\left(\frac{\sigma_2}{\sigma_1}\right) = \frac{1 - \frac{\sigma_2}{\sigma_1}}{1 - \alpha\frac{\sigma_2}{\sigma_1}}, \tag{11.10}$$

where for the Macrolon used by us the constant α equals 0.308.

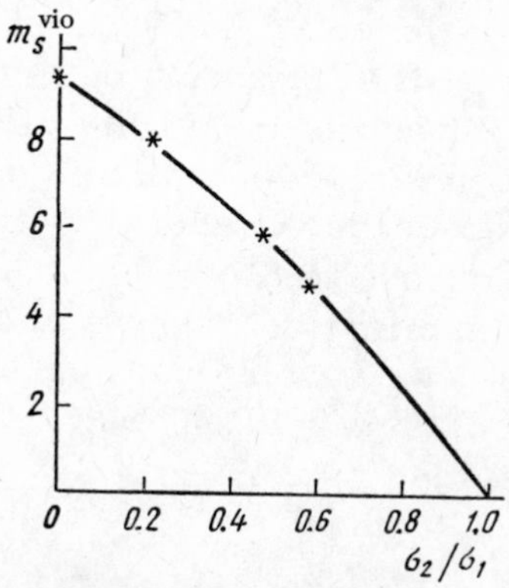

FIGURE 2.39.

In addition, the following equation must be satisfied at the boundary of the plastic range:

$$\varepsilon_1 - \varepsilon_2 = \frac{\varepsilon_{0el}}{h} m_s^{vio}. \tag{11.11}$$

Substitution of (11.11) in (11.6) yields

$$m_s^{vio} = Ah(\sigma_1 - \sigma_2) + B\varepsilon_{0el} m_s^{vio}. \tag{11.12}$$

If m_s^{vio} is expressed in terms of m_{s0}^{vio} and σ_2/σ_1 according to (11.9), we obtain an equation for determining the principal stresses at the boundary of the plastic range:

$$\sigma_1 - \alpha\sigma_2 = \frac{m_{s0}^{vio}(1 - B\varepsilon_{0el})}{Ah}. \tag{11.13}$$

By combining these equations with the Hencky-Mises condition $(\sigma_1 - \sigma_2)^2 + \sigma_1\sigma_2 = \sigma_s^2$, we determine the principal stresses and hence, from equation (11.12), the order of the bands m_s^{vio} at the boundary of the plastic range.

The above results permit one to formulate the following procedure for solving photoplastic problems on Macrolon models:

1. The model is loaded with constant increase in loading rate. The rate of load application is selected such that the rate of increase in the characteristic stress in the model does not exceed 1.5–2 kg/cm² per minute.
2. During some determined period of time, the interference bands in the model are photographed simultaneously, with two monochromatic light sources of different wavelength operating.
3. The boundary of the plastic range is determined with the aid of the characteristic optical effect, namely, the order of the interference bands at the inflection point on the $m \sim \varepsilon$ curve.
4. At an arbitrary point on the model the difference between the principal strains is determined by means of equations (11.8) and (11.12), and subsequently the difference between the principal stresses by means of equation (11.6).
5. For a separate determination of the stress and strain inside the plastic range, the stress-strain relation and the condition of existence of a single curve $\bar{\sigma}_u = \Phi(\bar{\varepsilon}_u)$ must be employed. The stress-strain relation yields

$$\bar{\sigma}_1 - \bar{\sigma}_2 = \frac{2\bar{\sigma}_u}{3\bar{\varepsilon}_u}(\bar{\varepsilon}_1 - \bar{\varepsilon}_2). \tag{11.14}$$

Since $\sigma_1 - \sigma_2$ and $\varepsilon_1 - \varepsilon_2$ are known, one can derive the values of $\bar{\sigma}_1 - \bar{\sigma}_2 = \frac{\sigma_1 - \sigma_2}{\sigma_s}$ and $\bar{\varepsilon}_1 - \bar{\varepsilon}_2 = \frac{\varepsilon_1 - \varepsilon_2}{\varepsilon_s}$. (For slow loading of the model one can choose as values of σ_s and ε_s constant values determined by calibrating tests under uniaxial state of stress.) Hence the ratio $\bar{\sigma}_u/\bar{\varepsilon}_u$ is obtained from equation (11.14). The values of σ_u/σ_s and $\varepsilon_u/\varepsilon_s$ are derived next, using the curve $\bar{\sigma}_u = \Phi(\bar{\varepsilon}_u)$. Thus the difference between the principal stress $\sigma_1 - \sigma_2$ the stress intensity σ_u, as well as the difference between the principal strains $\varepsilon_1 - \varepsilon_2$ and the strain intensity ε_u are known. These values suffice for determining the principal stresses σ_1 and σ_2 and the principal strains ε_1 and ε_2 in plane problems of photoplasticity.

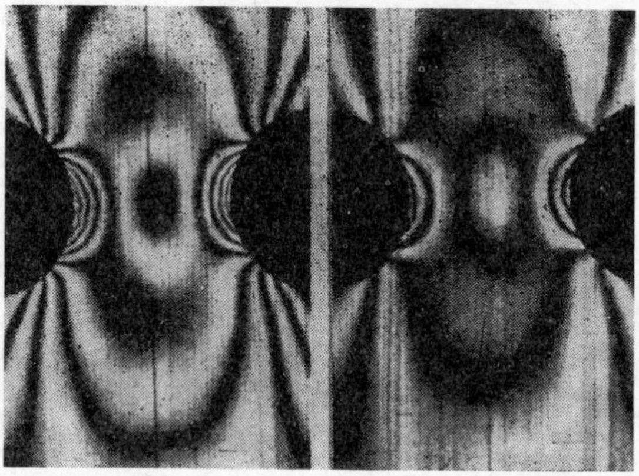

FIGURE 2.40.

Consider also the stress in plates with semicircular notches as an illustration of the application of Macrolon to the study of the stress-strain state under elastoplastic strain. The plates were of the following dimensions: width of the nominal cross-section 20 mm, notch radius 10 mm, plate thickness 0.38 mm. The stress and strain along the minimum cross-section were determined. A photograph of the interference bands in the model for $\sigma = 510$ kg/cm^2 is shown in Figure 2.40.

First, the difference between the bands at the boundary of the plastic range must be determined with the aid of (11.9), (11.12), (11.13), and the condition of plasticity $\sigma_u = \sigma_s$. The constants thus determined were: $\alpha = 0.308$, $B = \frac{1}{0.000426}$ cm^{-1}, $\varepsilon_{0el} = 0.000332$ cm, $A = 0.0541$ cm/kg, $\sigma_0^{1.0} = 4.75$ kg/cm, and $2G = 1.5 \cdot 10^4$ kg/cm^2.

The value of σ_s was found from the $\sigma \sim \varepsilon$ curve which was selected for a rate of change in the nominal stress $\sigma_n = 2.5$ kg/cm² per minute. It follows from the $m_{vio} \sim \varepsilon$ curve (Figure 2.38) that at the boundary of the plastic strain range $\varepsilon_s = 0.021$ and $m_{s0}^{vio} = 97$ cm^{-1}. The value of $\sigma_s = 386$ kg/cm² corresponds to the value ε_s on the $\sigma \sim \varepsilon$ curve. Computations show that $m_s^{vio} = 3.06$ at the boundary of the plastic strain range for the material of the model with thickness $h = 0.38$ mm.

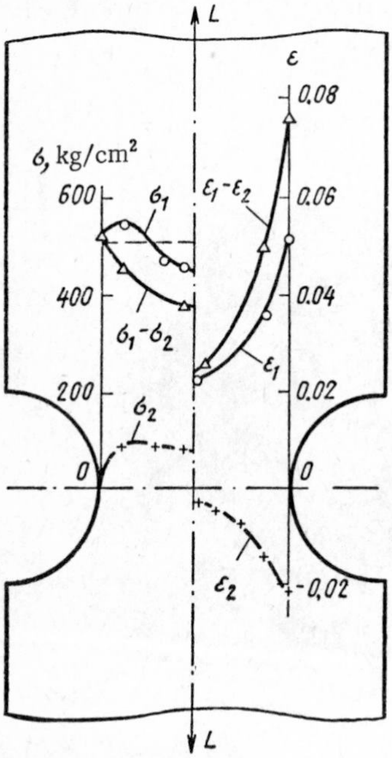

FIGURE 2.41.

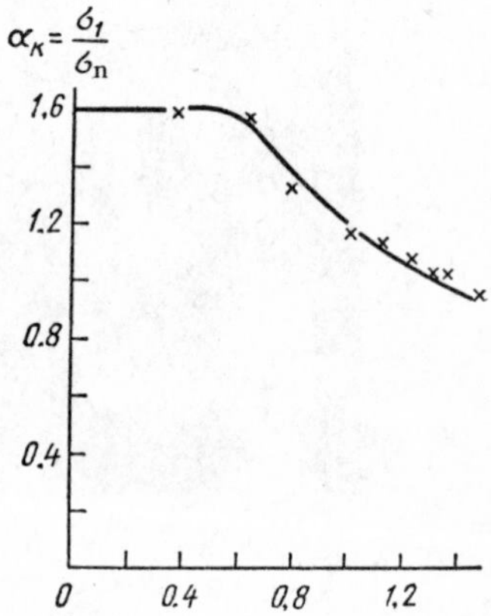

FIGURE 2.42.

The difference between the bands $(m_{vio} - m_{red})_s$ at the boundary of the plastic range is determined from known values of m_s^{vio}, on the assumption that for Macrolon, in the elastic range, the dispersion of birefringence $D = 1 - m_{red}\lambda_{red}/m_{vio}\lambda_{vio}$ possesses the constant value 0.115. Hence $m_{vio} - m_{red} = 1.36$. Then, expressions (11.8) and (11.6) determine the differences between the principal strains $\varepsilon_1 - \varepsilon_2$ and principal stresses $\sigma_1 - \sigma_2$ (Figure 2.41). Thus, at the edge of the notch $m_{vio} = 7.9$, $m_{red} = 4.4$, $\varepsilon_1 - \varepsilon_2 = 0.0766$, and $\sigma_1 = 521.3$ kg/cm². At a distance of 2.5 mm from the edge $m_{vio} = 5.37$, $m_{red} = 3$, $\sigma_1 - \sigma_2 = 451.8$ kg/cm² and $\varepsilon_1 - \varepsilon_2 = 0.0498$. At the boundary of the plastic range $m_s^{vio} = 3.06$, $\sigma_2 - \sigma_1 = 382.5$ kg/cm² and $\varepsilon_1 - \varepsilon_2 = 0.0259$.

Individual values of stresses σ_1 and σ_2 and strains ε_1 and ε_2 are determined by using equation (11.14) and the $\sigma_u \sim \varepsilon_u$ curve. On the edge of the notch $\varepsilon_1 = 0.0511$ and $\varepsilon_2 = -0.0255$. At a distance of 2.5 mm from the edge $\sigma_1 = 545$ kg/cm^2, $\sigma_2 = 93$ kg/cm^2, $\varepsilon_1 = 0.0366$, $\varepsilon_2 = -0.0132$, etc. The individual stresses and strains along the minimum cross-section are shown in Figure 2.41.

The stress coefficient α_k as a function of the loading parameter η was also determined for the same problem. The experimentally determined values of α_k were compared to those computed by Neuber /38/. Figure 2.42 shows experimental (points) and computed (solid line) values, which appear to be in sufficient agreement.

§12. SOME PROBLEMS OF MODELING THE STATE OF STRESS IN THE PHOTOPLASTIC METHOD

It has been shown above that plane problems of photoplasticity can can be solved completely with the aid of models, i. e., it is possible to determine the boundary of the plastic range and the stress tensor components within the elastic and plastic ranges. We now examine the similarity of the stress-strain state of models and actual members, and the conditions for passing from a stress in a model to a stress in an actual member subjected to elastoplastic strain.

The following requirements must be satisfied for the stress-strain states of a model and an actual member to be similar: a) the model must be geometrically similar to the actual member; b) the states of the actual member and the model, and the processes investigated must be expressed by the same differential equations; c) the solution of the differential equation of the actual member and the model must be determined with the same boundary conditions, i. e., the dimensionless boundary and initial conditions must be identical with the conditions pertaining to the actual member; d) the uniform dimensionless parameters entering the differential equations and the boundary and initial conditions in the model and actual member must be respectively equal.

When modeling stress-strain states of a body under elastoplastic strains, we must deal with the conditions for passing from a model to the actual member while satisfying the above-mentioned requirements.

The condition of geometric similarity is determined by the ratio of the characteristic dimension of the model to that of the actual member. This ratio is referred to as the scale of the linear dimensions, $l_v = l_m / l_a$. For rigorous geometric similarity, this scale must be identical for the model and the actual member in every direction. Moreover, the scale of the variation in linear dimensions, $\Delta l_v = \Delta l_m / \Delta l_a$, must equal the scale of the linear dimensions ($l_v = \Delta l_v$), i.e., the strain of the model and of the actual member must be the same.

In polarization-optical methods of investigating stresses, the condition of rigorous geometric similarity is practically never fulfilled even in the elastic range, since the strains at corresponding points generally exceed the strains of the actual member. When modeling the state of stress for elastoplastic strains, studies were conducted with strains of the model exceeding those of the actual member by a factor of almost ten.

Therefore, in polarization-optical methods, equality of strains in the model and actual member ($\varepsilon_m = \varepsilon_a$) is replaced by equality of relative strains, i.e., $\varepsilon_m / \varepsilon_s = \varepsilon_a / \varepsilon_o$. Any deviation from rigorous geometric similarity of the model and actual member is thus of no interest in the present problem. For example, in plane states of stress it is sufficient to specify the geometric similarity of the model and actual member by two dimensions (lying in the plane of a plate), i.e., an independent scale of linear dimensions on the plane ($\alpha = l_m / l_a$) can be selected together with a scale of the thickness ($\beta = h_m / h_a$).

In order to satisfy the second similarity requirement, the processes investigated on the model and actual member must belong to the same class. This means that the systems of all independent equations governing the model and actual member have the same form. We now consider isothermal static strain processes of homogeneous, initially isotropic bodies undergoing strains which are small in the general sense of strains referred to in the mechanics of strain of bodies. In such cases, the strain tensor ε_{ij} is related to the displacements by the Cauchy relationship

$$\varepsilon_{ij} = \frac{1}{2}\left(\frac{\partial u_i}{\partial x_j} + \frac{\partial u_j}{\partial x_i}\right) \quad (i, j = 1, 2, 3).$$

A complete closed system of equations for determining the stress-strain state under static isothermal strains includes differential equations of equilibrium, boundary conditions, the condition of compatibility, and equations of state (relationships between the stress and strain tensors).

The system of differential equations of equilibrium governing these processes is valid for different bodies, and consequently has the same form for the model and the actual member:

$$\frac{\partial \sigma_{ij}}{\partial x_j} = 0 \quad (i,\ j = 1,\ 2,\ 3). \tag{12.1}$$

The dimensionless boundary conditions of stress for the model are

$$\frac{\sigma_{im}^{\mathrm{m}}}{\sigma_s} l_m = \frac{S_{\nu i}^{\mathrm{m}}}{\sigma_s} \tag{12.2}$$

and for the actual member they are

$$\frac{\sigma_{im}^{\mathrm{a}}}{\sigma_0} l_m = \frac{S_{\nu i}^{\mathrm{a}}}{\sigma_0} (i,\ j = 1,\ 2,\ 3) \tag{12.3}$$

These conditions coincide, if at the corresponding points on the boundary of the model and actual member

$$\frac{S_{\nu i}^{\mathrm{m}}}{\sigma_s} = \frac{S_{\nu i}^{\mathrm{a}}}{\sigma_0}. \tag{12.4}$$

Here σ_s and σ_0 are characteristic stresses and l_m are the direction cosines.

When passing from the stress on the boundary of a body to the loads, we obtain the similarity condition for forces of the model and actual member. Hence the following equation must be fulfilled for the concentrated forces P^{m} and P^{a} and for uniformly distributed loads q^{m} and q^{a}:

$$\frac{P^{\mathrm{m}}}{\sigma_s} = l_v^2 \frac{P^{\mathrm{a}}}{\sigma_0}, \qquad \frac{q^{\mathrm{m}}}{\sigma_s} = l_v \frac{q^{\mathrm{a}}}{\sigma_0}. \tag{12.5}$$

Consider now the relationship between stress and strain in material of models (polymeric materials) and in actual bodies (metals and other structural materials). The mechanism of variation in polymers differs from that for metals. The total strain of metals is generally expressed as the sum of two components, elastic strain ε_{ij}^{e} and plastic strain ε_{ij}^{p}:

$$\varepsilon_{ij} = \varepsilon_{ij}^{e} + \varepsilon_{ij}^{p}.$$

It should be remembered that in isothermal processes each component remains constant with time, if the total strain is kept unchanged and if at constant stress the strain does not change with time. In analogy with metals, the total strain of a polymeric material can also be represented as the sum of two components /15/:

$$\varepsilon_{ij} = \varepsilon_{ij}^{e} + \varepsilon_{ij}',$$

where ε_{ij}^{e} is the tensor of elastic strain vanishing upon load removal, and ε_{ij}' is the tensor of residual strains occurring in instant removal of the load from the sample. However, in contrast to metals, the strain of polymeric materials varies with time for constant stress (it displays creep). The tensor of the instantaneous residual strain ε_{ji}' also varies with time.

Consequently, the fundamental difference between strain processes of metals and polymeric materials is that the isothermal strain processes in metals are processes of shifts of equilibrium states, and time is not an important variable in these processes; it only characterizes the sequence of the states. Time is an important variable in polymeric materials, as it signifies not only the sequence of the states but also the rate of the shifts of the states.

The time effect in strain processes of polymers can be eliminated by considering processes under "infinitely slow" (thermodynamically in equilibrium) loading. Vakulenko /15/ has shown that, in this case, the rheological law

$$\varepsilon_{ij} = \frac{1}{2G}\tilde{\sigma}_{ij} + \frac{1}{3K}\sigma\delta_{ij} + \int_{0}^{t} H[t-\tau,\ I_2(\tau)]\,\tilde{\sigma}_{ij}(\tau)\,d\tau$$

reduces to some kind of holonomic relationship between the stresses and strains of the element of the medium:

$$\varepsilon_{ij} = \omega(I_2)\tilde{\sigma}_{ij} + \frac{1}{3K}\sigma\delta_{ij},$$

where

$$\omega(I_2) = \frac{1}{2G} - \Omega_0(I_2).$$

It was shown above that under simple active loading the equations relating the relative stress and strain of polymeric materials can be expressed in the form of equations of the deformation theory of plasticity /10/:

$$\bar{\sigma}_{ij} - \bar{\sigma}\delta_{ij} = \frac{2\bar{\sigma}_u}{3\bar{\varepsilon}_u}\left(\bar{\varepsilon}_{ij} - \frac{1}{3}\bar{\theta}\delta_{ij}\right), \qquad (12.6)$$

$$\bar{\sigma}_u = \Phi(\bar{\varepsilon}_u), \qquad (12.7)$$

where

$$\bar{\sigma}_{mn} = \frac{\sigma_{mn}}{\sigma_0}, \quad \bar{\varepsilon}_{mn} = \frac{\varepsilon_{mn}}{\varepsilon_0}.$$

The problem of the $\bar{\sigma}_{ij} \sim \bar{\varepsilon}_{ij}$ relationship reduces to determining the functional relationship $\sigma_u \sim \varepsilon_u$ established experimentally. If the $\sigma_u \sim \varepsilon_u$ curves for the material of the model, $\sigma_u = \sigma_s \Phi(\varepsilon_u/\varepsilon_s)$, and for the actual member $\sigma_u = \sigma_0 F(\varepsilon_u/\varepsilon_0)$, are similar, i. e., if for all values satisfying $(\varepsilon_u/\varepsilon_s)^m = (\varepsilon_u/\varepsilon_0)^a$ the equality $\Phi(\varepsilon_u/\varepsilon_s = F(\varepsilon_u/\varepsilon_0)$ is valid, then the ratios between the relative strains in the materials of the model and actual member coincide.

Figure 2.43 presents the $\bar{\sigma}_u \sim \bar{\varepsilon}_u$ curve for celluloid, duralumin and 38-KhA (hardened) steel. The $\bar{\sigma}_u \sim \bar{\varepsilon}_u$ curves coincide for these materials. It is generally difficult to transform the $\sigma_u \sim \varepsilon_u$ curves for the material of the model and actual member into one another over the whole strain range with the aid of a suitable similarity factor. Hence one can speak only of an approximate transformation of the curves or of their agreement over a certain strain range. The latter can always be achieved by varying the characteristic stresses and strains (σ_s, σ_0, ε_s, ε_0).

Similarity of the plasticity conditions is necessary for both materials, so that transition from the material of the model to that of the actual member in the plastic state under a complex state of stress and the extent of the plastic range in the model and actual member should be similar. It has been shown above that for polymeric materials, as for metals, the Huber-Mises condition $\sigma_u = \sigma_s$ can be selected for the plasticity condition.

When modeling states of stress in the range of elastic and elastoplastic strains the Poisson condition of similarity must be satisfied, i. e., the Poisson ratios of the material of the model and of the actual member must be equal. Experimentation has shown that the Poisson ratios of polymeric materials, as of metals, are close to 0.5 in the range of plastic strain (Figure 2.44 shows the variation in Poisson ratio ν as a function of strain in the case of celluloid).

It follows that the fundamental requirements of similarity of the stress-strain state in the model and actual member under isothermal static deformations is fulfilled by the condition of simple loading in both cases. Hence the condition of transition from stress in the model to stress in the actual member can be formulated.

Suppose the elastoplastic problem has been solved for the model, i. e., we have determined the relative stresses σ_{mn}^{m}/σ_s, σ_u^m/σ_s and strains $\varepsilon_{mn}^{m}/\varepsilon_s$, $\varepsilon_u^m/\varepsilon_s$ at an arbitrary point of the model and the boundary of the range of plastic strain has also been found.

Then the corresponding relative stresses $\sigma^{a}_{mn}/\sigma_{o}$, $\sigma^{a}_{u}/\sigma_{o}$ and strains $\varepsilon^{a}_{mn}/\varepsilon_{o}$, $\varepsilon^{a}_{u}/\varepsilon_{o}$ and the boundary of the plastic range of the actual member are also determined, since $\sigma^{m}_{mn}/\sigma_{s}=\sigma^{a}_{mn}/\sigma_{o}$ and $\varepsilon^{m}_{mn}/\varepsilon_{s}=\varepsilon^{a}_{mn}/\varepsilon_{o}$ provided: (a) the model is geometrically similar to the actual member, i. e., the ratios of all characteristic linear dimensions in the model and actual member are measured on the same scale; (b) the load is applied to the model in a similar manner and at the corresponding points in proportion to the load applied to the actual member; (c) the curves of stress intensity versus strain intensity of the model, $\sigma_u=\sigma_s\Phi(\varepsilon_u/\varepsilon_s)$, and of the actual member, $\sigma_u=\sigma_0 F(\varepsilon_u/\varepsilon_0)$, are similar; (d) the plasticity condition is the same for both materials; (e) the Poisson ratios of the material of the model and actual member are identical.

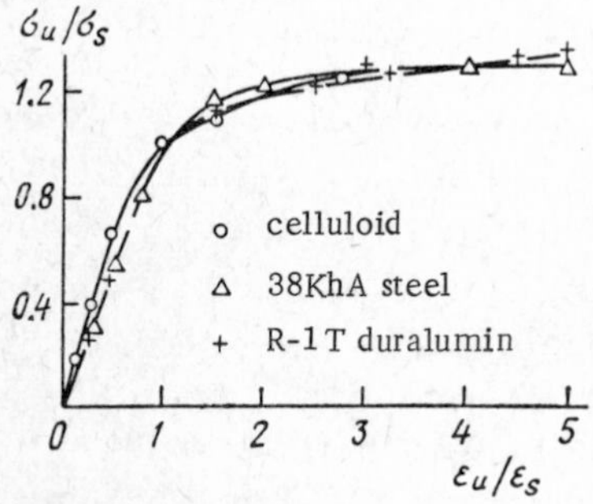

FIGURE 2.43.

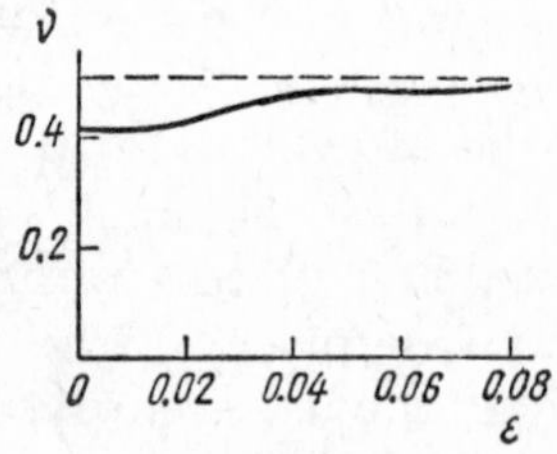

FIGURE 2.44.

In conclusion, note that the $\sigma\sim\varepsilon$ curves of polymeric materials obtained under different loading rates can be represented by a single curve in $\sigma/\sigma_s\sim\varepsilon/\varepsilon_s$ coordinates. Therefore a curve for the polymeric material subject to an arbitrary loading rate can be chosen when comparing the $\sigma\sim\varepsilon$ curves of the model and actual member. But in order to select a single curve characterizing the behavior of the material of the model at any point one must conduct tests on the model at low loading rates. In this case the curves for the polymeric material, and consequently also quantity σ_s, vary very little. Hence the mean value of σ_s in that region can be taken as the similarity factor.

§13. THE PHOTOCREEP METHOD

Metals at elevated temperatures, concrete, and polymeric structural materials have the property of undergoing strain with time under constant load, i. e., they display creep. The phenomenon of creep must be understood in order to assess the rational application of the rigidity properties of various machine parts and structural elements. A theoretical solution has so far turned out to be very complex, in particular at the onset of nonlinear creep. Hence, together with refining theoretical computation methods, experimental methods must be developed for solving these problems. In this section we consider possible applications of the polarization-optical method to the modeling of states of stress under creep. The polarization-optical investigation of stress in materials displaying appreciable nonlinear creep will be referred to as photocreep methods.

Several methods exist for computing creep when examining the state of stress in structural elements with the aid of polarization-optical methods. Some papers deal with an indirect method of modeling creep by means of elastic materials. For example, Akhmetzyanov /42/ developed a method based on the formal analogy of the equations governing creep with the equations for heterogeneous incompressible elastic bodies. The problem of creep formulation reduces to solving the problem of the elastic equilibrium of a fictitious heterogeneous model in which the elastic constant is proportional to the instantaneous modulus at corresponding points of the actual body. In plane problems, resort can be had to the analogy between solving the problem of plates with constant thickness and varying elasticity modulus, and plates with varying thickness and varying elasticity modulus.

Kharlab /43/ dealt with the modeling of creep in concrete. He proposed determining first the state of stress of the model by photoelastic methods, and then passing from the elastic model to the medium with creep by means of linear time operators. The second part of this paper treats the possibility of direct modeling of creep through the application of optically active materials, the creep of these materials obeying the same laws as the actual body. This method was applied to the modeling of nonlinear creep in concrete /44/. The modeling materials were prepared from epoxy resin hardened by Thiokol. This method was applied by Bugakov /45–48/ when modeling the state of stress in metallic structures at elevated temperatures. Standard technical celluloid, displaying appreciable creep at room temperature, was used as modeling material. These last papers will be examined in detail.

The optical and mechanical properties of celluloid under creep conditions were studied in both simple (uniaxial) and complex states of stress, in order to construct relationships linking the optical and mechanical quantities in celluloid and in order to be able to pass from measurement data on the model to the actual body.

The tests with uniaxial stress were carried out under constant and varying stress ($\sigma_1 =$ const, $d\sigma_1/dt =$ const, $\varepsilon_1 =$ const, $d\varepsilon_1/dt =$ const), and those with biaxial stress were carried out under constant stress. The fundamental tests were carried out at 20 ± 0.5°C over a period of 25 hours.

The test samples subjected to uniaxial tension were in the shape of a double blade with a gage length of 130 mm. The samples subjected to biaxial tension had the shape of a cross, the dimensions of the center part being 30 × 30 mm. Notches were cut on the branches of the cross in order to provide an almost homogeneous state of stress in the center part /48/. The samples were tested in loading devices constructed on the principle of a lever press. Uniaxial strain was measured by a Martens photometer and biaxial strain by a strain gage /48/. The optical path difference was measured with monochromatic light at 546.1 mμ by the St. Armand method.

We shall examine some mechanical properties of celluloid under creep, and problems of modeling. Here, following Bugakov, we consider the modeling of creep of metals.

The chief requirement of similarity theory is the identity of the system of equations describing the phenomena for the model and for the actual body. In a complete system of equations describing the macroscopic behavior of a continuous medium, only the stress-strain relations contain parameters which characterize the mechanical properties of the medium. Therefore, these relations must first be studied in order to examine the suitability of celluloid for modeling creep in metals.

The stress-strain relation in metals and alloys under creep conditions for constant stress assumes the form

$$\varepsilon_{ij} = e_{ij} + \Psi(T,\ t)\tilde{\sigma}_{ij},\quad i,\ j = 1,\ 2,\ 3. \tag{13.1}$$

Here ε_{ij} is the total strain, e_{ij} the elastic strain, $\tilde{\sigma}_{ij}$ the stress deviator, and T the intensity of tangential stresses.

Since the creep curves are geometrically similar, function $\Psi(T,\ t)$ can be expressed in the form

$$\Psi(T,\ t) = f(T)\varphi(t). \tag{13.2}$$

The investigation of celluloid creep under constant stress has shown that equation (13.1) is also valid in this case. Figure 2.45 presents a family of isochronic creep curves for celluloid derived from tests under conditions of uniaxial state of stress /46/. As for the creep curves of metals, these curves are geometrically similar in $\sigma_1 \sim (\varepsilon_1 - \varepsilon_1^\circ)$ coordinates, where ε_1° is the initial strain. Hence function $\psi(T, t)$ can be represented in the form (13.2) for celluloid too.

Thus the creep of celluloid and metals under a constant load is described by the same system of equations. In metals, for a heterogeneous stress field, steady-state creep can be attained for which the stress and strain rate are steady. Bugakov /47/ has shown that in celluloid models subject to certain boundary conditions (constant load acting over the whole surface of the body, or a given load acting over one part of the surface while the displacements of the remaining parts equal zero) quasi-steady-state creep is attained for which the stress is steady, the strain rate varies, and the creep equation assumes the form

$$\varepsilon_{ij} = \varphi(t) f(T) \tilde{\sigma}_{ij}. \tag{13.3}$$

where φ is a nonlinear function of time; for steady-state creep φ is a linear function of time. Note that φ does not enter the system of stress equations, and consequently the stress fields under steady-state and quasi-steady-state creep are identical for the indicated form of the boundary conditions.

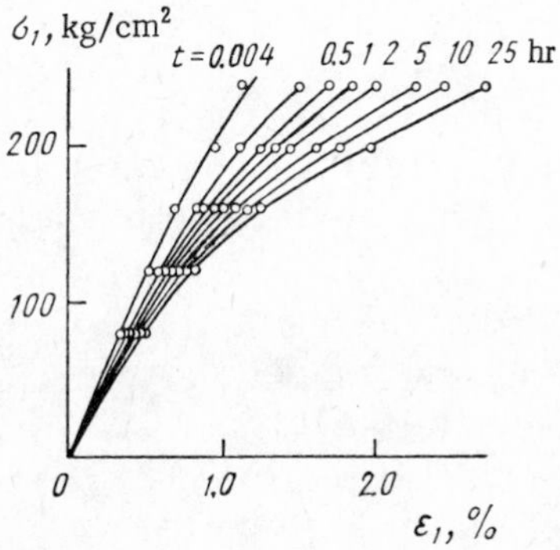

FIGURE 2.45.

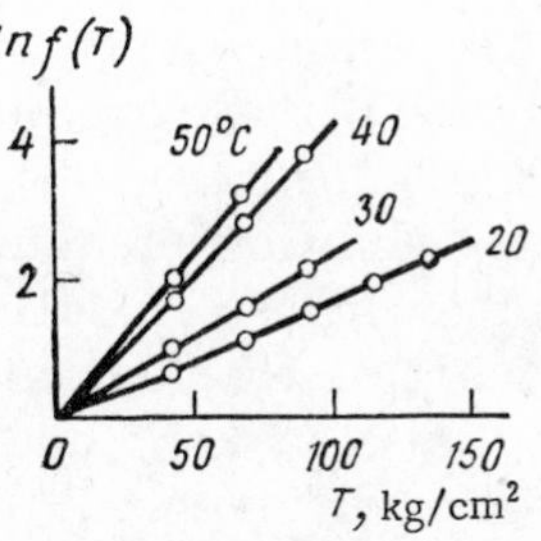

FIGURE 2.46.

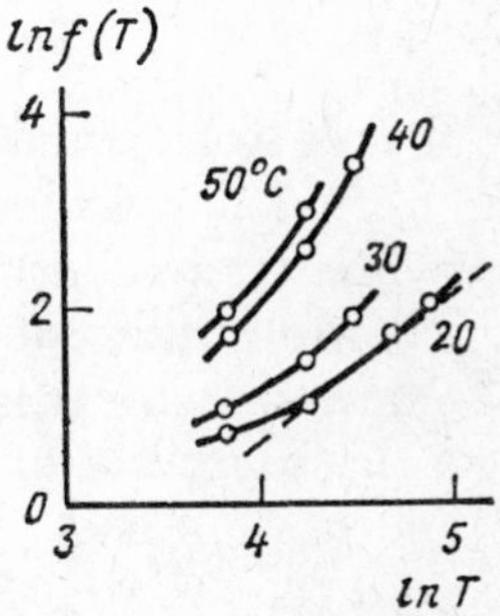

FIGURE 2.47.

The stress distribution in a body with specified shape under given boundary conditions depends on the form of function $f(T)$. Figures 2.46 and 2.47 illustrate $f(T)$ for celluloid at room temperature and elevated temperatures in semilogarithmic and logarithmic coordinates, respectively /46/. The points lie on the straight line $\ln f(T) \sim T$ (Figure 2.46). Hence function $f(T)$ can be approximated by the exponential relationship

$$f(T) = e^{bT} \tag{13.4}$$

The points on the $\ln f(T) \sim \ln T$ graph lie on a slightly curved line. With sufficient accuracy for practical purposes, the various parts of the curve can be replaced by straight lines, i. e., function $f(T)$ can be expressed as a power function (Figure 2.47):

$$f(T) = T^m. \tag{13.5}$$

When modeling creep, it is important that for many metals the form of function $f(T)$ is qualitatively analogous to the form of this function for celluloid. Therefore, the results obtained for models can be applied to the actual bodies by employing similarity theory. It follows from this theory that if expression (13.4) is employed, the external loads F_i on the model and actual body must be related by the relationship

$$F_i^{\mathrm{m}}/F_i^{\mathrm{a}} = \frac{b^{\mathrm{a}}}{b^{\mathrm{m}}}.$$

Hence the stress fields in the model and actual body must be similar. The results can be applied to actual bodies by means of the relations

$$\sigma_{xx}^{\mathrm{m}}/\sigma_{xx}^{\mathrm{a}} = \ldots = \ldots = \sigma_{xy}^{\mathrm{m}}/\sigma_{xy}^{\mathrm{a}} = \ldots = \frac{F_i^{\mathrm{m}}}{F_i^{\mathrm{a}}}. \tag{13.6}$$

If relationship (13.5) is employed, the stress fields in the model and actual body are similar if the materials of the model and actual body possess identical values of m.

Consider the equations relating measured optical quantities to mechanical quantities investigated in celluloid under creep, and also the methods of converting the former into the latter.

On the basis of creep tests at constant stress, Bugakov /46/ showed that the optical path difference in celluloid is given by

$$\delta = \delta_\tau + \delta_\gamma, \tag{13.7}$$

where $\delta_\tau = C\tau$ is a linear function of $\tau = \frac{\sigma_1 - \sigma_2}{2}$, while $\delta_\gamma = F(\gamma)$ is a function only of $\gamma = \varepsilon_1 - \varepsilon_2$.

It follows from the theory of piezo-optic effects /9/ that in plane problems the equation relating the optical path difference to the stress and strain assumes the form

$$\delta = \frac{\pi h}{\lambda \sqrt{\varkappa_0}} [A_\sigma (\sigma_1 - \sigma_2) + A_\varepsilon (\varepsilon_1 - \varepsilon_2)]. \tag{13.8}$$

Here, scalar coefficients A_σ and A_ε depend in general on the invariants of the mechanical quantities, but for certain stress and strain values this dependence can be neglected. It has also been shown that for small strains (of the order of 5%) the optical path difference δ_γ is small in comparison with δ_τ.

It follows that the quasi-principal directions of the dielectric constant tensor $\varkappa_{ij}$ are close to the quasi-principal directions of the stress tensor σ_{ij}, i.e., the parameters of the optical isoclines in the plane problem are determined by the directions of the quasi-principal stresses.

The deformation laws of the medium under consideration must be employed to express the optical path difference in terms of stress alone. By applying the law of celluloid creep in the form of (13.1), we obtain

$$\delta = \frac{\pi h}{\lambda \sqrt{\varkappa_0}} \left\{ A_\sigma + A_\varepsilon \left[\frac{1}{2G} + \varphi(t) f(T) \right] \right\} (\sigma_1 - \sigma_2). \qquad (13.9)$$

Evidently δ depends not only on time t, but also on the two variables T and $\sigma_1-\sigma_2$. Therefore, as noted above (§3), the single equation (13.9) is insufficient for determining the stress from a known optical path difference. Bugakov /146/ proposed overcoming this difficulty by replacing T by $(\sigma_1-\sigma_2)/2$. Equation (13.9) then becomes

$$\delta = \frac{\pi h}{\lambda \sqrt{\varkappa_0}} \left\{ A_\sigma + A_\varepsilon \left[\frac{1}{2G} + \varphi(t) f\left(\frac{\sigma_1 - \sigma_2}{2} \right) \right] \right\} (\sigma_1 - \sigma_2). \quad (13.10)$$

The relationship between T and $(\sigma_1-\sigma_2)/2$ depends on the form of the state of stress at the point. When the stresses σ_1 and σ_2 have identical sign, T and $(\sigma_1-\sigma_2)/2$ can differ greatly in magnitude. Therefore, in the general case such a replacement may introduce appreciable errors. However, it has been shown that in the case of small strain of celluloid such a replacement is admissible to a sufficient degree of accuracy. In this case it can be assumed that the optical path difference in celluloid is determined only by the difference between the principal directions, i.e., that the $\delta \sim (\sigma_1-\sigma_2)$ relationship does not depend on the form of the state of stress and the loading history.

Equation (13.10) corresponds to a family of isochronic lines in δ, $\sigma_1-\sigma_2$ coordinates (Figure 2.48), which can be used for converting measurements of δ into differences $\sigma_1-\sigma_2$. The curves in Figure 2.48 were constructed from data of tests for a uniaxial state of stress. One or another curve must be used, depending on the moment at which δ is measured.

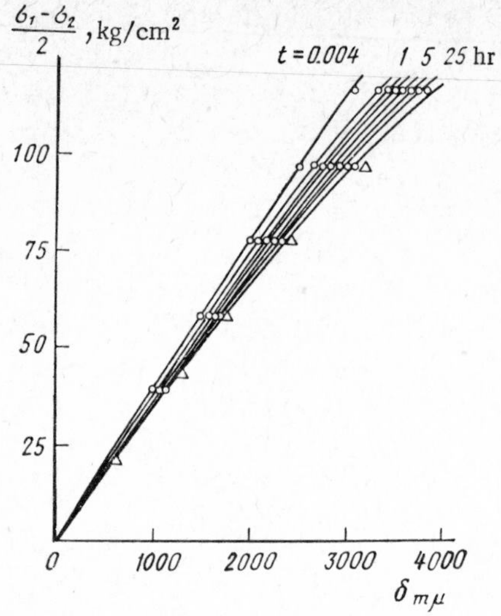

FIGURE 2.48.

The application of this method of determining the difference $\sigma_1-\sigma_2$ in a uniaxial constant state of stress yields accurate results. In the case of a complex state of stress and variable stresses it leads to approximate results.

The stress components can be determined from known values of $\sigma_1-\sigma_2$ and the isoclinic parameters, for example, by applying the method of numerical integration of the equations of equilibrium or of oblique transmission of light.

Comparison of the experimental solution (obtained by the photo-creep method with celluloid models) with theoretical solutions of two plane problems (pure bending of a rod and stress of a plate with circular holes) confirmed the satisfactory accuracy of the experimental solution /46/. Photocreep methods were used to investigate the stress concentrations in models of turbine disks with holes and in attachments of blades to disks in V-slots given in /49/.

§14. POLARIZATION-OPTICAL METHOD OF EXAMINING THE STRESS-STRAIN STATE OF ANISOTROPIC BODIES

Engineering, building construction, and other fields of modern technology make use of machine parts and structural members made from anisotropic materials, especially compositions of polymeric materials (glass-reinforced plastics). Hence it is of practical interest to develop methods for determining the state of stress of anisotropic bodies (photoelastic methods for anisotropic bodies).

First we consider the problem of selecting material for the model, since the derivation of the state of stress of the model from its known optical effects is based on the optical and mechanical properties of the material.

Single crystals and structural anisotropic polymeric material can be used for models in photoelastic methods for anisotropic bodies.

Transparent crystals (with the exception of crystals of the cubic system) exhibit anisotropic elastic properties and moreover are optically anisotropic in the single crystal state. This is an obstacle in their use as modeling material, since the initial birefringence complicates the measurements.

An optical method for solving problems of elasticity theory for orthotropic bodies by means of plates cut from cubic crystals parallel to the edges of the cube and parallel to the diagonal of a plane of the cube was considered by Krasnov /50, 51/. The stress component at any point of a plate could be determined in a particular case of anisotropy (the plate was parallel to the edges of the cube). In general, complex relationships linking the optical and mechanical quantities were obtained and so enabled one to determine the stress only on contours not subjected to external forces.

The use of structural anisotropic materials for modeling in photoelastic methods for anisotropic bodies was treated elsewhere /52–56/. It was shown that the application of structural anisotropic polymeric materials, especially materials based on epoxy resins and glass-fiber reinforced, permits the complete solution of plane photoelastic problems of orthotropic structures, i. e., the stress and strain can be determined at any point of the model.

In order that transparent orthotropic polymeric plates based on epoxy resins and glass fiber should be suitable for photoelastic studies, the following procedures are proposed:

a) The required number of glass-fiber layers is fastened not very tightly to a specially prepared frame, and the foundation prepared in this manner is set on glass placed in a bath with heated epoxy resin and curing agent. The glass fibers are then impregnated by resin, an additional layer of resin is applied, and a second glass is placed on top and weighted. The glass had beforehand been coated with an antiadhesion agent. The assembled form is placed in a thermostat, where the resin is polymerized in a conventional manner. Several layers of fiber are placed in the same direction, in order to obtain a material which displays different properties in different directions.

b) One layer of fibers is fastened not very tightly to a frame, impregnated with epoxy resin, and placed between glasses. Polymerization is then carried out in a thermostat at elevated temperatures or at room temperature, depending on the grade of the resin. The glass platelets thus prepared are glued to one another with a glue of the corresponding epoxy resin, in order to obtain plates of the required thickness.

The glass fibers act as reinforcement and give the composition anisotropic elastic properties. Materials of different anisotropic elastic properties can be obtained, depending on the number of glass-cloth layers. However, since the refractive index of epoxy resin differs from that of glass, the number of glass-fiber layers must be limited in order to obtain sufficiently transparent plates. For example, plates 1.5—2 mm thick provide good transparency and a clear picture of the interference bands, if 9—11 layers of E-40 glass fiber (0.04 mm thick) are selected. The above method of plate preparation can obviously be modified. In particular, epoxy resin can be replaced as matrix by a polyester of another resin.

Further research on materials used in photoelastic methods for anisotropic bodies should be directed toward obtaining completely transparent materials, i. e., materials whose matrix and reinforcement possess identical refractive indices. These materials should also be optically isotropic in the natural state and have sufficient optical activity.

Consider the mechanical and optical properties of plates in which the glass-fiber layers lying in the plane of the plate are oriented along two perpendicular directions alone. In addition, they are distributed symmetrically (by amount and orientation) about the center plane of the plate. Consequently, the plates considered are structurally orthotropic.

Note further that: (a) the composite material under consideration is quasi-homogeneous, and (b) the optical effects appearing in the material are caused only by the artificial birefringence on the polymer matrix while the glass fibers are optically inactive. The study will be conducted in the range of low elastic strain.

Hence the equations of the theory of elasticity of homogeneous orthotropic bodies can be employed to process experimental data while studying the mechanical properties. The investigation of the optical properties is reduced to determining the constants usually used in photoelasticity.

We recall the fundamental stress-strain relations. It is known /57/ that for orthotropic plates the equations of the generalized Hooke's law, linking the mean stress and strain components referred to the principal axes, assume the form

$$\begin{aligned}\varepsilon_1 &= \frac{\sigma_1}{E_1} - \frac{\nu_2}{E_2}\sigma_2,\\ \varepsilon_2 &= -\frac{\nu_1}{E_1}\sigma_1 + \frac{\sigma_2}{E_2},\\ \gamma_{12} &= \frac{1}{G}\tau_{12},\end{aligned} \qquad (14.1)$$

where E_1 and E_2 are the moduli of elasticity in tension and compression along the principal directions of elasticity; ν_1 and ν_2 are the Poisson's ratios and G is the shear modulus.

Relative to an arbitrary rectangular system of coordinates (x, y), rotated through angle θ with respect to the principal axes, the equations of the generalized Hooke's law for orthotropic plates are given by

$$\begin{aligned}\varepsilon_x &= \frac{\sigma_x}{E_1^1} - \frac{\nu_2^1}{E_2^1}\sigma_y + \alpha_1\tau_{xy},\\ \varepsilon_y &= -\frac{\nu_1^1}{E_1^1}\sigma_x + \frac{\sigma_y}{E_2^1} + \alpha_2\tau_{xy},\\ \gamma_{xy} &= \alpha_1\sigma_x + \alpha_2\sigma_y + \frac{1}{G^1}\tau_{xy}.\end{aligned} \qquad (14.2)$$

Here E_1^1, E_2^1, ν_1^1, ν_2^1, α_1, α_2 and G^1 are the elastic constants for the rotated system of coordinates x, y.

Several constants required below are expressed as follows:

$$\begin{aligned}\frac{1}{E_1^1} &= \frac{\cos^4\theta}{E_1} + \left(\frac{1}{G} - \frac{2\nu_1}{E_1}\right)\sin^2\theta\cos^2\theta + \frac{\sin^4\theta}{E_2},\\ \frac{\nu_1^1}{E_1^1} &= \frac{\nu_1}{E_1} - \frac{1}{4}\left(\frac{1+\nu_1}{E_1} + \frac{1+\nu_2}{E_2} - \frac{1}{G}\right)\sin^2 2\theta,\\ \alpha_1 &= \left[\frac{\sin^2\theta}{E_2} - \frac{\cos^2\theta}{E_1} + \frac{1}{2}\left(\frac{1}{G} - \frac{2\nu_1}{E_1}\right)\cos 2\theta\right]\sin 2\theta.\end{aligned} \qquad (14.3)$$

Thus the elastic state of orthotropic plates in any direction is determined in terms of the elastic constants for the principal directions, E_1, E_2, ν_1, ν_2 and G. Only four of these constants are unknown, since for the principal directions of orthotropic plates $E_1\nu_2 = E_2\nu_1$.

It is further known that three tests under uniaxial tension are sufficient for determining elastic constants E_1, E_2, ν_1, ν_2 and G.

The tests comprise two along the principal directions and one at angle θ to the principal direction. Thus, for tension along principal direction I ($\theta = 0°$)

$$\sigma_2 = \tau_{12} = 0, \quad \varepsilon_1 = \frac{\sigma_1}{E_1}, \quad \varepsilon_2 = -\frac{\nu_1}{E_1}\sigma_1, \tag{14.4}$$

for tension along principal direction II ($\theta = 90°$)

$$\sigma_1 = \tau_{12} = 0, \quad \varepsilon_1 = -\frac{\nu_2}{E_2}\sigma_2, \quad \varepsilon_2 = \frac{\sigma_2}{E_2}, \tag{14.5}$$

and for tension at angle θ to the principal direction

$$\sigma_y = \tau_{xy} = 0, \quad \varepsilon_x = \frac{\sigma_x}{E_1^1}, \quad \varepsilon_y = -\frac{\nu_1}{E_1^1}\sigma_x, \qquad \gamma_{xy} = \alpha_1\sigma_x. \tag{14.6}$$

Quantities E_1, ν_1, E_2 and ν_2 are derived from (14.4) and (14.5), if the longitudinal and transverse strains are measured in the tests under uniaxial tension; E_1^1 is derived from (14.6). The shear modulus G is obtained from the known values of E_1, E_2, ν_1 and E_1^1 by means of the first of equations (14.3):

$$\frac{1}{G} = \frac{4}{E_1^1 \sin^2 2\theta} - \left(\frac{\operatorname{ctg}^2\theta - 2\nu_1}{E_1} + \frac{\operatorname{tg}^2\theta}{E_2}\right). \tag{14.7}$$

In particular, when $\theta = 45°$

$$\frac{1}{G} = \frac{4}{E_{45}^1} - \left(\frac{1-2\nu_1}{E_1} + \frac{1}{E_2}\right). \tag{14.8}$$

The values of the elastic constants of several plates are stated below. For a plate 2 mm thick and containing 11 layers of E-40 glass cloth, of which 8 are placed in the same direction (the quantity of glass fibers with respect to resin is about 14% by volume), the elastic constants had the following values:

$$\begin{gathered} E_1 = 11.1\cdot 10^4 \text{ kg/cm}^2,\ E_2 = 4.69\cdot 10^4 \text{ kg/cm}^2, \\ \nu_1 = 0.292,\ \nu_2 = 0.169,\ E_{45} = 5.2\cdot 10^4 \text{ kg/cm}^2,\ G = 1.45\cdot 10^4 \text{ kg/cm}^2. \end{gathered} \tag{14.9}$$

For plates 1.4 mm thick and containing 9 layers of glass cloth, of which 4 layers are placed in the same direction and made from E-0.1 glass cloth and another 2 layers are placed in the same direction and made from E-40 glass cloth (the quantity of glass fibers is about 20% that of the resin), the elastic constants measured on samples cut from the plate at 0, 20, 45, 60 and 90° had the following values:

$$\begin{aligned}&E_1=11.5\cdot 10^4\ \text{kg/cm}^2;\ E_{20}=7.4\cdot 10^4\ \text{kg/cm}^2,\\&E_{45}=4.98\cdot 10^4\ \text{kg/cm}^2,\ E_{60}=5.1\cdot 10^4\ \text{kg/cm}^2,\\&E_2=6.4\cdot 10^4\ \text{kg/cm}^2,\ \nu_1=0.412,\ \nu_{20}=0.480,\ \nu_{45}=0.570,\\&\nu_{60}=0.490,\ \nu_2=0.228,\ G=1.86\cdot 10^4\ \text{kg/cm}^2.\end{aligned} \tag{14.10}$$

For a plate 1.25 mm thick and containing 6 layers of E-25 glass cloth, of which 4 are placed in the same direction (the quantity of glass fibers is about 10% that of the resin), the experimentally derived values of the elastic constants had the following values:

$$\begin{aligned}&E_1=8.43\cdot 10^4\ \text{kg/cm}^2,\ E_{20}=6.62\cdot 10^4\ \text{kg/cm}^2,\\&\nu_1=0.391,\ \nu_{20}=0.503,\ \nu_{45}=0.565,\ \nu_{60}=0.510,\\&\nu_2=0.312,\ G=1.56\cdot 10^4\ \text{kg/cm}^2.\end{aligned} \tag{14.11}$$

It is evident from these data that orthotropic plates with various values of the elastic constants lying within definite limits can be obtained by altering the plate thickness and the number of glass cloth layers. It is readily shown that the elastic constants of the plates vary in accordance with the laws of orthotropic elastic bodies. The modulus of elasticity and Poisson's ratio as a function of angle θ are plotted in Figure 2.49. Solid lines represent computations according to (14.3) for an orthotropic body. The experimentally determined results are shown by points. The experimental points lie sufficiently close to the computed curves.

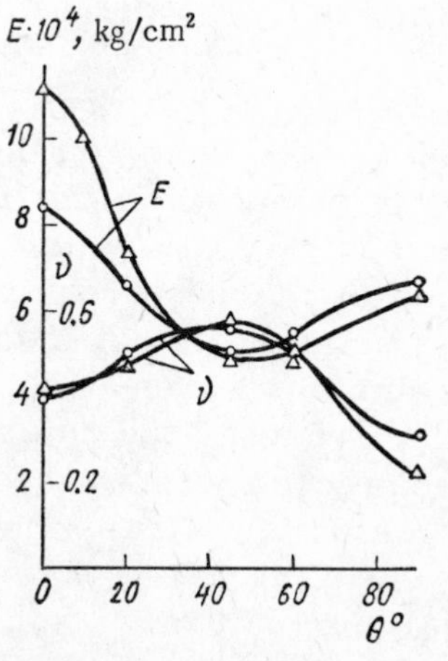

FIGURE 2.49.

Consider now the optical properties of structural anisotropic polymeric plates. The optical path difference formed in the matrix of an optically active polymer and glass fiber appears upon their deformation, primarily due to the effect of birefringence in the matrix. Optical path differences in glass fibers are small and can be neglected.

It is known that the optical properties of materials in photoelasticity are characterized by the values of the optical constants of the stresses and strains. The investigation of the optical properties of structural orthotropic polymeric materials is reduced to studying the optical properties of the polymeric matrix. Therefore, the optical properties of such materials are characterized by the optical constants of stress

$$\sigma_\theta^{1.0} = \frac{\sigma_p - \sigma_q}{m} h \tag{14.12}$$

and of strain

$$\varepsilon_\theta^{1.0} = \frac{\varepsilon_p - \varepsilon_q}{m} h, \tag{14.13}$$

where m is the order of the interference bands, $\sigma_p - \sigma_q$ is the difference between the principal stresses, and $\varepsilon_p - \varepsilon_q$ is the difference between the principal strains.

Quantity $\varepsilon_\theta^{1.0}$ is clearly constant, independent of the direction of the deformation. Indeed, since the optical path difference is determined only by the birefringence of the polymeric matrix, independent of the direction of the deformation, the optical path difference in samples should be the same for equal strain.

The optical constants of stress $\sigma_\theta^{1.0}$ should vary with changing direction of deformation since, depending on the direction, different forces must be applied to the sample in order to bring about the same deformation and consequently the same value of the optical path difference. The values of $\sigma_\theta^{1.0}$ and $\varepsilon_\theta^{1.0}$ can be determined from tests under uniaxial stress on samples cut from plates at different angles with respect to the principal axes, if the longitudinal and transverse strains and the order of the interference bands are determined simultaneously in each test.

We now present some values of optical constants for monochromatic light of wavelength 546.1 mμ in the case of the materials with elastic constants given in (14.10):

$$\sigma_0^{1.0} = 30 \text{ kg/cm}, \quad \sigma_{90}^{1.0} = 18.9 \text{ kg/cm}, \quad \sigma_{45}^{1.0} = 11.7 \text{ kg/cm},$$
$$\varepsilon_0^{1.0} = 0.000376 \text{ cm}, \; \varepsilon_{90}^{1.0} = 0.000372 \text{ cm}, \; \varepsilon_{45}^{1.0} = 0.000378 \text{ cm}. \tag{14.14}$$

For materials with elastic constants given in (14.11),

$$\sigma_0^{1.0} = 23.6 \text{ kg/cm}, \quad \sigma_{90}^{1.0} = 19.4 \text{ kg/cm} \quad \sigma_{20}^{1.0} = 15.9 \text{ kg/cm},$$
$$\varepsilon_0^{1.0} = 0.000380 \text{ cm}, \quad \varepsilon_{90}^{1.0} = 0.000372 \text{ cm}, \quad \varepsilon_{20}^{1.0} = 0.000371 \text{ cm}. \tag{14.15}$$

Evidently the optical constants for deformation are practically independent of the direction of the deformation and are material constants.

Consequently, the interference bands in the structural orthotropic materials are the geometric loci of points at which the values of the difference between the principal strains are the same.

Consider now the equations relating optical effects to mechanical quantities in structural orthotropic plates.

The above-mentioned experimentation has shown that the equation of the theory of piezo-optic effects, relating the dielectric constant to the mechanical quantities, can be expressed in the following form for the structural orthotropic plates under consideration /9/:

$$\varkappa_{ij} = (\varkappa_0 + A)\,\delta_{ij} + A_\varepsilon \varepsilon_{ij}, \tag{14.16}$$

where $\varkappa_0$ is the dielectric constant of the medium in the natural initial state; A is a scalar function of the invariants of the mechanical quantities, not affecting the birefringence; δ_{ij} is a unit tensor; A_ε is a constant within a certain range of strain.

The equations of the electrodynamics of continuous media and considerations similar to those used in §2 of the present chapter yield equations linking the optical path difference to the components of the dielectric constant tensor in the plane of the plate:

$$\delta \cos 2\varphi = \frac{h}{2\sqrt{\varkappa_0}}(\varkappa_{xx} - \varkappa_{yy}),$$
$$\frac{\delta}{2} \sin 2\varphi = \frac{h}{2\sqrt{\varkappa_0}}\varkappa_{xy}, \tag{14.17}$$

where φ is the angle between the x-axis and the principal value of the tensor $\varkappa_{ij}$.

For a plane state of stress, we derive from (14.16) the following relationships between the components of the dielectric constant tensor and the strain:

$$\varkappa_{xx} - \varkappa_{yy} = A_\varepsilon (\varepsilon_{xx} - \varepsilon_{yy}),$$
$$\varkappa_{xy} = A_\varepsilon \varepsilon_{xy}. \quad (14.18)$$

Substitution of these quantities in (14.17) gives a relationship between the optical path difference and the strains, expressible in the form

$$\varepsilon_{xx} - \varepsilon_{yy} = \frac{\varepsilon^{1.0} m}{h} \cos 2\varphi,$$
$$\varepsilon_{xy} = \frac{\varepsilon^{1.0} m}{2h} \sin 2\varphi, \quad (14.19)$$

where $\varepsilon^{1.0}$ is an optical constant of the material for deformation.

The angle of inclination of the principal strain to the x-axis is determined by the relationship

$$\tan 2\psi = \frac{2\varepsilon_{xy}}{\varepsilon_x - \varepsilon_y}. \quad (14.20)$$

Hence by substituting the expressions for $\varepsilon_{xx} - \varepsilon_{yy}$ and ε_{xy} given in (14.19) we obtain

$$\tan 2\psi = \tan 2\varphi,$$

i. e., the principal directions of tensors $\varkappa_{ij}$ and ε_{ij} coincide. Since the directions of plane polarization are determined by the quasi-principal directions of the dielectric constant, the optically measured isocline fully characterizes the direction of the principal strains.

It is thus possible to determine the differences between the normal components of the strain tensor $\varepsilon_{xx} - \varepsilon_{yy}$ and shearing strain tensor γ_{xy} from known values of the order of the interference bands m and the angle of inclination of the principal strains φ at any point of a model constructed from structural orthotropic material.

The difference between the principal strains $\varepsilon_p - \varepsilon_q$ at any point of the model is given by

$$\varepsilon_p - \varepsilon_q = \frac{\varepsilon^{1.0} m}{h}. \quad (14.21)$$

The stresses on the free contours of the model are also readily determined. Equation (14.19) and the equation of the generalized Hooke's law yield relationships between the stresses and optical quantities:

$$\frac{1+\nu_1^1}{E_1^1}\sigma_x - \frac{1+\nu_2^1}{E_2^1}\sigma_y + (\alpha_1 - \alpha_2)\tau_{xy} = \frac{\varepsilon^{1.0}m}{h}\cos 2\varphi,$$
$$\alpha_1\sigma_x + \alpha_2\sigma_y + \frac{1}{G^1}\tau_{xy} = \frac{\varepsilon^{1.0}m}{h}\sin 2\varphi. \tag{14.22}$$

Suppose the x-axis is selected in the direction along which the force acts. Then on the free contours $\sigma_y = \tau_{xy} = 0$ and equation (14.22) reduces to

$$\frac{1+\nu_1^1}{E_1^1}\sigma_x = \frac{\varepsilon^{1.0}m}{h}\cos 2\varphi,$$
$$\alpha_1\sigma_x = \frac{\varepsilon^{1.0}m}{h}\sin 2\varphi. \tag{14.23}$$

Hence

$$\sigma_x = \frac{\varepsilon^{1.0}m}{h\sqrt{\frac{(1+\nu_1^1)^2}{(E_1^1)^2} + \alpha_1^2}}. \tag{14.24}$$

In terms of the elastic constants for the principal directions, as given in (14.3), the latter expression becomes

$$\sigma_x = \frac{\varepsilon^{1.0}m}{h\sqrt{\left(\frac{1+\nu_1}{E_1}\cos^2\theta - \frac{1+\nu_2}{E_2}\sin^2\theta\right)^2 + \frac{1}{4G^2}\sin^2 2\theta}}. \tag{14.25}$$

Here, θ is the angle between the principal direction of elasticity I and the direction of the stress on the free contour.

Numerical computation can be used to determine the individual components of the strain and stress tensors at the interior points of the model, by combining equations (14.19) and (14.22) with the equilibrium equations of the plane theory of elasticity

$$\frac{\partial\sigma_x}{\partial x} + \frac{\partial\tau_{xy}}{\partial y} = 0,$$
$$\frac{\partial\tau_{xy}}{\partial x} + \frac{\partial\sigma_y}{\partial y} = 0, \tag{14.26}$$

and with the equations of the generalized Hooke's law (14.1) and (14.2).

We distinguish two cases: 1) the coordinate axes coincide with the principal directions of the orthotropic plates; 2) the coordinate axes lie at an arbitrary angle to the principal directions.

We shall examine the strain in the first case. By expressing stress in terms of strain by means of Hooke's law (14.1) and substituting it into equilibrium equation (14.26), we obtain

$$\frac{\partial}{\partial x}(\varepsilon_x+\nu_2\varepsilon_y)+\frac{G(1-\nu_1\nu_2)}{E_1}\frac{\partial\gamma_{xy}}{\partial y}=0,$$
$$\frac{\partial}{\partial y}(\varepsilon_y+\nu_1\varepsilon_x)+\frac{G(1-\nu_1\nu_2)}{E_2}\frac{\partial\gamma_{xy}}{\partial x}=0. \tag{14.27}$$

Since the shearing strain γ_{xy} is known at any point of the model, $\varepsilon_x+\nu_2\varepsilon_y$ and $\varepsilon_y+\nu_1\varepsilon_x$ are determined by integrating (14.27) along straight lines parallel to the coordinate axes. For instance, integration of the first of equations (14.27) along a line parallel to the x-axis yields

$$\varepsilon_x+\nu_2\varepsilon_y=(\varepsilon_x+\nu_2\varepsilon_y)_0-\frac{G(1-\nu_1\nu_2)}{E_1}\int_0^k\frac{\partial\gamma_{xy}}{\partial y}\,dx. \tag{14.28}$$

The integral is computed like in the method of differences between tangential stresses /3/. The components of the strain tensor are determined from the known values of $\varepsilon_x+\nu_2\varepsilon_y$ and $\varepsilon_x-\varepsilon_y$. Then, by applying Hooke's law, the components of the stress tensor are determined.

It is also possible to determine the stress along lines which exactly coincide with the principal directions, i. e., without first separating the strains.

The following equation relates stresses to optical quantities for the principal directions and is derived from (14.22):

$$\frac{1+\nu_1}{E_1}\sigma_1-\frac{1+\nu_2}{E_2}\sigma_2=\frac{\varepsilon^{1.0}m}{h}\cos 2\varphi,$$
$$\tau_{12}=\frac{G\varepsilon^{1.0}m}{h}\sin 2\varphi. \tag{14.29}$$

The problem of separating the stresses by applying these equations is solved like the corresponding photoelastic problem for isotropic bodies.

Equations (14.22) are used to separate the stresses along lines which do not coincide with the principal directions. The solution of these equations is

$$\sigma_x = \frac{K(x, y)}{D} - \frac{M}{D}\tau_{xy},$$
$$\sigma_y = \frac{L(x, y)}{D} - \frac{N}{D}\tau_{xy}. \qquad (14.30)$$

where

$$K(x, y) = \frac{\varepsilon^{1.0} m}{h}\left(\alpha_2 \cos 2\varphi + \frac{1+\nu_2^1}{E_2^1}\sin 2\varphi\right),$$

$$L(x, y) = \frac{\varepsilon^{1.0} m}{h}\left(\frac{1+\nu_1^1}{E_1^1}\sin 2\varphi - \alpha_1 \cos 2\varphi\right),$$

$$M = \alpha_2(\alpha_1 - \alpha_2) + \frac{1+\nu_2^1}{E_2^1 G^1},$$

$$N = \frac{1+\nu_1^1}{E_1^1 G^1} - \alpha_1(\alpha_1 - \alpha_2),$$

$$D = \frac{\alpha_2(1+\nu_1^1)}{E_1^1} + \frac{\alpha_1(1+\nu_2^1)}{E_2^1}.$$

Substitution of (14.30) in equilibrium equation (14.26) yields

$$M\frac{\partial \tau_{xy}}{\partial x} - D\frac{\partial \tau_{xy}}{\partial y} = \frac{\partial K(x,y)}{\partial x},$$
$$N\frac{\partial \tau_{xy}}{\partial y} - D\frac{\partial \tau_{xy}}{\partial x} = \frac{\partial L(x, y)}{\partial y}$$

from which we obtain

$$\frac{\partial \tau_{xy}}{\partial x} = \frac{N}{MN - D^2}\frac{\partial K}{\partial x} + \frac{D}{MN - D^2}\frac{\partial L}{\partial y}. \qquad (14.31)$$

Integration of this equation along the x-axis gives

$$\tau_{xy} = (\tau_{xy})_0 + \frac{N}{MN - D^2} K(x, y)\Big|_0^p + \frac{D}{MN - D^2}\int_0^p \frac{\partial L}{\partial y}\,dx. \qquad (14.32)$$

The value of the integral $\int \frac{\partial L}{\partial y}$ is determined approximately, as in the method of differences between tangential stresses /3/. The values of σ_x and σ_y are found after determining τ_{xy} from (14.30).

The above technique for separating stresses and strains involves measuring the order of the interference bands m and the angle of inclination φ of the principal strains at each point of the model.

A procedure for separating stresses has been developed in the photoelastic method for isotropic bodies, using only one picture of the interference bands in the model as starting data /58/.

It has been shown that one picture of the interference bands is sufficient also for separating the stresses in plane isotropic models along the lines forming an angle of 45° with the principal directions.

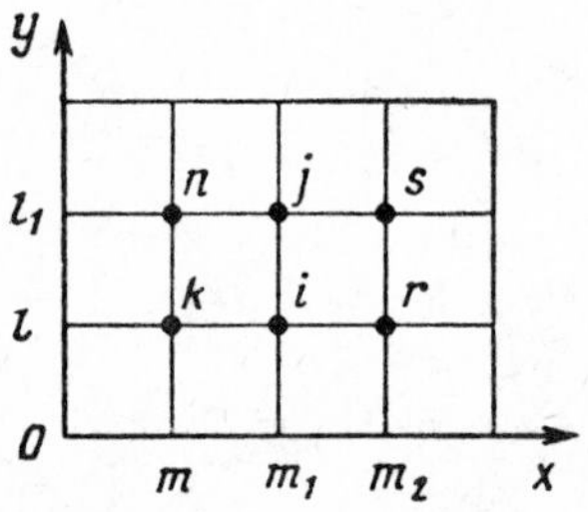

FIGURE 2.50.

Suppose the coordinate axes are directed at an angle of 45° to the principal directions and the region of the model is divided into rectangular elements by means of lines. The equilibrium equation expressed as finite differences for the points k of the separated element (Figure 2.50) assumes the form

$$\frac{\sigma_{x,k}-\sigma_{x,l}}{\Delta x}+\frac{\tau_{xy,k}-\tau_{xy,m}}{\Delta y}=0,$$
$$\frac{\sigma_{y,k}-\sigma_{y,m}}{\Delta y}+\frac{\tau_{xy,k}-\tau_{xy,l}}{\Delta x}=0. \tag{14.33}$$

The stresses at the points lying on the coordinate axes are assumed as known. For simplicity we set $\Delta x=\Delta y$. Then the difference between the stresses at the point k is derived from (14.33):

$$\sigma_{x,k}-\sigma_{y,k}=\sigma_{x,l}-\sigma_{y,m}+\tau_{xy,m}-\tau_{xy,l}. \tag{14.34}$$

When $\theta=45°$, $\frac{1}{E_1^1}=\frac{1}{E_2^1}$, $\frac{\nu_2^1}{E_2^1}=\frac{\nu_1^1}{E_1^1}$, $\alpha_1=\alpha_2$. Hence, we obtain from equation (14.2)

$$\varepsilon_{x,k} - \varepsilon_{y,k} = \frac{1+\nu_1^1}{E_1^1}(\sigma_{x,k} - \sigma_{y,k}). \tag{14.35}$$

Thus the difference between the normal strains $\varepsilon_{x,k} - \varepsilon_{y,k}$ at the point k is known. In addition, the differences between the principal strains at this point $(\varepsilon_p - \varepsilon_q)_k$ are determined by means of equation (14.21). Consequently, the angle of inclination of the principal strains is given by

$$\cos 2\varphi_k = \frac{\varepsilon_{x,k} - \varepsilon_{y,k}}{(\varepsilon_p - \varepsilon_q)_k}, \tag{14.36}$$

and subsequently the shearing strain is given by

$$\gamma_{xy,k} = \frac{m\varepsilon^{1.0}}{h} \sin 2\varphi_k. \tag{14.37}$$

Substitution of $\gamma_{xy,k}$ from (14.2) into (14.37) yields

$$\alpha(\sigma_{x,k} + \sigma_{y,k}) + \frac{1}{G^1}\tau_{xy,k} = \gamma_{xy,k}. \tag{14.38}$$

Moreover, the following equation can be derived from (14.33):

$$\sigma_{x,k} + \sigma_{y,k} + 2\tau_{xy,k} = \sigma_{x,l} + \sigma_{y,m} + \tau_{xy,m} + \tau_{xy,l} \tag{14.39}$$

The right-hand sides of equations (14.38) and (14.39) are known. Therefore

$$\sigma_{x,k} + \sigma_{y,k} = \frac{2G^1\gamma_{xy,k} - A}{2G^1\alpha - 1}, \tag{14.40}$$

$$\tau_{xy,k} = \frac{(\gamma_{xy,k} - \alpha A)\,G^1}{1 - 2G^1\alpha}, \tag{14.41}$$

where $A = \sigma_{x,l} + \sigma_{y,m} + \tau_{xy,m} + \tau_{xy,l}$.

Equations (14.40), (14.41) and (14.34) suffice for determining the components of the stress tensor at the point k. In addition, the stresses at the points n, i, j, etc. of the whole field are determined similarly. In conclusion, we note again that the method can be applied if the grid lines are inclined at 45° to the principal directions, since only then is equation (14.35) (required for deriving the solution) valid.

We now consider the application of the photoelastic method for anisotropic bodies to the investigation of the state of stress in some plane orthotropic bodies.

a) Tensile stress in a plate with a circular hole. Plates with circular holes at their center, prepared from structural orthotropic material, had the following constants: $E_1 = 8.43 \cdot 10^4$ kg/cm^2, $E_2 = 6.7 \cdot 10^4$ kg/cm^2, $\nu_1 = 0.391$, $\nu_2 = 0.312$, $G_1 = 1.56 \cdot 10^4$ kg/cm^2.

The plates possessed the following dimensions: width $l = 40$ mm, thickness 1.28 mm, hole diameter 10 mm.

The picture of the interference bands in a model under tension along the principal direction I with a force $P = 130$ kg is shown in Figure 2.51. The stresses on the edge of the hole were determined by means of formula (14.25). The experimental and theoretical /57/ stresses along the edge of the hole are listed in Table 2.4 (angle θ is taken from the direction perpendicular to that of the stress). Stress separation along the central horizontal cross-section by the method of the difference between tangential stresses was performed in the same case by employing equation (14.29). The results are given in Table 2.5.

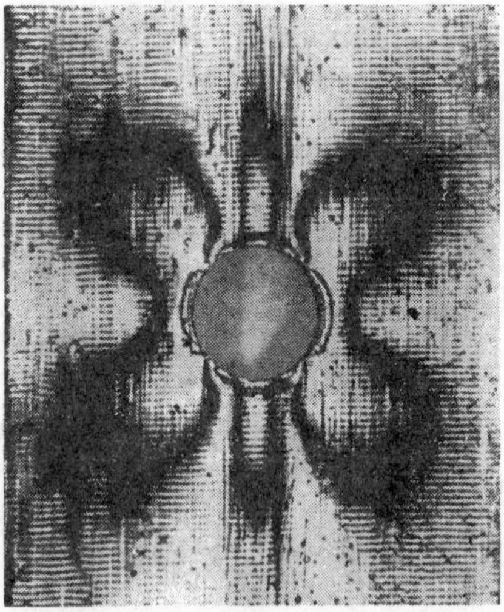

FIGURE 2.51.

Similar computations were carried out for plates with circular holes extended at 90° to the principal direction I. The plates had the same dimensions as those treated above and were prepared from the same material. The interference bands in the model for $P = 120$ kg is shown in Figure 2.52. The experimental and theoretical values of the stress along the edge are given in Table 2.6. Good agreement is seen to exist between experimental and theoretical values in both cases.

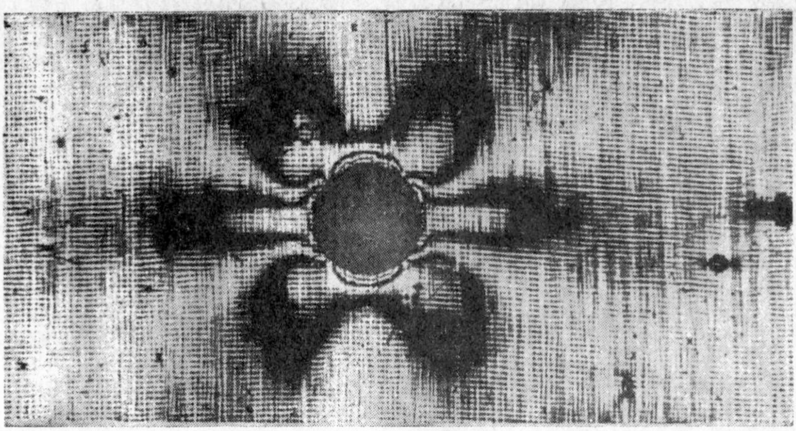

FIGURE 2.52.

TABLE 2.4

$\theta°$	0	10	20	30	40	50	60	70	80	90
$\frac{\sigma_\theta^T}{\sigma_{av}}$	3.62	3.22	2.40	1.61	0.99	0.486	0.0392	−0.384	−0.721	−0.890
$\frac{\sigma_\theta^E}{\sigma_{av}}$	3.56	3.10	2.27	1.60	0.986	0.434	0.0388	−0.426	−0.751	−0.913

TABLE 2.5

$\frac{x}{l}$	m_{fund}	m_{second}	$\varphi°\ \frac{\text{upper}}{\text{lower}}$	$\tau_{xy}\ \frac{\text{upper}}{\text{lower}}$	σ_x, kg/cm²	σ_y, kg/cm²
0	5	4.5	∓11.0	∓75.9	0	914.5
0.067	3.05	2.8	∓5.0	∓21.9	48.9	617.2
0.134	2.40	2.2	∓0.75	∓2.6	61.1	513.3
0.200	2.00	1.85	∓1.50	∓4.35	60.2	439.3
0.270	1.80	1.70	∓2.50	∓6.70	54.7	395.7
0.335	1.70	1.60	∓3.50	∓8.80	47.0	368.1
0.400	1.64	1.52	∓4.00	∓9.50	37.8	345.9
0.470	1.56	1.45	∓3.75	∓8.50	28.8	320.3
0.536	1.52	1.42	∓3.50	∓7.70	20.7	303.2
0.600	1.50	1.40	∓2.75	∓6.00	13.9	291.2
0.670	1.48	1.39	∓2.00	∓4.36	8.7	281.2
0.737	1.47	1.38	∓1.50	∓3.25	4.8	274.6
0.800	1.46	1.36	∓0.75	∓1.60	2.5	270.0
0.870	1.44	1.34	∓0.50	∓1.05	1.15	264.8
0.940	1.42	1.32	∓0.20	∓0.42	0.42	260.2
1.00	1.40	1.30	0	0	0.21	256.2

TABLE 2.6

$\theta°$	0	10	20	30	40	50	60	70	80	90
$\frac{\sigma_\theta^T}{\sigma_{av}}$	3.33	2.97	2.42	1.75	1.15	0.64	0.137	−0.392	−0.892	−1.12
$\frac{\sigma_\theta^E}{\sigma_{av}}$	3.28	2.96	2.25	1.60	1.06	0.65	0.180	−0.311	−0.873	−1.21

b) Tensile stress in a plate with semicircular notches. The plates were prepared from orthotropic material, the elastic constants of which had the following values: $E_1 = 9.37 \cdot 10^4$ kg/cm^2, $E_2 = 5.8 \cdot 10^4$ kg/cm^2, $\nu_1 = 0.440$, $\nu_2 = 0.274$, $G = 1.83 \cdot 10^4$ kg/cm^2. The geometrical dimensions of the plates were as follows: width $l = 40$ mm, notch radius 10 mm, thickness 1.9 mm. We shall examine tension of the plate at 45° to the principal directions. A picture of the interference bands of the model for $P = 100$ kg is given in Figure 2.53. Stress separation along the central horizontal cross-section was carried out by the above method for separating stresses along lines which do not coincide with the principal directions. The initial data for integration, the computed orders, and stresses σ_x, σ_y, τ_{xy} along the cross-section are presented in Table 2.7.

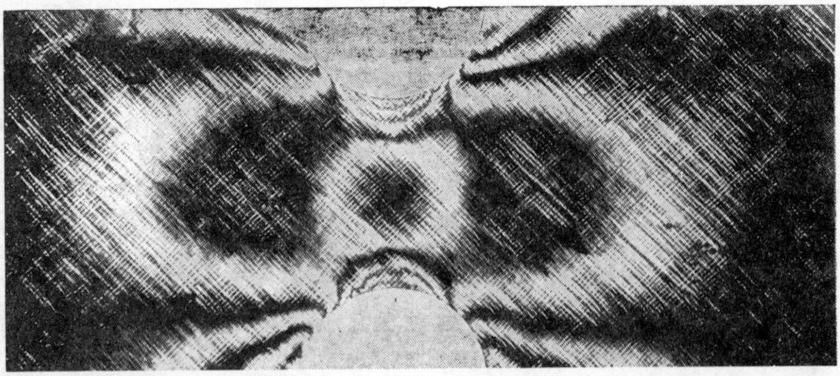

FIGURE 2.53.

TABLE 2.7

x/l	$\varphi^{\circ}_{\text{fund}}$	$\varphi^{\circ B}_{\text{second}}$	$\varphi^{\circ H}_{\text{second}}$	m_{fund}	m^{B}_{second}	m^{H}_{second}	$\tau_{xy'}$, kg/cm^2	$\sigma_{y'}$, kg/cm^2	$\sigma_{x'}$, kg/cm^2
0	3.50	5.00	2.75	5.90	5.80	5.85	0	427.2	0
0.1	2.50	4.00	2.00	5.00	4.85	4.85	−10.7	371.8	12.0
0.2	1.50	3.00	1.25	4.10	4.10	4.20	−18.0	314.3	18.6
0.3	1.00	2.00	0.65	3.50	3.50	3.55	−19.3	274.3	21.7
0.4	0.50	1.50	0	3.05	3.00	3.00	−21.0	246.2	26.0
0.5	0	0.9	−0.50	2.78	2.76	2.75	−22.5	230.0	30.1
0.6	−0.50	0.35	−0.75	2.50	2.55	2.50	−24.0	214.0	33.5
0.7	−0.75	0	−0.75	2.30	2.35	2.36	−24.3	201.8	35.7
0.8	−0.75	−0.25	−0.50	2.17	2.24	2.28	−23.0	193.2	36.4
0.9	−0.50	−0.50	−0.50	2.07	2.15	2.15	−21.2	186.0	36.9
1.0	0	0	0	2.00	2.10	2.10	−19.0	180.5	36.0

c) Tensile stress in a plate with three circular holes. The plates were prepared from material possessing the following mechanical and optical constants: $E_1 = 6.3 \cdot 10^4$ kg/cm^2, $E_2 = 5.0 \cdot 10^4$ kg/cm^2, $\nu_1 = 0.418$, $\nu_2 = 0.334$, $G = 1.42 \cdot 10^4$ kg/cm^2. The optical constant for deformation was $\varepsilon^{1.0} = 0.000793$ cm. The dimensions of the plate were as follows: width 100 mm, thickness 2 mm, distance between the hole centers $a = 25$ mm. The stresses and strains in the plate were determined for various ratios between the hole diameter d and distance between hole centers: $\lambda = d/a = 0.3$, 0.4, 0.49, 0.6, 0.712, 0.8. Figure 2.54 shows the interference bands in the model when $\lambda = 0.4$ (a) and $\lambda = 0.8$ (b).

The stresses on the hole edges were determined from the picture of the interference bands with the aid of formula (14.25) and the coefficient of stress concentration $k = \sigma_{\theta}/\sigma_{\text{av}}$. The variation in the latter quantity as a function of λ is shown in Figure 2.55. When $\lambda \leqslant 0.35$, the concentration coefficients are practically identical on all the hole edges; the values of the concentration coefficients in this case are equal to those for a plate with one hole. When $\lambda > 0.35$, the concentration coefficients increase, their largest value being attained on the edge of the innermost hole.

Strain separation along the central horizontal cross-section by integrating numerically equation (14.29). The stresses were deduced from the strains by means of Hooke's law. The results for $\lambda = 0.8$ are shown in Figure 2.56.

The stresses were also determined from the data of only one picture of bands for the same plates. Consider region OAC bounded by coordinate axes x', y', lying at 45° to the principal directions, and the contours of the model (Figure 2.57). We shall determine

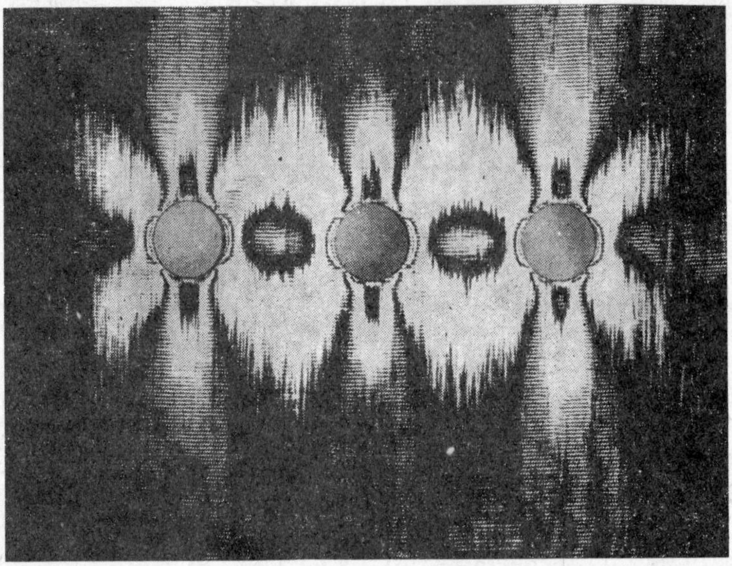

FIGURE 2.54a.

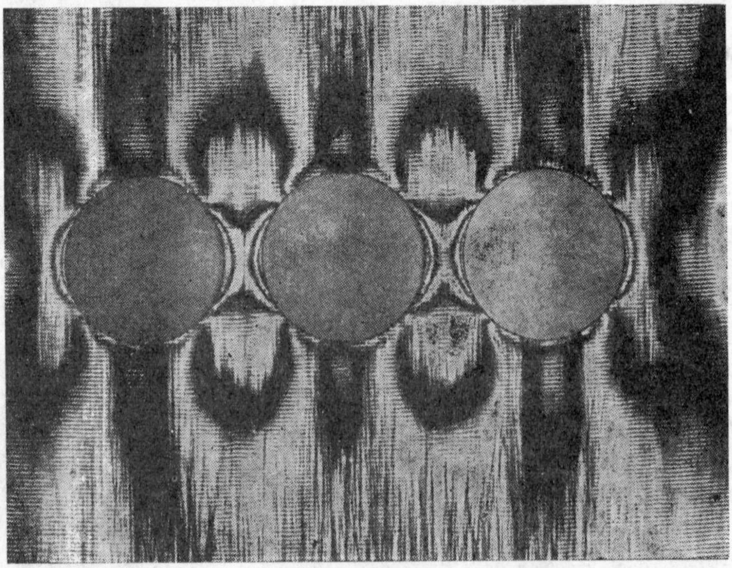

FIGURE 2.54b.

the stresses at the nodes formed by the lines of intersection parallel to the coordinate axes. The integration commences on the free contours, where the stress $\sigma_x^1 = \sigma_y^1 = -\tau_{xy}^1$ is determined from the orders of the interference bands. The values of these stresses are indicated on Figure 2.57. Next, the stresses at the nodes close to the contour are determined. As an illustration, we shall determine the stress at node k.

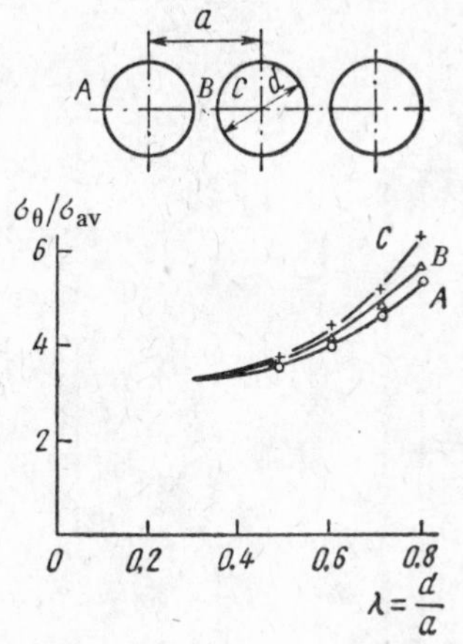

FIGURE 2.55.

The equilibrium equation yields

$$\sigma'_{x,k} - \sigma'_{y,k} = \sigma'_{x,c} - \sigma'_{y',p} + \tau'_{xy,p} - \tau'_{xy,c} = 8.7\ \text{kg/cm}^2.$$

According to the generalized Hooke's law

$$\varepsilon'_{x,k} - \varepsilon'_{y,k} = \frac{1+\nu_1^1}{E_1^1}(\sigma^1_{x,k} - \sigma^1_{y,k}) = 0.000306.$$

The difference between the principal strains at node k is determined from the known order of the interference bands $m = 1.85$:

$$\varepsilon_p - \varepsilon_q = \frac{m\varepsilon^{1.0}}{h} = 0.000363.$$

Hence $\cos 2\varphi_k = 0.0848$, $\sin 2\varphi_k = 0.9964$.

The known value of angle φ enables the shearing strain to be derived:

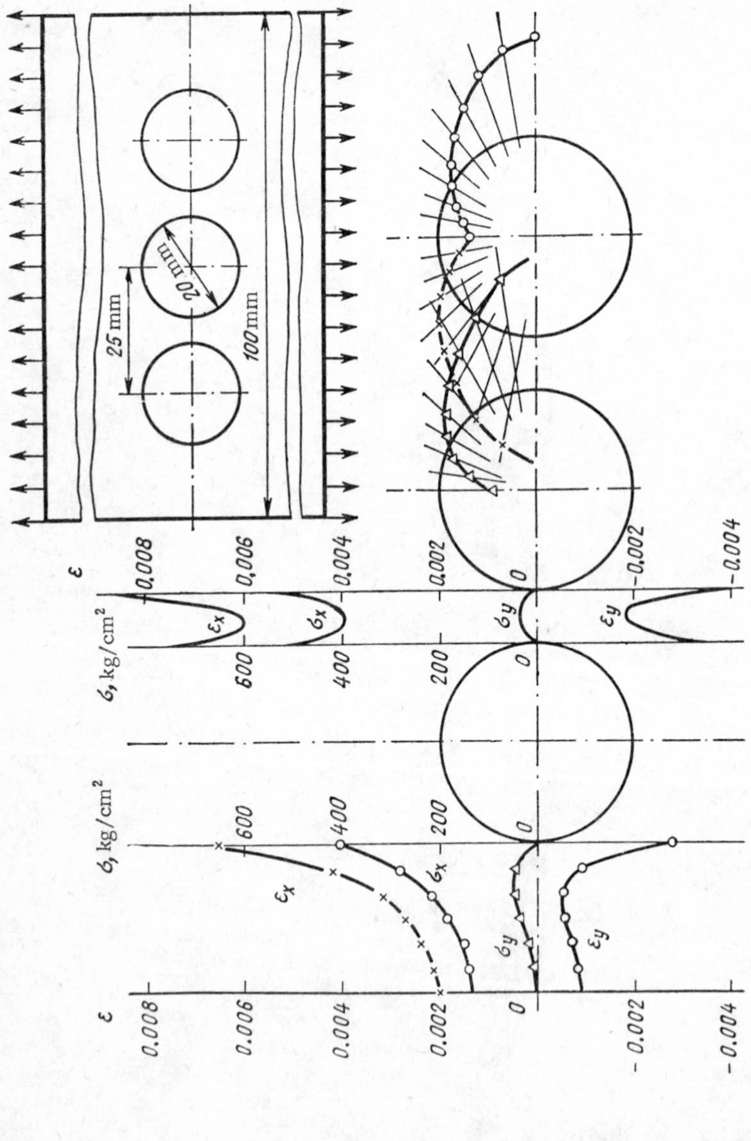
25 mm
20 mm
100 mm
ε
σ, kg/cm²
0.008
0.006
0.004
0.002
0
-0.002
-0.004
600
400
200
0
εx
σx
σy
εy

FIGURE 2.56.

$$\gamma'_{xy,\,k} = -\frac{m\varepsilon^{1.0}}{h}\sin 2\varphi_k = -0.00362.$$

Substitution for $\gamma'_{xy,\,k}$ in the equation of the generalized Hooke's law yields $0.02065\,(\sigma'_{x,\,k}+\sigma'_{y,k}) + 0.493\,\tau'_{xy,\,k} = -0.00362\cdot 10^4$ kg/cm². In addition, it follows from Hooke's law that

$$\sigma'_{x,k}+\sigma'_{y,k}+2\tau'_{xy,\,k}=0.$$

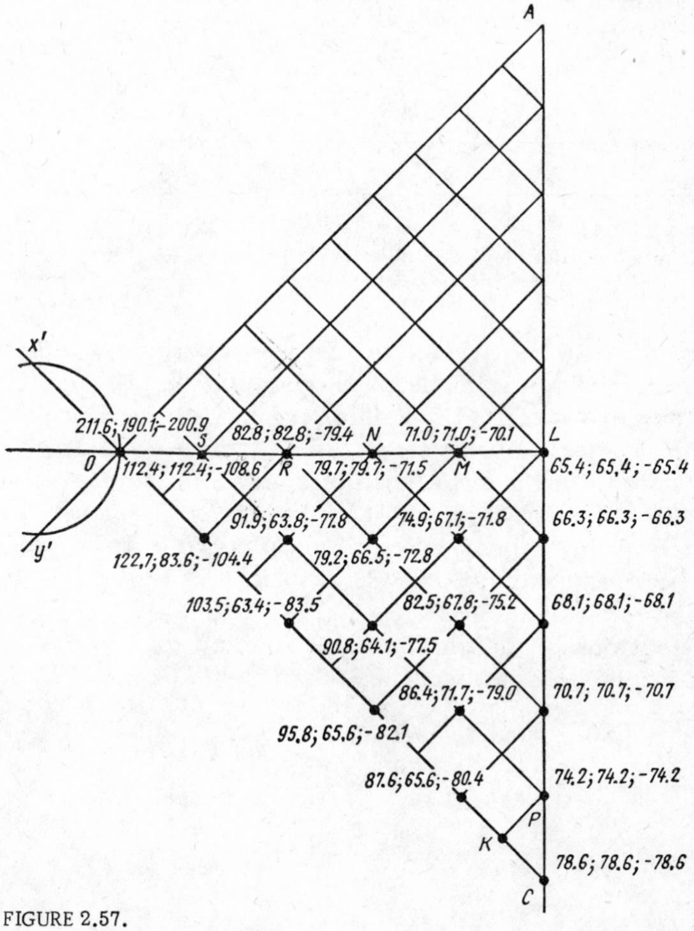

FIGURE 2.57.

The value $\tau'_{xy,k} = -80$ kg/cm² and the sum $\sigma'_{x,k}+\sigma'_{y,k} = 160.1$ kg/cm² were derived from the last two equations. Adding the difference of the normal stresses, we obtain

$$\sigma'_{x,k} = 84.4 \text{ kg/cm}^2; \ \sigma'_{y,k} = 75.7 \text{ kg/cm}^2.$$

The stresses at the other points are determined similarly.

The stresses σ'_x, σ'_y and τ'_{xy} at several nodes are indicated in Figure 2.57. Hence the stresses σ_x and σ_y were determined at the points L, M, N, R, S, O on the central axis of the model on planes perpendicular to the principal directions; use was made of known formulas for transforming the components of the stress tensor for a rotation of the coordinate axes. The values of stress σ_x at the points mentioned are tabulated in Table 2.8. The stresses derived as a result of strain separation are also cited.

TABLE 2.8

Point	L	M	N	R	S	O
σ_x, kg/cm^2 (by bands)	130.9	141.1	145.2	162.8	221.0	401.8
σ_x, kg/cm^2 (by strains)	131.0	142.0	168	202	252	403

Some divergence in the stress values was obtained at some points, due to inaccuracies in the methods applied. Errors in determining the angles of inclination of the principal directions may occur during strain separation. Moreover, errors may arise in the determination of the order of the bands in both cases. Nonetheless, it is evident from the computations cited that the method of determining stresses from one picture of the interference bands can be applied satisfactorily to stress investigations in orthotropic plates.

Other applications of the photoelastic method for anisotropic bodies are described elsewhere /55, 56/.

Chapter III

DETERMINATION OF LOCAL STRENGTH

The solution of technical problems frequently involves the determination of local strength, i. e., local fields of viscoelasto-plastic stresses and strains. The theoretical formulation and solution of such problems presents formidable mathematical difficulties which often cannot be overcome. Consequently, experimental methods are used widely in the qualitative and quantitative characterization of local strength. Some of these methods will be examined in this chapter.

§1. FEATURES OF MECHANICAL TESTS

By the term local strength we mean the strength at places of concentrated load application or at places of rapid variation in the shape of the surface of the structural member. Here, we examine the strength under the action of tangential forces (shear, warping, slip, cleaving), the effective concentration coefficients in the presence of several concentrators, and methods for determining hardness.

Several features of local stress are noteworthy. Under applied load, local stresses decrease very rapidly with distance from the loaded surface. Stress concentration at the edges of holes, notches and section corners not only bring about stress redistribution over the cross sections and the appearance of stress peaks in the immediate neighborhood of the concentrators, but also create (two- and three-dimensional) complex states of stress which can substantially affect the strength of the material at the place of stress concentration. The Saint-Venant principle cannot be applied to computing local stresses. Consequently, other hypotheses are required about the features of stress and strain distribution.

Structural polymers include reinforced plastics, organic glass, vinyl plastic, foam plastic, cellular plastics and various forms of fibrous plastics, i. e., both isotropic and anisotropic materials. This circumstance must be taken into consideration in mechanical tests.

Glass-fiber-reinforced plastics have attained very widespread use as structural materials, owing to their high specific strength. There are two approaches in the design of such materials: either relating the mechanical features of the reinforced material to the characteristics of its reinforcing material and matrix, or considering glass-fiber-reinforced plastics as a quasi-uniform and quasi-homogeneous continuous orthotropic medium and determining the material characteristics as a whole from test samples.

Henceforth the latter approach will be used for reinforced materials. Its advantage is that the methods of the theory of elasticity of anisotropic bodies can be applied in conjunction to compute the state of stress, and that with this approach allowance can be made for the effects of technological processing of the material on its mechanical properties.

The properties of the material under consideration depend on the temperature, loading rate, and time of loading. The strength of reinforced plates in particular depends essentially on the deformation rate, which enters the rheological relationships describing the sample behavior under load. Since the present chapter deals with short-duration tests, the calibration rates must be selected well. While some investigators regard short-term strength as pertaining to loading times of less than 1 minute /1, 2/, others assume that the sample must be subjected to breaking load for 10^{-4} hr.

The term short-duration strength was applied to strength established as a result of machine tests at rates equal or close to standard /13/. It is advisable that the selected strain rate should exclude the influence of Mackian-elastic strain on the elastic characteristics of the reinforced materials. Rates were established for a series of materials in which only elastic strain occurs /4/. Hence it should be borne in mind that under the action of standard loading rates different test procedures result in deformation rates which are not in agreement with one another.

In order to obtain comparable results, one must standardize the conditions under which the sample is stored before the test and also the specifications of the ambient medium during the test. The sample is stored so that it may attain physical equilibrium with the ambient medium and so that the effects of the previous history of the material can be eliminated.

The ASTMD 618-61 standards govern the storage of plastic test samples and contain six typical conditions for sample preparation before testing as dependent on the temperature and humidity conditions during the tests. In abbreviated form, these conditions are written in the form time/temperature/relative humidity. For example, in case *A*, which is typical for many tests, the conditions assume the following form: 40/23/50 for samples with $h \leqslant 7$ mm, 88/23/50 for samples with $h > 7$ mm. In other words, samples with thickness up to 7 mm are stored for 40 hours at 23°C and 50% relative humidity, and samples with thickness exceeding 7 mm are stored for 88 hours under the same conditions.

The samples are stored in a thermostat with forced circulation of air. Similar conditions have been worked out for samples at elevated temperatures and humidities and in water.

Generally speaking, the tests must be performed under standard conditions ($T = 23$°C, $\varphi = 50$%) immediately after aging of the sample.

If the tests are carried out at a higher or lower temperature, the samples are left alone for half an hour and then brought to the test conditions, after which they are stored under these conditions not longer than five hours and not less than the time required for attaining a state of temperature equilibrium /3/.

According to Goryainova /5/, glass-fiber Textolite is stored in two ways: 1) the sample is maintained for 5 days in a desiccator at a relative air humidity of 55 ± 2% and a temperature of 20 ± 2°C; 2) the sample is dried at 50 ± 3°C for 2 days and then cooled to room temperature in a desiccator containing calcium chloride or silica gel. These methods of sample storage are recommended when investigating the temperature dependence of the mechanical properties of glass-fiber Textolite.

At elevated or lower temperatures the samples must be kept in the test chamber for not less than 60 minutes. It is inadvisable to store the samples in the chamber longer than 90 minutes, since changes may occur in the properties of glass-fiber Textolite.

§2. DETERMINATION OF SHEAR STRENGTH

Low shear strength and rigidity are characteristic for many structural polymers, in particular reinforced materials. In these materials, the tensile elasticity modulus along the fibers and the shear modulus can differ by one order of magnitude.

These features were taken into account in strength calculations conducted elsewhere /6, 7/. The characteristic resistance of the material to shear stresses plays an important role in a series of strength criteria applied to structural polymers. A method for testing shear in glass-fiber-reinforced plastics and selecting the actual material for determining ultimate shear strength was treated by Smirnova et al. /8/.

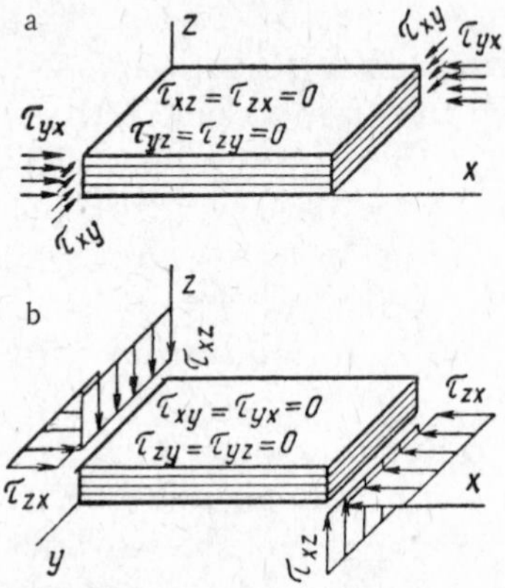

FIGURE 3.1.

As regards glass-fiber-reinforced plastics, two varieties of shear deformations must be distinguished depending on the orientation of the external shearing force with respect to the axis of elastic symmetry of the material:

1. Shear in the plane of the reinforcing material (Figure 3.1a) causing shear stresses τ_{xy} and τ_{yx} in mutually perpendicular planes normal to the shear plane. This is shear in the plane of the sheets.

2. Shear in planes perpendicular to the plane of the reinforcing material (Figure 3.1b). This shear causes shear stresses τ_{xz} and τ_{yz} in mutually perpendicular planes, one of which is parallel and the other perpendicular to the plane of the reinforcing material. This is slip or interlayer shear.

The following three aspects are examined when estimating strength in shear: 1) shear in the plane of the sheet, 2) shear perpendicular to the plane of the sheet, and 3) shear in the layers of glass-fiber-reinforced plastics (interlayer shear or slip). The last two points have the same deformation pattern by virtue of the law of conjugate shear stresses (see Figure 3.1b).

It was observed in a number of investigations that shear forces applied perpendicular to the plane of the reinforcing layers (slip) give rise to bending deformations in the sample, in addition to pure shear deformations. Hence the existing standard method for testing plastics of organic origin in the form of square 10 × 10 mm samples is in need of refinement when used to study the strength of glass-fiber-reinforced plastics subjected to shear. Substantial shortcomings also exist in other methods of testing for shear in line with Soviet and non-Soviet standards.

Consider the shear in the plane of the reinforcing fibers. Two test methods are suitable, namely for torsion of tubular samples or twisting of plane samples in the form of square plates subjected to pure shear (Figure 3.2). In order to ensure pure shear conditions, the sample is tested in a special hinged four-link mechanism which transforms the tensile stress into shear by inducing tension along one of the diagonals. In these tests the material of the central part of the sample is subjected to conditions approaching pure shear.

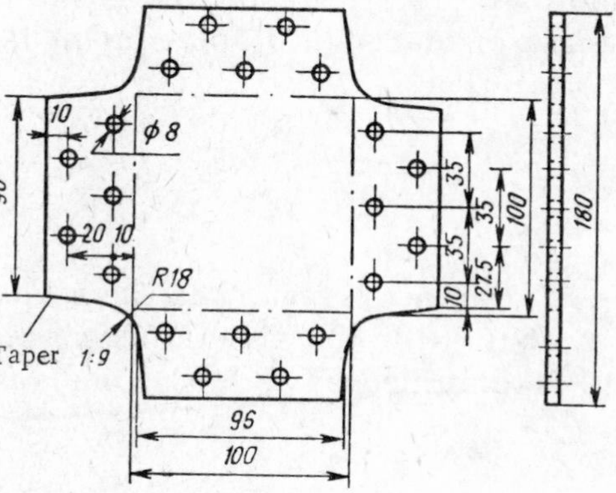

FIGURE 3.2.

During the loading process the strains at the center are measured along the tensioned and compressed diagonals on a gage length at a reasonable distance from the contact with the four-link mechanism. The changes in strain along the plate diagonals are readily measured by Type TA-2 Aistov strain gages.

The shear angle γ is computed from the measured strain by means of the formula

$$\gamma = \frac{\Delta l_1 - \Delta l_2}{l}, \qquad (2.1)$$

where Δl_1 and Δl_2 are the change in the gage length measured on the tensioned and compressed diagonals of the sample, respectively; l is the gage length. The shear modulus for specific orientations of the glass fibers is then computed by Hooke's law:

$$G = \frac{\tau}{\gamma} = \frac{Pl}{a\delta(\Delta l_1 - \Delta l_2)}, \tag{2.2}$$

where a is the length of the sample side, δ its thickness, and P the force acting on the four-link mechanism. The shear stress on the sample edge can be computed from the following equation with an accuracy sufficient for practical purposes:

$$\tau = \frac{P}{a\delta} \frac{\sqrt{2}}{2}. \tag{2.3}$$

In torsion tests on tubular samples the angle of torsion is measured on some gage length l with the aid of a Martens mirror strain gage. For known angle of torsion and geometrical dimensions of the sample, the angle of material displacement is computed by the expression

$$\gamma = \varphi \frac{r_{\mathrm{m}}}{l}, \tag{2.4}$$

where φ is the angle of displacement; r_{m} is the mean radius of the sample. The shear modulus for the specified orientation of the reinforcing fibers is determined by

$$G = \frac{2lM\varphi}{\pi r_{\mathrm{m}}^4}, \tag{2.5}$$

where M is the external torque. The shear stress is

$$\tau = \frac{M}{2\pi r_{\mathrm{m}}^2 \delta}. \tag{2.6}$$

Shearing tests with a four-link mechanism can be conducted with any apparatus which ensures reasonable accuracy in the load applied. Tests on tubular samples are conducted on special torsion apparatus. Measurement data pertaining to three-stage loading of the sample allow one to determine the shear modulus G between 0.05 and 0.20 of the breaking load. If the sample displays creep, it must be allowed to remain at rest for 50 minutes after each test.

In order to determine the ultimate shear strength in the plane of a plate τ_{B}, the sample is loaded monotonically until failure, so that the clamps of the testing apparatus move at 20 mm/min. The shear diagrams of glass-fiber-reinforced plastics of different grades are shown in Figure 3.3 /8/. The features of the failure of plane samples in shear are shown in Figure 3.4 /8/.

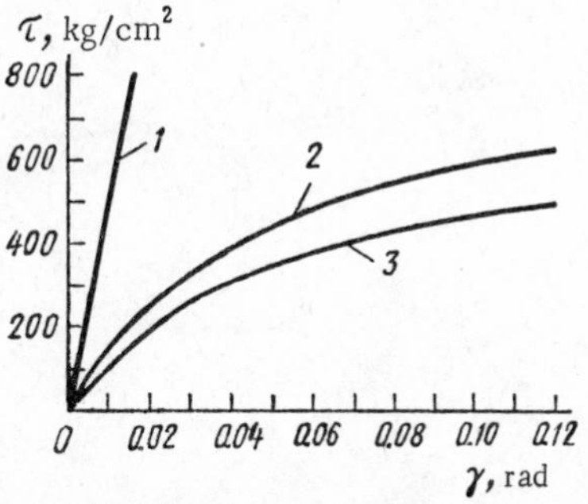

FIGURE 3.3. 1 — STER-1-30; 2 — ASTT (b)-S_2-V cloth and PN-3 resin; 3 — TZhS-0.85 cloth and PN-3 resin.

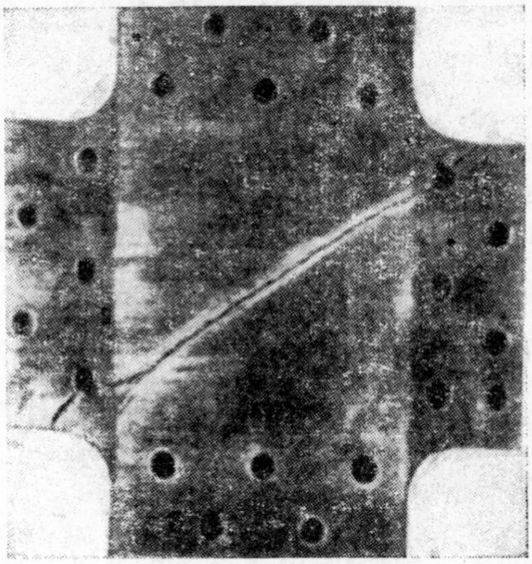

FIGURE 3.4.

It is evident from Figure 3.3 that the shear modulus G of glass-fiber-reinforced plastics is not constant but decreases slightly with increasing shear stress. The ultimate strength τ_{ult} of the material is determined by (2.3) or (2.6) depending on the tests employed.

The orientation of the external forces relative to the axes of elastic symmetry of the material has a considerable influence on the rigidity and deformation characteristics of glass-fiber-reinforced plastics in shear. This is evident from Table 3.1, which shows the results of torsion tests of tubular samples and plate-shaped samples tested in pure shear /8/. The samples had been prepared from ASTT (b)-S_2-O cloth and PN-1 polyester resin.

The experimental data show reasonably good agreement between values of the shear modulus determined on tubes and on plane samples with the same orientation of the glass fibers. The values of the ultimate shear strength τ_{ult} for plates are lower than the corresponding values obtained from tests on tubular samples. Figure 3.5 shows curves of the ultimate strength of glass-fiber-reinforced plastics as dependent on the direction of the stress with respect to the warp of glass cloth. The data on tubular samples are illustrated by curve 1 and of plane samples by curve 2.

There is a remarkable increase in the shear strength of glass-fiber-reinforced plastics in all directions differing from the principal one. The shear strength of glass-fiber-reinforced plastics is greatest when the warp of the glass cloth is positioned at 45° to the direction of action of the shear stresses.

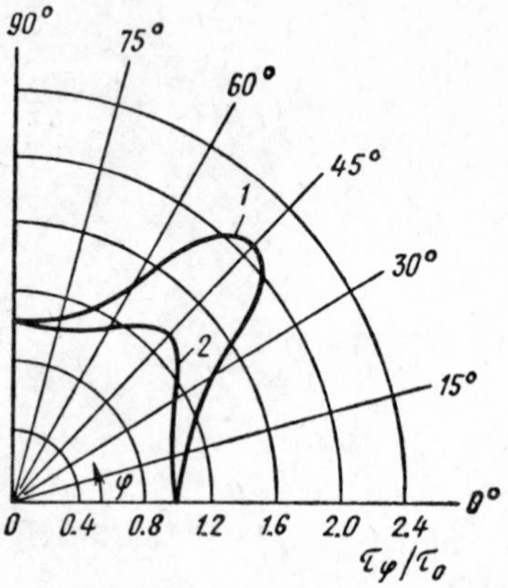

FIGURE 3.5.

TABLE 3.1. Results of testing samples for shear and torsion

Inclination of the warp of the sample to its axis in the direction of the tensioned diagonal, deg	Tubular samples		Plates		
	shear modulus, kg/cm^2	ultimate shear strength, kg/mm^2	shear modulus, kg/cm^2	ultimate shear strength, kg/mm^2	maximum shear angle, deg
0 (45)	$0.30 \cdot 10^5$	5.60	$0.27 \cdot 10^5$	6.8	2.50
30 (15)	$0.46 \cdot 10^5$	7.50	$0.45 \cdot 10^5$	7.6	0.86
45 0*/90	$0.65 \cdot 10^5$	11.5	$0.93 \cdot 10^5$* / $0.58 \cdot 10^5$	9.1* / 5.8	0.55
60 (105)	—	—	$0.45 \cdot 10^5$	7.6	0.86
90 (45)	$0.30 \cdot 10^5$	5.46	$0.27 \cdot 10^5$	6.8	2.50

* The numerator corresponds to the case when the warp of the cloth is directed along the tensioned diagonal; the denominator corresponds to the case when the warp lies at 90° to the tensioned diagonal.

The mechanical properties of some grades of glass-fiber-reinforced plastics obtained by shear tests with hinged four-link mechanisms are given in Table 3.2. The numerator refers to extreme values of shear determined by the tests and the denominator to their mean values.

Consider the shear strength of foam plastics. Such materials, which possess good heat and sound insulation properties in conjunction with low density, are good structural materials. Soviet PS-1 and PS-4 foam plastics are manufactured by pressing on the basis of polystyrene; PKhV-1 foam plastics are manufactured on the basis of polyvinylchloride. PSB foam plastic is manufactured without pressing.

Following Panferov and Kolpakov /9/, hollow tubular samples were tested in torsion to assess their shear strength. The sample dimensions were: external diameter 75 mm, wall thickness 20 mm, height 50–80 mm; the latter were determined by the thickness of foam plastic sheets of different grades. The samples were cut with a special milling cutter, held in the chuck of a drilling machine.

In order to fix a hollow cylindrical sample in the clamps of the tester, steel washers of the same diameter as the sample were glued to the butt ends of the sample by means of an epoxy glue. The strength of the joint where the steel washers were glued to the sample exceeded the shear strength of the sample.

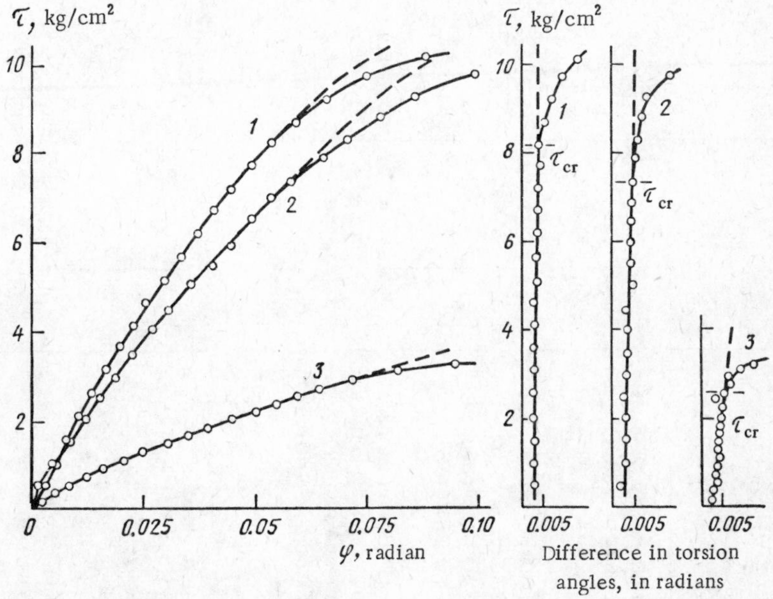

FIGURE 3.6.

The tests corresponded to the working conditions of the material in the capacity of the inner layer of a three-layer structure. The ratio of the height of the sample to its external diameter is

TABLE 3.2

Material	Angle of warp inclination		Sample thickness, mm	Shear strength of the material, kg/cm^2	Shear modulus of the material, kg/cm^2	Maximum shear angle, deg
	to the sample axis	to the tensioned diagonal				
Glass-fiber-reinforced plastics on the basis of PN-3 resin and KhZhK-3 glass cloth			$\frac{6.1-6.6}{9.35}$	$\frac{430-590}{555}$	$\frac{(3.06-3.38)\cdot 10^4}{3.34\cdot 10^4}$	$\frac{0.8-1.30}{1.05}$
			$\frac{3.7-4.0}{3.75}$	$\frac{649-707}{685}$	$\frac{(3.34-3.96)\cdot 10^4}{3.90\cdot 10^4}$	$\frac{1.2-1.50}{1.35}$
Glass-fiber-reinforced plastics on the basis of PN-1 resin and ASTT (b)-S_2-O glass cloth	0	45	$\frac{4.9-5.2}{5.15}$	$\frac{645-700}{675}$	—	—
Glass-fiber-reinforced plastics on the basis of NPS-609-22 resin and ASTT (b)-S_2-O glass cloth	0	45	$\frac{5.3-5.4}{5.35}$	$\frac{769-847}{810}$	—	—
Glass-fiber-reinforced plastics on the basis of PN-3 resin and ASTT (b)-S_2-O glass cloth	0	45	$\frac{5.8-5.9}{5.90}$	$\frac{723-880}{780}$	—	—
Glass-fiber-reinforced plastics on the basis of PN-3 resin and ASTT (b)-S_2-V glass cloth	0	45	$\frac{5.2-5.4}{5.25}$	$\frac{660-795}{725}$	$\frac{(32.60-3.10)\cdot 10^4}{2.90\cdot 10^4}$	$\frac{3.45-3.75}{3.60}$
	90	45	$\frac{5.1-5.5}{5.25}$	$\frac{650-740}{735}$	$\frac{(3.10-3.20)\cdot 10^4}{3.16\cdot 10^4}$	$\frac{3.30-4.35}{3.80}$
Heat-treated glass-fiber-reinforced STER-1-30 plastics on the basis of epoxy-phenol resin and ASTT (b)-S_1 glass cloth	0	45	$\frac{2.54-2.62}{2.57}$	$\frac{1460-1540}{1500}$	$\frac{(9.30-9.96)\cdot 10^4}{9.65\cdot 10^4}$	$\frac{3.25}{3.25}$
Heat-treated glass-fiber-reinforced STER-1-30 plastics on the basis of epoxy-phenol resin and ASTT (b)-S_2 glass cloth	0	45	$\frac{2.75-3.17}{2.96}$	$\frac{1105-1235}{1235}$	$\frac{(8.40-9.60)\cdot 10^4}{9.00\cdot 10^4}$	—
Glass-fiber-reinforced plastics on the basis of PN-3 resin and ZhTS-0.85 braided glass cloth	0	45	$\frac{6.5-6.9}{6.70}$	$\frac{700-770}{740}$	$\frac{(2.00-2.19)\cdot 10^4}{2.19\cdot 10^4}$	$\frac{5.5-6.25}{4.55}$

Glass-fiber-reinforced plastics on the basis of PN-3 resin and ASTT (b)-S_2-V glass cloth	45	45	$\frac{5.4-5.5}{5.45}$	$\frac{838-920}{885}$	$\frac{(5.90-6.05)\cdot 10^4}{6.00\cdot 10^4}$	$\frac{0.50-0.90}{0.70}$
	0	0	$\frac{5.2-5.4}{5.25}$	$\frac{885-1085}{950}$	$\frac{(8.00-8.66)\cdot 10^4}{8.32\cdot 10^4}$	$\frac{0.40-0.45}{0.42}$
	0	90	$\frac{5.2-5.4}{5.25}$	$\frac{555-700}{670}$	$\frac{(6.76-7.30)\cdot 10^4}{7.04\cdot 10^4}$	$\frac{0.30-0.35}{0.32}$
	90	0	$\frac{5.2-5.3}{5.25}$	$\frac{810-940}{870}$	$\frac{(7.64-6.80)\cdot 10^4}{8.22\cdot 10^4}$	$\frac{0.37}{0.37}$
	90	90	$\frac{5.2-5.3}{5.25}$	$\frac{690-690}{690}$	—	—
Heat-treated glass-fiber reinforced STER-1-30 plastics on the basis of epoxyphenol resin and ASTT (b)-S glass cloth	0	0	$\frac{3.75-5.20}{3.75}$	$\frac{1820-1900}{1870}$	$\frac{(1.38-1.43)\cdot 10^5}{1.41\cdot 10^5}$	$\frac{0.43}{0.43}$
	0	90	$\frac{3.75-5.20}{5.20}$	$\frac{1100-1180}{1145}$	$\frac{(1.20-1.41)\cdot 10^5}{1.20\cdot 10^5}$	—
Heat-treated glass-fiber-reinforced STER-1-30 plastics and ASTT (b)-S_2 glass cloth	0	0	$\frac{5.05-5.40}{5.20}$	$\frac{1380-1480}{1420}$	$\frac{(1.45-1.35)\cdot 10^5}{1.35\cdot 10^5}$	—
	0	90	$\frac{5.05-5.40}{5.20}$	—	$\frac{(1.10-1.18)\cdot 10^5}{1.15\cdot 10^5}$	—

Remarks. 1. The extreme values of the shear properties are stated in the numerator and the mean values (after excluding obviously incorrect data) in the denominator.

2. The angle between the direction of the warp of the glass cloth and the two adjacent reinforcing layers is zero.

admissible, because here the force is transmitted uniformly at each point of the cross-section through the glued joint, as opposed to the common method of gluing, when stress concentrations cannot be avoided in transmission of the force to the sample.

Short-time shear tests under torsion were conducted with K-6 machines by means of which a torque up to 10 kg · m can be induced. The sample was fixed with the aid of washers and screws in special collars which had square lugs in the center, the lugs being held by the grips of the machine.

The torsion angle of the annular section was measured by means of gages. The dependence of torsion angle on torque was obtained in the course of the tests. Figure 3.6 shows the strain of three types of foam plastics (PS-1 (1), PKhV-1 (2), PS-4 (3)) under torsion.

The samples of PS-1 and PKhV-1 foam plastics failed like brittle materials along a helical surface. The failure of the PS-4 sample was characterized by necking in the middle zone of the sample where the foam plastic became so plastic that the torque that could be applied dropped rapidly. The shear strength of the foam plastic was characterized by the stress corresponding to the inflection point on the diagrams of the difference in torsion angles. This stress, determining the initial development of appreciable strain, is termed the critical stress τ_{cr}. Another characteristic in shear tests is the ultimate strength τ_{ult}. Values τ_{cr} and τ_{ult} are listed in Table 3.3.

TABLE 3.3. Results of shear tests of control samples

Grade of foam plastic	Bulk weight, kg/m³	Number of samples	Mechanical properties, kg/cm²		$\frac{\tau_{cr,m}}{\tau_{ult,m}}$
			τ_{cr}	τ_{ult}	
PS-1	109	16	$\frac{6.08-8.95}{6.9}$	$\frac{9.8-13.1}{10.95}$	0.631
PS-4	42	15	$\frac{1.95-2.8}{2.15}$	$\frac{2.85-3.2}{2.9}$	0.74
PKhV-1	103	9	$\frac{5-6.95}{6.52}$	$\frac{8.4-9.65}{9.1}$	0.715

Foam and cellular plastics resemble honeycomb plastics in their properties, but display higher heat resistance and strength. Depending on the purpose, glass cloth, asbestos cloth, cotton or synthetic cloth and paper are used in preparing cellular plastics.

Shear tests on cellular plastics are carried out in order to determine the ultimate shear strength τ_{ult} in the direction parallel to the faces on which the cells are glued.

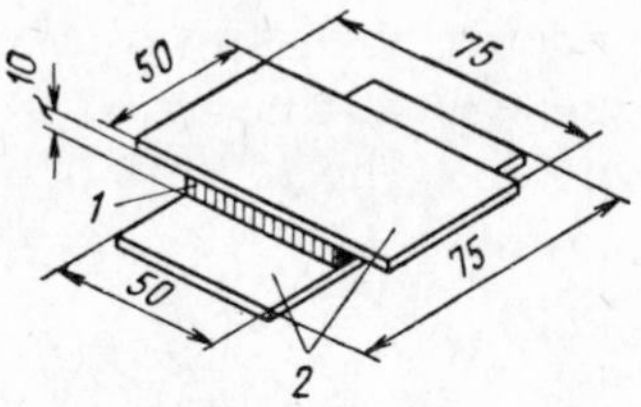

FIGURE 3.7.

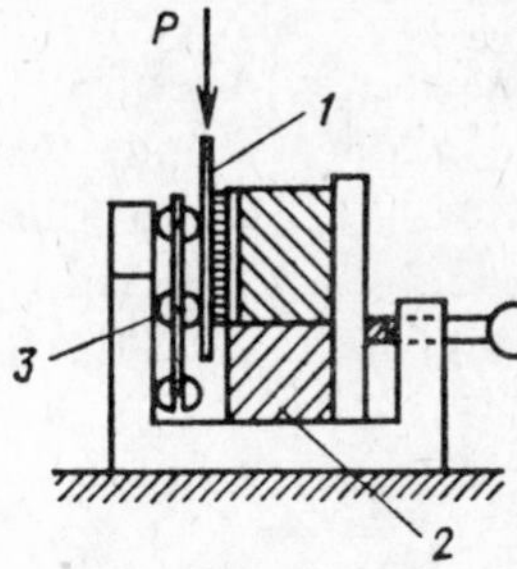

FIGURE 3.8.

TABLE 3.4

Type of cellular plastic	Bulk weight, tons/m^3	Cell dimension, mm	Ultimate compressive strength σ_c, kg/cm^2	Ultimate shear strength τ_{ult}, kg/cm^2
Cellular plastics on the basis of IP-63 paper saturated with MFF resin	0.024	25	1.5	‖ 0.731 ⊥ 0.56
The same	0.03	12	3.2	‖ 0.949 ⊥ 0.69
Cellular plastics on the basis of kraft paper saturated with carbamide resin	0.06	12	5.89	‖ 8.07 ⊥ 4.08
The same	0.09	12	13.46	‖ 10.68 ⊥ 6.22
Cellular plastics on the basis of cotton cloth saturated with R-21 phenolic resin	0.145	12	55.7	‖ 25.64 ⊥ 22.25

The recommended shape of the test sample /9/ is shown in Figure 3.7, where 1 denotes the cellular plastic, and 2 the aluminum plates with $\delta = 2$ mm. The shape was selected to attain optimum simulation of the pressure conditions to the natural working conditions of the structure. For tests, a special instrument (Figure 3.8) was designed to determine the cleavage stress in wood and glued joints between wood. Rollers (3) are inserted to induce a relatively pure shear stress in the glued joint.

Table 3.4 presents the test data on several types of cellular plastics. Since cellular plastics possess anisotropic structure, the ultimate shear strength was determined in two mutually perpendicular directions: for the shear stress in parallel ($\parallel$) and perpendicular ($\perp$) to the glued sides of the cells. Sample failure is characterized by the appearance of cracks propagating at 45° to the bordering planes, i. e., to the lines of action of the tensile stresses.

§3. DETERMINATION OF STRENGTH IN CUTTING

The limiting characteristic in shearing tests is the ultimate strength. To obtain the strength characteristics of materials in transverse cutting, samples are subjected to double or single shear. This test is essentially a technological sampling; a complex state of stress forms in the sample and in addition to pure shear there is also present bending and distortion. The samples used in cutting tests have the shape of a rectangular parallelepiped, the area of which in plan equals 20 × 80 mm; the sheet used is 4–6 mm thick. The sample is selected sufficiently wide to reduce distorting stresses on the surface. The test setup is shown in Figure 3.9.

The results of cutting tests perpendicular to the plane of the sheet are presented in Table 3.5 for three materials. The tests have shown that the "cutting strength" perpendicular to the plane of the sheet is greater than in the plane of the sheet. It is practically constant at all orientations of the sample relative to the glass fibers or cloth.

TABLE 3.5. Results of testing samples in cutting

Adhesive resin	Reinforcing material and ratio of fibers	Ultimate strength, kg/mm^2	Number of samples
PN-1	Cloth	8.5	20
Epoxy phenolic resin	Anisotropic glass-fiber material		
	1:5	13.3	26
	1:1	11.8	9

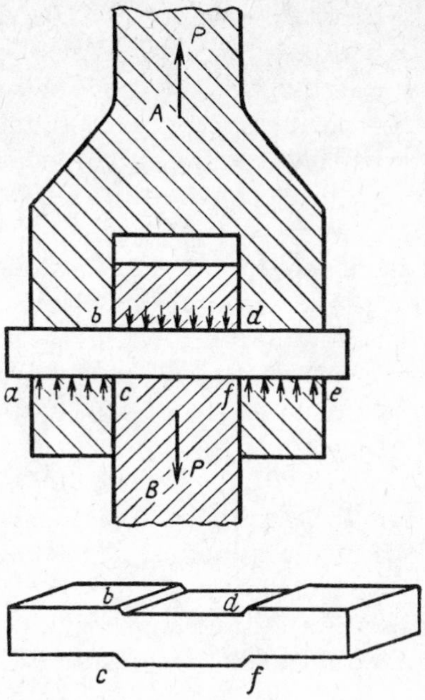

FIGURE 3.9.

It was discovered in cutting tests of several laminated plastics at −57 to +71°C that the cutting strength decreases with increasing temperature. This applies also to other mechanical properties of structural polymers with the exception of impact strength.

Two standard methods are most frequently applied when testing plastics at room temperature in double shear. In the first method rectangular samples cut from sheet are tested under compressive loading. In the second method cylindrical samples cut from sheet are tested for double shear in a three-plate setup under tensile load. Materials with properties differing in the transversal and perpendicular directions must be tested with samples cut in both directions.

It is advisable to keep the samples at a temperature of 25°C and 50% relative humidity for 48 hours or more before cutting tests, which should be conducted immediately after this conditioning. The average results are obtained on the basis of 5–10 samples. In thermosetting plastics there is no noticeable deformation before failure occurs and no influence of the thickness on the cutting strength was observed.

In cutting tests by compression the strength of thermoplastics increases with decreasing sheet thickness. This fact must be ascribed to the method of testing, since other properties of these thermoplastics depend little on thickness.

During cutting tests thermoplastics undergo greater compressive deformations before failure than thermosets. Since in a thinner sample the ratio of the bearing surface of the shear is larger than in a thicker sample, the compressive strain is smaller in the first case.

Most reinforced plastics have relatively smooth fracture surfaces, while in materials containing no filler this surface is irregular and jagged. The authors did not establish a definite relationship between cutting strength and tensile or compressive strength. Cutting strength at an angle of 45° is 10–15% greater than in the longitudinal direction.

The cutting strength of glass-fiber-reinforced plastics lies within the limits of compressive strength and depends on the structure and orientation of the filler, the adhesive, the method of preparation, and other factors.

According to the method explained by Goryainova /5/, the cutting strength of glass-fiber laminates is determined in the direction perpendicular to the plane of the sheet. The samples are circular with a diameter of 60 mm or square with sides of the same dimensions cut from sheet. A hole of 12 mm diameter is drilled in the middle of the sample for fixing it in a special device.

The testing apparatus consists of two plates with a center hole of 25 mm diameter, a punch, and two washers between which the sample is pressed, two guide pins and two fastening bolts.

The cutting edges of the lower plate and the upper washer must be sharp. The punch with the washers slipped over it without the sample must pass easily through the holes of the upper and lower plates.

The assembled device is placed on the testing machine and loading is effected at normal temperature at a rate of 12–20 mm/min to complete shearing off of the sample.

Cutting strength is determined by the relationship

$$\tau = P/F, \tag{3.1}$$

where P is the maximum load (in kg) and F the area of the shear (in cm^2). The area of shear is computed to within 0.01 cm by means of the formula

$$F = \pi dh, \tag{3.2}$$

where d is the diameter of the hole in the plate (equal to 25 mm) and h the thickness of the material (in cm).

In tests at elevated or low temperatures the device with the sample is immersed in a special chamber on the testing machine and conditioned there for 1.5 hours before testing.

Wood-fiber board is one of the structural materials used in building construction. As regards strength and other properties it is practically isotropic. Samples with symmetrical triangular notches (Figure 3.10) are recommended for cutting tests by tensile loading /9/. Failure of the sample in shear usually occurs simultaneously in two planes.

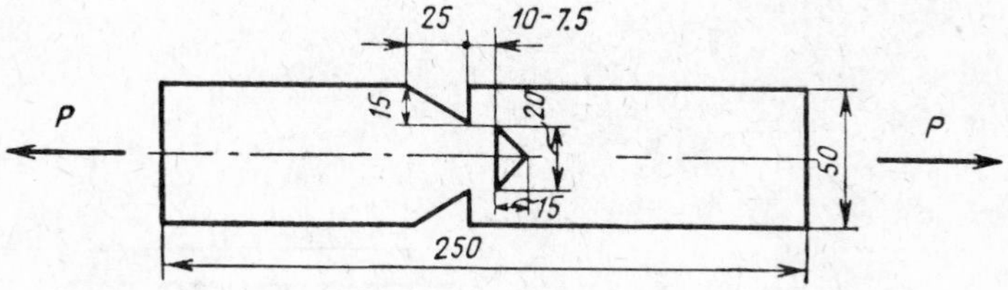

FIGURE 3.10.

When evaluating the behavior of materials in joints (bolted, riveted, etc.), in addition to the cutting strength of the joining elements, the crushing of the sheet must be taken into account. For this purpose the crushing strength is investigated. Crushing must not affect the reliability of the joint. It has been established that the strain curves of glass-fiber-reinforced plastics in crushing are analogous to the curves in tension and compression, but there are no reliable methods of directly determining crushing strength from the characteristics of tension or compression.

Crushing is tested under tensile or compressive load (relative to the longitudinal axis of the sample). Since compression tests indicate greater crushing strength than tensile tests, both forms of loading must be applied in order to completely evaluate the material.

Crushing tests are conducted as follows /3/. A metal pin is inserted into a calibrated hole of the sample to which the tensile or compressive load is applied. The displacement of the pin, i.e., the deformation of the hole in the material under investigation, is measured. The diameter of the hole is determined by the thickness of the sample. For accurate deformation measurements a special device and sensitive measuring apparatus are required.

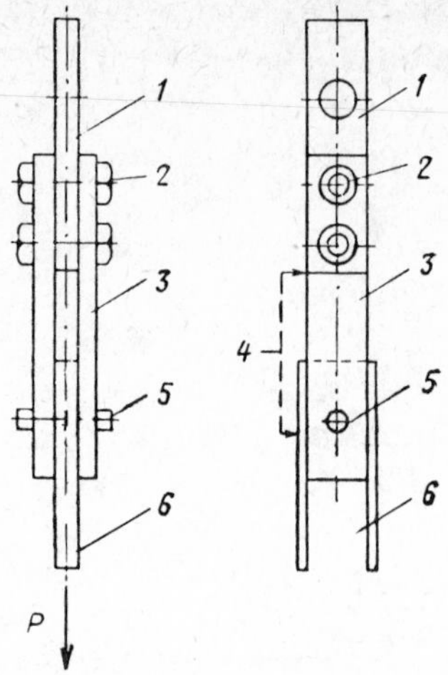

FIGURE 3.11.

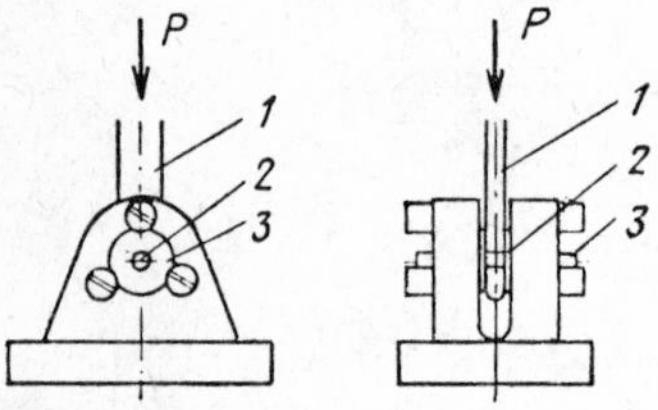

FIGURE 3.12.

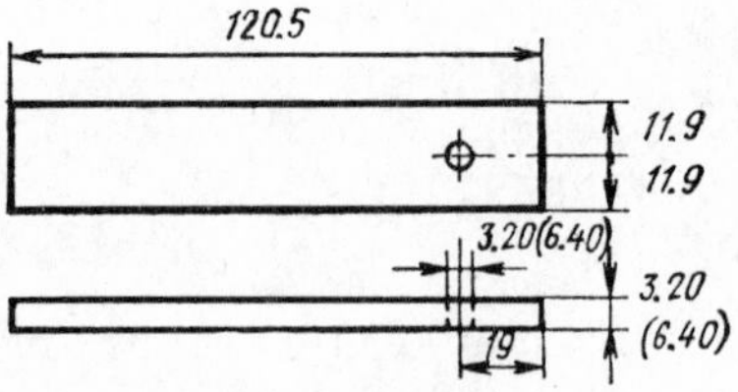

FIGURE 3.13.

Fixing of the sample for crushing tests under tension is shown in Figure 3.11, where 1 denotes the distance plate, 2 is a bolt, 3 a side plate, 4 the gage length, 5 a steel pin and 6 the samples. The setup for tests under compression is shown in Figure 3.12, where 1 denotes the sample, 2 a steel pin and 3 the thrust bush. Figure 3.13 shows a sample for crushing tests in line with the ASTMD 953-54 standard. Thick samples give more accurate results. However, in the case of glass-fiber-reinforced plastics displaying brittle failure it is an advantage to use thin samples which are less prone to premature destruction.

In crushing tests the strain is measured in steps up to a relative strain of the hole $\varepsilon = 4\%$, and then at maximum load. The following data are determined by the tests:

a) crushing stress $\sigma_{dis} = P/dh$,

b) tangential modulus of elasticity $E_t = \frac{\sigma_{dis}}{\varepsilon_{dis}} \approx 25\,\sigma_{dis}$, where P is the tensile or compressive load, d the hole diameter and h the sample thickness.

It is thus accepted conditionally that nonuniform pressure transmitted to the surface of the pin from the sheet is evenly distributed over the diametral cross-sectional plane of the pin. The stress in this plane is then approximately equal to the largest crushing stress σ_{dis} at the midpoint of the pin surface.

§4. DETERMINATION OF STRENGTH IN CLEAVING (FOR COMPOSITE MATERIALS)

In cleaving (interlayer shear), one layer of reinforcing cloth slides relative to the other. Hence the characteristics determining the strength of the material to interlayer shear are conditional and characterize basically the adhesion of the resin to the glass cloth. There exist a number of methods for conducting tests for interlayer shear, differing from each other with respect to sample shape and method of measuring the deformation.

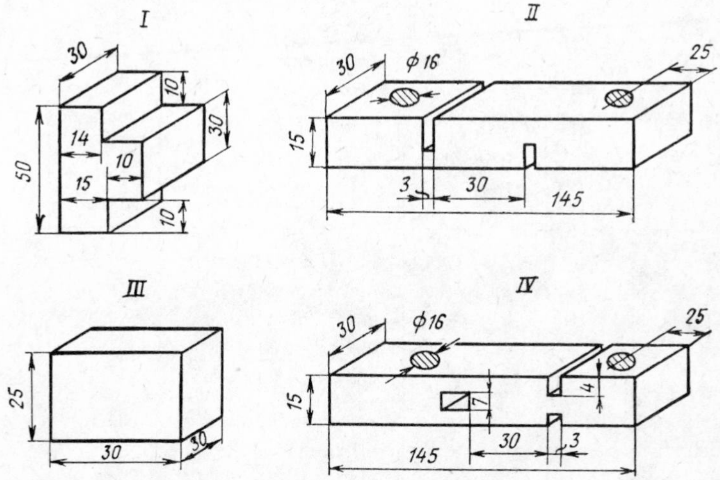

FIGURE 3.14.

Figure 3.14 shows four samples of glass-fiber-reinforced plastics for tests on interlayer shear. The samples are extended or compressed directly in the clamps of the testing machine by means of special fixtures. The samples of the fourth type were found to be most suitable for studying the strength of material in interlayer shear. When the sample is subjected to tension, slippage occurs in two planes. Resistance to slippage characterizes the resistance of the material to interlayer shear.

When determining the ultimate strength of the material in cleaving, the sample is loaded monotonically up to failure and the load upon failure is established. In this case

$$\tau_{cl} = \frac{P}{2bl_p}, \tag{4.1}$$

where b is the sample width and l_p the mean length of the slipping part of the sample.

Testing glass-fiber-reinforced plastics for cleaving can be carried out on ordinary all-purpose machines.

The characteristics of cleavage, determined by the above methods, are conditional and applicable only to a comparative evaluation of the materials. The question of a more correct experimental determination of the strength parameters of materials in interlayer shear is a very topical one.

Table 3.6 gives the ultimate strength in interlayer shear of a number of glass-fiber-reinforced plastics /8/.

TABLE 3.6. Ultimate strength of glass-fiber-reinforced plastics in interlayer shear

Material	Number of layers per 1 cm thickness	Ultimate strength, kg/mm²	Material	Number of layers per 1 cm thickness	Ultimate strength, kg/mm²
Glass-fiber-reinforced plastics with PN-1 resin and ASTT(b)-S_2-O glass cloth	20	1.02—1.47 1.37	Glass-fiber-reinforced plastics with PN-3 resin and TZhS-1.1 glass cloth treated with PVE and VTES lubricant	7.5	1.15—1.36 1.30
Glass-fiber-reinforced plastics with PN-1 resin and braided ASTT(b)-S_2-V glass cloth	20 20	2.60—2.85 2.75	Heat-treated glass-fiber reinforced STER-1-30 plastic with ASTT(b)-S_2 glass cloth	34.8	4.50
Glass-fiber-reinforced plastics with PN-3 resin and braided TZhS-0.6-O glass cloth	15	1.15—1.19 1.18			

TABLE 3.7. Strength in cleavage of matrices and glass-fiber-reinforced plastics based on their mechanical properties

Matrix material	Statistical characteristic	Strength in cleavage, kg/cm^2 test temperature 20°C	70°C	100°C	150°C	Cohesive tensile strength, at 20°C, kg/cm^2
K-156; TEA curing agent	$\overline{x}$ *	466	93.5	34.6	16.6	672
	σ **	31.4	10.3	0.56	1.6	12.2
	V †	6.7	11.0	1.6	10.0	1.8
Glass-fiber-reinforced plastics on K-156 with TEA	$\overline{x}$	376	113	50	30	—
	σ	35.7	9.5	4.7	1.0	—
	V	9.5	8.4	9.4	3.4	—
K-156; TEAT curing agent	$\overline{x}$	563	267	218	53	778
	σ	56.6	8.5	9.4	2.2	64
	V	10.0	3.2	4.3	4.2	8.2
Glass-fiber-reinforced plastics on K-156 with TEA	$\overline{x}$	516	333	184	85	—
	σ	38.2	10.9	13.7	6.2	—
	V	7.4	3.3	7.4	7.2	—
K-156; MFDA curing agent	$\overline{x}$	494	388	274	48	756
	σ	7.9	5.6	19.8	4.7	68.2
	V	1.6	1.4	7.2	9.8	9.0
Glass-fiber-reinforced plastics on K-156 with MFDA	$\overline{x}$	437	322	258	53	—
	σ	51.2	19.5	28.2	5.5	—
	V	11.7	6.1	10.9	10.4	—
PN-1	$\overline{x}$	421	139	36.6	16.7	595
	σ	15.7	20.5	3.0	0.75	—
	V	3.7	14.8	8.1	4.5	—
Glass-fiber-reinforced plastics with PN-1	$\overline{x}$	146	64	26	19	—
	σ	10.2	7.4	0.7	0.5	—
	V	7.0	11.5	2.7	2.8	—
Divinyl oligomer	$\overline{x}$	276	142	43.6	25.4	436
Glass-fiber-reinforced plastics with divinyl oligomer	$\overline{x}$	64.2	—	42.8	20.6	—
Glass-fiber-reinforced plastics on the basis of cloth treated with GVS-9 and divinyl oligomer	$\overline{x}$	200	—	87.1	48.4	—
ED-5; TEAT curing agent	$\overline{x}$	480	—	233	49	672
Glass-fiber-reinforced plastics with ED-5 and TEAT	$\overline{x}$	464	—	212	123	—
ED-5 + 30% Thiokol; TEAT curing agent	$\overline{x}$	420	—	91	14	650
Glass-fiber-reinforced plastics with EL-5 + 30% Thiokol; TEAT curing agent	$\overline{x}$	420	—	95	54	—

* $\overline{x}$ is the arithmetic mean (of 4—8 tests); ** σ is the standard deviation; † V is the coefficient of variation, %.

The strength of glass-fiber-reinforced plastics in cleavage and static bending is markedly lower than the initial value already at comparatively moderate temperatures (100–150°C). This is due to the fact that the strength of glass-fiber-reinforced plastics in cleavage between layers τ_{cl} and bending σ_{ben} is determined mainly by the type of matrix, and the adhesion between it and the reinforcing filler. In cleavage or bending, glass-fiber-reinforced plastics usually suffer rupture of the matrix situated between adjacent layers of the filler.

Below, following Yudin et al. /11/, we describe some methods and results of determining the correlation between the ultimate strength of glass-fiber Textolite in cleavage and the ultimate strength in cleavage of the polymeric matrix on the basis of which the specified reinforced plastics were prepared. The temperature range is 20–150°C.

In testing for cleavage, $10 \times 10 \times 60$ mm samples (cleavage area $F_{cl} = 100$ mm^2) with two notches 1.5–2 mm deep (forming a tooth in the middle part) were cut from castings of the matrix material; the tooth is subjected to cleaving. Samples measuring $10 \times 15 \times 60$ mm ($F_{cl} = 150$ mm^2) were cut from glass-fiber Textolite plate in the direction of the warp. The test results with $F_{cl} = 100$ and 150 mm^2 turned out to be practically identical. The loading method for cleavage is shown in Figure 3.15.

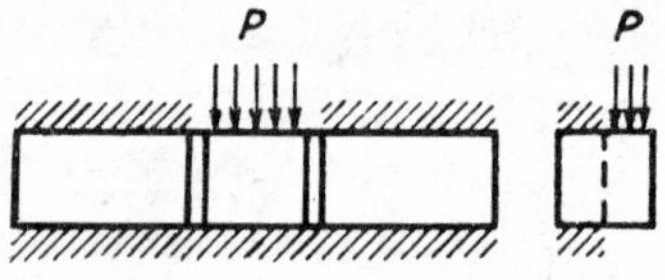

FIGURE 3.15.

In addition, the relationship between the cohesive strength of the matrix in tension σ_{ult} and the strength in cleaving σ_{cl} was established. The cohesive strength of the matrix in tension was determined using samples shaped as a dumbbell and cut from castings, the dimensions of the working part being $2 \times 8 \times 50$ mm.

The cleavage tests were conducted in a heat-controlled chamber. The prescribed temperature was maintained by means of an EPP-09 instrument. The samples were conditioned in the chamber before testing, at 70°C for 50 minutes, at 100°C for 30 minutes or at 150°C for 20 minutes.

Loading was effected by a mechanical drive, the lower grip of the machine moving at 20 mm/min. The load was determined with strain dynamometers.

Table 3.7 gives values of the ultimate strength of the matrix and glass-fiber-reinforced plastics on which the strength in cleavage is based /11/.

Known data show that the strength of glass-fiber Textolite in cleavage is to an appreciable extent determined by the strength in cleavage of the adhesive matrix without filler. The obtained feature is well adhered to if the matrix displays good adhesion to the glass filler.

§5. DETERMINATION OF EFFECTIVE CONCENTRATION COEFFICIENTS IN THE PRESENCE OF DIFFERENT STRESS RAISERS

High local stresses appear in regions where the shape of the surface of a deformed body changes rapidly, and also in the contact zone of elastic bodies. If one assumes an elastic distribution of stress propagation, then for given parameters of the stress raiser a stress can be characterized by the theoretical coefficient of stress concentration

$$K_t = \frac{\sigma_{\max}}{\sigma_n}, \qquad (5.1)$$

which is the ratio of the largest local stress to the nominal stress.

The term nominal is here applied to stresses computed by the simplest formulas under the assumption that there are no stress raisers. It should be noted that in computing nominal stress, the load can be related either to the whole cross-section without considering the stress raiser or to the dangerous cross-section weakened by a stress raiser. Therefore, when applying the term "nominal stress," its mode of determination must be indicated.

In the case of standardized structural elements, the theoretical stress concentration coefficient for isotropic materials is determined by solving problems of elasticity theory, and by employing experimental techniques and tabulated data /12/.

Theoretical solutions pertaining to the stress concentration in anisotropic plates with holes and notches of different shapes are included in the monographs by S. G. Lekhnitskii and G. N. Savin. These solutions were derived assuming a quasi-homogeneous composition of the material. Thus the theoretical stress concentration coefficient for an orthotropic plate of infinite width with a circular hole at the center is given by

$$K_t = 1 + 2\sqrt{\frac{E_0}{E_{45}} + \frac{1}{4}\left(\frac{E_0}{E_{90}} - 1\right)}, \qquad (5.2)$$

where E_0, E_{45} and E_{90} are the moduli of elasticity obtained in samples cut from sheet in the respective directions.

It is evident from (5.2) that, depending on the ratio of the elastic constants, a substantially higher stress concentration is possible than with isotropic material. Expression (5.2) can be applied also to plates of finite width if the width is more than five times larger than the hole diameter.

Experimental data have shown that many structural plastics are sensitive to stress concentration under static short-time loading, but hardly sensitive to them under prolonged or alternating loading. The sensitivity of reinforced plastics to stress concentrations also depends strongly on the fiber geometry. The strength in places of local concentrations can be regulated by means of a sensible distribution of reinforcing fiber; a reduction in strength near holes and notches can be especially avoided.

The effect of stress concentration on strength is referred to as the effective coefficient of stress concentration under static loading and is determined as the ratio of the ultimate strength of the structural member without a stress raiser to the ultimate strength of the same member with a stress raiser:

$$K_e = \frac{\sigma_{ult}}{\sigma_{ult.r}}. \qquad (5.3)$$

In addition, the area of the cross-section of the sample without a stress raiser must equal the corresponding area with the weakened cross-section. It is noteworthy that the time-dependent effective coefficient of stress concentration indicates how many times the fatigue limit of a sample without a stress raiser exceeds the fatigue limit of a sample with a stress raiser.

Effective concentration coefficients are usually represented as graphs or nomographs for the actual material and shape of stress raisers. Effective coefficients for plates made from glass-fiber-reinforced plastics with circular holes of different cross-sectional area are given in Table 3.8 /13/.

TABLE 3.8. Values of effective coefficients of stress concentration

Material	Area, mm^2	K_t	K_e 20°C	Material	Area, mm^2	K_t	K_e 20°C	K_e 150°C
4G-4S	18	3.0	1.13	33-18S	50	1.80	1.22	1.08
		3.6	1.30			2.75	1.29	1.10
		6.1	1.42			6.10	1.38	1.05
	200	3.7	1.48		100	2.30	1.25	1.02
		4.5	1.51			3.60	1.46	1.05
		7.3	1.62			7.40	1.56	1.20

Neuber, Peterson and Philip /14/ have developed methods for determining effective concentration coefficients. According to Neuber, K_e is computed as the ratio of the maximum stress $\sigma(x)$ averaged over a segment of length $2\delta_1$ near the apex of the stress raiser to the nominal stress σ_n:

$$K_e = \frac{\frac{1}{2\delta_1}\int_0^{2\delta_1} \sigma(x)\,dx}{\sigma_n}. \qquad (5.4)$$

According to Peterson and Phillip, K_e is determined as the ratio of the largest stress at a point distance $x=\delta_2$ from the apex of the stress raiser to the nominal stress:

$$K_e = \frac{\sigma(\delta_2)}{\sigma_n}. \qquad (5.5)$$

Consequently one, experimentally determined parameter δ_i is involved in these techniques of computing effective concentration coefficients.

Usually, the effective concentration coefficient K_e is less than the theoretical value; only in isolated cases does it approach K_t, in particular for brittle materials. In the case of materials with a high degree of plasticity the effective concentration coefficient is close to unity, and so justifies disregarding the effect of local stresses under static load.

By examining shallow and deep stress raisers it can be deduced that K_e oscillates between unity for very shallow notches and the value of the theoretical concentration coefficient for deep notches, but never exceeds the latter value. The notch sensitivity of the material q is expressed in the form

$$q = \frac{K_e - 1}{K_t - 1}. \qquad (5.6)$$

The presence of stress raisers in reinforced plastics such as holes, notches and recesses is detrimental to the monolithic structure and causes appreciable shear strains in the polymeric matrix which in turn causes shear stresses between the layers and an appreciable increase of the coefficient of normal stress concentration in comparison with homogeneous isotropic material. It has been shown experimentally /15/ that K_e for layered material is appreciably larger than for homogeneous anisotropic material.

The majority of glass-fiber-reinforced plastics possess a practically linear strain diagram up to failure. Owing to the brittle nature of the failure of these materials and insignificant stress redistribution in the cross-sections, stress concentrations must be taken into account in strength evaluations.

The effect of stress concentrations on the static strength of oriented glass-fiber-reinforced plastics is studied in detail elsewhere /16, 17/. Because of the above-mentioned properties in connection with the effect of anisotropy, K_e in glass-fiber-reinforced plastics is 2.5 to 3 times larger than in metals under otherwise identical conditions.

TABLE 3.9. Effective stress concentration coefficients of plates with notches

Material	Area, mm^2	K_t	K_e	
			$T = 20°C$	$T = 150°C$
AG-4S	18	3.00	1.13	—
		3.60	1.30	—
		6.10	1.42	—
	200	3.70	1.48	—
		4.50	1.51	—
		7.30	1.62	—
33-18S	50	1.80	1.22	1.08
		2.75	1.29	1.10
		6.10	1.38	1.05
	100	2.30	1.25	1.02
		3.60	1.46	1.05
		7.40	1.56	1.20

The effective concentration coefficient in tension is compared with the theoretical value in Table 3.9. The experimental data were obtained from tests on plates with hyperbolic notches on both sides. The materials used comprised glass-fiber-reinforced plastics with an AG-4S brittle matrix and also with a more plastic 33-18S matrix. Table 3.10 presents values of K_e for plates made from different materials with holes. The ratio between hole diameter d and width b of the plate was chosen constant (0.2).

TABLE 3.10. Effective concentration coefficients for plates with holes

Material	Matrix	K_e
KAST-V	VBF-1	1.20
ST-911S	Polyester	1.30
SVAM	BF-4	1.05
SVAM	Bakelite	1.54
33-18S	Epoxyphenol	1.25
AG-4S	Phenol formaldehyde modified with BF-4	1.33

The experimental results indicate attenuation in stress concentration with increasing K_t, the effect of stress concentrations being more pronounced in the region of large cross-sections. This can be explained by the peculiarity of stress transmission in oriented reinforced systems. In case of excessive stress, the shearing off of adhesive bonds close to the stress raiser may occur and the stress diminishes rapidly within a thin surface layer.

Stress concentration causes an increase in the scatter of the results. A number of investigators has shown that the scatter of experimental data is Gaussian.

It should be borne in mind that when designing stressed parts of glass-fiber-reinforced plastics with stress raisers, the permissible stresses must be selected with a view to the nonuniform stressed states and the ambient temperature. Tests on oriented glass-fiber-reinforced plastics with plastic or brittle matrix have shown that the effect of stress concentrations appears at temperatures between −69 and 100°C. Outside this range some attenuation of the effect of stress concentration on strength is observed (see Table 3.11).

In addition to the theoretical coefficient K_t, the stress distribution near the stress raiser can be characterized by another macroscopic parameter, stress gradient G. Thus for a plate with hyperbolic notches on both sides under uniaxial tension

$$G = \frac{\partial \sigma_y}{\partial x}\bigg|_{\sigma_y=\sigma_{max}} = \frac{2\sigma_{max}}{\rho}, \tag{5.7}$$

where ρ is the radius at the apex of the notch. In this case the relative stress gradient is

$$\overline{G} = \frac{\partial \sigma_y}{\partial x}\frac{1}{\sigma_{max}} = \frac{2}{\rho} \quad mm^{-1} \tag{5.8}$$

TABLE 3.11. Effective stress concentration coefficients at elevated temperatures /17/

Material	K_t	K_e		
		20°C	100°C	150°C
Oriented glass-fiber-reinforced	2.3	1.25	1.05	1.02
plastics with 33-18S plastic	3.6	1.46	1.04	1.05
matrix ($F = 100$ mm^2)	7.4	1.56	1.30	1.20

Smirnova /8/ drew attention to the fact that as a result of the actual heterogeneity of the material investigated, unreliable results are obtained in the study of concentrations on small-scale models made from glass-fiber-reinforced plastics (with errors of 200–300% toward the side of danger). Hence at present, consideration of the effects of the scale and stress concentrations in structural polymers has attained special importance.

Following Tarnopol'skii and Skudra /13/, a dimensionless stress gradient G_N is introduced for comparing test results in the study of the effects of stress concentration on samples of different absolute dimensions. This quantity is defined as the product of the relative stress gradient $\overline{G}$ by half the sample width at the notch location, a:

$$G_N = a\overline{G}. \tag{5.9}$$

Figure 3.16 illustrates the dependence of the maximum breaking stresses on the dimensionless stress gradient of two glass-fiber-reinforced plastics for different cross-sectional areas (a – glass-fiber-reinforced plastics with AG-4S matrix: × – 80 mm^2, ○ – 200 mm^2; b – glass-fiber-reinforced plastics with 33-18S matrix: ○ – 25 mm^2, △ – 50 mm^2, × – 100 mm^2).

In stress analysis of large parts the effect of the absolute dimensions and stress concentration must both be taken into account together. In this case it is advisable to determine the maximum breaking stress by means of an experimentally established dependence of the relative tensile breaking stress on the relative gradient:

$$\frac{\sigma_{\max}}{\sigma_{\text{ult}}} = f(\overline{G}_N) \tag{5.10}$$

and to determine the curve of the variation in the scale factor with respect to mean strength values. Relationship (5.10) for the materials considered is shown in Figure 3.17, where for AG-4S (stacking 1:1) △– 200 mm²; and for 33-18S □– 100 mm², ▲– 50 mm², ○– 25 mm².

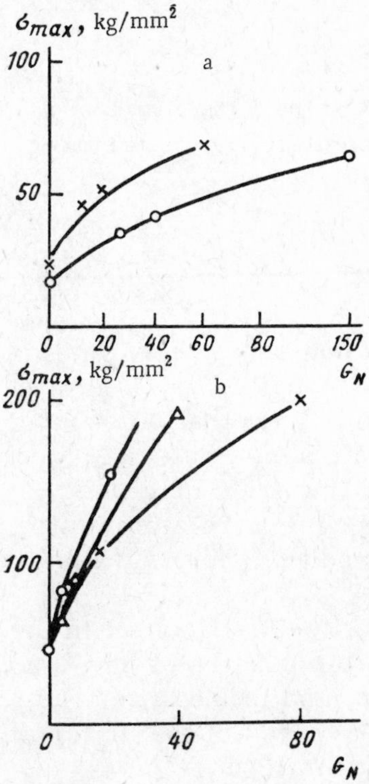

FIGURE 3.16.

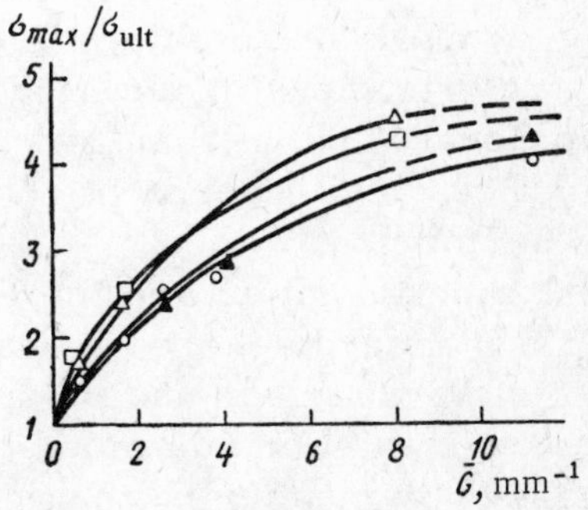

FIGURE 3.17.

The values of K_t and $\overline{G}$ can be derived from the corresponding solution of the elastic problem for a specified shape of the structural member.

Since

$$\frac{\sigma_{max}}{\sigma_{ult}} = \frac{K_t \sigma_{ult.r}}{\sigma_{ult}} = \frac{K_t}{K},$$

the effective stress concentration coefficient K_e is readily derived from (5.10).

The absolute dimensions are taken into account by means of the dependence of the coefficient of the effect of the absolute dimensions ε_σ on the cross-sectional area F:

$$\varepsilon_\sigma = f(F). \tag{5.11}$$

With allowance for the absolute dimensions, the ultimate strength σ_{ult} is given by

$$\sigma_{ult} = \varepsilon_\sigma R_T, \tag{5.12}$$

where R_T is the tabulated value of the strength of the material.

§6. METHODS OF DETERMINING HARDNESS

The hardness test is applied to make a comparative evaluation of the properties of a material. The term hardness is applied to the property of material to resist the mechanical penetration of foreign bodies. When a sharp object is pressed into some material, local plastic deformations occur in it, and when the force increases further, local rupture results. Hence hardness is related to strength and plasticity and depends on the actual conditions under which the test is performed.

Most widely applied are the Brinell and Rockwell tests. In the former a standard sphere of 10 mm diameter penetrates the surface of the member under investigation, and in the latter the penetrator is a sharp diamond tip. The hardness of the material is assessed by measuring the resulting indentation.

There are conversion tables by means of which the ultimate strength can be approximately derived from the hardness number. In nonhardenable and strain-hardened materials the yield point can also be derived from the hardness. The corresponding formulas are of the form $\sigma_{s,\,ult} = CH_B$, where H_B is the Brinell hardness, C a constant and $\sigma_{s,ult}$ the yield point (σ_s) or the ultimate strength (σ_{ult}). Thus the strength of a material can be determined by a hardness test without destroying the member.

There are also other methods for determining hardness, such as damaging the surface layer of the material by scratching, and hardness tests with a diamond cone or pyramid.

The determination of hardness of polymeric materials has its specific problems. First, hardness must be determined from the dimensions of the nonrecovered indentation because of the high elasticity and relaxation which vary for different materials. Therefore special presses must be used in hardness tests. Next, no reliable relationship between hardness and yield point or ultimate strength has been established for polymeric materials.

Methods and equations for computing strength and elastic properties of polymers from data of hardness tests have been developed /18/. Hardness was measured on a Rockwell instrument modified to measure the depth of the unrecovered indentation.

The indentors were spheres,5, 3.2 and 2 mm in diameter and cones with apex angles of 120, 90, 60 or 30°.

The hardness of the following materials was investigated: aminoplast, K-17-2, FKP-1 (thermosetting plastics with different fillers), polymethyl methacrylate, PVC (thermoplastic amorphous materials), polyethylene and teflon (crystalline material in the Mackian-elastic and brittle states at the test temperature). The tests were conducted at room temperature.

Samples of thermosetting plastics (25 mm in diameter, $h = 5$ mm) were prepared by molding from the corresponding molding powders. The polyethylene test sample was prepared by injection molding under pressure. The teflon, polymethyl methacrylate and PVC samples were cut from sheets.

The tests comprised: 1) determination of the depth of penetration as a function of the time of load application; 2) determination of the recovery as a function of time after unloading; 3) determination of the effect of the load magnitude on the results with a conical indentor; 4) determination of hardness H_B (load divided by indentation area) and H_M (load divided by indentation area projected onto the plane of the sample) at different penetration angles or ratios d/D (where d is the indentation diameter and D the ball diameter) for different ball diameters and cone apex angles. The areas were calculated from the measured depth of the unrecovered indentation.

In all cases the loading time was taken as one minute. For samples of different materials, the relationship between the penetration depth and the logarithm of the time of load application can be expressed by the linear equation

$$h = h_0 + a \log t, \tag{6.1}$$

where h_0 is the depth of ball penetration at $t=1$ min and a is a constant.

It is known that the Brinell hardness can be computed by the formula

$$H_B = \frac{P}{\pi D h},$$

where P is the load, D the ball diameter, and h the depth of penetration. Then equation (6.1) assumes the form

$$\frac{H_{B,0}}{H_{B,t}} = 1 + \frac{a}{h_0} \log t, \qquad (6.2)$$

where $H_{B,0}$ is the hardness at $t=1$ min and $H_{B,t}$ the hardness at a given instant.

The relative recovery one minute after load removal following loading for one minute at different penetration angles (for balls the penetration angle is $\alpha = 2 \operatorname{arc} \cos d/D$, for cones α is equal to the apex angle) is described by the equation

$$\frac{h - h_1}{h} = \frac{3(1-\nu^2)P}{4rhE}, \qquad (6.3)$$

where h_1 is the depth of indentation following removal of the load, ν is Poisson's ratio, E is the modulus of elasticity, and r is the radius of the indentation.

It should be noted that in general neither the elastic nor the strength properties of a material can be characterized by the size of the indentation at a certain instant.

TABLE 3.12

Material	H_B, kg/mm²	Compression σ_s/σ_{ult}, kg/mm²	Tension σ_s/σ_{ult}, kg/mm²	Compression $\frac{\sigma_{s,ult}}{H_B}$	Tension $\frac{\sigma_{s,ult}}{H_B}$	$\frac{\sigma_s}{E}$	E, kg/mm²	$\left(\frac{d}{D}\right)_{max}$	$\left(\frac{d}{D}\right)_{max}$ computed
FKP-1	15.5	12.0	2.55	0.77	0.16	0.081	23.0	0.87	0.84
K-17-2	35.6	20.0	7.0	0.50	0.20	0.056	47.5	0.82	0.83
Aminoplast	42.0	24.4	6.3	0.58	0.15	0.072	60.0	0.86	0.85
PVC	13.5	8.8	4.5	0.65	0.332	0.044	16.8	0.75	0.81
Plexiglas	18.5	12.8	8.0	0.69	0.43	0.052	25.0	0.90	0.81
Teflon	3.84	1.4	1.4	0.39	0.36	0.036	2.0	0.87	0.75
Polyethylene	1.55	0.4	0.4	0.26	—	—	1.9	0.85	0.83

Table 3.12 gives values of σ_s and σ_{ult} for tension and compression and the ratio between these values and maximum hardness. Ratio $\sigma_{s,ult}/H_B$ obtained in compression fluctuates between 0.44 and 0.82, i. e., it is always much greater than for most metals.

Table 3.12 also gives values of d/D at which Brinell hardness is independent of pressure. For all the materials tested d/D lay between 0.72 and 0.87.

The new All-Union State Standard (GOST) on methods of measuring the hardness of polymers states that the depth of ball penetration should be within the limits 0.2–0.6 mm. But even at $h = 0.6$ mm, $d/D = 0.7$ the hardness determined will depend on the load. Thus, different investigators may obtain different hardness values for the same material. Instruments with diamond pyramids possessing apex angles of 136° give hardness values far from the maximum values. Only at angles of 65–70° are the hardnesses with ball and pyramid indentors likely to be similar.

Thus, when using ball indentors, the hardness of polymeric materials should be measured at $d/D = 0.8$ by depth or diameter of the unrecovered indentation. If a pyramid or a cone is used, the apex angle should be 60–65°.

Rabinovich and Verkhovskii /4/ have established the following empirical formula for computing the strength and elastic properties from measurement data of hardness H_B in the elastic range:

$$\sigma_{s,ult} = 0.85\,(E')^{0.82}. \qquad (6.4)$$

This relationship links the ultimate strength or yield strength in compression to the tangent of the slope E' of the straight line $H_M(d/D)$. When employing expression (6.4), it is necessary to determine the hardness H_M by two loads and compute E' by the formula

$$E' = \frac{H_M'' - H_M'}{\left(\frac{d}{D}\right)'' - \left(\frac{d}{D}\right)'}.$$

The dependence of the ultimate strength or yield strength in compression on hardness H_B is given by

$$\sigma_{s,ult} = 0.87\,H_B^{0.93}. \qquad (6.5)$$

Quantity $\frac{E}{1-\nu^2}$ in the elastic range can be determined from penetration tests by means of the formula

$$\frac{E}{1-\nu^2} = 2.62\,\sigma_{av}\frac{D}{d}, \tag{6.6}$$

or, since $d^2 = Dh$,

$$\frac{E}{1-\nu^2} = 2.62\,\sigma_{av}\sqrt{\frac{D}{h}}. \tag{6.7}$$

Thus equations (6.4)–(6.6) can be used to derive the strength and elastic properties of polymeric materials from the results of hardness tests.

According to data cited elsewhere /19/, the hardness of the high-polymeric materials investigated turns out to be comparatively low (in the limits of 3 to 30 Brinell), i. e., it differs little from plastic metals. The polyethylene group has the lowest hardness. The hardness was determined by the Rockwell-Superficial instrument. The results of comparative tests on plastics and metals are presented in Table 3.13.

For a large number of thermoplastic polymers hardness does not depend on load. A marked difference between high-polymeric and metallic materials becomes evident upon comparing the hardness with the magnitude of the relative elastic recovery of the depth of indentation. For the metals tested the elastic recovery does not exceed 16%, while for high-polymeric materials it is very high (from 20 to 80%) and does not depend on hardness.

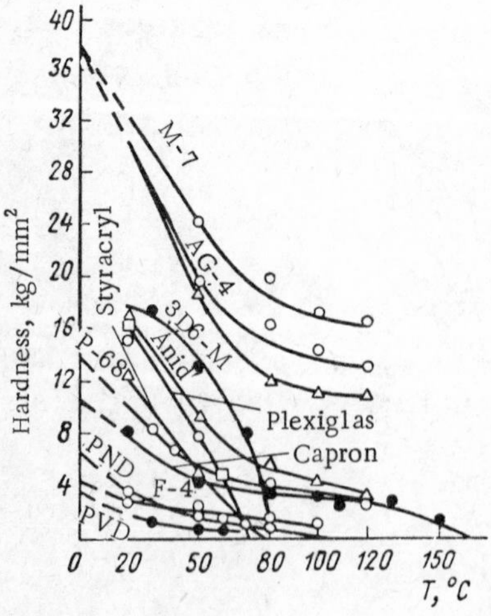

FIGURE 3.18.

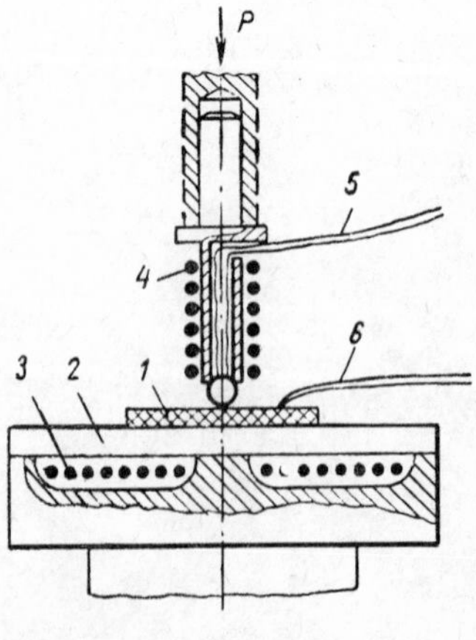

FIGURE 3.19.

TABLE 3.13. Results of determining hardness and relative elastic recovery on materials tested

Material	Hardness determination by depth of indentation				Relative elastic recovery		Hardness determination by diameter of indentation		
	P, kg	time, min	h_{full}, μ	H_B, kg/mm²	h_{res}, μ	h_{el}/h_{full}, %	P, kg	d, mm	H_B, kg/mm²
Armco iron (treated at 575°; 4 hours)	42	1	41	100.0	36.0	12	45	0.75	106.0
Cast tin	9	3	177	5.0	176.5	0	12	1.63	5.4
Cast aluminum	12	1	78	15.0	75.0	4	15	1.21	13.0
Cast copper	27	1	66	45.0	60.0	9	30	0.85	50.0
Cast copper	42	1	94	45.0	86.0	9	45	1.06	48.0
Technical Capron	5.5	2	153	5.5—5.2	71.0	50	—	—	—
Polycaprolactam	5	2	130	4.5—4.0	57.6	55	—	—	—
AK-7	12	2	151	8.0	77.0	49	—	—	—
AG-4	27	2	104	26.0	27.2	74	—	—	—
AG-4	42	2	134	31.0	39.4	71	—	—	—
R-49	12	2	77	15.5	28.7	62	—	—	—
R-49	27	2	154	17.0	53.5	65	—	—	—
M-7	12	2	44	27.0	11.0	75	—	—	—
M-7	27	2	90	30.0	21.0	77	—	—	—
M-7	42	2	127	34.0	29.8	76.5	—	—	—
ED6-M	12	2	72	16.7	24.0	67	—	—	—
ED6-M	27	2	153	17.0	60.6	60	—	—	—
Low density polyethylene	5.75	2	160	3.6—4.0	114.0	29	—	—	—
Plexiglas	12	2	86	14.0	36.0	58	—	—	—
Styrene-alkyd resin	12	2	114	10.5	58.0	49	—	—	—
Fluoroplast-4	5	2	148	3.3	120.0	19	—	—	—
P-68	8.5	2	109	8.0	52.0	52	—	—	—
P-68	12	2	130	9.1	61.0	53	—	—	—
High density polyethylene	3	4.5	164	1.8	112.0	32	—	—	—
P-54	8.5	—	170	4.6	77.0	55	—	—	—

The hardness of polymeric materials was also studied at elevated temperatures /20/. The hardness of plastics was measured at 20–150°C by a Rockwell-Superficial instrument; the results are given in Figure 3.18.

TABLE 3.14. Brinell hardness of structural polymers (ball 25 mm, load 50 kg)

Material	H_B, kg/mm^2	Material	H_B, kg/mm^2
Polystyrene	20—30	KAST	35
Polymethyl methacrylate	18—20	Asbotextolite	45
F-3 fluoroplast	10—13	Delta-wood	19
F-4 fluoroplast	3—4	Polyformaldehyde	40
PTK Textolite	34	PU polyurethane	12

The setup employed in measuring hardness at elevated temperatures is shown in Figure 3.19. The test sample (1) is placed on the table (2), which is heated by an electric heating coil (3). The indentor is heated by coil (4). The temperature of the ball indentor is measured by means of a (copper-constantan) thermocouple (5) and that of the test sample by thermocouple (6). The test sample is heated at a rate of 1° per minute. The hardness is measured after attaining the specified temperature in the indentor and sample and maintaining it for several minutes. The spherical indentor penetrated to a depth of 130–170 μ. The diameter of the ball indentor was 3.175 mm.

The Brinell hardness of a number of structural polymers is listed in Table 3.14.

Chapter IV

INITIAL, RESIDUAL AND TEMPERATURE STRESSES

Initial stresses are inevitable in structural polymeric materials during their production process. The terms initial and residual stress are applied to stresses in bodies in the absence of external load or temperature change. They can originate in pressing of parts, pressure casting, forming from sheet, welding and other technological processes. Initial stresses are particularly noticeable in composite materials in which different Poisson's ratios and coefficients of expansion of the resin and reinforcement cause stress concentrations around the fibers during the production of the material.

In addition, installations made from structural polymers frequently operate at elevated temperatures and so cause additional temperature stresses in them. In combination with the operating stresses, initial and temperature stresses can have an adverse effect on the strength and stability of the construction and parts and cause premature failure.

The present chapter deals with experimental data pertaining to the investigation of initial, residual and temperature stresses and examines efficient methods applied to evaluate their magnitudes and diminish their effects on the strength properties of the materials.

§1. INVESTIGATION OF INITIAL STRESSES OCCURRING IN THE PRODUCTION OF HOMOGENEOUS MATERIALS

One usually distinguishes two types of initial stresses, namely macroscopic and microscopic stresses. Physical and mechanical methods are applied to their detection and evaluation. Mechanical methods (removal of layers, trepanning, boring, etc.) involve the removal of part of the material in which microstresses are in equilibrium. Hence mechanical methods are essentially applied to measuring macrostresses. The joint effect of macro- and micro-stresses is measured by physical methods (X-rays, magnetic, etc.).

The effect of residual stresses is most frequently detected when they act jointly with other stresses, such as stress concentrations at the peak of a notch. The theory of mechanical methods of determining residual stresses is contained in Birger's monograph /1/. Although the book was written with reference to metals and alloys, the methods discussed are also applicable to the study of residual stresses in structural polymers.

Mechanical methods of measuring residual stresses are reviewed elsewhere /2/.

The method of preparing parts from amorphous polymers by pressure molding gives rise to initial stresses which in many cases cause crack formation. Dashko and Sporyagin /3/ used polarization-optical methods to study initial technological stresses appearing directly in the molding process or during cooling in the mold. It was established that when parts from grade D polystyrene from Kuskovsko Chemical Works are pressure molded, compressive stresses arise predominantly in thin-walled parts, tensile stresses in thick-walled parts. The kinds of initial stresses were determined by means of the "nail-test." In this technique, pressure is exerted on the section under investigation by means of a sharp object and the change in the features of the isochromes observed.

For the quantitative determination of initial stresses by Hardy's method the authors calibrated polystyrene by determining the values of the bands of the material, which express the dependence of the maximum shear stress on the path difference.

It was observed that initial tangential and normal stresses attain 34 and 60% of the mean values of ultimate strength, respectively, i. e., appreciable values which must not be neglected in stress analysis of structures and parts.

For reducing initial stresses the authors proposed heat treatment of finished products. This induces relaxation of internal stresses. The heat treatment consists in heating the part to a certain temperature, holding at that temperature and slow cooling.

Distilled water, distilled glycerol, industrial oil or furnace air are used as media for heat treatment. The temperatures are 80, 85 and 90°C, the rate of heating 15–60°C per hour and the rate of cooling 5–25°C per hour. Heat treatment in air has turned out to be most efficient, since it had no adverse effect on the optical properties of the part. In addition, heat treatment in air at 80 ± 2°C for 2–3 hours caused a 20–25% increase in the static strength of polystyrene.

The following data are given to illustrate the decrease in initial stresses as the result of heat treatment. In samples not heat-treated, five or six sets of bands were observed (qualitative isochromes counted starting from the center of the sample) corresponding to the values of the normal and tangential stresses: $\sigma_0 = 239$ kg/cm^2, $\tau_0 = 119.5$ kg/cm^2. Heat treatment for 2–3 hours reduced the set of isochromes to one, which corresponds to the following stresses: $\sigma_1 = 47.8$ kg/cm^2 and $\tau_1 = 23.9$ kg/cm^2, i. e., caused a substantial reduction in the initial stresses.

Increasing the holding time of heat treatment causes a certain increase in stress. The authors explain this by a consolidation of structure in structure formation of the polymer during long-term thermal action.

The effect of residual stresses on the failure of amorphous glassy polymers under the action of a liquid medium has been investigated /4/. The effect of the manufacturing technology of polystyrene and polymethyl methacrylate on the magnitude and character of the residual stresses was studied as well as the effect of residual stresses on the failure process of these materials under the simultaneous action of load and working media.

Samples of polystyrene were prepared by pressure molding at the melting temperature of 220–200°C and holding at that temperature for 15–20 minutes. Samples of polymethyl methacrylate were cut from sheet.

The residual stresses were determined by Davidenkov's method /36/. Let b be the initial thickness of the sample, l half the span between the supports relative to which the deflection of the sample is measured, E the elasticity modulus of the sample, a and c the distances between the initial surface of the sample at the side of the removed layer up to the basis of the corresponding layers of thickness Δa and Δc, φ a correction factor allowing for the final thickness of the layers and given by $\varphi = \frac{1}{1 + \frac{\Delta c}{b - c}}$, Δf the change in the deflection upon removal of the successive layer, and $f_{a-\Delta a}$ the total deflection of the sample after removing all the layers Δc overlaying layer Δa under consideration. Then the sought residual stress in this layer is given by the expression

$$\sigma = \frac{E}{l^2}\left\{\frac{(b-a)^2}{3}\frac{\Delta f}{\Delta a}\varphi - \sum_0^{a-\Delta a}\frac{(b-c)^2}{3}\frac{\Delta f}{\Delta c}\varphi\frac{\Delta c}{b-c} - \right.$$

$$\left. - \sum_0^{a-\Delta a} c\,\Delta f - (b - 2a + \Delta a)\,f_{a-\Delta a}\right\}. \qquad (1.1)$$

This expression was derived under the assumption that deflections Δf are positive if the sample is convex on the side at which the layers are removed. (Expression (1.1) was reproduced incorrectly by Soshko /4/.)

Tests have shown that there are compressive residual stresses in the surface layers of polystyrene samples, while in the inner layers the residual stresses are tensile. Internal cracks appear in working parts of polystyrene samples under the action of an external tensile load which increases continuously at the constant rate of $v = 10$ mm/min.

The principal reason for the appearance of cracks is a destructive process induced by external mechanical action. The mechanical destruction is caused by the localization of mechanical energy in separate sections of the polymeric chains resulting in scission of the chemical bonds.

About 100 samples were tested. In all cases internal cracking was propagated uniformly along the working parts of the samples. Brittle failure occurred upon further load increase. The tests were conducted at room temperature.

The tests have shown that initial failure occurs inside the sample. In polymethyl methacrylate samples free of residual stresses (having been annealed after mechanical treatment) and subjected to tensile stress, the formation and propagation of cracks starts at the surface. In this case the stress induced by external forces is distributed uniformly over the cross-section of the sample.

§2. INVESTIGATION OF INITIAL STRESSES ORIGINATING IN THE PRODUCTION OF COMPOSITE MATERIALS

The production of reinforced materials is accompanied by formation of appreciable initial (or residual) stresses. They are composed of stresses from chemical volume contraction during polymerization and stresses due to the difference in the linear thermal expansion coefficients α of the reinforcing material and the polymer.

During the forming of a polymeric part the state of aggregation of the glass fibers does not change, but the other component, the polymer matrix, undergoes curing, thereby changing its state of aggregation. This process is also accompanied by the formation of initial stresses in the glass – polymeric matrix system. The stresses appearing in the polymerization process of different matrixes have been investigated experimentally by many scientists (see references in /13/).

These results confirm that the principal factor causing the formation of initial stresses is the thermal shrinkage caused by the substantial difference in the thermal expansion coefficients of the polymer and glass fiber. According to Haslett and McGarry, the linear thermal expansion coefficient of E-glass equals $5.04 \cdot 10^{-6}$ deg^{-1} and of P-polyester resin, $43-63 \cdot 10^{-6}$ deg^{-1}, i. e., there is a difference of one order of magnitude. The purely chemical volume contraction in the polymeric matrix is of secondary importance.

It has been established by means of polarization-optical methods that the distribution of residual stresses along the fiber is parabolic. A certain smoothing of the maximum stresses with increasing number of fibers is observed. In Figure 4.1, 1 denotes one fiber and 2 denotes four fibers. The question as to whether the pressure appearing in the polymerization process is maintained for a long time or undergoes relaxation requires further experimental study.

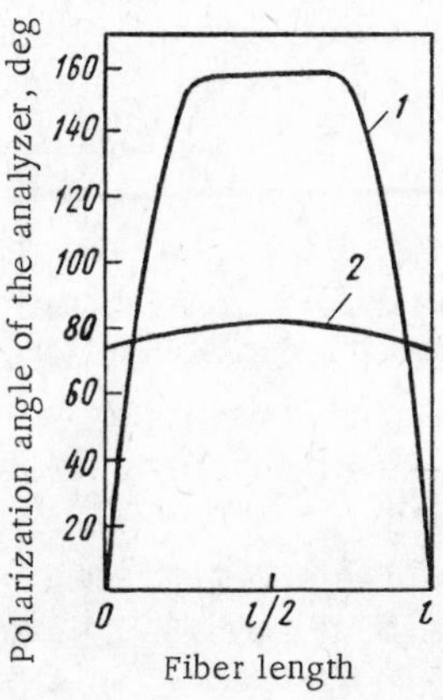

FIGURE 4.1.

The method of quantitative evaluation of the residual stress in ED-6 reinforced epoxy-resin polymer has been developed elsewhere /25/. The polarization-optical method of stress investigation was employed. A cylinder of 60-mm diameter and 100-mm length, reinforced by one, two and four rods of 10-mm diameter, was used as model. Cross-sections (of thickness 2–2.5 mm) of the cured polymer were taken and used to obtain the interference picture in the PPU-4 polarization projector. The data obtained was interpreted using graphic integration along isostatic curves.

The most important reasons for the formation of residual stresses are considered to be the change in volume upon curing, corresponding relaxation processes, and differences in the linear thermal expansion coefficients of the matrix and reinforcing element.

The effect of the indicated factors during the formation of residual stresses has been evaluated as follows. The stresses caused by all the factors are determined on models reinforced by aluminum alloy rods. The whole sample was subjected to heat treatment for two hours at 160°C in order to clarify the role of relaxation of volume change during curing.

The effect of chemical volume contraction was investigated on rod-reinforced models, the rods having been made from previously cured ED-6 polymer. Since in this case the effect of the difference in linear thermal expansion coefficients is eliminated, the formation of residual stresses can be explained only through the forced decrease in equilibrium intermolecular distances upon curing.

It has been established that the principal reason for the appearance of residual stresses upon curing and subsequent cooling of ED-6 reinforced polymer is the thermal volume contraction. It has also been shown that part of the residual stress, up to 10%, undergoes relaxation upon repeated heat treatment, but the remaining part is practically unchanged after numerous heat treatments.

The features of the stressed state were studied on a model elementary cell of regular structure with unidirectional glass-fiber-reinforced plastics, reinforced by four steel rods. It was established that residual stresses act in the cross-section of the model, increasing with decreasing resin content in the cell and attaining ~50–60% of ultimate strength.

Furthermore, upon investigating the stressed state of reinforced sections upon heating with simultaneous recording of half the difference between the principal stresses $(\sigma_1-\sigma_2)/2$ by means of the PPU-4 polarization-optical instrument, the same authors established /5/ that $(\sigma_1-\sigma_2)/2$ decreases with increasing temperature. There is a point or small temperature range ϑ^* at which $(\sigma_1-\sigma_2)/2=0$ (Figure 4.2). Quantity ϑ^* remains unchanged after repeated heat treatment. It can thus be assumed that the residual stresses in reinforced epoxy resin can be evaluated as thermoelastic, in proportion to the difference between the linear thermal expansion coefficient α of the polymer and reinforcing material $(\alpha_p-\alpha_{rein})$ and $\vartheta^*-\vartheta_{comp}$. That part of the stress undergoing relaxation as a result of heat treatment is disregarded here. Figure 4.2 illustrates the change in the number of bands upon heating the reinforced sample after curing (1), after the first heat treatment (2) and after the second heat treatment (3).

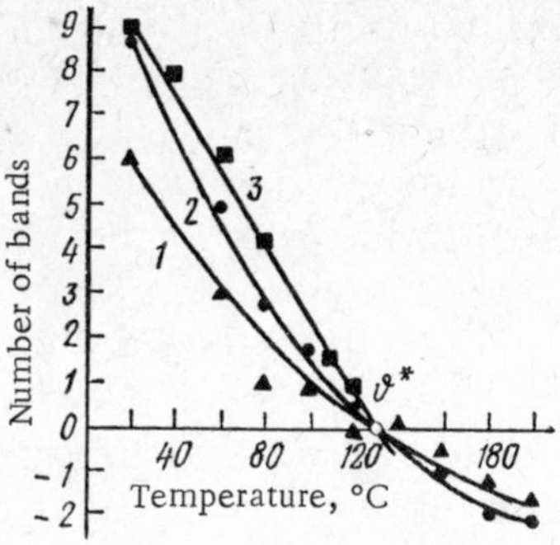

FIGURE 4.2.

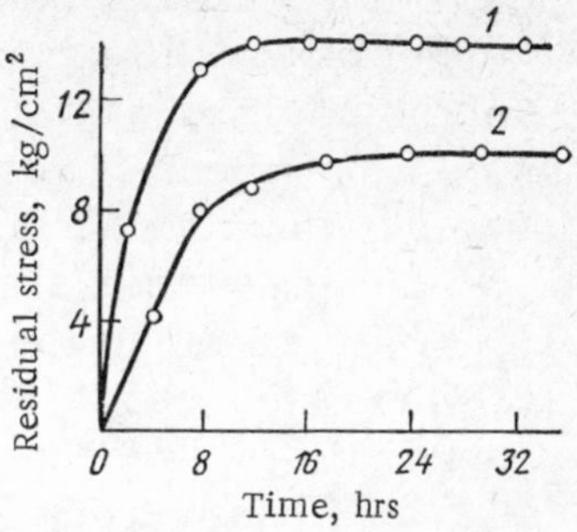

FIGURE 4.3.

Due to the application of glass-fiber-reinforced plastics as protective coating, the effect of the composition of the matrix, the structure of the reinforcing material and conditions of the coating formation on the resulting residual stresses and the strength of the reinforced coatings must be investigated. An account of the experimental study of the kinetics of growth and relaxation of residual stresses in coatings on the basis of polyester, epoxy and epoxy-phenol resins is given by Kiselev et al. /6/. The method of Zubov and Lepilkina for measuring residual stresses was applied /7/.

Measured data on the residual stresses in nonreinforced plates of epoxy-phenol matrix and in coatings reinforced by glass fabric and glass strips treated with paraffin emulsions show that residual stresses are decreased for coatings reinforced with glass fabric in comparison with nonreinforced coatings. In the case of reinforcement with glass strips the residual stresses measured in the direction perpendicular to that of the fiber appreciably exceed the stresses in the nonreinforced coatings.

Figure 4.3 shows the kinetics governing the buildup of residual stress appearing during the formation of a coating on the basis of polyester resin.

Reinforcing by glass-fiber mat (1) which is not treated with an emulsifier increases the initial stresses in the polyester coatings by a factor of 1.5 in comparison with nonreinforced plates (2). The stress distribution on the reinforced coatings is anisotropic. Maximum initial stresses appear in the direction perpendicular to the warp in the case of reinforcing with fabric and perpendicular to the fibers in the case of reinforcing with strip. Anisotropy is especially pronounced in the latter case.

For instance, in polyester coatings reinforced by glass strip the residual stresses measured along the fiber are less than one-tenth of the stresses measured perpendicular to the fiber. It has been shown that the anisotropy in stress distribution does not depend on the position of the surface of the glass fibers.

Thus, measurement of residual stresses in polyester coatings reinforced by glass fabric in the direction of the warp and the weft has shown that the stress along the weft is ten times larger than the residual stress along the warp, independent of the treatment of the glass-fiber surface.

The residual stresses in coatings reinforced with glass-fiber material, which has not been treated with an emulsifier or modified by a sizer in order to increase the adhesion of the matrix to the fiber, are appreciably higher than in the nonreinforced coatings. The mode of curing exerts a substantial influence on the residual stresses. In particular, the stresses in reinforced coatings increase rapidly with curing temperature. Adding a filler to the matrix that increases the adhesion of the polymeric matrix to the glass fibers causes an increase in the residual stresses and a decrease in the strength of the coating.

However, it is noteworthy that even when using glass fabric possessing small strength commensurable with that of the unfilled polymeric coating, the reinforced coating displays higher protective properties than the nonreinforced ones. For example, the strength of asbestos cement is increased 1.5–2 times by a protective polyester coating. The impermeability to water of the same asbestos cement protected by glass-fiber-reinforced plastics is increased one hundred times.

The application of fillers, which are modified by surfactants that diminish the adhesion of the polymeric matrix to the filler, are recommended in order to reduce residual stresses. Alkomon or octadecylamine are used as such modifiers. The tensile strength of a polyester coating reinforced by glass fabric was rapidly restored when the residual stresses dropped by one-third or one-half.

A decrease in the residual stresses can also be obtained by alternating the direction of the fibers of the reinforcing filler. In this case a less sharp increase in the residual stresses upon increasing the thickness of the coating is observed than in coatings in which all the fibers in one layer lie in the same direction.

In glass-fiber-reinforced plastics prepared on the basis of epoxyphenol resin, either unplasticized (EF) or plasticized with polyvinylbutyral (EFB-3), or prepared on the basis of epoxy resin, either unplasticized (K-82) or plasticized with Thiokol (K-97b) and reinforced with tape, the determination of the initial stresses by an optical method employing an automatic recorder /12/ has shown that maximum stresses appear in the direction perpendicular to that of the fibers. No stress was detected in the direction of the glass fiber.

The largest initial stresses in glass-fiber-reinforced plastics (reinforced by fabric) appear along the weft and the smallest along the warp. The kinetics of the buildup and relaxation of the initial stresses in glass-fiber-reinforced plastics are similar to those observed in reinforced coatings. Figure 4.4 illustrates data on glass-fiber-reinforced plastics using epoxyphenol adhesives filled with strip (1, 2, 3) and fabric (4, 5, 6) for a two-layer coating. Here the heat treatment method has a great effect.

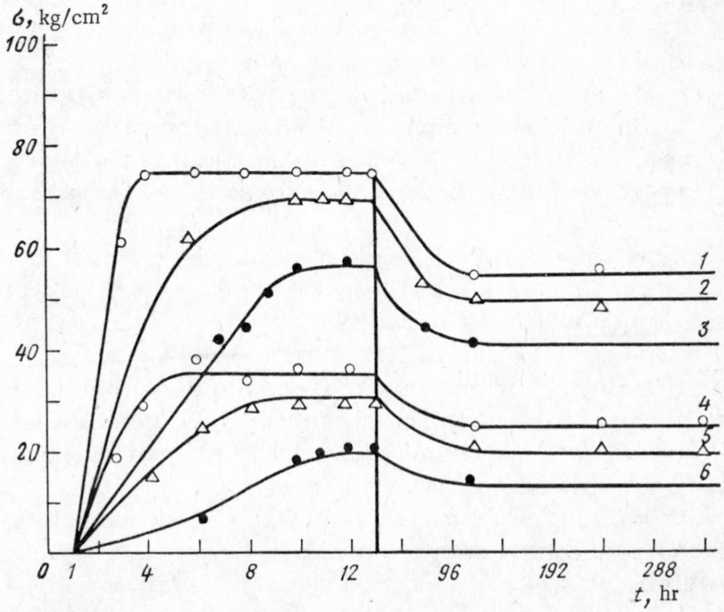

FIGURE 4.4.

The nature of the matrix also affects the initial stresses. Thus the largest stresses appear in samples on the basis of the less elastic K-82 and EF matrix. These glass-fiber-reinforced plastics also possess the worst strength properties. An increase in initial stresses in glass-fiber-reinforced plastics causes a decrease in their strength. The dependence of the initial stresses on the thickness of the plates was shown to be linear also for other matrixes /9, 10/.

A linear buildup of initial stresses was also observed in glass-fiber-reinforced plastics with increasing number of layers, having identical fiber orientation. In multilayer (as well as in single-layer) glass-fiber-reinforced plastics (reinforced by strip in the same direction) the maximum initial stresses are markedly larger than in glass-fiber-reinforced plastics on the basis of fabric.

The conclusions expounded above have been confirmed by other results /8/. The stresses appearing in glass-fiber-reinforced plastics as a result of volume contraction of the polymer matrix during curing were evaluated by means of photoelastic methods using models.

Samples cured at different temperatures were studied in order to establish the temperature dependence of the stresses. As in /6/, comparison of the band diagram shows that the formation of initial stresses is more intensive in samples cured at higher temperatures.

The investigation of the effect of the "interphase layer" (emulsion, sizer, antiadhesive coating) at the fiber-resin interface on the resulting initial stresses has shown that the largest stresses appear in samples with antiadhesion plates. Samples without "interphase layer" or paraffin emulsion possess comparatively small stresses.

The initial stresses are to a marked extent determined by the physicomechanical properties of the component materials, and can cause such phenomena as porosity, cracking of the material, and destruction of the surface of fibers.

The substantial effect of the initial stresses appearing in matrix layers near the glass fibers on the strength of the glass-fiber-reinforced plastics was examined by studying processes occurring at the glass-fiber-matrix boundary /11/.

Etching with various solvents was used to detect insufficiently cured or stressed sections of the matrix in glass-fiber-reinforced plastics. Acetone was used to etch epoxy, polyester and silicoorganic glass-fiber-reinforced plastics. Acetone, concentrated sulfuric acid, acetone—benzene mixtures and aqueous KOH solutions of different concentration were used to etch FN glass-fiber-reinforced plastics (with furfurol-formaldehyde resins).

Rings of decomposed resin formed around the fiber after etching the polished section of glass-fiber-reinforced plastic. The investigation of the curing process of a series of resins in the presence of fibers differing in surface treatment revealed no relationship between curing rate and type of glass-fiber treatment. Hence the decomposition of the resin around the fiber upon etching the polished surfaces of glass-fiber-reinforced plastics indicates only a high stress in the matrix layer adjacent to the glass fiber, i.e., qualitatively confirms the formation of initial stresses during curing of the material.

The preparation of an article from glass-fiber-reinforced plastics by means of winding is accompanied by the appearance of initial stresses. During winding of glass tape at constant winding force, owing to the stress decrease during winding and during the heat treatment, the stress in the turns at the end of the technological process is substantially different from the specified one at the time of winding and can be very nonhomogeneous /14/. This causes the appearance of marked initial stresses in the finished article.

The difference between the thermal expansion coefficients of the mandrel and wound material can also cause initial stresses. A tensile stress is induced in the article upon heating the mandrel with wound material. Portnov et al. /15/ noted that because of the large compliance of initially impregnated glass-fiber-reinforced plastics in the direction perpendicular to the reinforcing layer, circular, substantially irregular stresses are formed in the article. The rigidity of the matrix in the radial direction increases rapidly upon curing. When the article is cured on the mandrel, stresses in it are partially relieved. In this case the initial stresses are equal to the difference of these differently distributed stresses but correspond to the same tensile stress.

Heterogeneity of elastic and thermophysical properties in the section of thin-walled articles, such as polymerization conditions varying with the thickness of the article, or different glass content, can also be a cause of appreciable initial stresses upon cooling the finished article.

Methods for the experimental determination of initial stresses in a ring of glass-fiber-reinforced plastics are discussed and the effect of tensioning glass tape during winding on their value is investigated elsewhere /15/. It has been shown that by changing the tensile stresses during winding the stress pattern can be controlled to a considerable extent.

The samples investigated were rings of fiber-glass laminate with EDT-10 matrix prepared by winding with low stress on the strip (1 to 3 kg/cm^2).

The initial stresses in the rings were determined by two methods, namely cutting them radially and measuring the opening or closing of the gap and removing layers by boring or turning of the rings and measuring the deformations on opposite sides (Sachs's method). The second method, boring or turning, in the case of materials reinforced by glass fabric was replaced by layerwise unwinding of the fabric layers and measuring the deformation on opposite sides of the ring over a certain number of turns, for sufficiently thick rings. This makes it possible to enhance the accuracy of stress determination. One should, however, bear in mind that this method is applicable only when investigating sufficiently thick rings.

The method of cutting sections for determining initial stresses is applied on the assumption that their distribution is linear along the sections of the ring. Then the initial circumferential stresses σ_θ^0 in the ring, the thickness of which is small compared with the radius, is given by

$$\sigma_\theta^0 = \frac{E_\theta (r - r_0)}{2\pi r_0^2} \Delta h, \tag{2.1}$$

where r_0 is the mean radius of the ring and Δh the opening or closing of the gap after cutting. Rings of glass fabric with EDT-10 matrix of diameter 200 mm and thickness 5.5 mm wound with a different, but time constant tensile force have been investigated by this method. The dependence of the closing of the gap Δh on the tensile force τ is illustrated in Figure 4.5. The maximum stress computed from equation (2.1) varies from ± 230 to ± 780 kg/cm^2 (considering the change in modulus of elasticity from $2.7 \cdot 10^5$ to $3.5 \cdot 10^5$ kg/cm^2). In this case tensile stresses act on the inner surface of the ring and compressive stresses on the outer surface.

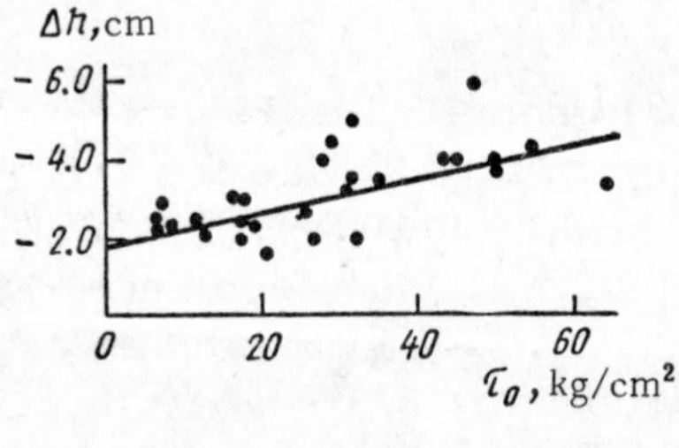

FIGURE 4.5.

The method of layer-by-layer removal enables one to determine not only the magnitude but also the nature of the distribution of the initial stresses.

The following expressions for circumferential and radial stresses were obtained for thick-walled rings made from material with cylindrical isotropy:

for unwinding over the external diameter (turning)

$$\sigma_\theta^0 = -\frac{E_\theta}{2\beta R_{\text{in}}^{\beta-1}}\left[\frac{\beta(r^{2\beta}+R_{\text{in}}^{2\beta})}{r^{\beta+1}}\varepsilon_\theta + \frac{r^{2\beta}-R_{\text{in}}^{2\beta}}{r^\beta}\frac{d\varepsilon_\theta}{dr}\right], \tag{2.2}$$

$$\sigma_r^0 = -\frac{E_\theta}{2\beta}\cdot\frac{r^{2\beta}-R_{\text{in}}^{2\beta}}{R_{\text{in}}^{\beta-1}\,r^{\beta+1}}\varepsilon_\theta, \tag{2.3}$$

where E_θ is the elasticity modulus of the ring in the circumferential direction, r the running radius, ε_θ the circumferential deformation at the inner radius R_{in} upon removing layers up to radius r, $\beta = \sqrt{E_\theta/E_r}$;

for unwinding over internal diameters (boring)

$$\sigma_\theta^0 = \frac{E_\theta}{2\beta R_{\text{out}}^{\beta-1}}\left[\frac{R_{\text{out}}^{2\beta}-r^{2\beta}}{r^\beta}\frac{d\varepsilon_\theta}{dr} - \frac{\beta(R_{\text{out}}^{2\beta}+r^{2\beta})}{r^{\beta+1}}\varepsilon_\theta\right], \tag{2.4}$$

$$\sigma_r^0 = \frac{E_\theta}{2\beta}\,\frac{R_{\text{out}}^{2\beta}-r^{2\beta}}{R_{\text{out}}^{\beta-1}\,r^{\beta+1}}\varepsilon_\theta; \tag{2.5}$$

where ε_θ is the circumferential deformation at the outer radius R_{out} upon removing layers up to radius r.

The deformation during unwinding in the corresponding surfaces of the ring can be measured by means of resistance strain gages. The deformation curves $\varepsilon_\theta \sim r$ are constructed according to the gage data. Upon finding the values of $d\varepsilon_\theta/dr$ by graphic differentiation, the stress curves can be plotted by employing expressions (2.2) to (2.5). It is noteworthy that an axisymmetric stress distribution is assumed and also that the material is linearly elastic and homogeneous with respect to elastic properties. Since in reality the elastic properties vary substantially with the height of the ring, the values of the stresses derived from (2.2)–(2.5) must be regarded as estimates.

In order to investigate the effect of the winding stress on the initial stresses, tests were carried out on rings having the same number of turns but obtained under different stretching conditions, constant for each ring, and also on rings with different numbers of turns obtained with the same winding stress.

The following conclusions can be derived from an analysis of the initial stresses:

1. Initial stresses increase considerably with increasing tensile stress (during winding $\tau_0 = \text{const}$). This indicates that the principal source of initial stresses is the tensile stress in the glass tape during winding.

2. Increase in ring thickness causes a marked increase in initial stresses. This can be ascribed to the unequal tensile stresses in the upper and lower soils.

3. Initial stresses also occur in rings made without tension, but they may be due to other causes which were discussed above.

4. The initial stresses may attain a considerable value, the most dangerous being the radial stresses as a result of the low tensile strength of the glass-fiber-reinforced plastic perpendicular to the layers. Changing the tensile stress in the glass strip during winding has been proposed as a means of regulating the initial stress distribution and attaining their optimum distribution from the standpoint of strength.

If a part of glass-fiber-reinforced plastics operates under conditions of constrained deformations, the relationship between the residual stresses in the finished article and the winding stress on the glass strip or glass fabric must be known. (The residual stresses appear during the winding of glass-fiber-reinforced plastics on parts owing to constrained deformation on the inner surface.)

It has been shown experimentally /14/ that the tensile stress of the winding changes during the forming process. A decrease in the total tensile stress occurs in the winding process due to radial deformation of previously wound turns as well as in the polymerization of the matrix.

A ring-shaped article was prepared from unidirectional glass-fiber-reinforced plastic wound on a thin-walled metallic dynamometric ring mandrel of the following dimensions: outer diameter of the ring 295 mm, width 100 mm and thickness of the ring 4 mm. The dynamometric ring was mounted in a special fixture ensuring its elastic mounting upon the transmission of a torque from the machine drive.

The LSB-F unidirectional glass strip reinforced with PE-933 epoxy polyester matrix was used as initial material. The ring had twenty turns applied in one layer under constant stress τ_0 during winding.

The deformation of the ring mandrel was measured with four heat-resistant sensors arranged symmetrically around the circumference of the ring at equal distance from its butt faces. The polymerization temperature of the LSB-F strip was 155°C.

Figure 4.6 shows the decrease in the previously specified stress upon the ring winding during its preparation. Here, 1—4 are the readings of the heat-resistant strain gages glued to the dynamometer ring, and T is the temperature of the ring during winding, polymerization and cooling. The total decrease in prestress for this material is shown in Figure 4.7, where 1 is after winding, 2 after polymerization ($T = 155°C$), and 3 after cooling to room temperature. Quantity τ_p is the prestress. It is evident from the figure that in the range of the usually applied tensile stresses the relative magnitude of the residual stress depends little on the initially given stress. The residual stress τ_{res} depends on the type of matrix, percentage of glass-fiber-content and initial stress τ_0. It has been noted elsewhere /17/ that for a series of wound glass-fiber-reinforced plastics

$$\tau_{res} \approx 0.3 - 0.6\tau_0.$$

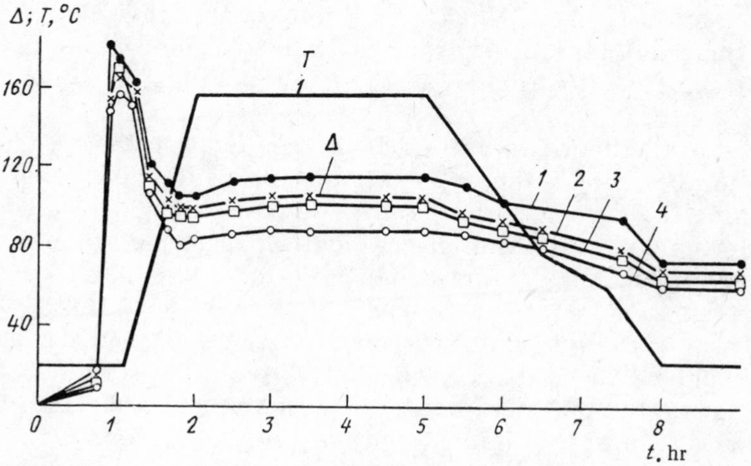

FIGURE 4.6.

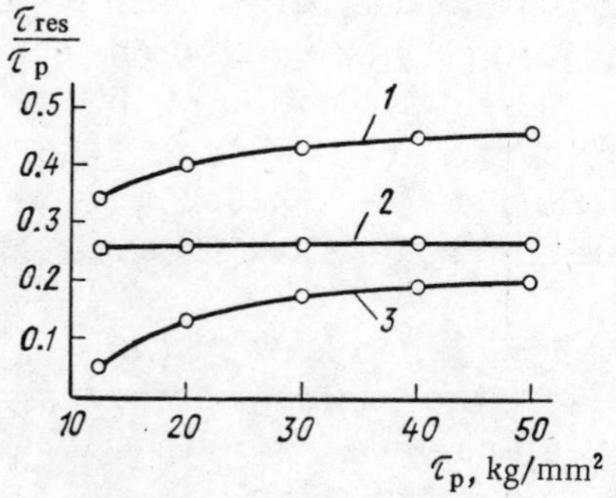

FIGURE 4.7.

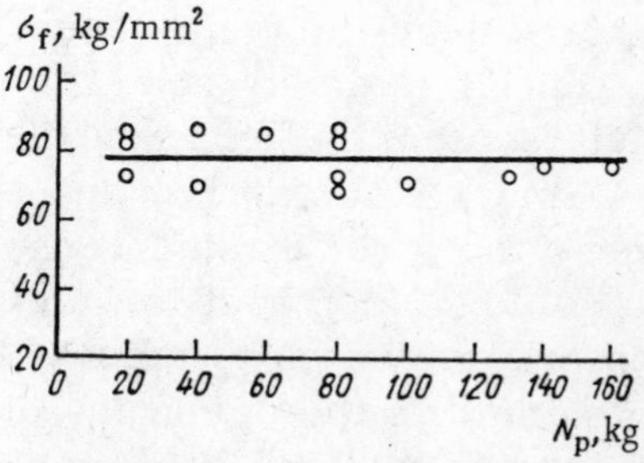

FIGURE 4.8.

The data specified above were obtained by R. E. Brivmanis from a study of the winding of annular samples. According to the data of I. G. Zhigun, winding of flat samples is also accompanied by a decrease in tensile stress. When prestressed flat samples of AG-4S material are pressed, the residual stress of the reinforcement is

$$\tau_{res} \approx 0.70 - 0.85\tau_0,$$

In this case the decrease in tensile stress during winding was eliminated by a special device.

The relationship between strength and winding force must be established in order to evaluate the strength of a structure. The experimental data on unidirectional glass-fiber-reinforced plastics with a plastic matrix /14/ (Figure 4.8) indicate that the tensile strength of the free rings σ_f is practically independent of the tensile stress N_p. Goldfein /20/ arrived at the same conclusion in the case of flat samples.

In addition to the absolute values of the residual stresses it is of importance in operation to know the sign of the residual stresses when assessing the strength of a part. The corresponding data in /18/ refer to the determination of residual stresses by boring in glass-fiber-reinforced elements produced either by winding or by hot pressing.

The analysis of the graphs of distribution of the circumferential stresses throughout the wall of a wound disk from AG-4S glass fiber has shown that their maximum positive values amount to ~100 kg/cm^2 in the middle layers of the disk. Negative residual stresses are maximal at the inner and outer surfaces of the disk and have the same order of magnitude.

Larger residual stresses appear in massive parts of AG-4S prepared by hot pressing and amount to 150–200 kg/cm^2. In this case tensile stresses of appreciable magnitude appear also on the inner surface near the edge of the hole. The distribution of the circumferential residual stresses over the wall thickness of the hub of a full-scale impeller made of material based on cotton liners and AG-4S matrix has shown that the maximum tensile stresses appear near the inner surface of the hole.

It can be concluded that for the parts investigated, which in operation are subjected to tensile stresses, the residual stresses are detrimental as the operating stresses are added to the residual stresses, and moreover, their maxima frequently coincide.

It is noteworthy that according to the data of /18/ the residual stresses are stable and relax within 1.5 years.

The transition to programmed winding often causes a change in the graph of the initial stresses in the finished part. Comparison of the data obtained in a ring wound at $\tau_0 =$ const with the case when the force in the tensioning device changes linearly /22/ has revealed that even switching over to such a simple program markedly reduces the initial stresses in the cross-sections of the ring.

Because the initial stresses are dependent on the tensile force, this force can be optimized in winding in line with the graph of the residual stresses. The selection of $\tau_0(r)$ should be such that after taking into account the polymerization process, the initial stresses should be minimal and obey in advance the specified law to provide the optimization of the properties of the wound articles. Tarnopol'skii and Portnov /23/ designed a program $\tau_0(r)$ which allows for changes in the deformation properties of the material during polymerization.

Prestressing of the reinforcement is an effective means for controlling the initial stresses appearing during the forming of an article from oriented reinforced plastics.

It has been shown experimentally /17/ that if an article is formed without tensioning the reinforcement, compressive forces which appear in the process of polymerization, acting along the glass fiber, cause its distortion. Prestressing the fibers protects them from loss of stability during curing and provides the possibility of raising the strength of the composite material.

Goldfein /20/ has discovered experimentally that a substantially higher bending strength (short- and long-term) and flexural rigidity are obtained by prestressing the fibers during processing and subsequent curing of the composition in the stressed state. In this case tensile and shear strength turn out to be practically independent of the prestress of the reinforcement. The strength properties of the prestressed composition in the direction perpendicular to the direction of the tension turn out to be lower than in the unstressed state.

The dependence of the flexural rigidity on the prestress for glass-fiber-reinforced polyester resin in the initial state (1) and after aging at room temperature for 13,000 hours (2) is shown in Figure 4.9 /20/.

The maximum strength increase by prestressing the reinforcement exceeds 50%. About 70% of the initial strength increase is preserved after aging for 7–19 months. Goldfein concluded from tests on polyester plastics with different percentage content of glass fibers that prestressing achieves a greater effect with plastics with a higher percentage of glass fibers.

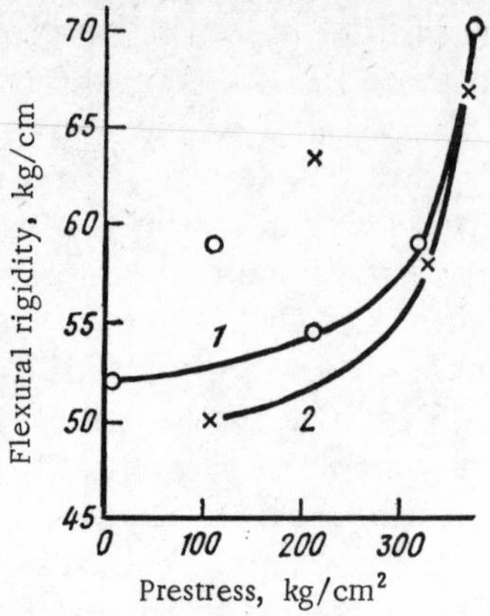

FIGURE 4.9.

The effect of the increased strength characteristics of the composition in question is mainly due to the advantageous redistribution of the initial stresses. Thus, if the filler is prestressed in tension during the forming of an article, then after load removal the filler contracts and compresses the matrix, which causes a decrease in the initial stresses and sometimes even the reversal of their sign.

Bartenev and Motorina /21/ investigated the effect of prestressing on the strength of glass fibers and established that the strength of the glass fibers can be enhanced by heat treatment under load. In this case increase in prestress doubles the strength of the original glass fibers. The strengthening effect is preserved even after cooling of the fibers, due to the diminished stress concentrations in the corners of microcracks as a result of induced elastic and plastic strain.

Because of the particular structure and production technology, glass-fiber-reinforced plastics have a considerable nonuniformity of mechanical properties which is more manifest than in metals. The following reasons may be regarded as the principal ones for the nonuniformity in their properties. A longitudinal tensile stress is exerted in the production of sheets of glass-fiber-reinforced plastics, but not a transverse stress. Since during production of the material polymerization occurs under longitudinal tensile stress, there is a difference in the scatter of data along and perpendicular to the fibers and the sheets may be nonorthotropic, the scatter in the perpendicular direction (weft) being larger.

The second cause of the increased nonhomogeneity in the properties of glass-fiber-reinforced plastics are stress concentrations around the fibers owing to the difference in Poisson's ratios and the temperature coefficients of resin and glass fibers. The polymerization ends with the longitudinal fibers under tensile stress. When the tension is removed, additional pressure on the transverse fibers and additional stress concentrations around them occur.

The scatter in properties of glass-fiber-reinforced plastics can be partially reduced by additional heat treatment. The additional heating may be even repeated several times.

However, it is known that the first heating has the greatest effect on the physicomechanical properties of the reinforced plastics and causes partial stabilization of their properties.

Heat treatment conducted while considering the conditions of polymerization of the matrix causes a decrease in the initial technological stresses and an increase in the adhesive bonds. In individual cases, additional polymerization may also cause an increase in the mechanical properties of the resin and increase the strength and rigidity of the composition /26/.

Heat treatment may also be combined with additional tensile stress which structures the material and enhances the stability of its properties. Therefore all the mechanical actions (tension, pressure) during mechanical treatment can play a positive role in obtaining material with stabler mechanical properties.

Volume contraction upon curing must be mentioned as one of those physical properties of resins on which the behavior of fiber-reinforced plastics is most dependent, since it is immediately related to the appearance of residual stresses. Material generalizing this subject has been published in a monograph /27/.

In typical cases the volume contraction upon curing of the epoxide and polyester resins amounted to 2–12%, which in conjunction with the thermal contraction upon cooling causes the appearance of residual stresses in the matrix and filler. In the matrix these stresses usually amount to between 70 and 240 kg/cm^2, being compressive in the radial direction and tensile in the tangential direction, and depending on the maximum curing temperature and volume contraction upon curing. As a result of the presence of frictional forces exerted on the perpendicular surfaces of the fiber all along its length, the residual stresses affect the adhesion on the fibers-matrix interface. It has been confirmed experimentally that the strength of the interface adhesion affects the properties of the plastics.

However, investigations by a number of scientists did not establish a linear relationship between the volume contraction of the resin and properties of the plastics. One of the principal difficulties in similar tests occurs when attempts are made to relate a certain physical property of the resin to the performance of the plastic.

It is obviously practically impossible to change the extent of the volume contraction of the resin without changing the other technological parameters and mechanical properties, which also affect the properties of the plastic. Thus, one should bear in mind that it is impossible to change one property of resin without changing other properties as well.

§3. INVESTIGATION OF THERMAL STRESSES

We shall now consider the stresses caused by changes of temperature in conjunction with residual stresses and stress raisers.

Residual thermal stresses appear in composite material under two conditions: 1) the linear expansion coefficient of the filler α_f differs from that of the matrix α_m, and 2) the temperature of the composition changes in the production process after curing of the matrix.

The temperature gradient is usually measured from the melting point of the crystalline material or from the glass transition temperature for amorphous material (noncrystalline polymers and glass). An analysis of residual temperature stresses in composite material for the case of plane deformation is contained elsewhere /27/.

The state of stress around a circular reinforced particle (cylinder) in an infinite matrix is expressed in polar coordinates in the form

$$\sigma_r = -p\left(\frac{a}{r}\right)^2; \ \sigma_\theta = p\left(\frac{a}{r}\right)^2; \ \tau_{r\theta} = 0, \qquad (3.1)$$

where a is the radius of the reinforced particle, r the radial distance to a certain point in the matrix, p the radial stress at the particle-matrix interface. The signs in (3.1) correspond to the case when $\alpha_m > \alpha_f$. Gerard and Gilbert have shown that

$$p = \frac{(\alpha_m - \alpha_f)\,\Delta T E_m}{(1+\nu_m)+(1+\nu_f)(E_m/E_f)}, \qquad (3.2)$$

where α_m and α_f are the mean values of the linear expansion coefficients of the matrix and filler, E_m and E_f are the moduli of elasticity; ν_m and ν_f are Poisson's ratios in the temperature range ΔT.

In the case of a large number of filler particles distributed close to one another, their stress fields interact. In this case the approximate solution of Haslett and McGarry is applied. Thus for hexagonal packing of equidistant cylindrical particles (assuming elastic behavior of the material), superposition of the radial stresses is examined along the lines joining two particles:

$$\sigma_r = -p\left[\left(\frac{a}{r}\right)^2 + \left(\frac{a}{2s-r}\right)^2\right]. \tag{3.3}$$

The radial stress σ_r found by means of superposition has an acceptable value when $s/a \geqslant 1.25$, where $2s$ is the distance between the centers of the two particles.

The investigation conducted by Daniel and Durelli by means of polarization-optical methods has confirmed the validity of expression (3.3). It was also observed that the distribution of tangential stresses σ_θ at the interface is sufficiently close to the distribution given by (3.1).

Equations (3.1)–(3.3) pertain to plane deformation. It has been noted /27/ that they apparently apply to long cigar-shaped particles and fibers. Relationships (3.1) give an approximate stress distribution for spherical or disklike particles, where p from (3.2) has a somewhat different value.

The analysis of the residual temperature stresses for individual particles under plane deformation reveals throughout a radial compressive stress σ_r if $\alpha_m > \alpha_f$ and a tensile stress if $\alpha_m < \alpha_f$. Similarly, the tangential stress components are tensile throughout when $\alpha_m > \alpha_f$ and compressive when $\alpha_m < \alpha_f$.

If not less than three fibers are in contact or almost in contact with each other, the sign of σ_r changes. West et al. have shown that upon contact of three particles the radial and tangential stresses are tensile if $\alpha_m > \alpha_f$ and compressive if $\alpha_m < \alpha_f$. For closely spaced noncontacting fibers ($1 < s/a < 1.45$) the axial stress may become compressive due to the effect of Poisson's ratio, but it is small in comparison with σ_r and σ_θ.

The strength of glass-fiber-reinforced plastic, as dependent on thermal stresses appearing in the resin–glass filler system during matrix curing, has been investigated /30/. Experimental temperature curves of the filler and matrix, the temperature distribution in the resin–glass system and the dependence of maximum resin temperature on the weight of the test sample were obtained. The temperature curves were recorded by means of thermocouples.

The results of investigating the temperature fields during unsteady one-sided heating are given in /31/. Based on experimentally obtained temperature distribution across the material, the temperature stresses have been computed for fiber-glass Textolite at 0, 45 and 90° to the warp. A relationship was established between increase in thermal stresses and rate and duration of heating.

The investigation of temperature distribution over the thickness was conducted on samples of 120 × 15 × 6 mm rectangular cross section. The study was carried out on FN glass-fiber Textolite on the basis of glass fabric. The number of layers of glass fabric equalled 18, its content by weight being 65–70%.

The one-sided heating was effected by the contact method using thermal elements with which the sample could be heated to +800°C at a rate of temperature increase up to 5°C per second. The temperature of the sample over the thickness was measured by five chromel-copel thermocouples 0.2 mm in diameter and attached to a PP-1 instrument. The thermocouples were sealed inside the test sample by resin, which had practically no detrimental effect on the monolithic nature of the material.

Thermal stresses can attain appreciable values. This has been shown experimentally in /28/, where the flexural thermal stresses in the case of clamped test samples of asbestos laminate were measured under intensive one-sided heating.

The test samples of rectangular cross section (180 × 15 × 17 mm) were placed freely on supports positioned 160 mm apart and heated at a rate of 8° per second with a nickel-plate heater pressed tightly to the sample from above. When the temperature of the sample at the surface attained 400°C, it was held. The deflection of the test sample was measured in the middle of the heating process and also upon cooling. The temperature was measured by means of three thermocouples placed, respectively, at the heated surface, at a depth of 7 mm, and on the opposite side of the test sample. The paper contains certain recommendations for experimental procedures with plastics in the case of one-sided heating.

Goldfein /29/ investigated the breaking stresses in reinforced plastics as a function of temperature and time.

The experimental procedure of investigating temperature deformation in glass-fiber-reinforced plastics is expounded in /32/. The state of stress was determined by strain gages which had been fixed together with the connecting leads between the layers of the material during production.

In the investigation of the state of stress of a square plate of glass-fiber-reinforced plastic, tensometers were attached in two mutually perpendicular directions and oriented along the directions of the sides of the plates.

In the investigation of stresses in articles of complex shape, where the direction of the principal stresses is unknown, the tensometers were positioned in the form of a rosette. Chromel-copel thermocouples for checking the temperatures were placed in the immediate neighborhood of the tensometers. Asbestos fabric was used as basic material for one part of the layers and glass fabric for the others. As a result the distribution of the relative residual deformations across the material in two mutually perpendicular directions was obtained.

It should be borne in mind that if glass-fiber-reinforced plastics are heated and then kept for a sufficiently long time at constant temperature, the thermal stresses relax considerably and their effect on the strength may be neglected /33/.

A simple method for the experimental determination of thermal stresses was developed in /34/. The stresses appearing in a rod of polymeric material with fixed ends under linear temperature changes in time and in the absence of axial and radial temperature gradients were investigated.

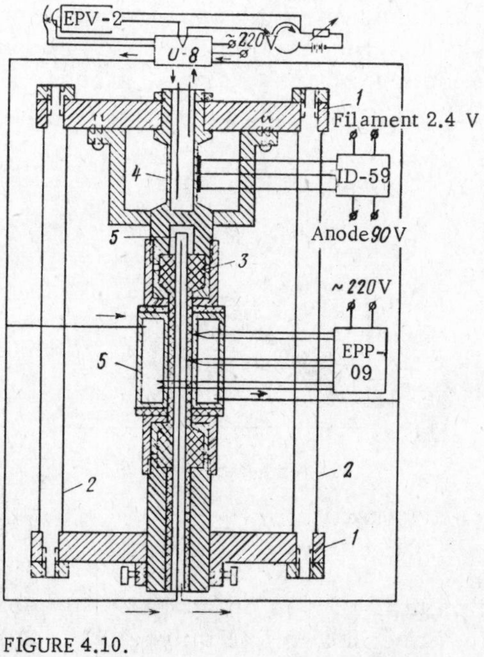

FIGURE 4.10.

A diagram of the setup is shown in Figure 4.10. Two rigid plates (1) are connected by rigid uprights (2). Dynamometer (4) is positioned between the upper plate and the sample (3). The other end of the test sample is rigidly attached to the lower plate. The deformations of the dynamometer are negligibly small in comparison with the thermal expansion of the free sample, but sufficient for making it possible to determine stress changes in the rod due to changes in temperature by means of the ID-59 electronic instrument. The dynamometer is thermostated internally and the sensors in it thermally insulated. A thin-walled tubular test sample with thickened ends is used. The test sample is heated and cooled from outside and inside by means of tubular heat exchangers (5). The internal heat exchanger is a copper tube. The external heat exchanger consists of two hollow hermetically sealed copper half-cylinders into which the heat carrier (glycerol) is fed from the U-8 thermostat providing heating or cooling at a constant rate, realized by means of a programming unit.

The selected shape of the polymeric test sample and design of the heat exchangers provide a homogeneous temperature field in the test sample throughout the test.

In order to relieve the initial stresses, the polymeric samples investigated had been annealed for 2—3 hours at a temperature somewhat below their glass point. The temperature of the test sample was checked by thin copper-constantan thermocouples connected to a three-point EPP-09 recording potentiometer. The dependence of the thermal stresses in the test sample on the heating and cooling rates can be obtained with this instrument.

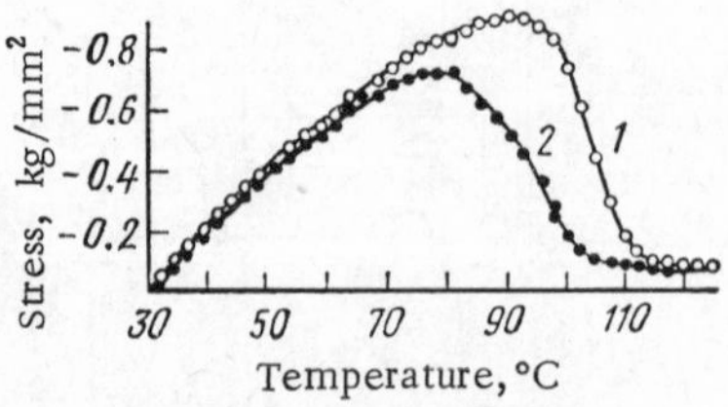

FIGURE 4.11.

Typical experimental curves on an EDT-10 epoxide composition at two heating rates are shown in Figure 4.11. Curve 1 corresponds to a heating rate of 4°C per minute and curve 2 to a rate of 1°C per minute. The first section shows a near-linear increase in stress with temperature and the second a stress relaxation practically down to zero.

The stress changes sign during the subsequent cooling of the test sample at constant rate and may attain larger values than upon heating, because relaxation processes in this region are impeded.

Analogous results have been obtained by Slonimskii and Askadskii /35/, who studied cylindrical polymeric test samples for stress relaxation at varying temperature. The samples were placed into the thermostated space between two working cylinders of a relaxometer. The initial strain of the test sample equaled zero. Consequently, no initial stress appeared in the test sample. Then the temperature was raised linearly at a rate of 80–90° per hour.

Since the working cylinders of the relaxometer were attached rigidly, temperature stresses appeared in the test sample. The experimental results were given by graphs which are similar to those presented in Figure 4.11. Such tests may also be conducted at different initial strains of the test samples.

The effect of elevated temperature on the strength of cured resins and materials based on them was treated elsewhere /16/.

Standard samples were examined, obtained by pressing phenol-formaldehyde resin of resol type (R-300 resin), phenol-aniline-formaldehyde resin modified by polyvinylacetate (R-2m resin), and phenol-aniline-formaldehyde resin modified by furfurol (FN resin). The presence of a thermoplastic fraction in the cured R-2m resin is indicated by the thermomechanical curve recorded with a Lazurkin instrument.

The compressive strength of resin heated to different temperatures and held for different times was studied. The heating was effected in a tubular furnace in air. Each set of tests was repeated three times.

It was established by investigating the relative change of weight and the compressive strength of the R-300 resin and R-2m and FN resins that upon thermal decomposition a sudden transition from the first to the second and third structural stages occurs with steadily increasing stability of the strength properties.

The creep strength of polymethylmethacrylate at temperatures from −120 to 150°C in air and vacuum was studied by Soshko et al. /24/. The test samples were tested for uniaxial tension by standard methods.

Chapter V

STRUCTURAL ANALYSIS AND METHODS OF DETERMINING ADHESIVE STRENGTH OF REINFORCED POLYMERS

The fundamental state of knowledge about the relationship between the supramolecular structure of polymers and their mechanical properties is dealt with briefly in the present chapter. The effect of adhesion bonds between filler and matrix in polymers with fillers (mainly with fibrous fillers) on the strength properties of the latter has been noted. An account is given of the main results of research in this field.

§1. INVESTIGATION OF STRUCTURAL SUPRAMOLECULAR FORMATIONS OF POLYMERS

The great length of polymer molecules in comparison with their "cross-sectional" area determines the flexibility of the chains of polymeric molecules. The flexibility determines the ability of the molecule to sustain considerable deformations without failure (up to 5% and sometimes even more), and subsequently recover its initial shape and dimensions. Material of small molecules can, after all, undergo large deformations, too, upon application of fairly large stresses. But in this case the process consists in sliding of atoms or molecules relative to one another as a result of which they occupy new positions. In this case the ratios between the forces acting on the particles and the interparticle distance are such that spontaneous reversible processes cannot occur if the deformation exceeds about 0.3%. Therefore nonpolymeric materials lack such properties as elasticity.

If the chemical bond joining monomeric units in the macromolecule forms a linear chain, such as that shown in Figure 5.1a in which a carbon atom chain is represented, the elongation of such molecules can be achieved simply, due to the mobility of the chain segments relative to the carbon-carbon bonds. In the above example the elongated shape of the chain represented in Figure 5.1b can be attained by the application of a mechanical field, the molecules being drawn out without any distortion in the length of the chemical bonds and valency angles.

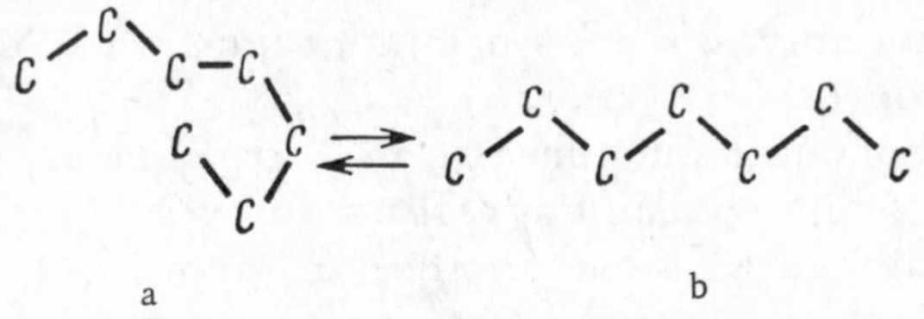

FIGURE 5.1.

The coiled conformation (Figure 5.1a) is a more probable one than the elongated conformation (Figure 5.1b). Consequently a spontaneous transition from state *b* to state *a* may take place immediately upon removing the tensile stress on the polymer chain, since this process involves a favorable change in the probability of the state of the system and consequently in the entropy (the entropy increases).

These considerations were derived on the basis of the theory of the Mackian elasticity of rubber-like materials which gives a quite satisfactory explanation of the ability of such materials to sustain reversible elongation up to 1000%. But rubber is only one group of polymeric materials and in many cases their ability to resist various deformations (i. e., their moduli) is small, at least one or two orders of magnitude lower than required. Therefore either glass-like or crystalline polymers are used as plastic materials.

In glass-like polymers which are amorphous substances in the glass state, the mobility of the macromolecules is limited so that they cannot pass from one conformation to another due to stress. The presence of crystalline regions in which strong interaction between macromolecules prevails causes an increase in the mechanical moduli of crystalline polymers. At the same time the polymers preserve their ability to sustain reversible deformations, which amount to about 5%. The great length of the macromolecules hampers the crystallization process. Therefore, crystalline polymers always contain amorphous regions in addition to crystalline regions. Because of this, crystalline polymers are frequently called amorphous-crystalline.

According to modern concepts there is a certain degree of regularity even in amorphous polymers. The concept, widespread in the early stages of development of polymer science, that amorphous polymers are completely disordered, at random forming something similar to felt, is at present unacceptable /2/. A system of macromolecules randomly oriented relative to one another would be very loose and energetically unfavorable. But the actual polymers have a density which does not differ much from that anticipated for dense packing. For example, the density of the initially amorphous polymer does not increase by more than 10% upon crystallization.

Following the concepts put forward by Kargin et al. /3/, the macromolecules of amorphous as well as amorphous-crystalline polymers are combined with one another to form bundles. The existence of bundles in polymer solutions was inferred by methods of electron microscopy, the bundles being visible under the electron microscope. The length of the bundle generally exceeds that of the individual macromolecule and is determined by its molecular weight. It is assumed that the bundles have the structure shown in Figure 5.2.

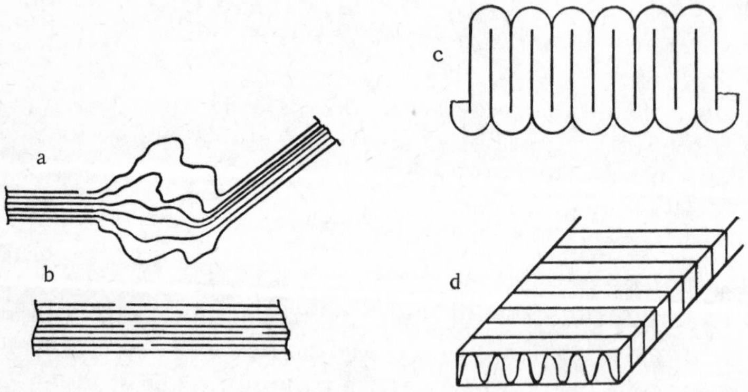

FIGURE 5.2.

According to the concepts of Kargin et al., the combination of macromolecules into bundles involves, for crystalline polymers, the crystallization of certain elements of the bundle. As already mentioned, the crystallization of polymers can never be complete.

Indeed, there is practically not one polymer with an ideal chain structure corresponding to the chemical formula for the whole extent of the chain. Thus in polyethylene, besides the groups

$-CH_2-CH_2-$ there are groups $-\underset{\underset{\displaystyle CH_3}{|}}{C}-$ and lateral branches of great length, and also groups $-CH{=}CH-$. A difference between individual molecular chains is noted even in molecular chains with side branches, in the absence of linear stereoregularity of the type "head to head" and "head to tail," and also in the absence of spatial stereoregularity.

Incomplete identity in chemical composition, absence of stereoregularity and the presence of admixtures cause the formation of internal stresses between the chains upon crystallization. The effect of these stresses becomes stronger as the crystallizing polymer chains are packed in parallel to one another in the bundle, so that starting from a certain point the differences in the mutual positions of neighboring chains become so substantial that the macromolecules cannot crystallize. An amorphous region appears in the bundle. This can be represented schematically as in Figure 5.2a.

The flexural rigidity of the bundle in the amorphous region is lower than in the crystalline one, just as the rigidity of boards placed loosely on top of one another is less than the rigidity of the same boards nailed together. Therefore the bundles can fold up by rotating their individual parts around the amorphous regions like a folding rule.

For two reasons the folded state of the bundle is energetically more favorable than the extended one. First, in the absence of a stress field the extended state of the bundle is hardly probable. The transition to a folded-up state is more probable and corresponds to less free energy and higher entropy. Second, the extended bundle in the solvent or in a medium of similar bundles has a higher surface energy owing to the larger surface area which divides the crystalline and amorphous phases.

Upon folding up, the bundles of the crystalline areas combine and the interface between them diminishes. A band, a one-dimensional crystal formation, is formed, the outline of which is shown in Figure 5.2b. The middle part of the band is crystalline while the edges are amorphous.

Further on, the separate bands are folded over next to each other to form the lobe or lamella (Figure 5.2c), whereby the free energy of the material is further decreased.

The lamellas are essentially single crystals, the length and width of which may attain macroscopic dimensions while their thickness amounts to 100–200 Å, i. e., very small in comparison with their length and width.

Furthermore, if certain conditions for normal crystallization are fulfilled, the lamellas are layered one next to the other to form a bulk polymeric single crystal (Figure 5.2d). In the actual processing of polymeric articles these ideal crystallization conditions are practically never fulfilled and in articles of plastics a structure of polymeric single crystals is never formed.

Under real conditions the crystallization usually occurs in the following manner. A crystallization germ (nucleus) is either present or formed in the crystallization center. Such a nucleus or artificial crystallization germ may be a grain of low-molecular substance, referred to as seeding. The crystallization of the polymer sets in around them. The latter situation may arise even in the absence of artificial crystallization nuclei. Incidental admixtures can act as nuclei or a polymeric microvolume in which incidental combination of macromolecules with microelements of crystalline structure takes place. Such an element becomes a crystallization center.

The absence of strict directivity in the structure formed and also lack of synchronism in the process of a larger number of forming and growing crystallization elements are, first, the reason why the crystallographic axes in different crystallization elements are oriented in different directions, and second, that the crystallization process at different points of the volume is completed at different stages of molecular organization: bundles, bands, lamellas or volumetric crystals.

Generally, articles of crystalline polymers have the spherulitic structure which is readily observed in an optical microscope under polarized light. Characteristic figures in the shape of the Maltese Cross are visible in the field of view. Spherulites are aggregates of acicular crystals. In the case of polymers they are long plates (lamellas). The lamellas can be flat plates or coiled into spirals, depending on the polymer composition.

Analogous structures can be formed even in amorphous polymers. However, the investigation of the latter is more complicated, perhaps because the fundamental methods of structure investigation based on X-ray diffraction do not supply conclusive and accurate information for amorphous material as in the case of crystalline material.

A lamellar structure is formed in crystalline polymers when crystallization proceeds without stresses. There is still another type of structure, namely the fibrillar structure, in which bundles have not been piled together and the individual macromolecules are joined up in the extended form. Upon orientation, a transition from the lamellar to the fibrillar structure occurs under cold or hot drawing. In cold drawing a loss in the stability of the individual lamellas or even their destruction occurs. A fibrillar structure forms and grows on the fragments /4/. The latter is formed also during the formation of polymeric filaments or films when a polymeric melt is subjected to tensile or shear stress during the formation of filaments or films.

The "defective crystal model" of the fibrillar structure of polymers, proposed by Hosemann, is shown in Figure 5.3 /5/. The individual atoms are represented by points. The valence angles are not indicated. The macromolecular chains are indicated by lines. The pattern in Figure 5.3 is flat, and must be mentally completed in the third dimension to obtain a spatial picture. The crystalline regions are bounded by dotted lines. Within the crystalline regions the macromolecules are positioned parallel to one another and the atoms are positioned at the nodes of a biperiodic crystalline spatial crystal lattice. In the amorphic region the regularity of the mutual position of the macromolecules and atoms is violated.

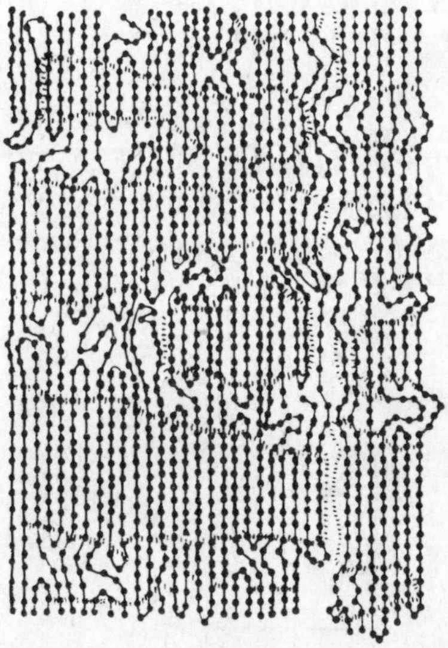

FIGURE 5.3.

The amorphous regions are first of all sections in which the macromolecules are subjected to bending. They are also the regions where the chain terminals, chain segments, cross-linking neighboring crystals, vacancy type holes, etc., are positioned.

Several scientists (such as Zaukelies /6/) are of the opinion that amorphous regions in highly ordered crystalline polymers are composed of vacancies and dislocations, i. e., of the very same defects as those of crystals of ordinary low molecular materials.

The model shown in Figure 5.3 to a certain degree contradicts the concept of the bundlewise structure of high polymers. Here, each macromolecule behaves as if it were isolated and independent of neighboring molecules. A pattern of the type shown in Figure 5.3 must not be conceived as immobile and rigid. The crystalline structure may become perfect or decay with time through thermal motion. In addition, certain segments in the crystalline region may pass into the amorphous one, and vice versa.

The conclusion to be drawn from the above account is that at present there is no concensus of opinion as to the supramolecular structure of polymers and more research is necessary in this field.

§2. DEPENDENCE OF THE MECHANICAL PROPERTIES OF POLYMERS ON THE SUPRAMOLECULAR STRUCTURES

Investigations into the effect of the structure of polymers (the supramolecular structure in the terminology advanced by Kargin /3/) on the mechanical properties started comparatively recently and continues.

It should first be noted that a high degree of order of the mutual distribution of macromolecules always enhances the mechanical properties of polymers.

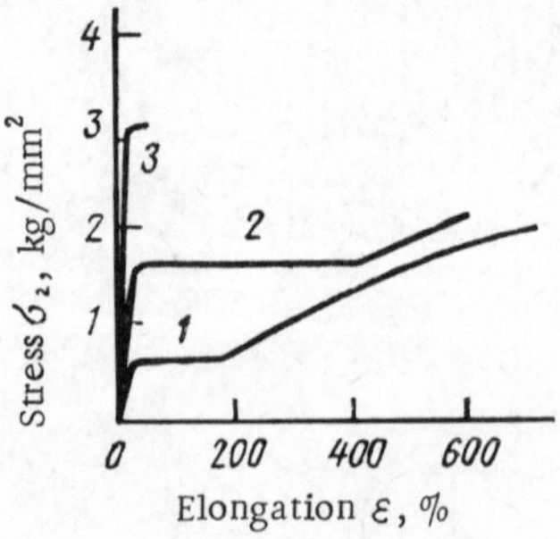

FIGURE 5.4.

For comparison, Figure 5.4 shows the $\sigma \sim \varepsilon$ diagram recorded at 80°C for test samples of the same fluoroplast-3 with various degrees of crystallization /7/. Curve 1 was obtained on a sample with a 30–40% degree of crystallization, curve 2 with a 60% degree of crystallization and curve 3 with a degree of about 80%. It is evident from the figure that a higher degree of crystallization substantially increases the limit of coercive elasticity, whereby the ultimate strength is also somewhat enhanced.

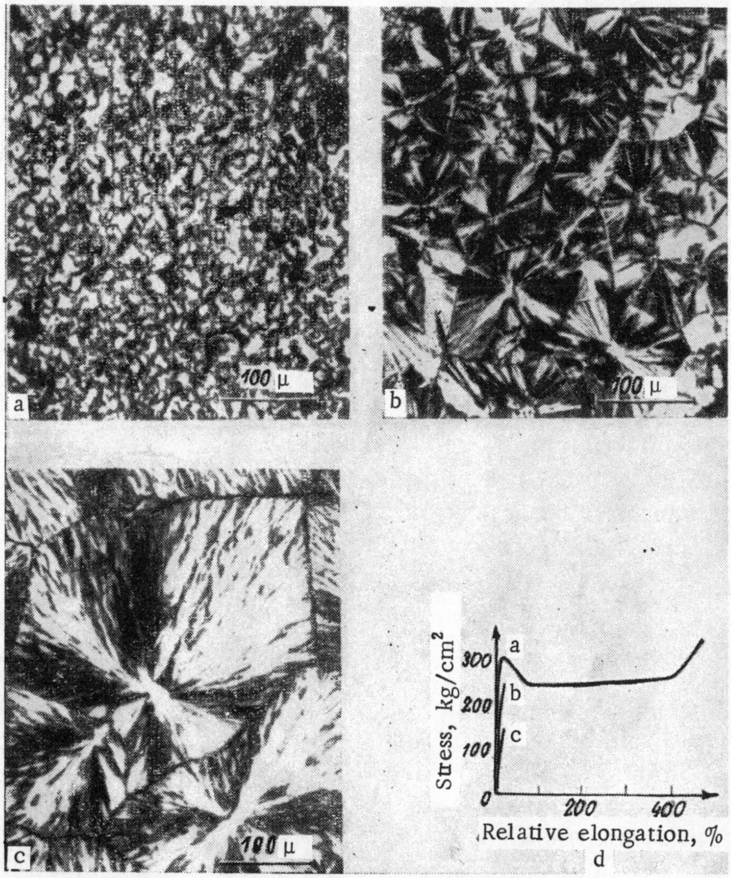

FIGURE 5.5.

An increased regularity in the spatial distribution of macromolecule side groups also causes improved mechanical properties of polymers. For instance, according to Krentsel' and Sidorova /8/, isotactic polypropylene is a fairly rigid material and maintains its rigidity up to 130°C. Thereafter, softening starts and at 174°C melting of the crystals takes place and the material passes into the viscous state. The glass-transition temperature T_g of atactic polypropylene is −10°C. Since it is a linear product, it displays appreciable flow already at room temperature.

According to Kargin /9/, isotactic polystyrene displays high rigidity and strength, which are maintained up to 220°. At higher temperatures a transition to the viscous state occurs. According to the data of the same paper, the glass point of atactic polystyrene is +80°C. At elevated temperatures the Mackian-elastic state sets in and the rigidity is decreased to about one-hundredth or less. In addition, as a linear polymer the atactic polystyrene also displays a noticeable fluidity at $T > T_c$.

The effect of the supramolecular structure of a polymer on its mechanical properties is evident in Figure 5.5 /3/, which presents pictures (observed by means of a polarization microscope) of crystalline polypropylene held at 180°C for (a) 5 seconds, (b) 20 seconds and (c) 60 seconds. The dimensions of the spherulites are increased and the structure becomes more coarse-grained with increased holding time at 180°C. Figure 5.5d shows the $\sigma \sim \varepsilon$ diagram of the polymers, the structure of which is shown in Figures 5.5a, b, c. Evidently, with increasingly coarse-grained structure the strength of the polymer decreases and, what is more important, its brittleness is enhanced.

More comprehensive data on the effect of the supramolecular structure on the mechanical properties of high polymers are contained in the book by Gul' and Kuleznev /2/ which treats this problem.

§3. INVESTIGATION OF THE ADHESION STRENGTH ON BULKY SPECIMENS

Most plastic materials contain fillers which are incorporated into the polymer material in order either to strengthen it, or to make the material cheaper, or to modify the physical, physico-chemical or other properties of the matrix. Very frequently the filler particles have higher strength properties than the polymeric matrix. The greatest possible increase in the utilization of the strength properties of the filler for higher product strength is desirable.

The reinforcing action of the filler can be achieved only when concurrent functioning of filler and polymeric matrix is provided for, i. e., when the material is a monolithic product. Mechanical stresses appear at the boundary between the filler particles and matrix when the composite material works as a monolithic unit. The reinforcing action of the filler can be achieved if the adhesion bonds between the filler and matrix are of sufficiently high strength.

Adhesion is the sticking together of the surfaces of two nonsimilar solid or liquid bodies. Adhesion is characterized quantitatively by the work expended on separating the bodies. In applications to composite material other adhesion characteristics are frequently employed, such as the adhesion strength, which is the stress that must be applied at the interface of the nonsimilar bodies in order to separate one from the other.

Occasionally adhesion is larger than cohesion, which characterizes the coupling force of the particles inside the particular body. In this case cohesive rupture occurs, namely inside the weaker of the contacting bodies. For example, while investigating adhesion rupture of glass-fiber-reinforced plastics Gul' et al. /10/ established that with an epoxide matrix, the rupture takes place in such a way that the resin tears off part of the glass or glass tears off part of the resin.

Adhesion problems may be of decisive importance in the gluing of solid bodies, in reinforcing composite material (as mentioned above), and in many other processes. In this context adhesion problems drew much attention and led to the publication of many papers. By necessity only an outline of a discussion of those problems is given in the present monograph. Should the reader intend to specialize in the field of polymer adhesion, then for a preliminary guide monographs /11–13/ can be recommended. The problems of adhesion in filled polymers and glass-fiber-reinforced plastics are considered in detail elsewhere /14, 15/.

Two methods are nowadays widely applied to the quantitative determination of adhesion, namely tearing off and peeling. When the method of tearing off is used, it is assumed that the separation of the glued solid (substrate) from the glue layer (adhesive) takes place simultaneously over all the surface of the glued joint. The force overcome in the simultaneous tearing off over the whole contact area per unit surface is called adhesion strength (dimensions: dyne/cm^2 or kg/cm^2). Sometimes, instead of adhesion strength, other terms are used, such as adhesion pressure, or specific adhesion /13/.

When tests by the tear method /13, 15/ are conducted, identical elements are prepared from the substrate material, usually in the shape of cylinders or in the form of a mushroom (hence the mushroom method). These are glued together at meticuously treated butt surfaces by means of the adhesive under study. After curing the glue, the tear test is carried out on the specimen. The adhesion strength is determined from the force causing the separation of the halves of the test pieces as a result of destruction of the adhesion bonds at the substrate—adhesive boundary. (The destruction may have other causes.) Several investigators used test pieces in the shape of rectangular prisms glued crosswise /15/.

In testing for shear /13, 15/, two strips of the investigated solid bodies (substrates) were glued together by an adhesive. In the test, one is sheared relative to the other in the direction of the longitudinal axis of the strip. The adhesion strength in shear is determined by the ratio of the maximum forces causing rupture of the glue joint to the area of the latter.

Tear or shear tests are conducted on various machines of the type described in the second chapter of the first part. The TsNIKZ adhesiometer, described in detail by Voyutskii /13/, has also found widespread application for this purpose.

The determination of adhesion strength in tear and shear involves certain inaccuracies connected with the nonuniform stress distribution over the cross section of the glue layer caused by the different properties of the adhesive and substrate. As to carrying out shear tests on a lap joint of strips, the corresponding problem of determining the distribution of shear and strain along the glue joint was considered by Rabotnov /16/. With increasing length of the lap joint, the rupture load approaches a certain constant value /17/. An analogous picture was also obtained with tear tests, which in particular was confirmed experimentally by the results of investigating the stress distribution in the glued joint by means of the polarization-optical method /15/.

Bikerman /22/ noted certain inaccuracies in the tear method consisting in the fact that due to the unevenness of the surface of the substrate of the test sample the force applied to the microsections is practically never exactly perpendicular. Besides, the values obtained are inaccurate because, due to the general roughness of the substrate, the actual surface upon testing does not equal the nominal one. Unfortunately, however meticulously the treatment of the substrate is carried out, the effect of the roughness cannot be eliminated in the experimental determination of adhesion strength by shear and tear methods as well as in the actual structural elements that are glued together.

The adhesive shear strength can also be determined by torsion tests on tubular /15/ or solid /19/ test specimens. In this case the halves of the specimens of hard material (substrate) in the form of tubes or solid cylinders are glued together at meticulously treated butt faces. In the tests one half of the test piece is fixed in working clamps connected to a torsion dynamometer and a torque is applied to the other half.

The adhesion strength in shear is determined by the maximum torque at which the glued joint fails. The computations are carried out with the conventional formulas of material resistance. Naturally, due to the inelastic behavior of the adhesive, which considering the material of the first part of the present monograph is very possible, the computation in regard to solid test specimens is very inaccurate.

The advantage of the above-mentioned method of peeling or cleaving is that the adhesive film is removed successively from the substrate. In this case adhesion is determined by the force required for peeling the film in relation to the width of the latter (the dimensions are dyne/cm, erg/cm^2 or g/cm). The theoretical basis of the peeling method was worked out by Deryagin /11/. Bikerman /18/ expressed doubts about the correctness in determining adhesion by the peeling method, because in his opinion appreciable work is expended on bending the peeled adhesive film. However, as shown in Deryagin's investigations which are cited in /13/, the work expended on the deformation of sufficiently thin films during their peeling is not substantially reflected in the adhesion work.

Very frequently, a cohesion rupture of the substrate material occurs in the determination of adhesion by the methods of shear and tear /15/. Besides, large scatter is observed in the values of adhesion strength as well as a decrease in measured adhesion values, apparently because of the nonuniform stress distribution and appearance of a complex state of stress, with normal and transverse forces and a bending moment applied to the adhesive layer /15/.

Cleaner test conditions are provided for by ultrasonic and ultracentrifugal methods when accelerations appear in the adhesive layer exceeding the acceleration of gravity 10^5 to 10^6 times /13, 15/. Similar accelerations are also attained by the "pneumatic gun" method, in which a layer of adhesive is applied to the surface of a bullet fired from a pneumatic gun. The adhesive is separated from the substrate when the bullet hits the obstacle /15/.

So-called nondestructive test methods /15/ are very promising for strength tests of the glued system without destroying it. When applying nondestructive methods the properties of each article are examined without its destruction, while rigidity and strength are determined indirectly by other indexes of material properties /20/. The work of Dietz, cited in /15/, establishes the changes in strength according to the changes of the elasticity modulus of the adhesive determined by ultrasonic oscillations and belongs to works in which the nondestructive methods are applied in the determination of the strength of a glued joint. In the same monograph /15/ works are mentioned in which attempts of an indirect determination of a glued joint are made, for example, according to the electrical capacity, as well as works on flaw detection in glued joints.

§4. INVESTIGATION OF THE STRENGTH OF THE ADHESION BOND BETWEEN FIBERS AND POLYMER ADHESIVE

The investigation of the adhesion of the polymer matrix to the surface of the reinforcing fibers is of general interest, since it provides an approximation to the actual conditions prevailing in reinforced systems. Besides, as pointed out by Andreevskaya /15/, the methods of determining adhesion directly in the fibers have several advantages over methods of measuring adhesion of polymers to the surface of massive test samples made from the filler material.

The determination of adhesion of various polymers to bulky test samples of reinforcing material is difficult for the following reasons /15/.

The strength and elastic properties of the reinforcing material (such as glass in blocks) are very small and it is practically impossible to determine the value of the adhesion to massive test samples of resins with high adhesion, such as epoxide resins, because of cohesive destruction of the substrate material, such as cleaving or cracking. Besides, the surface of the sample of the substrate prepared for the measurement of adhesion undergoes large changes in comparison with a freshly formed surface. This occurs as the result of polishing processes, i. e., the phenomenon of flow upon treating with abrasive powders, and polishing, namely the effect of chemical corrosion by the action of aggressive polishing media.

On the other hand, reinforcing fibers, such as glass fiber, display a mechanical strength which is sometimes two orders of magnitude larger than that of bulky test samples and generally has a clean, smooth surface not contaminated by any impurity. Especially because of this, nowadays, in studying adhesion to the reinforcing fibers, attempts are made to determine the strength of gluing directly on the fibers.

Deryagin /11/ has developed a method, based on measuring the adhesive force of two quartz filaments glued together crosswise at an angle of 90° in media of various materials. Aslanova (cited in /15/) applied this method to determine the adhesive force of several glues to glass fibers, for which one of the fibers was coated with a film of the applied glue. This method does not always provide clear-cut reproducible results, since under the experimental conditions it is very difficult to achieve point contact between two fibers. Even the area of adhesion between fibers covered with a glue film and glass fibers with a clear surface cannot be determined.

Of all mechanical test methods, namely tear, shear and peeling, the shear method is the most convenient one when developing a method for determining polymer adhesion to the glass fibers. The contact between fiber and polymer should be over a short section, otherwise in testing polymers with high adhesion to glass the glass fiber itself will fail, rather than the contact between polymer and fiber /15/. For this purpose a high-molecular joint polymerized around the fiber was studied, so that the test sample assumed the shape of a thin disk through which the fiber under study passed at the center perpendicular to the surface of the disk. When determining adhesion strength a shear stress appears either upon axial displacement of the resin disk relative to the fiber /15, 21/, or upon rotation of the disk relative to the fiber /15/.

Broutman's review /21/ examines methods for determining the strength of adhesion bonds in tension and shear based on test samples at the central part of which polymerization of one fiber was carried out. In the first case a flat test sample with curved edges was used. The adhesion failure in compression of such samples is due to the different Poisson's ratios of the resin and glass. The test piece was loaded with a constant force, but the stress varied at different points along the length of the test sample as the latter had a variable cross-section. The point at which failure occurred was recorded by means of a microscope (under lateral illumination the light scattering intensity increases rapidly upon adhesion failure). For measuring shear strength, a test sample in the shape of a rectangular parallelepiped was used. Maximum shear stresses occur close to the ends of the fibers; their magnitude was determined on the basis of corresponding design problems.

The method for determining adhesive shear strength as applied by McGarry is investigated elsewhere /15/. The fiber investigated was polymerized in a pyramidal block of resin. Upon compressing the pyramid, compressive stresses varying with height were induced in it. Shear stresses, which were determined by optical methods, appeared close to the surface of the fiber. When the stresses approached the value of adhesion strength in shear, the fiber was separated from the polymeric matrix.

The method of measuring adhesion strength on the surfaces of fibers, developed by Andreevskaya, has been treated in detail /15/. The essence of the method is the following. Two thick glass fibers of 120–150 μ diameter (or thin metal wires) are stretched in parallel and covered by a resin film of uniform thickness. The thin fiber under investigation, of 7–20 μ diameter, is stretched between these fibers at right angles. After curing of the resin, the shear adhesion strength is determined by the force required to tear the thin fiber from the resin layer.

§5. DETERMINATION OF THE STRENGTH OF THE ADHESION BOND AS DEPENDENT ON THE COMPONENTS OF THE JOINT, LOADING PATTERN AND TEMPERATURE

The problems of the strength of adhesion bonds are very important in glued joints, in filling, reinforcing, and so on. It is impossible to consider in this section the problems of adhesion applied to the strength of glued joints. Readers interested in this problem are referred to specialized literature /11, 12, 18, 22/.

It has been established by a number of investigators /10, 23/ that the strength of glass-fiber-reinforced plastics under otherwise equal conditions increases with increasing strength of the adhesion bonds between resin and glass. Therefore, to obtain high-strength glass-fiber-reinforced plastics, first polymers having good adhesion to glass are selected, and second, an increase in adhesion strength is achieved either by suitable treatment of the fiber surface or by adding a surfactant to the matrix /15/.

Investigations /10, 15/ have shown that the adhesion strength of polymers to glass depends on the composition of the resin as well as on the composition of the glass. Gul' et al. studied four types of matrix, namely polyestermaleate, epoxyphenol, epoxypolyester-maleate and epoxide. They established that epoxide has the strongest adhesion to glass and polyester resin the weakest. According to a number of papers cited by Andreevskaya /15/, high adhesion strength of epoxy resins in bonds with glass surface is explained by the presence of functional groups in the resin able to form chemical bonds. At the same time, according to other data (see /15/) the low adhesion of polyester resin to glass is explained by the great shrinkage upon curing and the appearance of large internal stresses in the composition (shrinkage stresses).

It is noteworthy that the interaction mechanism between the components of reinforced polymers is distinguished by being very involved. The phenomena occurring in the formation of adhesion bonds are caused by forces of a chemical as well as a physical nature, which have not yet been fully investigated.

The effect of the chemical composition of glass on the strength of the adhesion bond between glass and resin has been studied /15/. It was established in particular that polar glues have the best adhesion to quartz and alkali-free fibers and the worst adhesion to fibers of glass of alkaline composition.

The adhesion of resin to glass can be substantially increased by treating the glass fibers with a sizer. For instance, sizing of fibers caused a 30–50% increase in adhesion strength /23/. According to Alksne et al. /24/, fiber sizing, even if it does not raise markedly the short-time strength of polyester glass-fiber reinforced plastics, increases substantially the strength of the material after prolonged soaking (for 30 days) in distilled water. For example, in the case of glass-fiber-reinforced plastics, the fibers of which were not treated by a sizer, the loss in strength after soaking in distilled water amounted to 86.7%, while for sized fibers the loss in strength in certain cases amounted to only 9.4–19.4%.

The physicochemical mechanism of adhesion bond formations between a sized fiber and matrix is presently unknown. Some (see /25/) believe that the sizer improves the properties of the glass-fiber-reinforced plastics as a result of physical processes occurring at the glass–matrix interface, namely the formation of a hydrophobic film preventing penetration of moisture, changes in wettability, adsorption, friction, etc.

However, all these phenomena which doubtless occur at the glass–matrix interface do not fully account for the effect of the sizer. For instance, according to some data /25/, when two sizing compositions impart the same degree of hydrophobicity to a glass surface, better results were obtained upon applying a sizer with functional groups which can interact with the matrix.

Others believe /15, 25/ that the sizer enhances adhesion and consequently also the strength of the glass-fiber-reinforced plastics as a result of the formation of chemical bonds between the glass fibers and the matrix. It has been established /25/ by means of infrared spectroscopy that ES and AGM-9 sizers actually interact chemically with the carbamide resin matrix.

The loading program and the temperature affect the adhesion strength. Andreevskaya /15/ has established that adhesion strength of the joints investigated by her was substantially lower in shear than in tear.

As regards temperature–time dependences of adhesion strength, first of all the physical mechanism of adhesive bond formation and destruction under the action of mechanical stresses should be considered. These mechanisms are presently not fully clear. There are different points of view leading to various theories of adhesion /13/. Nowadays the adsorption, electrical and diffusion theories of adhesion are widely accepted /13/.

The adsorption theory explains adhesion by Van der Waals interaction between the surface molecules of the adhesive and of the substrate. In the electrical theory of adhesion (see Deryagin /11/) it is assumed that the interaction between the layers of adhesive and substrate is caused by electrostatic forces. According to the diffusion theory (see Voyutskii /13/), it is assumed that, as a result of diffusion, the macromolecules of the adhesive penetrate into the substrate and cause the interface to become diffuse. According to yet another theory, advanced recently /26/, it is assumed that the adhesion bond between the polymeric adhesive and substrate is formed as the result of polymer penetrating into the microscopic defects in the surface of the substrate.

If the destruction of the adhesion bonds occurs in accordance with a thermal fluctuation mechanism, as does ordinary failure, then these two different processes have certain traits in common. This assumption was confirmed in investigations by Malinskii et al. /27/. They have shown that, as a rule, adhesion strength is lower at higher temperatures or lower loading rates, although extrema were observed with some polymeric materials over certain narrow temperature and speed ranges. For example, full analogy between the thermomechanical curve and the temperature dependence of the adhesion strength ($\sigma_{adh} \sim T$) was established for BF-4 glue. The presence of a maximum over a certain temperature range is due to enhancement in the crosslinked structure of the polymeric network. In other cases the presence of a maximum is explained by non-uniformity in tear, crystallization of the polymer and the effect of filler and stress raisers. Bartenev and Marinina /28/ studied the adhesion of polyvinylbutyral to glass. There were no extrema on the $\sigma_{adh} \sim T$ curves, but there was a break in the curve near $T = 92°$. Above this temperature failure was cohesive, while at lower temperatures it was adhesive.

Chapter VI

METHODS OF PROCESSING TEST DATA

The present chapter contains a brief account of methods of processing experimental results. A general account is given of the derivation of data characterizing the expectation and confidence interval from repeatedly performed tests. General principles underlying the mathematical treatment of lengthy tests are illustrated by constructing long-term strength diagrams from test data. In addition, the method of determining the viscoelastic properties of polymers on the basis of the time-temperature equivalence of the generalized temperature-invariant characteristics is examined when the initial data have a certain scatter.

§1. MATHEMATICAL TREATMENT OF EXPERIMENTAL RESULTS

The selection of mathematical methods of processing experimental data is very important for a comprehensive analysis of test results and a correct evaluation of the qualitative and quantitative large-scale effects. As an example the statistical approach is discussed.

The coefficient of variation ν and the coefficient of variation of the mean of the sampling distribution $\tilde{p}$ are defined by

$$\nu = \frac{s}{\bar{x}}, \quad \tilde{p} = \frac{\nu}{\sqrt{n}}. \tag{1.1}$$

Here $\bar{x}$ is the arithmetic mean of a random variable x, determined from n individual values of x_i:

$$\bar{x} = \frac{1}{n}\sum_{i=1} x_i,$$

$s=s[x]$ is the standard deviation of x computed from the variance dispersion $\tilde{D}=\tilde{D}[x]$, where

$$s=\sqrt{\tilde{D}},\quad \tilde{D}=\frac{1}{n-1}\sum_{i=1}^{n}(x_i-\bar{x})^2.$$

Strictly speaking $s[x]$ is the evaluated standard deviation of $\bar{x}$ determined from an unbiased estimate of the variance $\tilde{D}[x]$ /1/, while quantity $\widetilde{px}=s/\sqrt{n}$ is the standard deviation of $\bar{x}$ or the mean error s.

It is known from the theory of probability that for sufficiently large s and confidence coefficient β, the confidence interval $(\bar{x}-\varepsilon_\beta,\ \bar{x}+\varepsilon_\beta)$ is determined by the approximate relationships

$$\varepsilon_\beta=\widetilde{px}t_\beta,\quad t_\beta=\sqrt{2}\,\Phi^{-1}(\beta),$$

where $\Phi^{-1}(\beta)$ denotes the inverse Laplace function /1/. For measurable values, we have with probability β

$$x=\bar{x}(1\pm\tilde{p}t_\beta). \tag{1.2}$$

In particular, for a confidence coefficient $\beta=0.997$ tabulated values of function $\Phi^{-1}(\beta)$ yield $t_\beta=3$. Hence

$$x=\bar{x}(1\pm 3\tilde{p}). \tag{1.3}$$

The minimum number of test samples required n_{min} can be determined by using the second of formulas (1.1), setting the desired limits of deviation of the measurable values from the arithmetic mean at the desired accuracy, $(x-\bar{x})\,\bar{x}$, for the given confidence coefficient. In other words, we use (1.2) and determine the value of $t_\beta\,\tilde{p}_{min}$, and use the experimental value of ν. Consequently

$$n_{min}=\frac{\nu^2}{\tilde{p}^2_{min}}. \tag{1.4}$$

For example, if

$$\frac{x-\bar{x}}{\bar{x}}=\pm 0.15=\pm 15\%,$$

then for a confidence coefficient $\beta=0.997$ ($t_\beta=3$) (1.2) yields $t_\beta\,\tilde{p}_{min}=\pm 0.15$, whence $\tilde{p}_{min}=\pm 0.05$. Applying the mean value of the coefficient of variation from experimental tables, for example $\nu=0.2$, we derive from (1.4) that $n_{min}=16$. But even for a confidence coefficient of 0.98 ($t_\beta = 2.32$), an analogous sequence of computations yields $\tilde{p}_{min} = 0.065$ and $n_{min} = 10$.

Thus, judging by the data of experimental tables, the minimum required number of test samples should lie in the range $n_{min} = 10-15$. It is understood that a better technique and preparation will decrease the scatter in the properties and decrease the coefficient of variation, so that n_{min} will be less than the indicated value.

§2. MATHEMATICAL PROCESSING OF LENGTHY EXPERIMENTS

Statistical processing of test results for long-term strength is more involved than that of data pertaining to tests with ordinary testing machines, where one deals only with one population of random variables, namely the population of σ_B. The distribution of these random variables can be represented by a curve in a plane, where the values of σ_B are plotted along the abscissa and the probability density $\psi(\sigma_B)$ along the ordinate.

In processing experimental data for long-term strength we deal with two populations, namely σ_B and t. According to Bolotin /2/, the distribution of these random variables can be expressed in a $\sigma_B \sim t \sim \psi(\sigma_B, t)$ system of coordinates. The statistical processing consists in determining function $\psi(\sigma_B, t)$, finding the scatter, and establishing the "confidence" of the evaluation. These problems of modern probability theory are very complicated and have not been solved completely.

It was established by Serensen /3/ that the life-times of test samples in long-term tests usually obey a lognormal distribution law. Thus for computing ease $x = \log t$ can be selected as random variable. The most probable value of x is the expectation $M(x) = \bar{x} = \sum_{i=1}^{n} x_i/n$, where n is the number of tests /2, 4/. The scatter is characterized by the variance s^2 defined by the formula

$$s^2 = \frac{\sum_{i=1}^{n} (x_i - \bar{x})^2}{n-1}. \tag{2.1}$$

The expectation $M(\log t)$ obtained at various stress levels is plotted in a diagram constructed in $\sigma_B \sim t$ (or $\sigma_B \sim \log t$) coordinates. This represents the curve of the most probable long-term strength.

Each stress level possesses a confidence interval $x = \log t$ for some probability or other. In processing the data presented below, for example, a confidence interval was selected within which the random variables have a probability of 0.95.

It is known that the most general normal probability distribution is given by /4/

$$\psi(x) = \frac{1}{s\sqrt{2\pi}}\, e^{-\frac{(x-\bar{x})^2}{2s^2}}. \qquad (2.2)$$

The variable x is replaced by the expression

$$\xi = \frac{x-\bar{x}}{s}. \qquad (2.3)$$

We have to determine some value of ξ for which the probability $p\{-\xi_0<\xi<+\xi_0\}$ of the value ξ in the interval $-\xi_0<\xi<+\xi_0$ equals 0.95.

For the normal distribution /4/,

$$p\{-\xi_0<\xi<\xi_0\} = \Phi(\xi_0), \qquad (2.4)$$

where $\Phi(\xi_0)$ is the error function, the values of which have been tabulated. Since $\Phi(\xi_0) = 0.95$, $\xi_0 = 1.96$. The width of the confidence interval is $\Delta x = 2\xi_0 s$; the ends of this interval lie on the $\sigma_B \sim \log t$ curve and are equidistant from $M(x)$ on the $\log t$ axis.

Occasionally, difficulties arise during the statistical processing of tests for long-term strength, because at low stresses some of the test samples do not fail within the maximum test duration. In this case it is impossible to construct a comprehensive cumulative curve, as the points in its upper right-hand corner are missing. A histogram can also not be constructed and the expectation M and variance s^2 cannot be computed by ordinary methods. In this case two methods can be applied for computing M and s.

The first method is based on the following hypothesis. Evidently M does not change during a sufficiently large number of tests, provided the edges of the probability distribution curve are intersected at equal distances from the distribution center. Therefore when determining $M(x)$ for the variational series x_i the first few terms are rejected, their number equaling the number of tests in which failure has not occurred within the maximum test duration. The shape of the histogram is near-symmetrical and the expectation of the series with equal amounts cut off approximately equals M for the whole series.

Another difficulty appears in determining the variance s^2 for such an incomplete series. If s^2 is computed by equation (2.1) only for those terms at which failure occurred, low values are deliberately obtained as the extreme terms are excluded. The standard error will be more marked if these values are included. It is assumed that for a large number of tests the histogram edges have an approximately symmetrical shape relative to the distribution center. The right edge of the histogram is missing, but the histogram is extrapolated to the end. In this case its left end is added to the right hand with mirror-image representation about the vertical axis through the distribution center.

When computing values of s^2 this operation is carried out as follows. All the terms in formula (2.1) corresponding to the terms of the incomplete variational series are counted once, and to them are added repeatedly those terms which were formed by terms previously rejected in computing the expectation. The expectation and variation are denoted by $M_1(x)$ and $s_1^2(x)$, respectively. Naturally, when failure occurs at a certain stress on all test pieces we have a complete variational series and $M_1(x)$ and $s_1^2(x)$ are determined by standard methods.

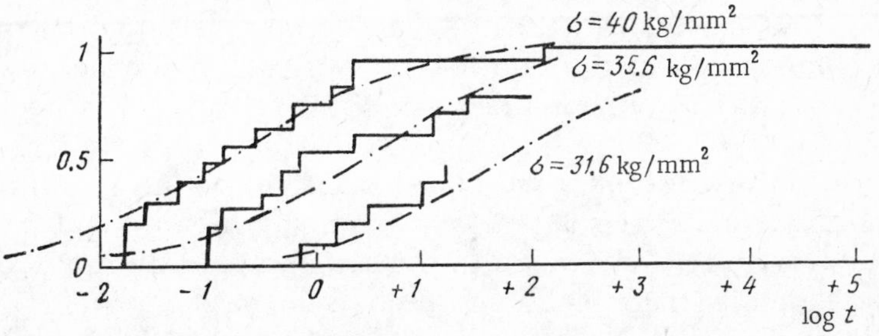

FIGURE 6.1.

Another method for determining $M(x)$ and $s^2(x)$ is as follows. The cumulative curve of the type shown in Figure 6.1 is constructed from the test results. Then that curve is selected from the family of integral distribution curves $F(\xi)=\Phi(\xi)+\frac{1}{2}$ for all possible $\bar{x}$ and s. This curve deviates least from the points of the cumulative curve. The curve $F(\xi)$ is plotted in $F\sim x$ coordinates. In this case parameter s is determined by (2.3) and the expectation is the abscissa of the point at which $F=0.5$. The values of $M(x)$ and $s(x)$ determined by this method are $M_2(x)$ and $s_2(x)$, respectively.

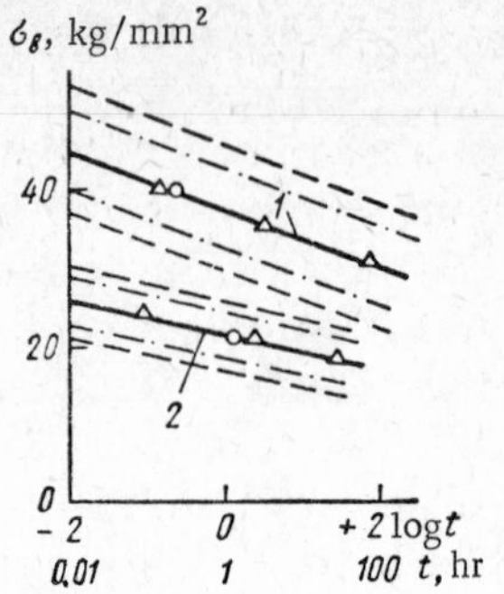

FIGURE 6.2.

As an illustration, Figure 6.2 shows graphs of the long-term strength obtained in this manner for unidirectional (1) and equal-strength (2) AG-4S cited from /5/. Values of $M_1(x)$ are denoted by circular points and $M_2(x)$ by triangles.

It is seen that the values of $M_1(x)$ differ little from $M_2(x)$. This indicates that the second method is reasonably accurate. In the case of low stresses only the points $M_2(x)$ are given, as failure occurred rarely and the number of terms in the variational series were insufficient for determining $M_1(x)$.

Figure 6.2 also shows the confidence regions. Dashed lines indicate the boundaries of the confidence region as obtained by the first method, and dash-dot lines are the limits as obtained by the second method.

The second method gives a narrower confidence interval, since it is less sensitive to sharp deviations from the mean result. The difference between the confidence intervals obtained by the above methods decreases with increasing number of tests.

§3. METHOD OF CONSTRUCTING TEMPERATURE-INVARIANT CHARACTERISTICS OF THE VISCOELASTIC PROPERTIES OF POLYMERS ON THE BASIS OF TEMPERATURE-TIME SUPERPOSITION

Time-temperature superposition, widely employed to predict the behavior of polymers in regions of either very large or very small times (frequencies), is based on experimental facts first observed by Aleksandrov, Gurevich, Kobeko, Kuvshinskii and Lazurkin (see /7–9/). Their work has shown that the value of equilibrium Mackian-elastic deformations of a polymer at a specified stress depends little on temperature. But the time for the development of viscoelastic deformation decreases very rapidly with increasing temperature.

In line with the temperature-time superposition principle (abbreviated as TTS) the dependence of a mechanical parameter P on $\log t$ (or the logarithm of the frequency, $\log \omega$) does not change with temperature. There is only a displacement of the $P \sim \log t$ curve (or the $P \sim \log \omega$ curve) along the $\log t$ axis (or $\log \omega$ axis) by an amount a_T. Here P can be creep, relaxation modulus, or the real or imaginary part of the complex compliance or complex modulus. The value of a_T determines by how many times the rate of the relaxation process at temperature T is diminished in comparison with the rate at some reference temperature.

Williams, Landel and Ferry /10/ proposed a relationship for coefficient a_T:

$$\log a_T = -\frac{8.86\,(T - T_s)}{101.6 + T - T_s}, \tag{3.1}$$

where T_s is the characteristic temperature.

When the paper by Williams, Landel and Ferry was published, many papers appeared in which the temperature-time superposition principle and the Williams–Landel–Ferry formula (3.1) (the WLF formula) were applied for processing experimental data on the viscoelastic properties of polymers. A series of studies in this field is discussed elsewhere /11/.

By employing temperature-time superposition, Ferry proposed making allowance for the increase in the polymer equilibrium modulus with temperature T in the elastic state in accordance with the kinetic theory of elasticity. However, in most works no such consideration was made, i. e., no temperature correction was considered. It was shown /12/ that this correction is usually insignificant.

In the construction of the $P \sim \log t$ (or $P \sim \log \omega$) generalized function by the method of reduced variables (see /13/), much arbitrariness is possible due to the scatter of the experimental data and the incomplete fulfillment of the TTS principle in some region. Suppose we have two relationships $P \sim \log t$ at temperatures T_i and T_j. By carrying out the reduction, for instance, at temperature T_i, we can connect any arbitrary points on the $P \sim \log t$ curve and determine a_T as t_j/t_i, where t_j is the time corresponding to some value P at $T = T_j$, while t_i is the same at $T = T_i$. But we shall derive different values a_{T_j} for different values of P. Arbitrary choice of a_{T_j} may lead to the fact that the relationship thus obtained using the TTS principle differs substantially from the experimentally confirmed ones.

Below, a method for processing experimental data by the TTS principle is proposed which, to a marked extent, is free from these errors. This method involves knowing the initial $P \sim \log t$ (or $P \sim \log \omega$) curves for temperatures in the interval under study. It is assumed that the temperatures are above the glass point T_g. (Formula (3.1) is not valid when $T < T_g$ /13/.) It is advantageous to operate with averaged functions $P \sim \log t$, in order to reduce the effect of errors in each individual experiment. In this case P at a specified t is the mean result of at least three to five tests.

The procedure is as follows:

1. The experimental curves of the dependence of the mechanical parameters on time t (or frequency ω) plotted with coordinate $\log t$ or $\log \omega$ as abscissa are intersected by a number of equally spaced straight lines parallel to the $\log t$ or $\log \omega$ axis. These straight lines will henceforth be referred to as horizontals.

2. The coefficient a_{T_i}, determining the retardation of the rate of the relaxation mechanism at some temperature T_i in comparison with the rate at a higher temperature T_{i+1}, is defined by the intersection of the horizontals with the $P \sim \log t$ or $P \sim \log \omega$ graphs. The distance between the horizontals and the points of intersection of two neighboring $P \sim \log t$ or $P \sim \log \omega$ graphs gives the value of $\log a_{T_i}$.

3. If neighboring $P \sim \log t$ or $P \sim \log \omega$ graphs are intersected by several horizontals, $\log a_{T_i}$ is determined for each horizontal and the mean value of $\log a_{T_i}$ is found.

4. The averaged values of $\log a_{T_i}$ obtained are used to construct the function $\log a_T \sim T$. The highest temperature T_n is determined as well as the $P \sim \log t$ (or $P \sim \log \omega$) graph which intersects one of the horizontals. The point $(T_n, 0)$ is plotted in $\log a_T \sim T$ coordinates. The value of $\log a_{T_{n-1}}$ is determined by the method outlined in paragraphs 2 and 3 as the distance between the points of intersection of the $P \sim \log t$ (or $P \sim \log \omega$) graphs at temperatures T_n and T_{n-1} (T_{n-1} is less than T_n and the graph of function P at T_{n-1} is adjacent to the analogous graph at T_n). The point $(\log a_{T_{n-1}}, T_{n-1})$ is plotted in $\log a_T \sim T$ coordinates.

Then the process is continued, whereby for each temperature T_i quantity $\log a_{T_i}$ is plotted from the ordinate of the preceding point of the $\log a_T \sim T$ graph. After the whole temperature range under investigation has been dealt with, we obtain the curve of the $\log a_T \sim T$

function. On this curve each value at some temperature T shows by how many times slower the relaxation mechanism at that particular value of T takes place than at the maximum temperature T_n of the range under study.

5. Construction of the generalized temperature-invariant $P \sim \log t$ (or $P \sim \log \omega$) function is carried out as follows. First, reduction is carried out to the highest testing temperature T_n. In this case the plot is started with the available $P \sim \log t$ curve at temperature T_n, which is left unchanged unless temperature corrections are made. The subsequent curve, i. e., at temperature T_{n-1}, is transposed by the value $\log a_T$ along the logarithm of time axis in the direction of smaller times (or higher frequency). In this case $\log a_T$ is chosen from the graph, the plotting technique of which is described in §4. Subsequently, all the curves at the various T_i are plotted on the same generalized diagram. The generalization is carried out with respect to the points obtained, i. e., the $P \sim \log t$ curve is reduced to the temperature T_n.

6. On the basis of the $\log a_T \sim T$ experimental relationship the characteristic temperature T_s in relationship (3.1) is determined by the least squares method. The way of applying the least squares method to this problem is examined below. In this case, in addition to T_s the value of $\log a_{T_{ns}}$ is also obtained ($a_{T_{ns}}$ is a coefficient determining by how many times the rate of relaxation mechanisms at temperature T_s is slower than the rate at temperature T_n).

7. The generalized $P \sim \log t$ (or $P \sim \log \omega$) relationship, previously reduced to temperature T_n, is now reduced to characteristic temperature T_s. In this case the origin of the graph obtained in paragraph 5 is transposed to the left along the abscissa axis by the value $\log a_{T_{ns}}$, if the graph is constructed in $P \sim \log t$ coordinates, and to the right if in $P \sim \log \omega$ coordinates.

Below, such an approach is followed for poly-n-octylmethacrylate, the frequency dependence of the real part of the complex shear compliance being taken from Ferry's book (/13/, p. 235). Figure 6.3 shows $\log I' \sim \log \omega$ graphs for temperatures from −14.3 to +129.5°C. The horizontals were drawn through each 0.1 decimal order of the compliance I'. The uppermost temperature amounted to +129.5°C; this temperature was taken as the reference temperature in constructing the $\log a_T \sim T$ graph, illustrated in Figure 6.4.

Data processing by the TTS method also provided an opportunity of checking to which degree the WLF formula (3.1) applies to the material investigated and also of determining the value of the characteristic temperature T_s. The least squares method is resorted to for this purpose (see, e. g., /6/, pp. 150–158). For simplicity, we substitute x for T and y for $\log a_T$ as regards the experimentally determined quantities. The computed values are expressed by $f(x)$, where

$$f(x) = A_1 - \frac{8.86(x - A_2)}{101.6 + x - A_2}. \tag{3.2}$$

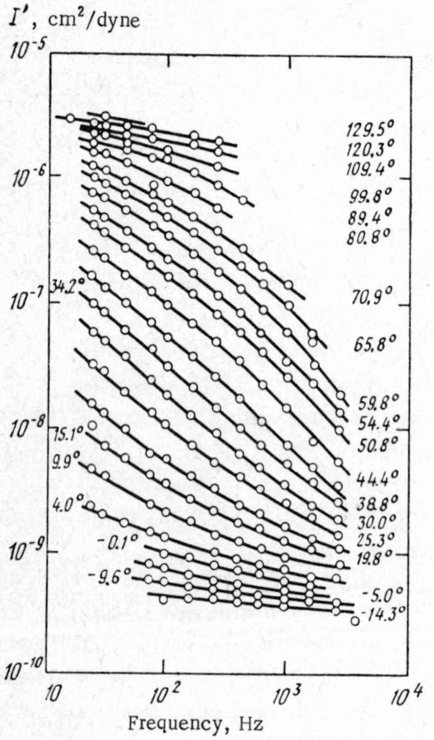

FIGURE 6.3.

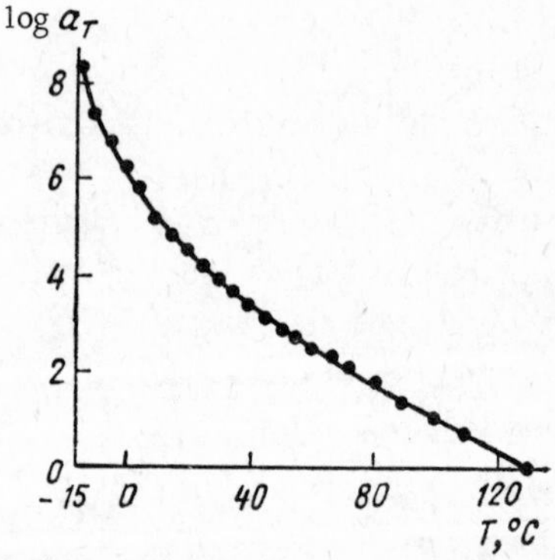

FIGURE 6.4.

In general, the best approximation of function $y=f(x)$ to experimental data implies that the sum of the squares of the deviation of the computed values

$$f(x_1),\ f(x_2),\ \ldots,\ f(x_n)$$

from the empirical values

$$y_1,\ y_2,\ \ldots,\ y_n$$

should be minimal. The mean square principle consists in minimizing the quantity

$$S=\sum_{k=1}^{n}[y_k-f(x_k)]^2. \qquad (3.3)$$

Quantity A_2 in (3.2) represents T_s. Knowing A_2, A_1 is found from the conditions for minimum S, namely

$$\frac{\partial S}{\partial A_1}=-2\sum_{k=1}^{n}\left[y_k-A_1+\frac{8.86(x_k-A_2)}{101.6+x_k-A_2}\right]=0. \qquad (3.4)$$

The value of A_1 is determined from (3.3):

$$A_1=-\frac{1}{n}\sum_{k=1}^{n}\left[y_k+\frac{8.86(x_k-A_2)}{101.6+x_k-A_2}\right] \qquad (3.5)$$

When finding the value of A_2 from the condition that the sum (3.3) be a minimum, i. e., from the condition

$$\frac{\partial S}{\partial A_2}=0,$$

the value of A_1 in (3.4) must be substituted from (3.5). The resulting equation must be differentiated with respect to A_2, the derivative $\partial S/\partial A_2$ set equal to zero, and the algebraic equation thus obtained solved. The latter is an algebraic equation of degree $3n-2$, the formulation and solution of which for $n>1$ is difficult. It is therefore proposed that the minimum of functions S be determined by trial and error.

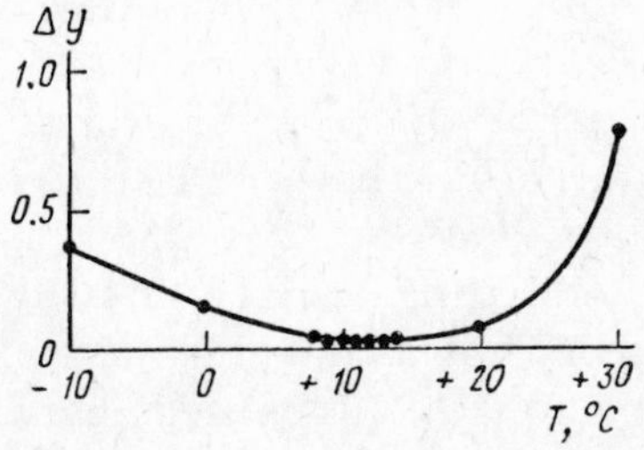

FIGURE 6.5.

We insert reasonable values of A_2 and derive A_1 by means of equation (3.5), and then find the standard error $\Delta y = \sqrt{S/n}$. Subsequently, we plot the dependence of Δy on A_2. Since A_2 is a temperature, Δy is plotted as a function of temperature. The required value of A_2 is that at which the dependence of Δy on T is least. In this case the value of A_1 is $\log a_{T_{ns}}$.

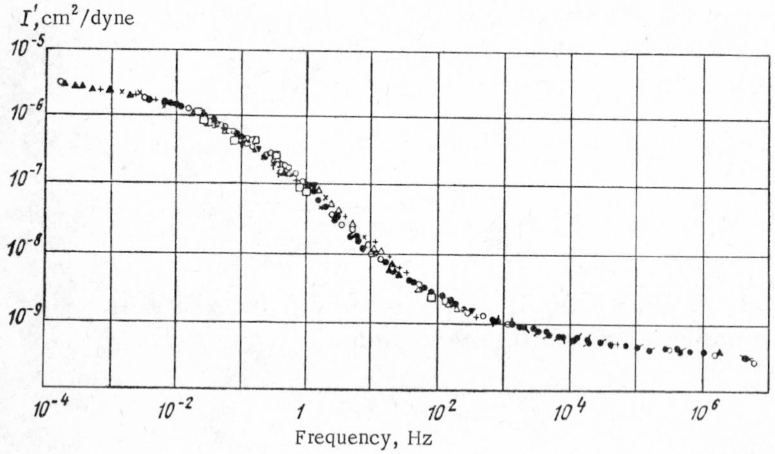

FIGURE 6.6.

The results of the mathematical processing of the data presented in Figures 6.3 and 6.4 for poly-n-octylmethacrylate are shown in Figures 6.5 and 6.6. In Figure 6.4, the experimental data y_k were considered as those points at which the function intersects the ordinates -10, 0, +10, +20, . . ., +130°C. In this case n equaled 15. The values of Δy at different temperatures were determined by trial and error. The results obtained were plotted on the graph in Figure 6.5. The value $\Delta y = 0.0256$ was minimum at $A_2 = T_s = 12$°C. Since Δy is the standard error of $y = \log a_T$, and a_T is the ratio of the relaxation mechanism rates, the error in obtaining $\log a_T$ must be regarded as small.

It is noteworthy that according to data cited by Ferry /13/, poly-n-octylmethacrylate is not a material for which the WLF formula is most suitable. Better agreement between experimental data and the WLF formula has been obtained for a number of other amorphous polymers. This result was confirmed when some other polymeric materials were subjected to computation by the method described.

The relatively low values of the error Δy obtained are no basis for confirming that each test sample of those tested at the temperatures under investigation would display only small errors. Here all the computations were carried out with averaged values. The error in an individual test can be larger than the obtained value of Δy.

Figure 6.6 illustrates the generalized $I' \sim \log \omega$ graph obtained by the TTS superposition principle for poly-n-octylmethacrylate. The reference temperature was 12°C.

The fundamental ideas underlying the method are due to A. S. Nikolaevskii.

BIBLIOGRAPHY

Chapter I

1. Rabotnov, Yu. N. and S. A. Shesterikov. Stability of Rods and Lamina in Creep Conditions. — Prikl. Mat. Mekh., 21, No. 3. 1957.
2. Shanley, F.R. Inelastic Column Theory. — J. Aeronaut. Sci., Vol. 14. 1947.
3. Rabotnov, Yu. N. On the Equilibrium of Compressed Rods Outside the Proportionality Limit. — Inzhenernyi Sbornik, Vol. 11. 1952.
4. Shesterikov, S. A. Dynamic Criterion of Stability for Creep of Rods. — Prikl. Mekh. Tekh. Fiz., No. 1. 1961.
5. Shesterikov, S. A. On a Stability Criterion for Creep. — Prikl. Mat. Mekh., AN SSSR, 22, No. 6. 1959.
6. Shesterikov, S. A. Stability of Plates for Creep Following the Flow Theory. — Prikl. Mekh. Tekh. Fiz., No. 5. 1961.
7. Ivanov, G. V. On the Equilibrium Stability of Compressed, Curved and Thin Rods with Inelastic Deformations. — Prikl. Mekh. Tekh. Fiz., No. 3. 1961.
8. Rabotnov, Yu. N. The Theory of Creep and its Applications. — In: Plasticity, pp. 338—346. Oxford—London—New York—Paris, Pergamon Press. 1960.
9. Shesterikov, S. A. The Stability of Rectangular Plates During Creep. — Prikl. Mekh. Tekh. Fiz., No. 4. 1961.
10. Hoff, N. J. Creep Bending and Buckling of Thin Circular Cylindrical Shells. — PIBAL Report, No. 555. July 1956.
11. Hoff, N. J. Buckling at High Temperature. — J. Roy. Aeronaut. Soc., 61, No. 563. 1957.
12. Rabotnov, Yu. N. Creep of Structural Elements. — Moscow, "Nauka." 1966.
13. Teters, G. A. Stability of Plates and Shells Made from Polymeric Materials (Survey). — Mekhanika Polimerov, No. 1. 1969.
14. Teters, G. A. Combined Loading and the Stability of Shells Made from Polymeric Materials. — Riga, "Zinatne." 1969.
15. Teregulov, I. G. Bending and Stability of Plates and Shells During Creep. — Moscow, "Nauka." 1969.
16. Ogibalov, P. M. and Yu. V. Suvorova. Mechanics of Reinforced Plastics. — Izd. MGU. 1965.
17. Ogibalov, P. M. and V. F. Gribanov. Thermal Stability of Plates and Shells. — Izd. MGU. 1968.
18. Bolotin, V. V. Local Buckling of Compression Struts Made from Laminated Viscoelastic Material. — Mekhanika Polimerov, No. 5. 1968.
19. Bolotin, V. V. On the Theory of Laminar Plates. — Izv. AN SSSR, Otdel. Tekh. Nauk, Mekh. Mash., No. 3. 1963.
20. Bolotin, V. V. — In: Raschety na prochnost', Vol. 2. Moscow, "Mashinostroenie." 1965.
21. Bland, D.R. The Theory of Linear Viscoelasticity. — Oxford, Pergamon Press. 1965.
22. Lavrent'ev, M. A. and B. V. Shabat. Methods of the Theory of Functions of a Complex Variable. — Moscow, "Nauka." 1965.

23. Kominar, V. A. and N. I. Malinin. On the Stability of a Rectangular Plate Made from Orthotropic Glass-Fiber-Reinforced Plastic Allowing for Creep. — Vestn. Mosk. Univ., Ser. Mat. Mekh., No. 1. 1968.
24. Bryzgalin, G. I. On Estimating Creep of Plates Made from Glass-Fiber-Reinforced Plastic. — Prikl. Mekh. Tekh. Fiz., No. 4. 1963.
25. Rabotnov, Yu. N. Equilibrium Elastic Media with Aftereffect. — Prikl. Mat. Mekh., 12, No. 1. 1948.
26. Bryzgalin, G. I. On the Description of Anisotropic Creep of Glass-Fiber-Reinforced Plastic. — Prikl. Mekh. Tekh. Fiz., No. 6. 1963.
27. Vol'mir, A. S. Stability of Elastic Systems. — Moscow, Fizmatgiz. 1963.
28. Lekhnitskii, S. G. Anisotropic Plastics. — Moscow, Gostekhizdat. 1947.
29. Krush, I. I. On Applying the Method of Integral Operators to the Study of the Steady State of Elastic-Hereditary Media. — Dokl. Akad. Nauk SSSR, 158, No. 4. 1964.
30. Bryzgalin, G. I. On the Stability of a Thin Rectangular Plate Made from Glass-Fiber-Reinforced Plastics. — Inzh. Zhurn., MTT, No. 3. 1966.
31. Pelekh, B. L., G. A. Teters, and R. V. Mel'nik. On the Stability of Glass-Fiber-Reinforced Plastics Connected with an Elastic Foundation. — Mekhanika Polimerov, No. 6. 1968.
32. Koltunov, M. A. On the Problem of Selecting Kernels for Solving Problems Allowing for Creep and Relaxation. — Mekhanika Polimerov, No. 4. 1966.
33. Il'yushin, A. A. and P. M. Ogibalov. Some Fundamental Problems of Polymer Mechanics. — Mekhanika Polimerov, No. 3. 1965.
34. Il'yushin, A. A. and P. M. Ogibalov. On a Criterion of Long-Term Strength of Polymers. — Mekhanika Polimerov, No. 6. 1966.
35. Ogibalov, P. M. and M. A. Koltunov. Stability of Orthotropic Viscoelastic Shells. — Prikladnaya Mekhanika, 3, No. 8. 1967.
36. Koltunov, M. A. On Designing Flexible, Mildly Sloping, Orthotropic Shells with Linear Heredity. — Vestn. Mosk. Univ., Ser. Mat. Mekh., No. 5. 1964.
37. Vol'mir, A. S. and L. N. Smetanina. Study of the Dynamic Stability of Glass-Fiber-Reinforced Plastic Shells. — Mekhanika Polimerov, No. 1. 1968.
38. Agamirov, V. L. and A. S. Vol'mir. The Behavior of Cylindrical Shells upon Dynamic Application of Uniform Pressure and Axial Compression. — Izv. AN SSSR, Otdel. Tekh. Nauk, Mekh. Mash., No. 3. 1959.
39. Antipov, V. A., M. K. Smirnov, B. P. Sokolov, and N. P. Trunin. On Methods for an Experimental Study of the Stressed State of Shells Made from Glass-Fiber-Reinforced Plastics. — Mekhanika Polimerov, No. 1. 1969.
40. Gumenyak, V. S. and V. S. Kravchuk. Study of the Stability of Cylindrical Shells Made from Glass-Fiber-Reinforced Plastics. — Mekhanika Polimerov, No. 5. 1969.
41. Ivanov, V. V. Study of the Stability of Closed, Circular, Cylindrical Shells Manufactured from Glass-Fiber-Reinforced Plastics. — Plasticheskie Massy, No. 4. 1964.
42. Kravchuk, V. S. Study of the Stability of Orthotropic Cylindrical and Conical Shells. — Proc. 2nd Scientific and Technical Conference on Structural Mechanics of Shipbuilding, Devoted to the Memory of Acad. Yu. A. Shimanskii, No. 66. Nauch. Tekh. Otdel, Sudprom. 1965.
43. Shchigolev, B. M. Mathematical Processing of Observations. — Moscow, Gos. Izd. Fiz.-Mat. Literat. 1962.
44. Makarov, B. P. Applying a Statistical Method to the Analysis of Experimental Data on Shell Stability. — Izv. AN SSSR, Otdel Tekh. Nauk, Mekh. Tekh., No. 1. 1962.
45. Rakhmatulin, Kh. A. and Yu. A. Dem'yanov. Strength During Intensive, Instantaneous Loading. — Moscow, Gos. Izd. Fiz.-Mat. Literat. 1961.

46. Kolsky, H. Stress Waves in Solids. — Oxford, Clarendon Press. 1953.
47. Sokolovskii, V. V. Propagation of Cylindrical Shear Waves in Elastoviscoplastic Media. — Dokl. Akad. Nauk SSSR, 10, No. 8. 1948.
48. Sokolovskii, V. V. Propagation of Elastoviscoplastic Waves in Rods. — Prikl. Mat. Mekh., 12, No. 3. 1948.
49. Sokolovskii, V. V. One-Dimensional Unsteady Motion in Viscoplastic Media. — Prikl. Mat. Mekh., 12, No. 6. 1949.
50. Richter, G. Die elastisch-plastische Reflexion eines Stabes. — Z. angew. Math. Mech., 33, No. 11. 1953.
51. Kokoshvili, S. M. Propagation of Perturbation Waves in a Linear Polymeric Rod. — Mekhanika Polimerov, No. 2. 1966.
51a. Kokoshvili, S. M. Experimental Study of the Propagation of Perturbation Waves in a Long Polyethylene Rod. — Mekhanika Polimerov, No. 4. 1966.
51b. Kokoshvili, S. M. Study of the Propagation of Longitudinal Waves in a Polyethylene Rod. — Mekhanika Polimerov, No. 1. 1970.
52. Il'yushin, A. A. and B. E. Pobedrya. Fundamentals of the Mathematical Theory of Thermoviscoelasticity. — Moscow, "Nauka." 1970.
53. Ogibalov, P. M. and M. A. Koltunov. Fundamental Theories and Methods of Polymer Mechanics. — Mekhanika Polimerov, No. 1. 1969.
54. Vol'mir, A. S. and A. T. Ponomarev. The Stability of Cylindrical Shells upon a Thermal Shock. — Dokl. Akad. Nauk SSSR, 192, No. 4. 1970.
55. Vol'mir, A. S. Stability of Deformable Systems. — Moscow, "Nauka." 1967.
56. Sneddon, I. N. — Proc. Roy. Soc. Edinburgh, A, 65, No. 2. 1959.

Chapter II

1. Aleksandrov, A. Ya. and M. Kh. Akhmedzyanov. Polarization-Optical Method in the Mechanics of Rigid Deformable Bodies. — Moscow, "Nauka." 1972.
2. Vorontsov, V. K. and P. I. Polukhin. Photoplasticity. — Moscow, "Metallurgiya." 1969.
3. Frocht, M. M. Photoelasticity, Vol. 1. — New York, Wiley. 1941.
4. Coker, E. G. and L. N. G. Filon. Treatise on Photo-Elasticity. — Macmillan. 1932.
5. Durelli, A. J. and W. F. Riley. Introduction to Photomechanics. — Prentice-Hall. 1965.
6. Landau, L. D. and E. M. Lifshits. Electrodynamics of Continuous Media. — Moscow, Fizmatgiz. 1959.
7. Nye, J. F. Physical Properties of Crystals. — Oxford, Clarendon Press. 1957.
8. Mindlin, R. D. A Mathematical Theory of Photoviscoelasticity. — J. Appl. Phys., 20, No. 2. 1949.
9. Bugakov, I. I. On the Piezo-Optic Effect in Polymers with Simple Loading. — In: "Issledovaniya po uprugosti i plastichnosti," No. 3. Izd. LGU. 1964.
10. Il'yushin, A. A. Plasticity. — Moscow, Gostekhizdat. 1948.
11. Il'yushin, A. A. Plasticity. — Moscow, Izd. AN SSSR. 1963.
12. Il'yushin, A. A. Mechanics of Continuous Media (Textbook). Part V. — Izd. MGU. 1965.
13. Ginzburg, V. L. Propagation of Electromagnetic Waves in Plasma. — Moscow, Fizmatgiz. 1960.
14. Aben, H. K. Photoelastic Phenomena upon Uniform Rotation of Quasi-Principal Directions. — Izv. AN SSSR, Otdel. Tekh. Nauk, Mekh. Mash., No. 3. 1962.
15. Bakulenko, A. N. On Features of the Fundamental Laws of High Polymer and Metal Deformation in Relation to the Problems of Modeling. — In: "Polyarizatsionno-opticheskii metod issledovaniya napryazhenii." Izd. LGU. 1966.

16. Mönch, E. Die Dispersion der Doppelbrechung bei Zelluloid als Plastizitätsmass in der Spannungsoptik. — Z. angew. Phys., 6, No. 8. 1954.

17. Mönch, E. Die Dispersion der Doppelbrechung als Mass für die Plastizität bei spannungsoptischen Versuchen. — Forsch. Geb. IngWes., 21, No. 1. 1955.

18. Mönch, E. and R. Jira. Studie zur Photoplastizität von Zelluloid am Rohr unter Innendruck. — Z. angew. Phys., 7, No. 9. 1955.

19. Jira, R. Das mechanische und optische Verhalten von Zelluloid bei zweiachsiger Beanspruchung und der Nachweis seiner Eignung für ein photoplastisches Verfahren. — Konstruktion, 9, No. 11. 1957.

20. Mönch, E. and R. Loreck. A Study of the Accuracy and Limits of Application of Plane Photoplastic Experiments. — In: Photoelasticity, Oxford–London-New York– Paris, Pergamon Press. 1963.

21. Nisida, M., M. Hondo, and T. Hasunuma. Studies of Plastic Deformation by Photoplastic Methods. — Proc. Sixth Japan. Nat. Congr. Appl. Mech., 1956. Tokyo. 1957.

22. Frocht, M. M. and R. A. Thomson. Studies in Photoplasticity. — Proc. Third U.S. Nat. Congr. Appl. Mech., 1958. New York. 1958.

23. Frocht, M. M. and R. A. Thomson. Experiments on Mechanical and Optical Coincidence in Photoplasticity. — Exp. Mech., No. 2. 1961.

24. Frocht, M. M. and Y.F. Cheng. An Experimental Study of the Laws of Double Refraction in the Plastic State in Cellulose Nitrate Foundations for Three-Dimensional Photoplasticity. — In: Photoelasticity. Oxford—London—New York—Paris, Pergamon Press. 1963.

25. Frocht, M. M. and Y.F. Cheng. On the Meaning of Isoclinic Parameters in the Plastic State in Cellulose Nitrate. — Trans. Am. Soc. Mech. Engrs., No. 29. 1962.

26. Netrebko, V. P. Photoelastoplastic Properties of Celluloid. — Vestn. Mosk. Univ., Ser. Mat. Mekh., No. 6. 1960.

27. Netrebko, V. P. Fundamental Relationships of Photoplasticity for the Plane-Stressed State of Celluloid. — Vestn. Mosk. Univ., Ser. Mat. Mekh., No. 2. 1962.

28. Netrebko, V. P. A Photoplastic Method for Solving Plane Elastoplastic Problems. — Vestn. Mosk. Univ., Ser. Mat. Mekh., No. 4. 1966.

29. Netrebko, V. P., V. D. Kopytov, and Yu. G. Mesnyankin. Photoelectric Polarization Instrument. — Patent No. 200223. 1967.

30. Netrebko, V. P. Photoelectric Method of Determining the Optical Path Difference and Inclination of Principal Stresses. — Vestn. Mosk. Univ., Ser. Mat. Mekh., No. 5. 1965.

31. Ambronn, H. Dispersion der Doppelbrechung in zweiphasigen Systemen. — Kolloidzeitschrift, Vol. 9. 1911.

32. Raumspeck. Anomalien der accidentellen Doppelbrechung bei Zelluloid. — Annln. Phys., 4, No. 74. 1924.

33. Netrebko, V. P. Study of the Photoplastic Method. Author's Summary of Thesis. — Moscow. 1968.

34. Kachanov, L. M. Mechanics of Plastic Media. — Moscow, Ob"ed. Gos. Izdat. 1948.

35. Javornicky, J. Ein Beitrag zur Doppelbrechungsanalyse in der Photoplastizität. — Z. angew. Phys., 14, No. 3. 1962.

36. Javornicky, J. Photoplastische Versuche am Werkstoff Zelluloid. — Abh. dt. Akad. Wiss. Berl., Klasse Math. Phys. Technik, No. 4. 1962.

37. Javornicky, J. Die Photoplastizität und ihre Anwendung in der Materialprüfung. — Materialprüfung, 5, No. 12. 1963.

38. Neuber, H. Theory of Stress Concentration for Shear-Strained Prismatical Bodies with Arbitrary Non-Linear Stress-Strain Law. — J. Appl. Mech., 28, No. 3. 1961.

39. Akhmetzyanov, M. Kh. Study of Stress Concentrations in the Plastic Region by Means of Photoelastic Coating. — Izv. AN SSSR, Otdel. Tekh. Nauk, Mekh. Mash., No. 1. 1963.

40. Kopytov, V. D. Study of the Stress-Strain State During Elastoplastic Deformation of a Band with a Double-Ended Semicircular Notch by the Method of Photoelastic Coating. — Vestn. Mosk. Univ., Ser. Mat. Mekh., No. 2. 1967.

41. Netrebko, V. P. Optical and Mechanical Properties of Macrolon and its Application for Solving Photoplastic Problems. — Vestn. Mosk. Univ., Ser. Mat. Mekh., No. 1. 1970.

42. Akhmetzyanov, M. Kh. Techniques of Polarization. — Optical Research on Problems of Plasticity and Creep on Elastic Models. — Proc. 5th All-Union Conf. on Polarization-Optical Methods. Izd. LGU. 1966.

43. Kharlab, V. D. Modeling of the Stress-Strain State of Concrete Structures Allowing for Creep of Concrete. — Proc. 5th All-Union Conf. on Polarization. — Optical Methods. Izd. LGU. 1966.

44. Vardanyan, G. S., L. S. Musatov, and V. V. Pavlov. Modeling of Creep of Structural Elements by a Polarization-Optical Method. Modeling of Problems of Dynamics and Statics by a Polarization-Optical Method. — Sbornik Trudov Mosk. Inzh. Stroit. Inst., No. 73. 1970.

45. Bugakov, I. I. The Application of Plastic for Modeling of Creep. — 18th Scientific Conference, Leningr. Inzh. Stroit. Inst., Leningrad. 1960.

46. Bugakov, I. I. Study of Photocreep Methods. — In: "Issledovaniya po uprugosti i plastichnosti," No. 1. Izd. LGU. 1961.

47. Bugakov, I. I. Utilization of Polarization-Optical Methods for Studying Stresses during Inelastic Deformations. — Proc. 5th All-Union Conf. on Polarization-Optical Methods. Izd. LGU. 1966.

48. Bugakov, I. I. On Apparatus for Testing Creep of Plastic. — In: "Issledovaniya po uprugosti i plastichnosti," No. 1. Izd. LGU. 1961.

49. Bugakov, I. I., V. P. Smirnova, and S. P. Shikhobalov. Stress Concentration in Turbine Disks with Vents and in T-Shaped Fixing of Blades to Disks. — Proc. 5th All-Union Conf. on Polarization-Optical Methods. Izd. LGU. 1966.

50. Krasnov, V. M. On the Determination of Stresses in Cubic Crystals by an Optical Method. — Uchen. Zap. LGU, Issue 13, No. 87. 1944.

51. Krasnov, V. M. On the Anisotropy Problem of Photoelasticity. — In: "Issledovaniya po uprugosti i plastichnosti," No. 1. Izd. LGU. 1961.

52. Hayashi, T. Photoelastic Method of Experimentation for Stress Analysis in Orthotropic Structures. — 24th Intern. Sympos. Space Technol. Sci., Tokyo. 1963.

53. Bugakov, I. I. and I. I. Grakh. Study of the Photoelastic Method for Anisotropic Bodies.— Vestn. Leningr. Univ., Issue 11, No. 19. 1968.

54. Netrebko, V. P., L. S. Zlenko, and S. S. Kapshaninova. Study of the Stress-Strain State of Anisotropic Bodies by a Photoelastic Method. — Vestn. Mosk. Univ., Ser. Mat. Mekh., No. 6. 1969.

55. Netrebko, V. P. Polarization-Optical Method of Studying the Stressed State of Anisotropic Bodies. — MTT, No. 1. 1971.

56. Netrebko, V. P. and L. S. Zlenko. Determination of the Stress-Strain State of Plane Orthotropic Bodies by Polarization-Optical Methods. — Vestn. Mosk. Univ., Ser. Mat. Mekh., No. 5. 1971.

57. Lekhnitskii, S. G. Anisotropic Plastics. — Moscow, Gostekhizdat. 1957.

58. Akhmetzyanov, M. Kh. Separation of Stresses without Employing Isoclines. — Trudy NIIZhTa, No. 24. 1961.

Chapter III

1. Panshin, B. I., G. M. Bartenev, and G. I. Finogenov. Strength of Plastics under Repeated Loading. — Plasticheskie Massy, No. 11. 1960.
2. Oberbach, K. and H. Paffrach. — Materialprüfung, 2, No. 9. 1960.
3. Tarnopol'skii, Yu. M. and A. M. Skudra. Structural Strength and Deformability of Glass-Fiber-Reinforced Plastics. — Riga, "Zinatne." 1966.
4. Rabinovich, A. L. and I. A. Verkhovskii. On the Elastic Constants of Oriented Glass-Fiber-Reinforced Plastics. — Inzh. Zhurn., 4, No. 1. 1964.
5. Goryainova, A. V. Glass-Fiber-Reinforced Plastics in Mechanical Engineering. — Gos. Nauch. Tekh. Izd. 1961.
6. Tarnopol'skii, Yu. M. et al. Computation of Shear During Bending of Glass-Fiber-Reinforced Plastics. — Mekhanika Polimerov, No. 2. 1965.
7. Tarnopol'skii, Yu. M. and A. V. Roze. Strength of Oriented Glass-Fiber-Reinforced Platics During Bending. — Mekhanika Polimerov, No. 4. 1966.
8. Smirnova, M. K. et al. Strength of Ship Hulls Made from Glass-Fiber-Reinforced Plastics. — Leningrad, "Sudostroenie." 1965.
9. Study of Structural Plastics and Structures Built on their Basis. — Trudy Tsentr. Nauchn. Issled. Inst. Stroit. Konstruktsii, No. 11. Moscow, Gosstroiizdat. 1962.
10. Ashkenazi, E. K. On Methods of Studying Mechanical Properties of Structural Plastics. — Zavodskaya Laboratoriya, 26, No. 6. 1960.
11. Yudin, V. F. et al. Comparative Strength of Polymeric Binders and Glass-Fiber-Reinforced Plastics on their Basis During Slip. — Mekhanika Polimerov, No. 2. 1967.
12. Neuber, H. Theory of Notch Stresses. — Edwards Bros. 1946.
13. Serensen, S. V. and V. S. Strelyaev. Static Structural Strength of Glass-Fiber-Reinforced Plastics. — Kiev, Inst. Tekh. Inform. 1961.
14. Ratych, L. V. and S. Ya. Yarema. Effect of the Loading Method on Specimen Strength with Stress Raisers. — Fiz. Khim. Mat. Met., 3, No. 1. 1967.
15. Vinogradov, R. I. et al. Experimental Study of the Stress Concentration in Structural Plastics. — Mekhanika Polimerov, No. 4. 1969.
16. Strelyaev, V. S. Static Structural Strength of Oriented Glass-Fiber-Reinforced Plastics. Author's Summary of Candidate Thesis. — Moscow. 1963.
17. Strelyaev, V. S. and G. P. Zaitsev. Scatter of the Characteristics of Short-Lived Static Strength of Glass-Fiber-Reinforced Plastics in View of the Effect of the Absolute Dimensions and Nonuniformity of the Stressed State. — Izv. Vyssh. Uchebn. Zaved., Mash., No. 3. 1964.
18. Ainbinder, S. B. and M. G. Laka. On the Hardness of Polymeric Materials. — Mekhanika Polimerov, No. 3. 1966.
19. Kuritsyna, A. D. and P. G. Meinster. Techniques for Determining the Hardness and Coefficient of Elastic Restitution of Plastics. — Zavodskaya Laboratoriya, 27, No. 8. 1961.
20. Kuritsyna, A. D.. and P. G. Meinster. Determination of the Hardness of Polymeric Materials at Elevated Temperatures. — Zavodskaya Laboratoriya, 28, No. 4. 1962.

Chapter IV

1. Birger, I. A. Residual Stresses. — Moscow, Mashgiz. 1963.
2. Osgood, W. R. (Editor). Residual Stresses in Metals and Metal Construction. — Reinhold. 1954.
3. Heat Treatment of Structural and Polymeric Materials in Chemical and Petroleum Mechanical Engineering. Synopses of Reports. — Moscow, Izd. VDNKh SSSR. 1969.

4. Soshko, A. I. and A. N. Tynnyi. The Influence of Residual Stresses on the Fracture of Amorphous Glassy Polymers under the Action of Liquid Media. — Fiz. Khim. Mot. Met., 1, No.5. 1965.
5. Abibov, A. L. and G. A. Molodtsov. Method of Computing Residual Stresses in Monodirectional Glass-Fiber-Reinforced Plastics. — In: "Fiziko-khimiya i mekhanika orientirovannykh stekloplastikov." Moscow, "Nauka." 1967.
6. Kiselev, M. R., L. A. Sukhareva, V. V. Paturoev, and P. I. Zubov. Study of Physicomechanical Properties of Reinforced Coatings. — In: "Fiziko-khimiya i mekhanika orientirovannykh stekloplastikov." Moscow, "Nauka." 1967.
7. Zubov, P. I. and L. A. Lepilkina. A Device for Studying Polymeric Coatings. — Vestn. AN SSSR, No. 3. 1962.
8. Gil'man, T. P., N. T. Bukhtiyarov, and K. S. Zatsepin. Study of Glass-Fiber-Reinforced Plastics by a Photoelastic and Differential-Thermal Method. — In: "Fiziko-khimiya i mekhanika orientirovannykh stekloplastikov," Moscow, "Nauka." 1967.
9. Zubov, P. I., L. A. Lepilkina, and T. P. Gil' man. The Effect of Lubricants and Sizing Agent on the Internal Stresses and Adhesive Properties of Polyester Coatings. — Kolloid. Zhurn., 24, No. 2. 1962.
10. Zubov, P. I., L. A. Lepilkina, T. P. Gil'man, and A. Z. Leites. Study of Internal Stresses During Hardening of Polyester Resins. — Kolloid. Zhurn., 23, No. 5. 1961.
11. Trostyanskaya, E. B., A. M. Poimanov, and Yu. N. Kazanskii. Study of the Effect of Processes Originating at the Boundary of Fiber-Glass Binder on the Strength of Glass-Fiber-Reinforced Plastics. — Mekhanika Polimerov, No.1. 1965.
12. Kiselev, M. R., P. I. Zubov, L. A. Sukhareva, E. E. Zaborovskaya, and E. P. Dontsova. Study of Internal Stresses in Glass-Fiber-Reinforced Plastics. — Mekhanika Polimerov, No. 1. 1965.
13. Tarnopol'skii, Yu. M. and T. Ya. Kintsis. On the Mechanism of Stress Transmission During Deformation of Glass-Fiber-Reinforced Plastics. — Mekhanika Polimerov, No.1. 1965.
14. Brivmanis, R. E. Experimental Determination of Residual Stresses during Winding of Monodirectional Glass-Fiber-Reinforced Plastics. — Mekhanika Polimerov, No. 1. 1966.
15. Portnov, G. G., V. A. Goryushkin, and A. G. Tilyuk. Initial Stresses in Rings Made from Glass-Fiber-Reinforced Plastics Prepared by Winding. — Mekhanika Polimerov, No. 3. 1969.
16. Trostyanskaya, E. B., V. U. Novikov, and Yu. N. Kazanskii. Effect of Elevated Temperature on the Strength of Hardened Resins and Materials Made on their Basis. — Mekhanika Polimerov, No. 1. 1966.
17. Tarnopol'skii, Yu. M. and A. M. Skudra. Structural Strength and Deformability of Glass-Fiber-Reinforced Plastics. — Riga, "Zinatne." 1966.
18. Timofeev, L. F. and V. S. Strelyaev. Residual Stresses in Parts Made from Glass-Fiber-Reinforced Plastics. — Mekhanika Polimerov, No. 6. 1966.
19. Avilov, T. I. Determination of Residual Stresses in Plastics. — Mekhanika Polimerov, No. 5. 1967.
20. Goldfein, S. Prestressed Reinforced Plastics. — Modern Plastics, 33, No. 8. 1956.
21. Bartenev, G. M. and L. I. Motorina. The Effect of Tensile Stresses on the Strength of Fiber Glass. — Mekhanika Polimerov, No. 1. 1965.
22. Tarnopol'skii, Yu. M. and A. V. Roze. Characteristic Features of the Design of Parts Made from Reinforced Plastics. — Riga, "Zinatne." 1969.
23. Tarnopol'skii, Yu. M. and G. G. Portnov. Programmed Winding of Glass-Fiber-Reinforced Plastics. — Mekhanika Polimerov, No. 1. 1970.

24. Soshko, A. L., Yu. N. Kholitskii, and A. N. Tynnyi. Problem of the Time and Temperature Dependence of the Strength of Polymethyl Methacrylate. — Fiz. Khim. Mat. Met., 3, No. 1. 1967.
25. Abibov, A. L. and G. A. Molodtsov. Study of Residual Stresses in Reinforced Epoxy Polymer. — Mekhanika Polimerov, No. 4. 1965.
26. Kishkin, B. P. Effect of Heat Treatment on the Physicomechanical Characteristics of Glass-Fiber-Reinforced Plastics and on their Stability (in /3/).
27. Broutman, L. J. and R. H. Krock (Editors). Modern Composite Materials. — Addison-Wesley. 1967.
28. Iskhanov, G. V., Yu. M. Rodichev, and V. V. Vengzhen. Thermal Stresses in a Straight Bar Made from Reinforced Plastic under the Effect of Uniaxial Heating. — Problemy Prochnosti, No. 2. 1969.
29. Goldfein, S. Fracture Strength in Reinforced Plastics as Dependent on Temperature and Time. — Khimiya i Khimicheskaya Tekhnologiya, No. 3. 1956.
30. Nosov, G. G. Thermal Stresses in Reinforced Plastics. — Sbornik Trudov Mosk. Vyssh. Tekh. Uchilishcha im. Baumana, No. 4. 1964.
31. Litvinenko, Yu. A., N. N. Guchar, and V. M. Il'man. Temperature Fields and Thermal Stresses in Glass-Fiber-Reinforced Plastics under Uniaxial Thermal Effects. — In: "Gidroaeromekhanika i teoriya uprugosti. Respublikanskii mezhvedomstvennyi nauchno-tekhnicheskii sbornik," No. 10. Kiev. 1969.
32. Lebedev, I. V. and I. A. Kozlov. Experimental Study of the Stressed State of Glass-Fiber-Reinforced Plastics at Elevated Temperature. — In: "Teplovye napryazheniya velementakh konstruktsii, No. 4. Kiev, "Naukova dumka." 1964.
33. Antans, V. P. and A. M. Skudra. Some Problems of Thermal Rheology of Reinforced Polymers. — Prikladnaya Mekhanika, 2, No. 5. 1966.
34. Turusov, R. A. and V. F. Babich. Thermal Stresses in Polymers. — In: "Fiziko-khimiya i mekhanika orientirovannykh stekloplastikov," Moscow, "Nauka." 1967.
35. Slonimskii, G. L. and A. A. Askadskii. Determination of the Parameters of the Temperature Dependence of Stress Relaxation Time. — Mekhanika Polimerov, No. 1. 1965.
36. Davidenkov, N. N. and E. M. Shevandin. Study of Residual Stresses Created by Bending. — Zhurn. Tekh. Fiz., 9, No. 12. 1939.

Chapter V

1. Sharples, A. Introduction to Polymer Crystallization. — Arnold, E. and Co. 1966.
2. Gul', V. E. and V. N. Kuleznev. Structure and Mechanical Properties of Polymers. — Moscow, "Vysshaya shkola." 1966. 2nd edition. 1971.
3. Kargin, V. A. and G. L. Slonimskii. Brief Surveys on the Physics and Chemistry of Polymers. — Moscow, "Khimiya." 1967.
4. O'Léary, K. and P. H. Geil. Deformation of Bulk Polyoxymethylene. — J. Macromolec. Sci. Phys., B2, No. 2. 1968.
5. Geil, P. H. Polymer Single Crystals. — Interscience. 1963.
6. Zaukelies, D. A. Observation of Slip in Nylon 66 and 610 and its Interpretation in Terms of a New Model. — J. Appl. Phys., 33, No. 9. 1962.
7. Chegodaev, D. D., Z. K. Naumova, and Ts. S. Dunaevskaya. Teflon (or Related Plastics). — Leningrad, Goskhimizdat. 1960.
8. Krentsel', B. A. and L. G. Sidorova. Polypropylene. — Kiev, "Tekhnika." 1964.

9. Kargin, V. A., V. A. Kabanov, and I. Ya. Marchenko. Synthesis and Mechanical Properties of Isotactic Polystyrene. — Vysokomolekulyarnye Soedineniya, 1, No. 1. 1959.
10. Gul', V. E., E. E. Zaborovskaya, E. P. Dontsova, and B. G. Bubnova. Study of Adhesion of Thermosetting Polymers to Glass. — Vysokomolekulyarnye Soedineniya, 5, No. 2. 1963.
11. Deryagin, B. V. and N. A. Krotova. Adhesion. — Moscow—Leningrad, Izd. AN SSSR. 1949.
12. Krotova, N. A. On Adhesion and Agglutination. — Moscow, Izd. AN SSSR. 1960.
13. Voyutskii, S. S. Autohesion and Adhesion of High Polymers. — Interscience. 1963.
14. Lipatov, Yu. S. Physics and Chemistry of Filled Polymers. — Kiev, "Naukova dumka." 1967.
15. Andreevskaya, G. D. High-Strength Oriented Glass-Fiber-Reinforced Plastics. — Moscow, "Nauka." 1966.
16. Rabotnov, Yu. N. Strength of Materials. — Moscow, Fizmatizdat. 1962.
17. Malyshev, B. M. and R. L. Salganik. Study of the Fracture of Brittle Splices by Methods of Crack Theory. — Prikl. Mekh. Tekh. Fiz., No. 5. 1964.
18. Glue and Technology of Glueing. — Moscow, Oborongiz. 1960.
19. Kalnin', M. M., V. P. Karlivan, and M. O. Metnietse. Determination of the Adhesion of Filled Polyethylene to Steel for Static Breaking, Shear and Torsion Using the Same Type of Models. — Mekhanika Polimerov, No. 2. 1967.
20. Latishenko, V. A. Diagnostic of the Hardness and Strength of a Material. — Riga, "Zinatne." 1968.
21. Broutman, L. I. Measurement of the Fiber-Polymer Matrix Interfacial Strength. — In: "Interfaces Composites." Sympos. 71st. Annual Meet. Am. Soc. Test. Mater., San Francisco, Calif. 1968. Philadelphia, Pa. 1969.
22. Bikerman, Ya. O. Theory of Adhesive Binding. — Vysokomolekulyarnye Soedineniya, 10, No. 4. 1968.
23. Shiryaeva, G. V., G. D. Andreevskaya, and L. V. Belunova. Adhesion of Polyester Resin to a Glass Surface and the Mechanical Strength of Glass-Fiber-Reinforced Plastics. — In: "Adgeziya polimerov." Moscow, Izd. AN SSSR. 1963.
24. Alksne, V. I., K. P. Grinevich, and I. E. Yakobson. The Effect of Organosilicon Dressing on Physicomechanical Properties of Glass-Fiber-Reinforced Plastics. — Mekhanika Polimerov, No. 5. 1967.
25. Krivonosov, A. I., M. S. Akutin, M. L. Kerber, S. N. Nikonova, L. I. Golubenkova, and G. N. Shebeko. — Vysokomolekulyarnye Soedineniya, B12, No. 11. 1970.
26. Gul', V. E., S. V. Genel', and L. L. Fomina. On the Effect of Microrheological Processes on Adhesion. — Mekhanika Polimerov, No. 2. 1970.
27. Malinskii, Yu. M., V. V. Prokopenko, and V. A. Kargin. On the Nature of the Extremal Dependence of the Strength of Adhesive Binding and Polymer Materials on Temperature and Strain Rate. — Vysokomolekulyarnye Soedineniya, 6, No. 10. 1964.
28. Bartenev, G. M. and V. T. Marinina. Effect of the Scale Factor and Temperature on the Adhesive Strength of Polymer to Glass. — Vysokomolekulyarnye Soedineniya, 3, No. 5. 1961.

Chapter VI

1. Venttsel', E. S. Theory of Probability. — Moscow, Fizmatgiz. 1962.
2. Bolotin, V. V. Statistical Methods in Structural Mechanics. — Moscow, Gosstroiizdat. 1961.
3. Serensen, S. V. and N. A. Borodin. Statistical Processing of Results of Long-Term Static Tests. — Zavodskaya Laboratoriya, 25, No. 6. 1959.

4. Rumshiskii, L. Z. Elements of the Theory of Probability. — Moscow, Fizmatgiz. 1960.
5. Malinin, N. I. Study of Long-Term Strength of Glass-Fiber-Reinforced AG-4S Plastics. — Plasticheskie Massy, No. 9. 1964.
6. Dlin, A. M. Mathematical Statistics in Engineering. — Moscow, "Sovetskaya Nauka." 1958.
7. Kobeko, P. P., E. V. Kuvshinskii, and G. I. Gurevich. Study of the Amorphous State. Elasticity of Amorphous Bodies. — Izv. AN SSSR, Ser. Fiz., No. 3. 1937.
8. Aleksandrov, A. P. and Yu. S. Lazurkin. Study of Polymers. I. High-Elastic Deformation of Polymers. — Zhurn. Tekh. Fiz., 9, No. 14. 1939.
9. Gurevich, G. I. and P. P. Kobeko. Study of Polymers. III. Techniques for Mechanical Testing of Rubber Vulcanizers and Plastics. — Zhurn. Tekh. Fiz., 9, No. 14. 1939.
10. Williams, M. L., R. F. Landel, and J. D. Ferry. The Temperature Dependence of Relaxation Mechanisms in Amorphous Polymers and Other Glass-Forming Liquids. — J. Amer. Chem. Soc., 77, No. 14. 1955.
11. Treloar, L. R. G. Physics of Rubber Elasticity. — Oxford, Clarendon Press. 1949.
12. Volodin, V. P., S. P. Kabin, and E. V. Kuvshinskii. Applicability of the Method of Reduced Variables to the Temperature and Frequency Dependence of Dynamic Mechanical Properties of Filled Resins. — In: "Relaksatsionnye yavleniya v tverdykh telakh." Moscow, "Metallurgiya." 1968.
13. Ferry, J. D. Viscoelastic Properties of Polymers. — Wiley. 1961.

SUBJECT INDEX for Volume I and Volume II